Get the eBook FREE!

(PDF, ePub, Kindle, and liveBook all included)

We believe that once you buy a book from us, you should be able to read it in any format we have available. To get electronic versions of this book at no additional cost to you, purchase and then register this book at the Manning website.

Go to https://www.manning.com/freebook and follow the instructions to complete your pBook registration.

That's it!
Thanks from Manning!

Deep Learning with JAX

GRIGORY SAPUNOV

MANNING
SHELTER ISLAND

For online information and ordering of this and other Manning books, please visit www.manning.com. The publisher offers discounts on this book when ordered in quantity.

For more information, please contact

> Special Sales Department
> Manning Publications Co.
> 20 Baldwin Road
> PO Box 761
> Shelter Island, NY 11964
> Email: orders@manning.com

Manning Publications Co.
20 Baldwin Road
PO Box 761
Shelter Island, NY 11964

Development editor:	Frances Lefkowitz
Technical editor:	Nicholas McGreivy
Review editor:	Kishor Rit
Production editor:	Andy Marinkovich
Copy editor:	Kari Lucke
Proofreader:	Katie Tennant
Technical proofreader:	Kostas Passadis
Typesetter:	Tamara Švelić Sabljić
Cover designer:	Marija Tudor

ISBN 9781633438880
Printed in the United States of America

To my parents, who encouraged me to follow my passions,
surrounded me with great books, and got me my first computer
when it was still a luxury (and mostly an entertainment)

brief contents

PART 1 FIRST STEPS 1

    1 ▪ When and why to use JAX   3

    2 ▪ Your first program in JAX   18

PART 2 CORE JAX 45

    3 ▪ Working with arrays   47

    4 ▪ Calculating gradients   85

    5 ▪ Compiling your code   119

    6 ▪ Vectorizing your code   152

    7 ▪ Parallelizing your computations   176

    8 ▪ Using tensor sharding   215

    9 ▪ Random numbers in JAX   237

    10 ▪ Working with pytrees   265

PART 3 ECOSYSTEM 285

    11 ▪ Higher-level neural network libraries   287

    12 ▪ Other members of the JAX ecosystem   324

iv

contents

preface   *x*

acknowledgments   *xii*

about this book   *xiv*

about the author   *xviii*

about the cover illustration   *xix*

PART 1   FIRST STEPS..1

1   *When and why to use JAX*   *3*

1.1   Reasons to use JAX   6

Computational performance   7 ▪ Functional approach   9
JAX ecosystem   10

1.2   How is JAX different from NumPy?   12

JAX as NumPy   12 ▪ Composable transformations   13

1.3   How is JAX different from TensorFlow and PyTorch?   15

2   *Your first program in JAX*   *18*

2.1   A toy ML problem: Classifying handwritten digits   19

2.2   An overview of a JAX deep learning project   20

2.3   Loading and preparing the dataset   22

v

2.4   A simple neural network in JAX   24

*Neural network initialization   27 ▪ Neural network forward
pass   27*

2.5   vmap: Auto-vectorizing calculations to work with batches   30

2.6   Autodiff: How to calculate gradients without knowing about
        derivatives   33

*Loss function   34 ▪ Obtaining gradients   35 ▪ Gradient
update step   36 ▪ Training loop   37*

2.7   JIT: Compiling your code to make it faster   38

2.8   Saving and deploying the model   40

2.9   Pure functions and composable transformations: Why are they
        important?   41

Exercise 2.1   42

PART 2   CORE JAX 45

3 *Working with arrays   47*

3.1   Image processing with NumPy arrays   48

*Loading an image into a NumPy array   49 ▪ Performing basic
preprocessing operations with an image   53 ▪ Adding noise to the
image   54 ▪ Implementing image filtering   55 ▪ Saving a tensor
as an image file   61*

3.2   Arrays in JAX   61

*Switching to JAX NumPy-like API   61 ▪ What is Array?   63
Device-related operations   65 ▪ Asynchronous dispatch   69
Running computations on TPU   71*

3.3   Differences from NumPy   74

Immutability   74 ▪ Types   78

3.4   High-level and low-level interfaces: jax.numpy and jax.lax   80

Control flow primitives   81 ▪ Type promotion   83

Exercise 3.1   84

4 *Calculating gradients   85*

4.1   Different ways of getting derivatives   86

*Manual differentiation   88 ▪ Symbolic differentiation   89
Numerical differentiation   90 ▪ Automatic differentiation   91*

4.2   Calculating gradients with autodiff   93

*Working with gradients in TensorFlow   95 ▪ Working with
gradients in PyTorch   96 ▪ Working with gradients in JAX   97
Higher-order derivatives   104 ▪ Multivariable case   106*

4.3   Forward- and reverse-mode autodiff   108

*Evaluation trace   109 ▪ Forward mode and jvp()   110
Reverse mode and vjp()   114 ▪ Going deeper   117*

5   *Compiling your code*   119

5.1   Using compilation   120

*Using JIT compilation   121 ▪ Pure functions and compilation
process   128*

5.2   JIT internals   130

*Jaxpr, an intermediate representation for JAX programs   130
XLA   138 ▪ Using AOT compilation   143*

5.3   JIT limitations   147

*Pure and impure functions   147 ▪ Exact numerics   147
Conditioning on input parameter values   147
Slow compilation   147 ▪ Class methods   149
Simple functions   150*

Exercise 5.1   151

6   *Vectorizing your code*   152

6.1   Different ways to vectorize a function   153

*Naive approaches   154 ▪ Manual vectorization   156
Automatic vectorization   157 ▪ Speed comparisons   158*

6.2   Controlling vmap() behavior   160

*Controlling array axes to map over   160 ▪ Controlling output
array axes   163 ▪ Using named arguments   164 ▪ Using
decorator style   166 ▪ Using collective operations   166*

6.3   Real-life use cases for vmap()   168

*Batch data processing   168 ▪ Batching neural network
models   170 ▪ Per-sample gradients   171
Vectorizing loops   172*

7 *Parallelizing your computations   176*

7.1   Parallelizing computations with pmap()   177

Setting up a problem   178 ▪ *Using pmap (almost) like vmap   180*

7.2   Controlling pmap() behavior   186

Controlling input and output mapping axes   187
Using named axes and collectives   192

7.3   Data-parallel neural network training example   199

Preparing data and neural network structure   200
Implementing data-parallel training   203

7.4   Using multihost configurations   208

8 *Using tensor sharding   215*

8.1   Basics of tensor sharding   217

Device mesh   218 ▪ *Positional sharding   219* ▪ *An example with 2D mesh   220* ▪ *Using replication   223* ▪ *Sharding constraints   226* ▪ *Named sharding   227* ▪ *Device placement policy and errors   228*

8.2   MLP with tensor sharding   230

Eight-way data parallelism   230 ▪ *Four-way data parallelism, two-way tensor parallelism   232*

9 *Random numbers in JAX   237*

9.1   Generating random data   238

Loading the dataset   240 ▪ *Generating random noise   242*
Performing a random augmentation   245

9.2   Differences with NumPy   248

How NumPy works   248 ▪ *Seed and state in NumPy   249*
JAX PRNG   253 ▪ *Advanced JAX PRNG configuration   258*

9.3   Generating random numbers in real-life applications   260

Building a complete data augmentation pipeline   260
Generating random initializations for a neural network   261

10 *Working with pytrees   265*

10.1   Representing complex data structures as pytrees   266

10.2   Functions for working with pytrees   271

      Using tree_map()   271 ▪ Flatten/unflatten a pytree   274
      Using tree_reduce()   276 ▪ Transposing a pytree   277

10.3   Creating custom pytree nodes   280

PART 3 ECOSYSTEM 285

11 *Higher-level neural network libraries*   287

11.1   MNIST image classification using an MLP   288

      *MLP in Flax   289 ▪ Optax gradient transformations
library   294 ▪ Training a neural network the Flax way   297*

11.2   Image classification using a ResNet   301

      *Managing state in Flax   302 ▪ Saving and loading a model
using Orbax   307*

11.3   Using the Hugging Face ecosystem   310

      *Using a pretrained model from the Hugging Face Model Hub   311
Going further with fine-tuning and pretraining   317
Using the diffusers library   318*

12 *Other members of the JAX ecosystem*   324

12.1   Deep learning ecosystem   325

      *High-level neural network libraries   325 ▪ LLMs in JAX   326
Utility libraries   328*

12.2   Machine learning modules   330

      *Reinforcement learning   330 ▪ Other machine learning
libraries   331*

12.3   JAX modules for other fields   333

appendix A   Installing JAX   335

appendix B   Using Google Colab   339

appendix C   Using Google Cloud TPUs   342

appendix D   Experimental parallelization   346

      index   378

preface

JAX is a powerful Python library created by Google for deep learning and high-performance computing. It's widely used in machine learning research and ranks as the third most popular deep learning framework, trailing only behind TensorFlow and PyTorch. Notably, it's the go-to framework for companies like DeepMind, and Google's research increasingly relies on JAX.

What I really appreciate about JAX is its emphasis on functional programming in deep learning. It offers robust function transformations, including gradient computation, JIT compilation via XLA, auto-vectorization, and parallelization. JAX supports both GPUs and TPUs, delivering impressive performance.

Now is an exciting time to dive into JAX, as its ecosystem is rapidly expanding. Despite being around for a few years, there's a noticeable lack of comprehensive resources for beginners. While JAX's website offers solid documentation and a supportive community, piecing everything together, especially when integrating other libraries, can be daunting.

This book is crafted for those eager to master JAX. My goal is to consolidate crucial information in one place and guide you through understanding JAX concepts, enhancing your skills and ability to apply JAX in your projects and research.

A basic understanding of deep learning and proficiency in Python are expected. This book doesn't cover deep learning basics, as there are plenty of resources available. Instead, it focuses solely on JAX, although I'll briefly touch on key deep learning concepts when necessary. This should benefit individuals from non–deep learning backgrounds, like physics.

JAX is more than just a deep learning framework. Its expanding range of modules beyond deep learning suggests its potential in differentiable programming, large-scale physics simulations, and more. My hope is that this book will also serve those interested in these applications.

JAX continues to evolve, and I've had to update several chapters significantly. Don't worry about possible changes in the future; the core knowledge you'll gain remains applicable to future versions of JAX.

acknowledgments

The book took longer than I expected. I changed a few countries along the way; JAX versions also changed. Some chapters had to be rewritten significantly. But now everything is done!

First and foremost, I want to thank my family, my wife Mila, and my kids, Danya and Fedya. You suffered from a lack of my attention for so long! Yet you constantly supported me all along the way.

I want to thank the people of Armenia, where we lived for some time, for their kindness and hospitality. Special thanks go to the Yerevan tech startup community for their help and support. To Hrant Khachatrian, Zaven Navoyan, Arsen Yeghiazaryan, Andranik Khachatryan, Ashot Arzumanyan, Ash Vardanian, Adam Bittlingmayer, Artur Aleksanyan, Erik Arakelyan, Karén Gyulbudaghyan, and many others—thank you a lot!

Thank you, Enterprise Armenia, the National Investment Promotion Agency of Armenia. You do a great job, and your help was invaluable.

I'd also like to acknowledge my editors at Manning, Patrick Barb, Becky Whitney, and Frances Lefkowitz. Even with three successive editors and many changes along the way, each of you added value to the book. Thanks also go to Mike Stephens and Marjan Bace, who believed in the book since my earliest proposal.

I thank my technical editor Nick McGreivy, who, in addition to being a PhD student at Princeton University where he studies plasma physics, uses JAX in his research for optimization of scientific experiments and for integrating deep learning into numerical simulations. Thanks also go to technical proofreader Kostas Passadis and to my reviewers, Arslan Gabdulkhakov, Chansung Park, Fillipe Dornelas, James Black, James Wang, Jun Jiang, Keith Kim, Lucian-Paul Torje, Maxim Volgin, Najeeb Arif, Or Golan, Ritobrata Ghosh, Seunghyun Lee, Simone De Bonis, Stephen Oates, Tony Holdroyd, Vidhya Vinay, and Vojta Tuma. You all provided so many valuable comments and suggestions that helped to improve this book. With that said, any remaining errors in the book are entirely my own.

And, finally, I thank my GDE (Google Developer Experts) friends and Google for supporting such a great initiative. The GDE community is fantastic! Many GDEs looked at early versions and provided helpful feedback. Special thanks go to David Cardozo for his exceptional feedback!

about this book

Deep Learning with JAX is written to help you understand and start using JAX in your projects and research. It consolidates crucial information in one place and guides you through understanding JAX concepts through a series of easy-to-digest examples that build your intuition in the subject.

Who should read this book?

Deep Learning with JAX targets deep learning practitioners and researchers familiar with frameworks such as PyTorch and TensorFlow who want to start using JAX. Readers should have a basic grasp of deep learning and be proficient in Python. Researchers from other areas (e.g., physics or optimization) or graduate students focused on deep learning, numerical optimization, or distributed computations will also find this book beneficial to their learning and practice.

How this book is organized: A roadmap

The book has three parts that cover 12 chapters.

Part 1 is the introduction and a showcase for JAX:

- Chapter 1 answers the crucial question, "Why JAX?" We'll explore what JAX is, its strengths and weaknesses compared to other frameworks like TensorFlow and PyTorch, and when it might be the best tool for your project.
- Chapter 2 guides you through your first hands-on experience with JAX. We'll build a simple neural network for image classification, introducing key concepts like JAX transformations for auto-vectorization, gradient calculation, and just-in-time (JIT) compilation. You'll also learn how to save and load models and understand the difference between pure and impure functions in JAX.

Part 2 covers the core functionalities of JAX:

- Chapter 3 explores the workhorse of deep learning: tensors or multidimensional arrays. We'll compare NumPy arrays and JAX arrays, discuss how to work with them on different hardware like CPUs, GPUs, and TPUs, and explain the nuances of adapting code between NumPy and JAX.
- Chapter 4 tackles the critical task of calculating gradients, which is essential for training neural networks. We'll compare various differentiation methods, dive deep into JAX's automatic differentiation capabilities, and explore both forward and reverse autodiff modes.
- Chapter 5 teaches how to optimize your code for performance using JIT compilation. We'll examine how JIT works under the hood, its interaction with the XLA compiler, and how to address potential limitations.
- Chapter 6 introduces automatic vectorization, a powerful technique for efficiently processing batches of data. We'll explore different vectorization approaches, discuss how to control JAX's `vmap()` transformation, and analyze real-life scenarios where auto-vectorization shines.
- Chapter 7 delves into parallelization, enabling you to run computations on multiple devices simultaneously. We'll discuss how to use the `pmap()` transformation for parallel execution, control its behavior, and implement data parallel neural network training. We'll also explore running code on multihost configurations for large-scale tasks.
- Chapter 8 introduces tensor sharding, a modern and efficient approach to parallelization in JAX. We'll explain how to leverage XLA for automatic parallelization and implement data and tensor parallelism for neural network training, as well as the advantages of this technique.
- Chapter 9 tackles the important topic of generating random numbers in JAX. We'll explore the differences between JAX and NumPy in this regard, discuss the role of keys in representing the state of random number generators, and explain how to apply these concepts in real-world applications.
- Chapter 10 introduces pytrees, a powerful tool for representing complex data structures in JAX. We'll discuss how to work with pytrees effectively, utilize functions for manipulating them, and even create custom pytree nodes for specialized needs.

Part 3 covers the rich and diverse ecosystem of libraries and tools built around JAX:

- Chapter 11 introduces higher-level neural network libraries like Flax and Optax, which provide convenient abstractions for building and training complex models. We'll use Flax to build both a simple MLP and a more advanced residual network for image classification and explore how to leverage Hugging Face libraries for working with transformers and diffusion models.

- Chapter 12 takes a broader look at the JAX ecosystem, showcasing libraries for various machine learning tasks, including training large language models (LLMs), reinforcement learning, and evolutionary computations. We'll also explore JAX modules for other scientific fields like physics, chemistry, and more.

If you're a manager, I suggest reading the first two chapters to get a grasp of JAX's strengths, how it stands out from PyTorch and TensorFlow, and what a typical JAX machine learning project looks like. Chapter 12 is also non-technical and can give you insight into where JAX shines.

For developers eager to start crafting neural networks with JAX, focus on chapter 2 for a straightforward deep learning example, chapters 3 to 6 for JAX's foundational concepts, and chapter 11 for an overview of the high-level libraries in the ecosystem. You can tackle the rest of the book in any order, depending on your specific interests. Feel free to skip chapters 7 and 8 if parallelization isn't on your radar yet—you can always circle back. Dive into chapters 9 and 10 if you're curious about random numbers and pytrees, though the earlier chapters provide enough groundwork to get you started.

About the code

This book contains many examples of source code both in numbered listings and in line with normal text. In both cases, source code is formatted in a `fixed-width font like this` to separate it from ordinary text. Sometimes code is also **in bold** to highlight code that has changed from previous steps in the chapter, such as when a new feature adds to an existing line of code.

In many cases, the original source code has been reformatted; we've added line breaks and reworked indentation to accommodate the available page space in the book. In some cases, even this was not enough, and listings include line-continuation markers (➥). Additionally, comments in the source code have often been removed from the listings when the code is described in the text. Code annotations accompany many of the listings, highlighting important concepts.

You can get executable snippets of code from the liveBook (online) version of this book at https://livebook.manning.com/book/deep-learning-with-jax. The complete code for the examples in the book is available for download from the Manning website at www.manning.com and from GitHub at https://github.com/che-shr-cat/JAX -in-Action.

Almost every chapter has a corresponding Colab notebook (or several of them). The code was tested with JAX version 0.4.14.

liveBook discussion forum

Purchase of *Deep Learning with JAX* includes free access to liveBook, Manning's online reading platform. Using liveBook's exclusive discussion features, you can attach comments to the book globally or to specific sections or paragraphs. It's a snap to make notes for yourself, ask and answer technical questions, and receive help from the author and other users. To access the forum, go to https://livebook.manning.com/book/deep-learning-with-jax/discussion. You can also learn more about Manning's forums and the rules of conduct at https://livebook.manning.com/discussion.

Manning's commitment to our readers is to provide a venue where a meaningful dialogue between individual readers and between readers and the author can take place. It is not a commitment to any specific amount of participation on the part of the author, whose contribution to the forum remains voluntary (and unpaid). We suggest you try asking the author some challenging questions lest their interest stray! The forum and the archives of previous discussions will be accessible from the publisher's website for as long as the book is in print.

Other online resources

The most important source of information is the JAX documentation (https://jax .readthedocs.io/en/latest/). It updates frequently, and you may find answers there. Other important sources of information are GitHub Discussions (https://github .com/google/jax/discussions) and Issues (https://github.com/google/jax/issues).

about the author

GRIGORY SAPUNOV is a cofounder and the CTO of Intento. He is a software engineer with more than 20 years of experience, holds a PhD in artificial intelligence, and is a Google Developer Expert in Machine Learning.

about the cover illustration

The figure on the cover of *Deep Learning with JAX* is captioned "La Bearnaise," or "The Bearnese," referring to a people from a specific region in the French Pyrenees mountains. Taken from a collection by Jacques Grasset de Saint-Sauveur, published in 1797, the illustration is finely drawn and colored by hand.

In those days, it was easy to identify where people lived and what their trade or station in life was just by their dress. Manning celebrates the inventiveness and initiative of the computer business with book covers based on the rich diversity of regional culture centuries ago, brought back to life by pictures from collections such as this one.

Part 1

First steps

Embark on a journey into the world of JAX, a cutting-edge library that's revolutionizing deep learning and high-performance computing. In this opening part of *JAX for Deep Learning*, we lay the groundwork for understanding why JAX is a pivotal tool in the ever-evolving landscape of machine learning frameworks. Through two foundational chapters, you'll gain insights into the unique advantages of JAX over other popular libraries like TensorFlow, PyTorch, and NumPy and learn how to harness its power for your deep learning projects.

Chapter 1 introduces you to the core concepts and strengths of JAX. It sets the stage by delving into the history of deep learning frameworks, highlighting the evolutionary path that led to the birth of JAX. This chapter illuminates JAX's niche in the ecosystem, showcasing its adeptness at compiling and parallelizing code for a wide range of applications, from ocean simulation to large-scale neural networks. By comparing JAX with TensorFlow, PyTorch, and NumPy, you'll understand the strategic scenarios that call for JAX's utilization, laying a robust foundation for the rest of the book.

Chapter 2 is a hands-on exploration that walks you through the development of a simple neural network application. This chapter is your gateway to experiencing JAX's transformative capabilities firsthand. You'll learn about the high-level structure of a JAX project, from loading datasets to creating neural networks, and discover the power of JAX transformations. The chapter concludes with a dive into saving and loading models and the distinction between pure and impure functions, equipping you with the knowledge to embark on more complex projects.

Together, these chapters serve as your initiation into the potent world of JAX, ensuring you're well prepared to tackle more advanced topics in deep learning and beyond. Whether you're a seasoned developer or new to the field, part 1 of *JAX for Deep Learning* offers a comprehensive guide to starting your journey with confidence and clarity.

When and why to use JAX

This chapter covers

- An introduction to JAX
- When and where to use JAX
- A comparison of JAX with TensorFlow, PyTorch, and NumPy

One more deep learning library? Are you serious?! After everything has converged to the beloved-by-everyone PyTorch and the well-established ecosystem around Tensorflow, why should I bother about JAX? And if I wanted a low-level neural network development, there's good old NumPy or its alternatives with GPU support. Why would I even want to look at JAX?

The history of deep learning frameworks shows that no framework lasts forever. For instance, where is Theano, which shaped the field significantly? For me, it was the first deep learning library in the modern sense, after the long-forgotten PyBrain2 and others. And where is Caffe? It was hugely popular many years ago, especially for production deployments. Years ago, I developed a driver assistant tool to recognize road signs in real time, running on old Android smartphones with much less power than contemporary phones; Caffe was the best choice for this job back then.

3

And what about good old Torch7, which many image style transfer models used around 2015? I participated in one such project back then, and we used many of these models on our backends. For that matter, where is Chainer, TensorFlow 1, CNTK, Caffe2, and so many others?

Those were all remarkable frameworks; they did not fall out of use because they were bad. It's just that time flies, context evolves, and requirements change. These frameworks (or libraries; the boundary is sometimes unclear), however, are alive in their descendants. Thanks to Torch7 and Caffe2, we now have PyTorch. Thanks to TensorFlow 1, we have Keras, which is now the default high-level API for TensorFlow 2. Thanks to Chainer, DyNet, and others, we now have dynamic computation graphs and eager execution.

If you assume that PyTorch or Tensorflow 2 is the end of evolution, think again. There is already a newcomer in the field: JAX and its rich ecosystem.

JAX is a Python library developed by Google for high-performance array computing. Some people call it "NumPy on steroids," and it is used for large-scale and high-performance computations thanks to its ability to compile and parallelize your code, no matter whether it is deep learning code or, say, ocean simulation (https://mng.bz/MZAE), weather forecasting (https://arxiv.org/abs/2212.12794), or cosmology (https://arxiv.org/abs/2302.05163; https://arxiv.org/abs/2305.06347). Many exciting applications and libraries on top of JAX are built for physics, including molecular dynamics, fluid dynamics, rigid body simulation, quantum computing, astrophysics, ocean modeling, and more. There are libraries for distributed matrix factorization, streaming data processing, protein folding, and chemical modeling, with other new applications emerging constantly.

No surprise, JAX is widely used for deep learning applications. In fact, JAX is often considered a deep learning framework, the third after PyTorch and TensorFlow.

The well-known State of AI 2021 report (https://mng.bz/aEYx) calls JAX a new framework challenger, and indeed, more and more deep learning research is being conducted with JAX. Among the recent research are Google's essential papers on applying transformers and modern versions of multilayer perceptrons (MLPs) for vision tasks (namely, Vision Transformer [ViT] and MLP-Mixer; https://mng.bz/gvjZ). DeepMind has announced it is using JAX to accelerate research, and the company contributes significantly to the JAX ecosystem (https://mng.bz/eo6w). Let's look at some more ways JAX is currently gaining momentum.

Because JAX has enabled rapid experimentation with novel algorithms and architectures, it now underpins many of DeepMind's recent publications. Among them, I'd highlight

- A new approach to self-supervised learning called BYOL (Bootstrap Your Own Latent; https://arxiv.org/abs/2006.07733)
- A general transformer-based architecture for structured inputs and outputs called Perceiver IO (https://mng.bz/OZ02)

- Research on large language models (LLMs), with the 280-billion-parameters Gopher model (https://mng.bz/Y7Be) and the 70-billion-parameters Chinchilla (https://mng.bz/r1yg)

One of the first large, open source GPT-like models, EleutherAI's GPT-J-6B, the 6-billion-parameter transformer language model, was trained with JAX on Google Cloud. The authors of the GPT-J paper state it was the right set of tools to develop large-scale models rapidly. Google internally uses JAX to train its LLMs, such as PaLM 2, Gemini, and Gemma. In 2023, xAI (https://x.ai/) began training its Grok LLM (https://github.com/xai-org/grok-1) using a custom training and inference stack based on Kubernetes, Rust, and JAX.

Furthermore, in 2021, Hugging Face made JAX and Flax (the high-level neural network library on top of JAX) the third officially supported framework in their well-known Transformers library. The Hugging Face collection of pretrained models (as of June 2024) already has the number of JAX models comparable to the number of TensorFlow models. PyTorch is still ahead of both, but porting models from PyTorch to JAX/Flax is already happening.

JAX on its own might not be very suitable for production deployment, as it primarily focuses on the research side, but that was precisely how PyTorch went. The gap between research and production will likely be closed soon. There is already a JAX2TF package that provides support for JAX native serialization and interoperation between JAX and TensorFlow. A JAX model could be converted to TensorFlow's SavedModel so you can serve it with TensorFlow Serving, TFLite, or TensorFlow.js.

Given Google's weight and the rapid expansion in the community, I expect a bright future for JAX. It is easy to adopt since Python and NumPy are widely used and familiar to most developers. Its composable function transformations help support machine learning research. It has a vivid ecosystem and a high degree of expressiveness and can provide high performance and computational efficiency. It uses the familiar NumPy API and promotes a functional programming approach. The code can run efficiently on multiple backends, including CPUs, graphics processing units (GPUs), and tensor processing units (TPUs). And if you happen to be developing LLMs or training other large-scale neural networks, JAX is a good choice for these. (Find more on LLMs in chapter 12, where I provide you with a list of JAX modules for high-performance LLM training.)

Why Is it called JAX?

According to the paper that first presented JAX, "Compiling Machine Learning Programs Via High-Level Tracing" (https://mlsys.org/Conferences/doc/2018/146.pdf), the acronym JAX stands for "Just After eXecution," since to compile a function, we first monitor its execution once in Python.

Before we move on to the specific ways JAX is useful, let's clarify a bit about this book. Although there are many fascinating areas in which to use JAX (including cosmology, protein folding, and ocean modeling), this book focuses mostly on deep learning. It targets developers, engineers, and researchers who already understand deep learning concepts and have some experience with one of the other frameworks. If you are a newbie to the field, you can still use the book to learn JAX, but you will need a separate book that teaches you deep learning.

Although many examples are tailored for deep learning uses, a reader interested in using JAX for other purposes can also learn JAX from the eight chapters on core JAX in part 2. I added sidebars explaining deep learning concepts in simple language for these readers. Forgive me, deep learning experts; for you, these added notes may be too basic, but I believe they could be extremely helpful for people from other fields who want to learn JAX. Feel free to skip any sidebar that looks like "Deep Learning 101."

I deliberately did not include cases outside of deep learning, like astronomy. Although there are beautiful examples of using JAX in other fields, I don't feel it is worth mixing such cases into the book. They won't add much value for the deep learning people, and they also won't be much help to the physics people as they likely need much more, likely a separate book or a workshop on the topic. I still want to focus on JAX essentials, which are useful everywhere, and deep learning people, to help them get a taste of the new framework and start using it. However, I mention JAX's applicability to such fields many times and provide some relevant links (especially in the last chapter about the ecosystem).

The book builds your core JAX understanding from the ground up, diving deeply into all the essential concepts, each explained with numerous examples and bite-sized projects. This may sometimes look pretty low-level, but this approach gives you a solid understanding of how things work and provides a strong basis to explore JAX's rich ecosystem. As you begin your exciting journey with JAX, let *Deep Learning with JAX* be your indispensable guide.

In this chapter, I will introduce JAX and its vibrant ecosystem and explain what JAX is and how it relates to NumPy, PyTorch, and TensorFlow. We will review JAX's strengths to understand how they combine to give you a powerful tool for deep learning research and high-performance computing.

1.1   *Reasons to use JAX*

There are several reasons why you might want to use JAX. First is its outstanding performance and the ability to execute computations on multiple backends, including CPUs, GPUs, and TPUs, while having a familiar NumPy-style API for ease of adoption by researchers and engineers. Second is its functional nature and a set of composable function transformations for compilation, batching, automatic differentiation, and parallelization. Third is its composability and the rich ecosystem of modules and libraries built on top of JAX.

Before we get into these three reasons for using JAX, it's important to state that JAX is not always the best option for every problem. If you work with very special settings, like mobile or embedded deployments, keeping your current framework, such as TFLite, is probably best (though there is the JAX2TF converter if needed). Similarly, if you have a vast and established code base using your current framework, such as PyTorch, it may not make the most sense to switch to JAX (though, if the speed is super important for you, that still might be a good option). Now to those JAX advantages.

1.1.1 *Computational performance*

First, JAX provides excellent computational performance. Some benchmarks show that JAX is faster than TensorFlow (https://mng.bz/0GDm). Others state that "the performance of JAX is very competitive, both on GPU and CPU. It is consistently among the top implementations on both platforms" (https://github.com/dionhaefner/pyhpc-benchmarks) And even the world's fastest transformer of 2020 was built with JAX (https://mng.bz/KZO4).

Many things fit into this section, including the ability to use modern hardware such as GPUs or TPUs (and JAX is probably the best choice if you want to achieve the maximum performance on TPUs), just-in-time (JIT) compilation with Accelerated Linear Algebra (XLA), auto-vectorization, easy parallelization across the cluster, and ability to use data- and model-parallel training, while scaling your program from your laptop CPU to the largest TPU Pod in the cloud. We will discuss all these topics in different chapters of the book.

You can use JAX as accelerated NumPy by replacing `import numpy as np` with `import jax.numpy as np` at the beginning of your program. It is, in some sense, an alternative to switching from NumPy to CuPy (for using GPUs with NVIDIA CUDA or AMD ROCm platforms), Numba (to have both JIT and GPU support), or even PyTorch, if you want hardware acceleration for your linear algebra operations. Not all NumPy functions are implemented in JAX; sometimes, you need more than just replacing an import. We will touch on this topic in chapter 3.

Hardware acceleration with a GPU or TPU can speed up matrix multiplications and other operations that can benefit from running on this massively parallel hardware. To start using this type of acceleration, you only need to perform computations on multi-dimensional arrays you have put in the accelerator memory. Chapter 3 will show how to manage data placement.

Acceleration can also stem from JIT compilation with the XLA compiler that optimizes the computation graph and can fuse a sequence of operations into a single efficient computation or eliminate some redundant computations. It improves performance even on the CPU, without any other hardware acceleration (yet, CPUs are different, and many modern CPUs provide special instructions suitable for deep learning applications).

Figure 1.1 shows a screenshot with a simple (and pretty useless) function with some amount of computations that we will evaluate with pure NumPy, with JAX using a CPU and GPU (in my case, Tesla-P100) and with JAX-compiled versions of the same function for CPU and GPU backends. I will describe all the relevant things and dive deeper into this topic in chapter 5. The corresponding code can be found in the book's code repository: https://mng.bz/9dRa.

```python
import jax
import numpy as np
import jax.numpy as jnp

# a function with some amount of calculations
def f(x):
  y1 = x + x*x + 3
  y2 = x*x + x*x.T
  return y1*y2

# generate some random data
x = np.random.randn(3000, 3000).astype('float32')
jax_x_gpu = jax.device_put(jnp.array(x), jax.devices('gpu')[0])
jax_x_cpu = jax.device_put(jnp.array(x), jax.devices('cpu')[0])

# compile function to CPU and GPU backends with JAX
jax_f_cpu = jax.jit(f, backend='cpu')
jax_f_gpu = jax.jit(f, backend='gpu')

# warm-up
jax_f_cpu(jax_x_cpu)
jax_f_gpu(jax_x_gpu);
```

Figure 1.1   A simple (and pretty useless) function with some amount of computations that we will evaluate with pure NumPy, with JAX using a CPU and GPU, and with JAX-compiled versions of the same function for CPU and GPU backends. We will evaluate the time to calculate f(x).

Figure 1.2 compares the different ways of calculating our function. Please ignore the specific things like `block_until_ready()` or `jax.device_put()` for now. The former is needed because JAX uses asynchronous dispatch and does not need to wait for the computation to complete. In that case, the measurement would be wrong because it only counts some computations. The latter is needed to stick an array to the specific device. We will talk about this in chapter 3.

```
%timeit -n100 f(x)

100 loops, best of 5: 49.8 ms per loop

%timeit -n100 f(jax_x_cpu).block_until_ready()

100 loops, best of 5: 59.5 ms per loop

%timeit -n100 jax_f_cpu(jax_x_cpu).block_until_ready()

100 loops, best of 5: 10.5 ms per loop

%timeit -n100 f(jax_x_gpu).block_until_ready()

100 loops, best of 5: 1.87 ms per loop

%timeit -n100 jax_f_gpu(jax_x_gpu).block_until_ready()

100 loops, best of 5: 649 µs per loop
```

Figure 1.2   Time measurements for different ways of calculating our function f(x). Line 1 is a pure NumPy implementation; line 2 uses JAX on CPU; line 3 is a JAX JIT-compiled CPU version; line 4 uses JAX on GPU; and line 5 is a JAX JIT-compiled GPU version.

In this particular example, the CPU-compiled JAX version of the function is almost five times faster than the pure NumPy original, yet a noncompiled JAX CPU version is a bit slower. You do not need to compile your function to use GPUs, and we might also ignore all these direct transfers to the GPU device as, by default, all the arrays are created on the first GPU/TPU device if available. The noncompiled JAX function that still uses a GPU is 5.6 times faster than the JAX CPU–compiled one. And the GPU-compiled version of the same function is another 2.9 times faster than the noncompiled one. Compared to the original NumPy function, the total speedup is close to 77 times—decent speed improvements without changing the function code so much!

Another tool that might help in acceleration is auto-vectorization, which converts a single-element function to a function that can process a batch of elements. Its main goal is simplifying your developer life and writing efficient vectorized code faster. Still, it can also provide another way to speed up your computations if your hardware resources and program logic allow you to perform computations for many items simultaneously. We will discuss auto-vectorization in chapter 6.

Finally, you can also parallelize your code across the cluster and perform large-scale computations in a distributed fashion, which is impossible with pure NumPy but can be implemented with something like Dask, DistArray, Legate NumPy, or others. Training large-scale models (like GPT-like LLMs or text-to-image diffusion models) is a very hot topic. The ability to do it efficiently may be a game changer, saving you hours and days of computing time and, as a result, a lot of money. Chapters 7 and 8 are dedicated to different aspects of parallelization.

And, of course, you can benefit from all the mentioned things simultaneously, which is the case for training large distributed neural networks, doing large physical simulations, performing distributed evolutionary computations, and so on.

1.1.2 *Functional approach*

In JAX, everything is in plain sight and explicit. Thanks to the functional approach, there are no hidden variables or side effects (more on side effects here: https://mng .bz/jXQy). The code is clear; you can change anything you want, and doing something off the road is much easier. As I've mentioned, researchers love JAX, and much new research is being done with it.

Such an approach requires you to change some habits. In PyTorch and TensorFlow, the code is typically organized in classes. Your neural network is a class with all its parameters being an internal state. Your optimizer is another class with its internal state. If you work with reinforcement learning, your environment is usually another class with its state. Your deep learning program looks like an object-oriented program with class instances and method calls.

In JAX, code is organized as functions instead. It's wrong to say JAX does not allow the use of classes; all the high-level libraries provide you with class abstractions similar to traditional deep learning frameworks. The difference is that classes and functions do not use an internal state. You need to pass any internal state as a function parameter, so all the model parameters (sets of weights in the case of neural networks or even seeds for random numbers) are passed into functions directly. The random number generating functions now require you to explicitly provide the random generator state (we will dive into JAX random number generators in chapter 9). Gradients are calculated explicitly by calling a special function (obtained with the `grad()` transformation of your function of interest, the topic of chapter 4). The optimizer state and calculated gradients are also parameters of an optimizer function, and so on. There is no hidden state; everything is visible. Side effects are also bad because they do not work with JIT.

JAX forces you to change habits regarding `if` statements and `for` loops because of how it complies. We will discuss this topic in chapter 5.

The functional approach also brings rich compositionality. JAX provides rich composable function transformations (more on that in section 1.2.2), like automatic differentiation, auto-vectorization, end-to-end compilation with XLA, and parallelization, which are easy to combine. JAX's rich composability and expressivity lead to its powerful ecosystem.

1.1.3   *JAX ecosystem*

JAX provides a strong foundation for building neural networks, but its real power comes from its constantly growing ecosystem. Together with its ecosystem, JAX provides an exciting alternative to the two current state-of-the-art deep learning frameworks: PyTorch and TensorFlow.

With JAX, it is easy to compose a solution from different modules. You do not have to use an all-in-one framework like TensorFlow or PyTorch, where everything is included. These are powerful frameworks, but replacing one tightly integrated thing with a different one is sometimes hard. In JAX, you can build a custom solution by combining the blocks you want.

Long before JAX, the deep learning field resembled the LEGO approach, where you had a set of blocks of different shapes and colors for creating your solutions. Deep learning is a LEGO-style thing on different levels, from the lower levels of activation functions and types of layers to high-level engineering blocks of architecture primitives (like self-attention), optimizers, tokenizers, and so on.

With JAX, you have even more freedom to combine different blocks that best suit your needs. For example, you can take a high-level neural network library you want and a separate module that implements the optimizers you wish to use. Then you can customize the optimizer to have custom learning rates for different layers, use PyTorch data loaders you love, use a separate reinforcement learning library, add Monte-Carlo Tree Search, and use some other things for meta-learning optimizers from another library.

Combining a solution using JAX and its ecosystem resembles the Unix way of simple and modular design, as Eric Raymond stated: "Write programs that do one thing and do it well. Write programs to work together. Write programs to handle text streams because that is a universal interface." (*Basics of the Unix Philosophy*, Addison-Wesley Professional,

2003) Except for the text streams, this is relevant to JAX philosophy. However, text communication might also become the universal interface between different (large) neural networks someday. Who knows? And here emerges the ecosystem.

The ecosystem is already huge, and that's just the beginning. There are excellent modules for

- High-level neural network programming, including, among others,
  - Flax by Google (https://github.com/google/flax)
  - Equinox, with easy-to-use PyTorch-like syntax (https://github.com/patrick-kidger/equinox)
  - Keras 3, a brand-new multi-backend (https://github.com/keras-team/keras)
- A module with state-of-the-art optimizers (Optax; https://github.com/deepmind/optax)
- Reinforcement learning libraries
  - RLax by DeepMind (https://github.com/deepmind/rlax)
  - Coax by Microsoft Research (https://github.com/coax-dev/coax)
- A graph neural network library (Jraph; https://github.com/deepmind/jraph),
- A library for molecular dynamics (JAX, M.D.; https://github.com/google/jax-md)

Please note, the list does not pretend to be a complete list of all the modules, it's just to give you a first glimpse of the ecosystem.

The JAX ecosystem contains hundreds of modules already and evolves quickly. New libraries constantly emerge. I recently noticed

- EvoJAX (https://github.com/google/evojax) and `evosax` (https://github.com/RobertTLange/evosax) for evolutionary computations
- FedJAX for federated learning (https://github.com/google/fedjax)
- Paxml (https://github.com/google/paxml) and MaxText (https://github.com/google/maxtext) for training LLMs
- The Scenic library for computer vision research (https://github.com/google-research/scenic)

DeepMind already developed a set of libraries on top of JAX (some already mentioned earlier). New libraries are available for Monte Carlo Tree Search, neural network verification, image processing, and many others. But it is far from the whole picture. I do not intend to mention all of them in the first chapter as that's not realistic and not the goal; the first chapter is not supposed to be an exhaustive list of everything in the ecosystem. There are many popular libraries, briefly described in chapter 12. However, there is a good chance that some useful new library will emerge or become widely used after this book is printed. If you understand JAX, it's easy to start using these modules.

The number of JAX models in the Hugging Face repository grows constantly, as JAX is among the three supported frameworks there. We will touch on this topic in practice in chapter 11.

So, JAX is gaining momentum, and its ecosystem is constantly growing. It's an excellent time to jump in!

1.2   How is JAX different from NumPy?

Strictly speaking, JAX is a Python mathematics library with a NumPy interface developed by Google (the Google Brain team, to be specific). It is heavily used for machine learning research, but it is not limited to it, and many other things can be solved with JAX.

JAX creators describe it as Autograd and XLA brought together for high-performance numerical computing. Do not be afraid if you are unfamiliar with these names; it's expected, especially if you are just entering the field.

Autograd (https://github.com/hips/autograd) is the library that efficiently computes derivatives of NumPy code, the predecessor of JAX. By the way, the Autograd library's main developers are now working on JAX. In a few words, Autograd means you can automatically calculate gradients for your computations, which is the essence of deep learning and many other fields, including numerical optimization, physics simulations, and, more generally, differentiable programming.

XLA (Accelerated Linear Algebra) is Google's domain-specific compiler for linear algebra. It compiles Python functions with linear algebra operations to high-performance code for running on GPU or TPU. Let's start with the NumPy part.

1.2.1   JAX as NumPy

NumPy is a workhorse of Python numerical computing. It is so widely used in the industry and science that NumPy API became the de facto standard for working with multidimensional arrays in Python. JAX provides a NumPy-compatible API but offers many new features absent in NumPy. That's why some people call JAX "NumPy on steroids."

JAX provides a multidimensional array data structure called `Array` that implements many typical properties and methods of the `numpy.ndarray`. There is also the `jax.numpy` package that implements the NumPy API with many well-known functions like `abs()`, `conv()`, `exp()`, and so on.

JAX tries to follow the NumPy API as closely as possible, and in many cases, you can switch from `numpy` to `jax.numpy` without changing your program. There are still some limitations; not all the NumPy code can be used with JAX. JAX promotes a functional programming paradigm and requires pure functions without side effects. As a result, JAX arrays are immutable, yet NumPy programs frequently use in-place updates, like `arr[i] += 10`. JAX provides a purely functional alternative API that replaces in-place updates with an indexed update function. For this particular case, it will be `arr = arr.at[i].add(10)`. There are a few other differences, and we will address them in chapter 3.

So you can use almost all the power of NumPy and write your programs as you are accustomed to when using NumPy. But you have new opportunities here.

1.2.2 Composable transformations

JAX is much more than NumPy. It provides a set of *composable function transformations* for Python + NumPy code. At its core, JAX is an extensible system for transforming numerical functions with four main transformations (but it doesn't mean no more transformations are to come!):

- *Taking the gradient* of your code or differentiating it. This is the essence of deep learning. JAX uses an approach called *automatic differentiation* (or *autodiff* for short). Automatic differentiation helps you focus on your code and not take derivatives by hand; the framework takes care of it. It is typically done by the `grad()` function, but other advanced options exist. We will give more context on automatic differentiation and dive deeper into the topic in chapter 4.

- *Compiling* your code with `jit()` or JIT compilation. JIT uses Google's XLA to compile and produce efficient code for GPUs (typically NVIDIA ones through CUDA, though AMD ROCm platform support is in progress) and TPUs (Google's Tensor Processing Units). XLA is the backend that powers machine learning frameworks, originally TensorFlow, on various devices, including CPUs, GPUs, and TPUs. We will dedicate the whole of chapter 5 to this topic.

- *Auto-vectorizing* your code with `vmap()`, which is the vectorizing map. You probably know what a map is if you are familiar with functional programming. If not, do not worry; later, we will describe what it means. `vmap()` takes care of batch dimensions of your arrays and can easily convert your code from processing a single item of data to processing many items (called a *batch*) at once. You may also call it auto-batching. By doing this, you vectorize the computation, which typically gives you a significant boost on modern hardware that can efficiently parallelize matrix computations. We will discuss auto-vectorizing in chapter 6.

- *Parallelizing* your code to run on multiple accelerators, say, GPUs or TPUs. It is done with `pmap()`, which helps write single-program multiple-data (SPMD) programs. `pmap()` compiles a function with XLA, then replicates it and executes each replica on its XLA device in parallel. This topic will be discussed in chapters 7 and 8.

Each transformation takes in a function and returns a function, so you can take one function and automatically obtain a compiled or vectorized version of the function without writing much code for it. You focus only on what's important. You can mix different transformations as you like if you use functionally pure functions. We will talk about this later, but in short, a functionally pure function is a function whose behavior is determined only by its input data. It has no internal state, and it should produce no side effects. For those who came from functional programming, it should be a natural thing to do. For others, it's not hard to adopt this way of writing programs, and I will help you with it.

If you respect these constraints, you can mix, chain, and nest transformations and create complicated pipelines if needed. JAX makes all those transformations arbitrarily composable.

For example, you can prepare a function for processing an image with a neural network and then automatically generate a highly optimized, vectorized, and distributed version of the function, which can be automatically differentiated. Hence, you have everything you need for neural network training while writing only the core computation part. Technically, it means that using the original function and `vmap()`, you obtain another function that processes a batch of images. Then with `jit()`, you compile it into efficient code to run on GPU or TPU (or many of them in a parallel fashion with `pmap()`). Finally, you generate a function to calculate gradients with `grad()` to train our image processing function with gradient descent. In NumPy, you'd have to write a lot of code for it. We will see some exciting examples along the way.

You do not want to implement these transformations in pure NumPy. You don't need to calculate derivatives by hand; the powerful framework takes care of that, no matter how complicated your functions are—the same goes for auto-vectorization and parallelization.

Figure 1.3 (left side) shows NumPy as an engine for working with multidimensional arrays with many useful mathematical functions. JAX (right side) has a familiar NumPy-compatible API with its multidimensional arrays and many functions, so it's easy for researchers and engineers to adopt JAX. Besides this, NumPy-like API JAX provides a set of powerful function transformations, which saves a lot of time and effort compared with implementing the same things with pure NumPy.

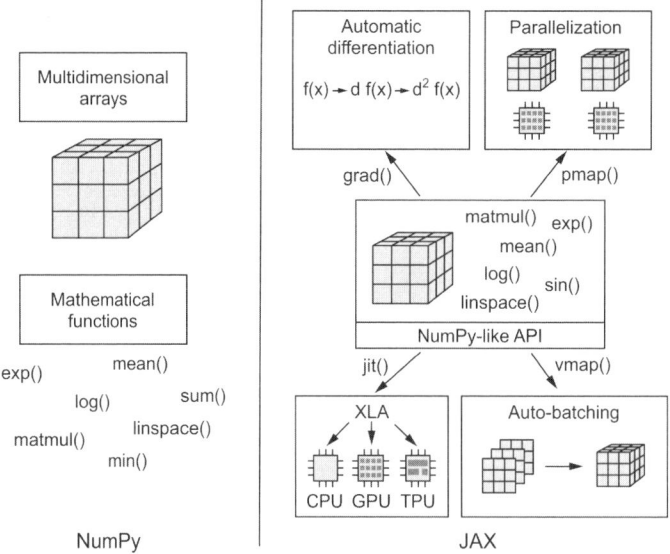

Figure 1.3   JAX (right) is much more than NumPy (left). It provides a set of composable function transformations for Python + NumPy code for compilation, vectorization, parallelization, and automatic differentiation.

In some sense, JAX resembles Julia. Julia also has JIT compilation, good automatic differentiation capabilities, machine learning libraries, and rich hardware acceleration with parallel computing support. But with JAX, you can stay within your well-known Python world. Sometimes it matters.

1.3 How is JAX different from TensorFlow and PyTorch?

We've already discussed how JAX compares to NumPy. Let's compare JAX with the two modern deep learning frameworks, PyTorch and TensorFlow.

We mentioned that JAX promotes the functional approach compared to the object-oriented approach common to PyTorch and TensorFlow. It is the first very tangible thing you face when you start programming with JAX. It changes how you structure your code and requires some changing of habits. At the same time, it gives you powerful function transformations, forces you to write clean code, and brings rich compositionality. If you like the functional programming approach or want these automatic function transformations, then JAX may be your choice. High-level neural network libraries on top of JAX, say Flax, still provide you with a set of functionally pure classes that look familiar to anyone with experience in Keras or PyTorch. You will see this in chapter 11.

JAX-like composable function transforms for PyTorch

JAX composable function transformations heavily influenced PyTorch. In March 2022, with the PyTorch 1.11 release, its developers announced a beta release of the functorch library (https://github.com/pytorch/functorch), providing JAX-like composable function transforms for PyTorch. The reason for doing this is that many use cases were tricky to do in PyTorch at that time—say, computing per-sample gradients, running ensembles of models on a single machine, efficiently batching tasks in the meta-learning inner loops, and efficiently computing Jacobians and Hessians and their batched versions. Now functorch is integrated into PyTorch as torch.func APIs (https://pytorch.org/docs/master/func.html), and the functorch APIs are deprecated as of PyTorch 2.0. The torch.func library is still in beta.

Another tangible thing you soon notice is that JAX is pretty minimalistic. It does not implement everything. TensorFlow and PyTorch are the two most popular and well-developed deep learning frameworks, with almost all possible batteries included. Compared to them, JAX is a very minimalistic framework, and it's even hard to call it a framework. It's rather a library.

For example, JAX does not provide any data loaders just because other libraries (e.g., PyTorch or Tensorflow) do this well. JAX authors do not want to reimplement everything; they want to focus on the core. And that's precisely the case where you can and should mix JAX and other deep learning frameworks. It is okay to take the data loading stuff from, say, PyTorch and use it. PyTorch has excellent data loaders, so why not use it?

In JAX, you may miss some things you liked that were included in your current framework, and you will need some time to find an alternative from the JAX ecosystem (or even use it from your current framework, like with data loaders). The good news is if something was missing from your original framework, or you didn't like it but could not change it, you have the freedom to mix whatever you want in JAX.

Another noticeable thing is that JAX primitives are pretty low-level, and writing large neural networks in terms of matrix multiplications could be time consuming. Hence, you need a higher-level language to specify such models. It's similar to wanting something like `torch.nn` instead of just `torch`. JAX does not provide such high-level APIs outside the box (as did TensorFlow 1 before the high-level Keras API was added to TensorFlow 2). No such batteries are included, but it is not a problem as there are high-level libraries for the JAX ecosystem. Flax, Equinox, and Keras provide all the required high-level abstractions you might need, and your resulting model definitions may look very similar to the same model definitions in PyTorch or TensorFlow. You don't need to write your neural networks with the NumPy-like primitives. We will touch on high-level libraries in chapter 11 after we cover all the core JAX.

Figure 1.4 visualizes the differences between PyTorch/TensorFlow and JAX.

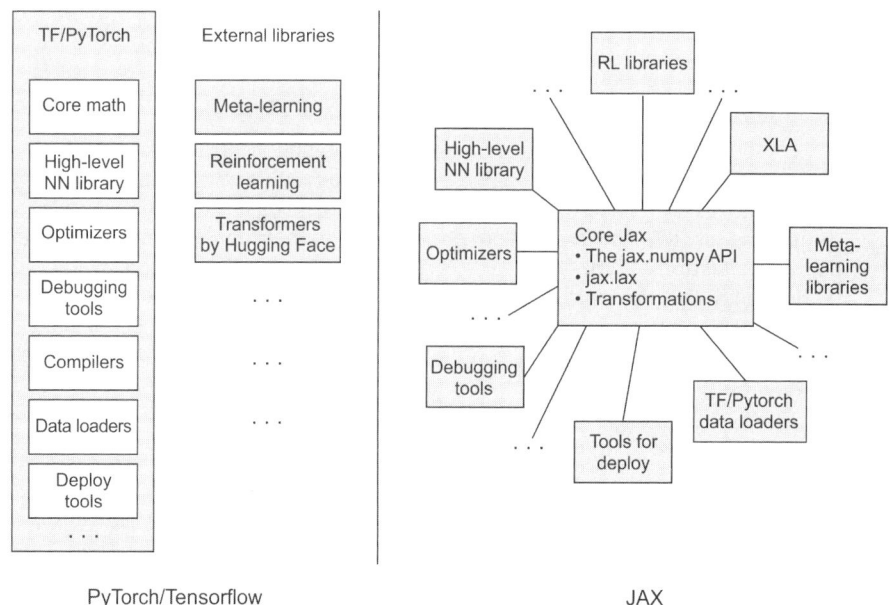

Figure 1.4   Compared to PyTorch/TensorFlow, JAX is a minimalistic framework. However, many components included in PyTorch/TensorFlow are available as separate modules from the JAX ecosystem.

Because JAX is an extensible system for composable function transformations, it is easy to build separate modules for everything and mix them in any way you want.

To conclude this introduction to JAX, if computational performance is crucial for you, if you value functional programming and clean code, if you are involved in deep learning research, or if you are interested in controlling every aspect of your code, JAX is a great option for you! At the same time, JAX is not always the best option for every problem, and in some cases, like embedded deployments or vast legacy codebases that use other frameworks, PyTorch or TensorFlow could be a better option.

The next chapter provides a more technical introduction to JAX for those who like to see the code. We will examine an example deep learning project that uses JAX for image classification.

Summary

- JAX is a low-level Python library from Google that is heavily used for machine learning research (but can also be used in other fields like physics simulations and numerical optimization).

- JAX provides a NumPy-compatible API for its multidimensional arrays and mathematical functions.

- JAX has a powerful set of function transformations, including automatic differentiation (autodiff), JIT compilation, auto-vectorization, and parallelization, which are arbitrarily composable.

- JAX provides good computational performance thanks to its ability to use modern hardware such as TPU or GPU, JIT compilation with XLA, auto-vectorization, and easy parallelization across the cluster.

- JAX uses a functional programming paradigm and requires pure functions without side effects.

- JAX has a constantly growing ecosystem of modules, and you have the freedom to combine different blocks that best suit your needs.

- Compared to TensorFlow and PyTorch, JAX is a pretty minimalistic framework, but thanks to its constantly growing ecosystem, there are many good libraries to fit your particular needs.

Your first program in JAX

This chapter covers

- The high-level structure of a JAX deep learning project
- Loading a dataset
- Creating a simple neural network in JAX
- Using JAX transformations for auto-vectorization, calculating gradients, and just-in-time compilation
- Saving and loading a model
- Pure and impure functions

JAX is a library for composable transformations of Python and NumPy programs. Though it is not limited to deep learning research, it is often considered a deep learning framework, sometimes the third after PyTorch and TensorFlow. Therefore, many people start by learning JAX for deep learning applications.

In this chapter, we'll do a deep learning Hello World exercise. We will build a simple neural network application demonstrating the JAX approach to building a deep learning model. It's an image classification model that works on the MNIST handwritten digit dataset—a problem you've likely seen or addressed with PyTorch or

TensorFlow. This project will introduce you to three of the main JAX transformations: `grad()` for taking gradients, `jit()` for compilation, and `vmap()` for auto-vectorization. With just these three transformations, you can build custom neural network solutions that do not need to be distributed on a cluster (for distributed computations, there is a separate `pmap()` transformation).

The chapter provides an overall, big-picture view, highlighting JAX features and essential concepts. I will explain the details of these concepts in later chapters.

The code for this chapter can be found in the book's code repository. I use Google Colab notebook with GPU runtime. It is the easiest way to start using JAX. Colab has JAX preinstalled, and JAX can use hardware acceleration. Later in the book, we will also use Google TPU with JAX. So, I'd recommend running this code in the Colab notebooks. Appendix B contains instructions on how to start with Colab.

You may run the code on a different system, so you might need to install JAX manually. To do so, check appendix A. It contains instructions on how to install JAX.

Let's start with defining a toy problem we want to solve.

2.1   *A toy ML problem: Classifying handwritten digits*

The task of image classification is ubiquitous among computer vision tasks: you can classify foods from a photo of a grocery shelf, determine the type of galaxy in astronomy, determine animal species, or recognize a digit from a ZIP code.

Imagine you have a labeled set of images, each one being assigned a label—say, "cat," "dog," or "human"—or a set of images with numbers from 0 to 9 with the corresponding labels. This is usually called *the training set*. Then you want a program that will take a new image without a label, and you want it to assign one of the predefined, meaningful labels to the photo. You typically test your final model on the *test set*, which the model did not see during training. Sometimes, there is also a *validation set* to tune model hyperparameters during training and choose the best ones.

In the modern deep learning era, you typically train a neural network to perform this task. You then integrate the trained neural network into a program to feed the network with data and interpret its outputs. For example, this might be a program for butterfly classification. When you take a photo of a butterfly, the photo is processed by a neural network that produces output (technically, output neuron activations for each butterfly class known to the network). Then, the program interprets this data, for example, by choosing the class with the maximum activation and displaying a label with a butterfly name in the interface.

Classification and regression tasks

Classification is one of the standard machine learning tasks that, together with regression, falls under the umbrella of supervised learning. In both tasks, you have a dataset of examples (a training set) that provides the supervision signal (hence, the name "supervised learning") of what is correct for each example.

(continued)

In classification, the supervision signal is a class label, so you must distinguish between a fixed number of classes. It could be classifying a dog breed by a photo or a tweet sentiment by its text or marking a specific card transaction as a fraud by its characteristics and previous history.

A special case of a multiclass classification called *binary* classification is when you need to distinguish an object between only two classes. Classes can be mutually exclusive (say, animal species) or not (say, assigning predefined tags to a photo). The former case is called a *multiclass* classification and the latter, a *multilabel* classification.

In regression, a supervision signal is usually a continuous number; you need to predict this number for new cases. It could be a prediction of room temperature at some point by other measurements and factors, a house price based on its characteristics and location, or the amount of food on your plate based on its photo.

We will take a well-known MNIST dataset (https://www.tensorflow.org/datasets/catalog/mnist) of handwritten digits. Figure 2.2 shows some example images from the dataset.

Now, we introduce a mental model of the process and then explore its steps in more detail. The chapters of the book explain the steps even further; I will point to specific chapters along the way.

2.2   An overview of a JAX deep learning project

A typical JAX deep learning project consists of the following steps:

1 Choose a dataset for your particular task. In our example, we use the MNIST dataset.

2 Create a data loader to read your dataset and transform it into a sequence of batches. We will use the data loader from TensorFlow Datasets.

3 Define a model that works with a single data point. JAX needs pure functions (more on this later in the chapter) without state and side effects, so you separate model parameters from the function that applies the neural network to data. A neural network model is defined as (a) a set of model parameters and (b) a function performing computations given the parameters and input data. You can also use high-level neural network libraries on top of JAX to define your models.

4 Define a model that works with a batch of data. In JAX, this is typically done by auto-vectorizing the model function from step 3.

5 Define a loss function that takes in model parameters and a batch of data. It calculates the loss value, which is usually some error we want to minimize. We will use the categorical cross-entropy loss, which is frequently used for multiclass classification.

6 Obtain gradients of the loss function with respect to the model parameters. The gradient function is evaluated on the model parameters and the input data and produces gradients for each model parameter. We will use JAX's `grad()` transformation for this.

7 Implement a gradient update step. The gradients are used to update the model parameters with some gradient descent procedure. You can update model parameters directly (as we'll do) or use a special optimizer from a separate library (say, Optax; we will use it later in chapter 11).

8 Implement the complete training loop.

9 The model is compiled to the target hardware platform using JIT compilation. This step may significantly speed up your computations.

10 You may also distribute model training across a cluster of computers.

11 After running the training loop for several epochs, you get a trained model (an updated set of the parameters) that can be used for predictions or any other task you designed the model for.

12 Save your trained model.

13 Use the model. Depending on your case, you can deploy the model using some production infrastructure or just load it and perform calculations without specialized infrastructure:

 a For saving and restoring model weights, you may use standard Python tools like `pickle` or safer solutions like `safetensors`. Higher-level libraries on top of JAX may also provide their own means for loading/saving models.

 b For deployment, there are several options available. For example, you can convert your model to TensorFlow or TFLite and use their well-developed ecosystem for model deployment.

Step 1 of our process is already done. Let's continue going through this process step by step, starting with loading the dataset and preparing it for the solution we will develop in the chapter. See figure 2.1 for a depiction of these steps.

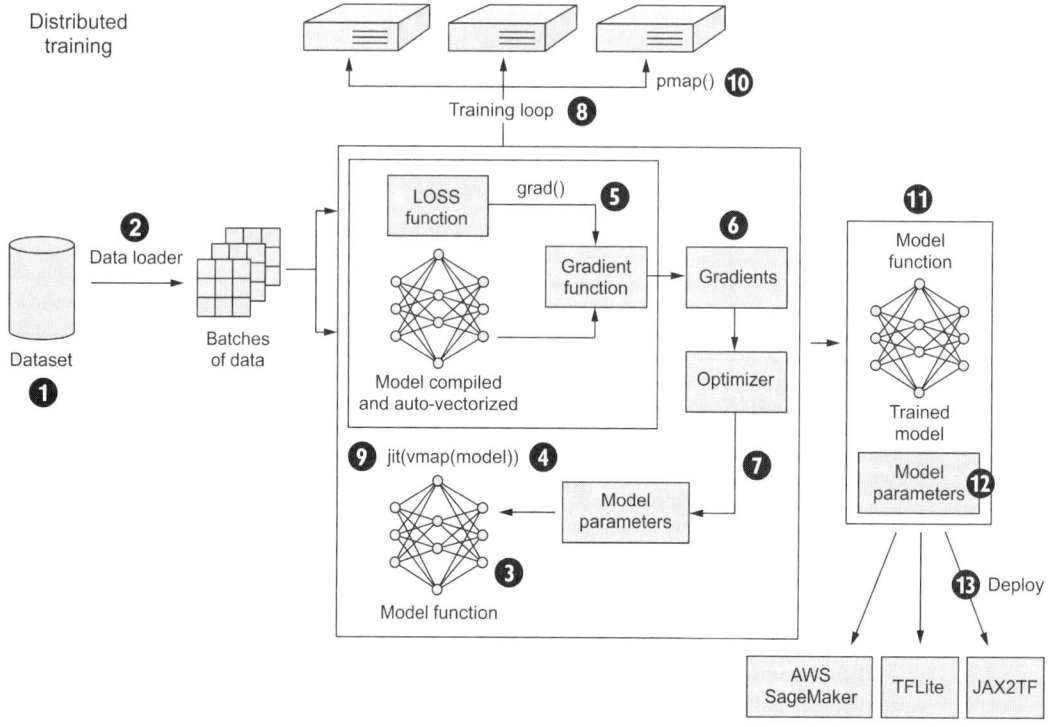

Figure 2.1   High-level structure of a JAX project, with data loading, training, and deployment to production

2.3   *Loading and preparing the dataset*

As mentioned in chapter 1, JAX does not include any data loaders, as JAX tends to concentrate on its core strengths. You can easily use TensorFlow or PyTorch data loaders, whichever you prefer or are more familiar with. JAX official documentation contains examples of both of them. We will use TensorFlow Datasets with its data loading API for this particular example. In the JAX documentation, you can find an example of how to use PyTorch data loaders.

TensorFlow Datasets contain a version of the MNIST dataset, not surprisingly under the name `mnist`. The total number of images is 70,000. The dataset provides a train/test split with 60,000 images in the train and 10,000 in the test part. Images are grayscale with a size of 28×28 pixels.

Listing 2.1   Loading the dataset

```
import tensorflow as tf                          Imports relevant modules
import tensorflow_datasets as tfds               from TensorFlow

data_dir = '/tmp/tfds'          ◄──────    A temporary directory for
                                           downloading the data
```

Loads the MNIST dataset using a function from TensorFlow Datasets. The as_supervised=True parameter returns the data as an (image, label) tuple instead of a dict.

```
data, info = tfds.load(name="mnist",
                       data_dir=data_dir,
                       as_supervised=True,
                       with_info=True)

data_train = data['train']
data_test  = data['test']
```

Extracts train and test splits from the data

After loading the data, we can look at the samples from the dataset with the following code.

Listing 2.2   Showing samples from the dataset

```
import numpy as np
import matplotlib.pyplot as plt
plt.rcParams['figure.figsize'] = [10, 5]

ROWS = 3
COLS = 10

i = 0
fig, ax = plt.subplots(ROWS, COLS)
for image, label in data_train.take(ROWS*COLS):
    ax[int(i/COLS), i%COLS].axis('off')
    ax[int(i/COLS), i%COLS].set_title(str(label.numpy()))
    ax[int(i/COLS), i%COLS].imshow(np.reshape(image, (28,28)), cmap='gray')
    i += 1

plt.show()
```

Imports Matplotlib drawing module and sets the canvas size

Parameters for image layout: we want to present images in a grid of 3 rows and 10 columns.

Displays each example at the corresponding position inside the grid, turning off the axis coordinates, providing a class label as an image title, and displaying each image with the grayscale palette

The preceding code generates the image in figure 2.2.

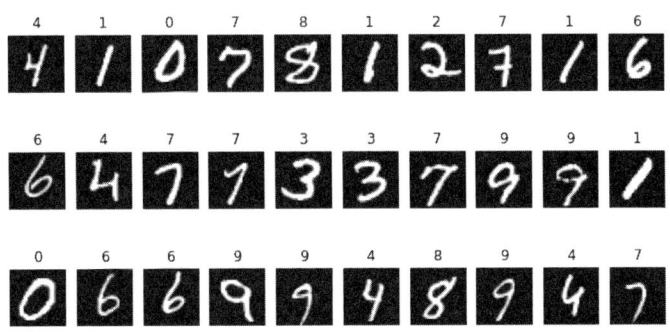

Figure 2.2   Examples from the MNIST dataset. Each handwritten image has a class label displayed above it.

As the images are the same size, we can work with them similarly and pack multiple images into a batch. The only preprocessing we might want is normalization. It converts the pixel byte values (`uint8`) from integer values in the range of [0, 255] into the floating type (`float32`) with the range of [0,1].

Listing 2.3   Preprocessing the dataset and splitting it into batches

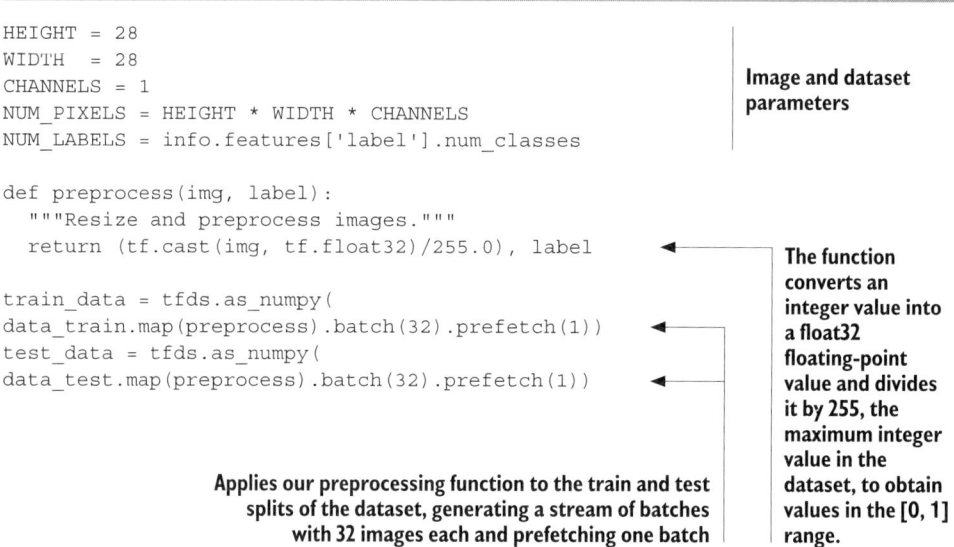

```
HEIGHT = 28
WIDTH  = 28
CHANNELS = 1
NUM_PIXELS = HEIGHT * WIDTH * CHANNELS
NUM_LABELS = info.features['label'].num_classes

def preprocess(img, label):
  """Resize and preprocess images."""
  return (tf.cast(img, tf.float32)/255.0), label

train_data = tfds.as_numpy(
data_train.map(preprocess).batch(32).prefetch(1))
test_data = tfds.as_numpy(
data_test.map(preprocess).batch(32).prefetch(1))
```

Image and dataset parameters

The function converts an integer value into a float32 floating-point value and divides it by 255, the maximum integer value in the dataset, to obtain values in the [0, 1] range.

Applies our preprocessing function to the train and test splits of the dataset, generating a stream of batches with 32 images each and prefetching one batch

We ask the data loader to apply the `preprocess` function to each example, pack all the images into a set of batches of 32 items, and prefetch a new batch without waiting for the previous batch to finish processing on the GPU.

Step 2 is done, and it is enough now. We can switch to developing our first neural network with JAX. Along the way, we will highlight the differences between JAX and more traditional frameworks like NumPy, TensorFlow, and PyTorch.

2.4   *A simple neural network in JAX*

Now step 3. Here, we use a feed-forward neural network known as a multilayer perceptron (MLP). It is a very simple (but far from being the best) network chosen for demonstrating important concepts without too much complexity. We will use a more advanced solution in chapter 11.

Our solution will be a simple two-layer MLP, a typical Hello World example for neural networks. The neural network we will develop is shown in figure 2.3.

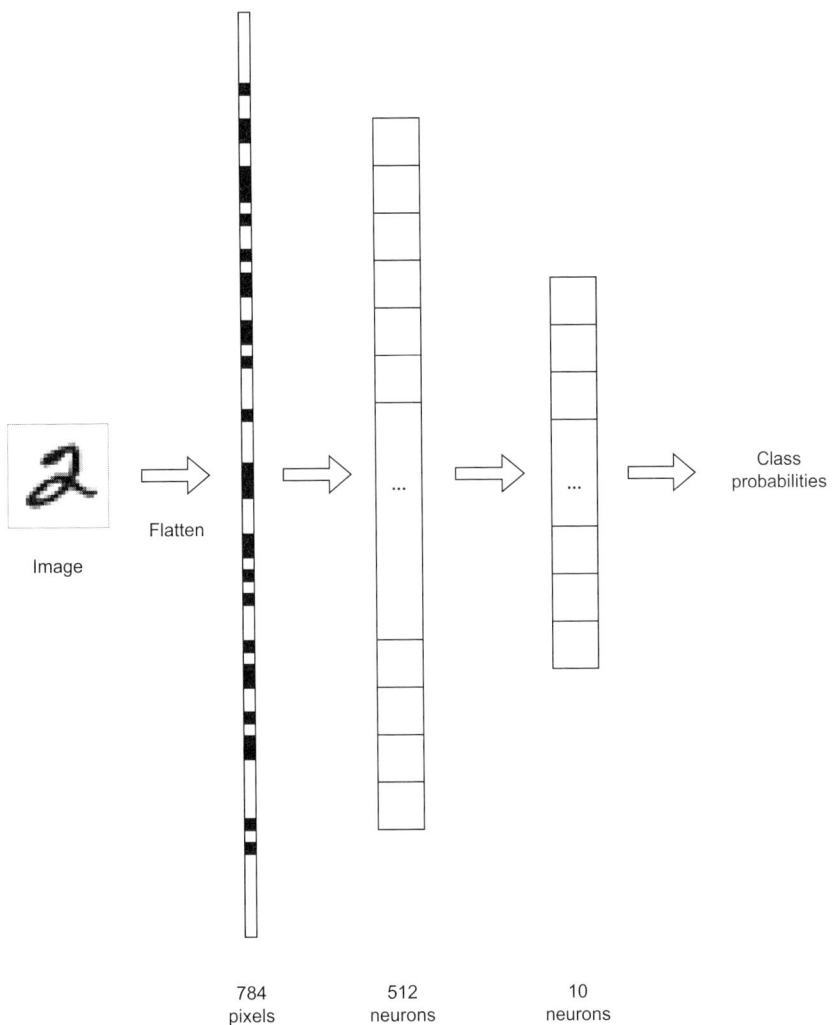

Image   Flatten

784   512   10
pixels   neurons   neurons

Class probabilities

Figure 2.3   Structure of our neural network. The image of 28 × 28 pixels is flattened into 784 pixels without a 2D structure and passed to the network's input layer. Then a fully connected hidden layer with 512 neurons follows, and another fully connected output layer with 10 neurons produces target class activations.

The image is flattened into a 1D array of 784 values (because a 28 × 28 image contains 784 pixels), and this array is the input to the neural network. The *input layer* maps each of the 784 image pixels to a separate input unit. Then a fully connected (or dense) layer with 512 neurons follows. It is called the *hidden layer* because it is located between the input and output layers. Each of the 512 neurons "looks" at all the input elements simultaneously. Then, another fully connected layer follows. It is called the *output layer*. It has 10 neurons, the same number as there are classes in the dataset. Each output neuron is responsible for its class. Say neuron #0 produces the probability of the class 0, neuron #1 for the class 1, and so on. Hence, the output layer produces a probability distribution with the probability values predicted by the neurons in the output layer summing to 1.

Each feed-forward layer implements a simple function $y = f(x \times w + b)$, consisting of weights w, that multiplies incoming data x and biases b, which are added to the product. Activation function $f()$ is a nonlinear function applied to the result of multiplication and addition.

The process of creating a neural network in JAX is different from the same process in PyTorch/TensorFlow in several ways, namely, in using random number generators for model parameter initialization and in how model code and parameters are structured.

Regarding the first difference, random number generators in JAX require their state to be provided externally to be functionally pure (the PRNGKey in figure 2.4 plays this role). Regarding the second difference, the forward pass function must also be stateless and functionally pure, so model parameters are passed there as some input data. This is not the case in PyTorch and Tensorflow, where model parameters are stored inside some objects together with code. In other aspects, a forward pass function looks pretty much the same.

I visualized the process of creating a model in figure 2.4.

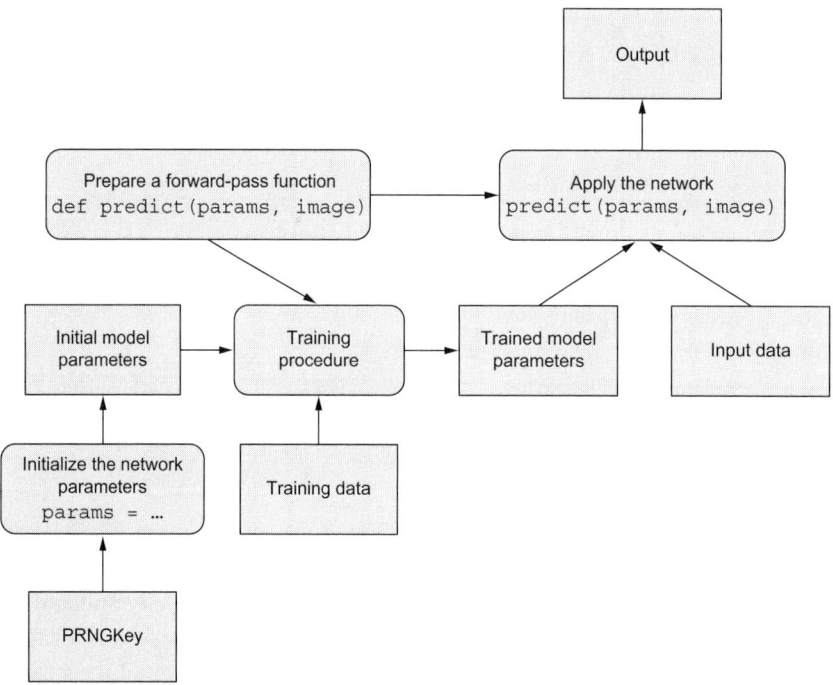

Figure 2.4   The process of initializing and applying a neural network in JAX

First, we need to initialize the layer parameters.

2.4.1 Neural network initialization

Before training a neural network, we need to initialize all the `b` and `w` parameters with random numbers.

Listing 2.4 Initializing the neural network

```
from jax import random                          The list with layer sizes

LAYER_SIZES = [28*28, 512, 10]                  Parameter for scaling
PARAM_SCALE = 0.01                              random values

def init_network_params(sizes, key=random.PRNGKey(0), scale=1e-2):
  """Initialize all layers for a fully-connected
neural network with given sizes"""

                                                Generates random keys
  def random_layer_params(m, n, key, scale=1e-2):   (more on this in chapter 7)
    """A helper function to randomly initialize
  weights and biases of a dense layer"""
    w_key, b_key = random.split(key)            Generates random
    return scale * random.normal(w_key, (n, m)),  values for the layer
scale * random.normal(b_key, (n,))              parameters w and b

  keys = random.split(key, len(sizes))
  return [random_layer_params(m, n, k, scale)   Running generation
for m, n, k in zip(sizes[:-1], sizes[1:], keys)]  for all the layers

params = init_network_params(
LAYER_SIZES, random.PRNGKey(0), scale=PARAM_SCALE)
```

Working with random numbers in JAX differs from NumPy because JAX requires pure functions, and the NumPy random number generators (RNG) are not pure because they use a hidden internal state. TensorFlow and PyTorch RNGs usually also use an internal state. JAX implements random number generators that are purely functional, and I will talk about them in depth in chapter 9. For now, it's enough to understand that you must provide each call of a randomized function with an RNG state, which is called a *key* here, and you should use every key only once, so each time you need a new key, you split an old key into the required number of new ones. Step 3a is done.

2.4.2 Neural network forward pass

Then, you need a function that performs all the neural network computations, the forward pass. This is almost the same function as `forward(self, x)` in PyTorch or `call(self, x)` in Tensorflow/Keras, except how you pass model parameters there. In JAX, it looks like `predict(params, x)`. The function name doesn't matter; you may call it `forward()`, `call()`, or anything else. What matters is that it's not a class function but a function with model parameters passed as a function parameter (sorry for the tautology). So, you have `params` instead of `self`.

For the forward pass, we already have initial values for the `b` and `w` parameters. The only missing part is the activation function. We will use the popular Swish activation function from the `jax.nn` library.

Activation functions

Activation functions are essential components in the deep learning world. Activation functions provide nonlinearity in neural network computations. Without nonlinearity, a multilayer feed-forward network will be equivalent to a single layer. Because of simple mathematics, a linear combination of linear combinations of inputs is still a linear combination of inputs, which is what a single neuron does. We know that single-neuron capabilities for solving complex classification problems are limited to linearly separable tasks (you have probably heard of the well-known XOR problem that is impossible to solve with a linear classifier). So, activation functions ensure neural network expressivity and prevent collapse to a simpler model.

Many different activation functions have been discovered. The field started with simple and easy-to-understand functions like the sigmoid or the hyperbolic tangent. They are smooth and have properties mathematicians love, such as being differentiable at each point.

$$\text{Sigmoid}(x) = \frac{1}{1 + e^{-x}}$$

$$\text{Tanh}(x) = \frac{2}{1 + e^{-2x}} - 1$$

Then a new kind of function emerged, a rectified linear unit (ReLU). ReLU was not smooth, and its derivative at the point x = 0 does not exist. Yet, practitioners found that neural networks learn faster with ReLU.

$$\text{ReLU}(x) = \max(0, x)$$

Then many other activation functions were found—some experimentally and others by rational design. Among the popular designed functions are Gaussian error linear units (GELUs, https://arxiv.org/abs/1606.08415) and scaled exponential linear units (SELUs, https://arxiv.org/abs/1706.02515).

$$\text{Selu}(x) = scale * \begin{cases} x, & x > 0 \\ \alpha e^x - \alpha, & x \leq 0 \end{cases}$$

Among the latest trends in deep learning is automatic discovery. It is typically called the Neural Architecture Search (NAS). The idea of the approach is to design a rich yet manageable search space that describes components of interest. It could be activation functions, layer types, optimizer update equations, etc. Then, we run an automatic procedure to search through this space intelligently. Different approaches may also use reinforcement learning, evolutionary computations, or even gradient descent. The Swish (https://arxiv.org/abs/1710.05941) function was found this way.

$$\text{Swish}(x) = x \cdot \text{sigmoid}(\beta x)$$

NAS is an exciting story, and I believe that JAX's rich expressivity can significantly contribute to this field. Maybe some of our readers will make an exciting advancement in deep learning!

Here, we develop a forward-pass function, often called a *predict* function. It takes an image to classify and performs all the forward-pass computations to produce activations on the output layer neurons. The neuron with the highest activation determines the class of the input image (so, if the highest activation is on neuron 5, then, according to the most straightforward approach, the neural network has detected that the input image contains the handwritten number 5).

Listing 2.5   The forward pass of a neural network

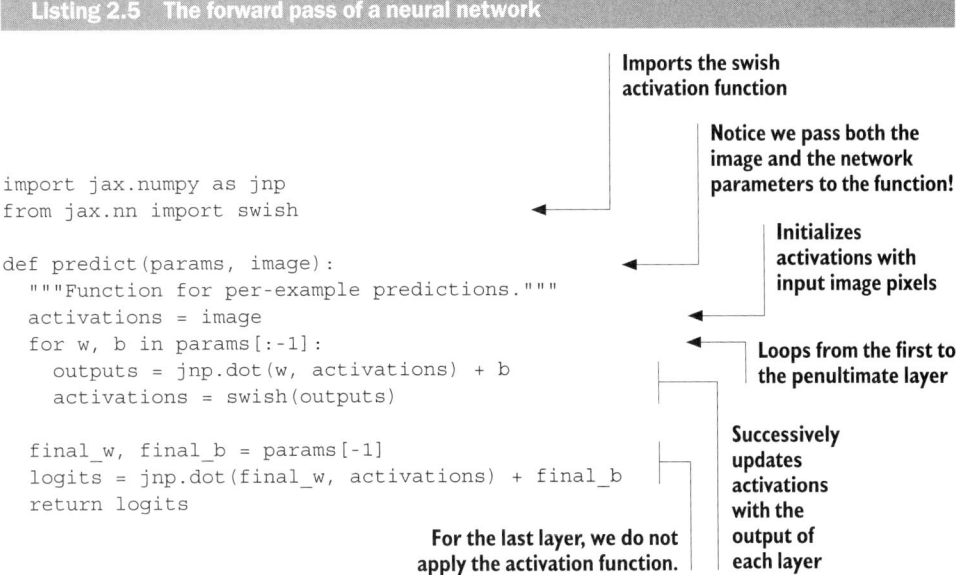

```
import jax.numpy as jnp
from jax.nn import swish

def predict(params, image):
  """Function for per-example predictions."""
  activations = image
  for w, b in params[:-1]:
    outputs = jnp.dot(w, activations) + b
    activations = swish(outputs)

  final_w, final_b = params[-1]
  logits = jnp.dot(final_w, activations) + final_b
  return logits
```

Imports the swish activation function

Notice we pass both the image and the network parameters to the function!

Initializes activations with input image pixels

Loops from the first to the penultimate layer

Successively updates activations with the output of each layer

For the last layer, we do not apply the activation function.

Notice how we pass the list of parameters here. It differs from a typical program in PyTorch or TensorFlow, where these parameters are usually hidden inside a class, and a function uses class variables to access them.

Keep an eye on how the neural network calculations are structured. In JAX, you typically have two functions for your neural networks: one for initializing parameters and another one for applying your neural network to some input data. The first function returns parameters as some data structure (here, a list of arrays; later, it will be a special data structure called *pytree*). The second one takes in parameters and the data and returns the result of applying the neural network to the data. This pattern will appear many times in the future, even in high-level neural network frameworks.

That's it. We can use our new function for per-example predictions. Here, in listing 2.6, we generate an image of the same size as in our dataset and with random pixel values. We then pass it to the `predict()` function. You can use a real image from the dataset as well. Do not expect good results, as our neural network is not trained yet. Here, we are only interested in the output shape, and we see that our prediction returns a tuple of 10 activations for the 10 classes.

Listing 2.6   Making a prediction

```
random_flattened_image = \
    random.normal(random.PRNGKey(1), (28*28*1,))    ◄──  Generates an image of size
                                                          28 × 28 pixels with a
                                                          single color channel and
                                                          random pixel values
preds = predict(params, random_flattened_image)     ◄──  Passes an image to the
                                                          prediction function
print(preds.shape)

>>> (10,)                                            ◄──  The prediction contains a
                                                          tuple of activations for
                                                          the 10 classes.
```

Step 3b is also done.

So, everything looks okay, but we want to work on batches of images, yet our function was designed to work only with a single image. Auto-batching can help here!

2.5   *vmap: Auto-vectorizing calculations to work with batches*

Interestingly, our `predict()` function was designed to work on a single item, and it will not work if we pass in a batch of images. To test what happens with batches, we may generate a random batch of 32 images, 28 × 28 pixels each, and pass it to the `predict()` function. You can see the modified code in listing 2.7. We added some exception processing as well, but this is only to reduce the size of an error message and to highlight the most crucial part.

Listing 2.7   Making a prediction for a batch

```
random_flattened_images = \
    random.normal(random.PRNGKey(1), (32, 28*28*1))    ◄──  Generates a batch of 32
                                                            random images of size 28
                                                            × 28 pixels and a single
                                                            color channel each
try:
    preds = predict(params, random_flattened_images)   ◄──  Passes a batch of
                                                            images to the
                                                            single-element
                                                            prediction function
except TypeError as e:
    print(e)

>>> dot_general requires contracting dimensions
    to have the same shape, got (784,) and (32,).      ◄──  The error message shows
                                                            that the single-element
                                                            prediction function cannot
                                                            process a batch of images.
```

Getting this error is not surprising, as our `predict()` function was a straightforward implementation of matrix calculations, and these calculations assume specific array shapes. The error message says the dimension along which the dot product is calculated must be the same shape. It expected 784 numbers for calculating a dot product with the weights array, and the new batch dimension (here, the size of 32) confuses it. We must change something to fix the problem and adapt the program to work with this additional dimension.

Tensors, matrices, vectors, and scalars

In deep learning, multidimensional arrays are the primary data structures used to communicate between neural networks and their layers. They are also called *tensors*. In mathematics or physics, tensors have a stricter and more complicated meaning; just do not be embarrassed if you find something difficult about tensors. Here, in deep learning, they are just synonyms for multidimensional arrays. And if you worked with NumPy, you know almost everything you need.

There are particular forms of tensors or multidimensional arrays. A matrix is a tensor with two dimensions (or rank-2 tensor), a vector is a tensor with one dimension (rank-1 tensor), and a scalar (or just a number) is a tensor with zero dimensions (rank-0 tensor). So, tensors are generalizations of scalars, vectors, and matrices to an arbitrary number of dimensions (a rank).

For example, your loss function value is a scalar (just one number). An array of class probabilities at the output of a classification neural network for a single input is a vector of size k (the number of classes) and one dimension (do not confuse size and rank). An array of such predictions for a batch of data (several inputs at once) is a matrix of size k × m (where k is the number of classes and m is the batch size). An RGB image is a rank-3 tensor with three dimensions (width, height, and color channels). A batch of RGB images is a rank-4 tensor (the new dimension being the batch dimension). A stream of video frames can also be considered a rank-4 tensor (with time being the new dimension). A batch of videos is a rank-5 tensor, and so on. In deep learning, you usually work with tensors with no more than four or five dimensions.

What are our options to fix the problem?

First, there is a naive solution. We can write a loop that decomposes the batch into individual images and process them sequentially. It will work, but it would be inefficient, as most hardware can potentially do many more calculations in a unit of time. In such a case, it will be significantly underutilized. If you have already worked with MATLAB, NumPy, or something similar, you are familiar with the benefits of vectorization. It would be an efficient solution to the problem.

So, the second option is to rewrite and manually vectorize the `predict()` function so it can accept batches of data as its input. It usually means our input tensors will have an additional batch dimension, and we need to rewrite the calculations to use it. It is straightforward for simple calculations, but it can be complicated for sophisticated functions. You usually work this way when writing neural networks on top of NumPy or using low-level primitives of TensorFlow and PyTorch. Higher-level libraries in the TensorFlow/PyTorch ecosystem may provide you with an interface that hides this complexity.

And here comes the third option: automatic vectorization. JAX provides the `vmap()` transformation that transforms a function that works with a single element into one that can work on batches. This is what you'll probably use most of the time in JAX, as it is the most convenient way and produces excellent performance. I bet you'll like it. However, nothing prohibits you from using other options as well.

Listing 2.8   Auto-vectorizing a function

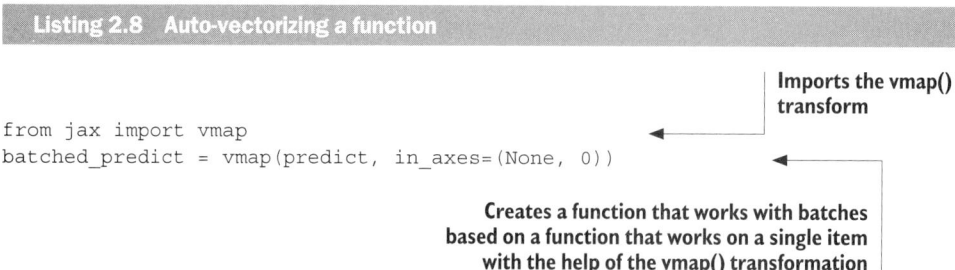

```
from jax import vmap
batched_predict = vmap(predict, in_axes=(None, 0))
```

Imports the vmap() transform

Creates a function that works with batches based on a function that works on a single item with the help of the vmap() transformation

It's just a one-liner. You may skip the following paragraph, as we will explain everything in detail in chapter 6. For those interested, we briefly describe the meaning of this code.

The `in_axes` parameter controls which input array axes to map over (or to vectorize). Its length must equal the number of positional arguments of the function. `None` indicates we need not map any axes, and in our example, it corresponds to the first parameter of the `predict()` function, which is `params`. This parameter stays the same for any forward pass, so we do not need to batch over it (yet, if we used separate neural network weights for each call, we'd use this option). The second element of the `in_axes` tuple corresponds to the second parameter of the `predict()` function, `image`. The zero value means we want to batch over the first (zeroth) dimension, the dimension that contains different images. In the hypothetical case when the batch dimension will be in another position in a tensor, we'd change this number to the proper index.

Now we can apply our modified function to a batch and produce the correct outputs.

Listing 2.9   Using the `vmapped` function

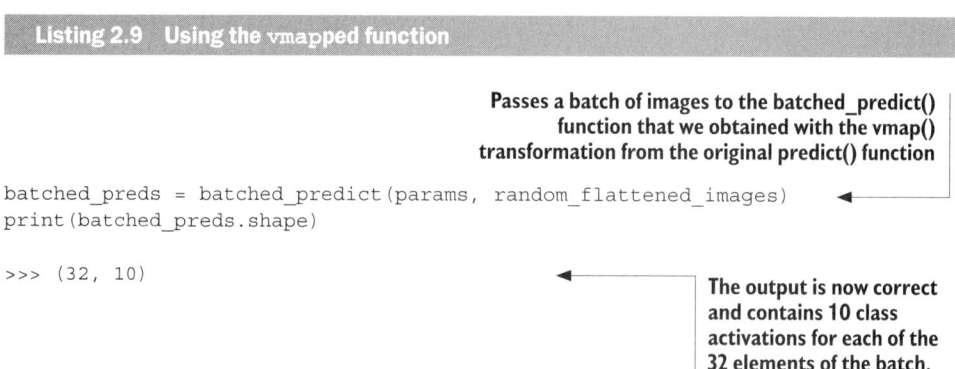

Passes a batch of images to the batched_predict() function that we obtained with the vmap() transformation from the original predict() function

```
batched_preds = batched_predict(params, random_flattened_images)
print(batched_preds.shape)

>>> (32, 10)
```

The output is now correct and contains 10 class activations for each of the 32 elements of the batch.

Notice the significant thing. We did not change our original function. We created a new one.

vmap() is a beneficial transformation, as it frees you from doing manual vectorization. Vectorization might not be a very intuitive procedure as you have to think in terms of matrices or tensors and their dimensions. It is not easy for everyone, and it might be an error-prone process, so it is fantastic that we have automated vectorization in JAX. You write a function for a single example, then run it for a batch with the help of vmap().

Step 4 is done. We created a neural network that can work with batches. The only missing part now is training. Here comes another exciting part. We need to train it.

2.6 *Autodiff: How to calculate gradients without knowing about derivatives*

We typically use a gradient descent procedure to train a neural network. While the general idea is still the same as for PyTorch/Tensorflow, this process significantly differs from those frameworks. I provide a thorough description and comparison in chapter 4.

We will use an almost straightforward mini-batch gradient descent with an exponentially decaying learning rate and without momentum, similar to a vanilla stochastic gradient descent (SGD) optimizer in any deep learning framework.

Gradient descent procedure

Gradient descent is a simple iterative procedure for finding the local minima of a differentiable function. For a differentiable function, we can find a gradient, the direction of the most significant change of a function. If we go opposite the gradient, this is the direction of the steepest descent. We go to a local minimum of a function by taking repeated steps.

Neural networks are differentiable functions determined by their parameters (weights). We want to find a combination of weights that minimizes some loss function, which calculates the discrepancy between the model prediction and the ground truth values. If the difference is smaller, the predictions are better. We can apply gradient descent to solve this task.

We start from some random weights, a chosen loss function, and a training dataset. Then, we repeatedly calculate the gradient of the loss function with respect to current weights on the training dataset (or some batch from the dataset). After calculating a gradient for each weight in a neural network, we can update each weight in the opposite direction, subtracting some part of the gradient from the weight value. The procedure stops after some predefined number of iterations, when loss improvement stops, or by other criteria. The process is visualized in the following figure.

The loss function is the curve where there is a corresponding loss value for any weight value. This curve is also called a *loss curve* or a *fitness landscape* (this makes sense in more complex cases with more than a single dimension).

Here, we started from some initial random weight (W_0) and, after a series of steps, came to the global minimum corresponding to some specific weight (W_k). The special parameter called a *learning rate* determines how great or small an amount of the gradient we take.

(continued)

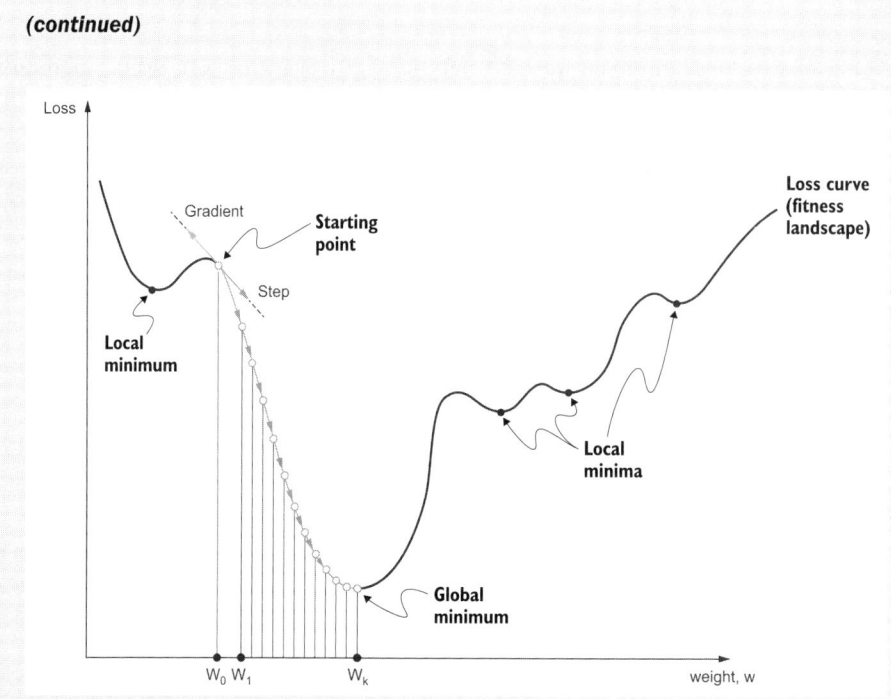

Visualizing gradient descent steps along the loss landscape

Repeating such steps, we follow the trajectory that leads to a local minimum of the loss function. And we hope this local minimum is the same as the global one, or at least not significantly worse. Strangely enough, this works for neural networks. Why it works so well is an interesting topic on its own.

In this figure, for demonstration purposes, I have chosen a "good" starting point for which it is easy to come to the global minimum. Starting in other places of the fitness landscape may lead to local minima, and there are few of them in the image.

This vanilla gradient descent procedure has many improvements, including gradient descent with momentum and adaptive gradient descent methods such as Adam, Adadelta, RMSProp, LAMB, etc. Many of them help in overcoming some local minima as well.

To implement such a procedure, we need to start with some random point in the parameter space (we already did when we initialized the neural network parameters in the previous section).

2.6.1   Loss function

Now, we need a loss function to evaluate our current set of parameters on the training dataset. The loss function calculates the discrepancy between the model prediction and the ground truth values from the training dataset labels. There are many different loss functions for specific machine learning tasks, and we will use a simple loss function suitable for multiclass classification, the categorical cross-entropy function.

It is almost the same loss function as for other frameworks but with the same difference as for the forward-pass function—it should be functionally pure, and we need to provide it with the model parameters.

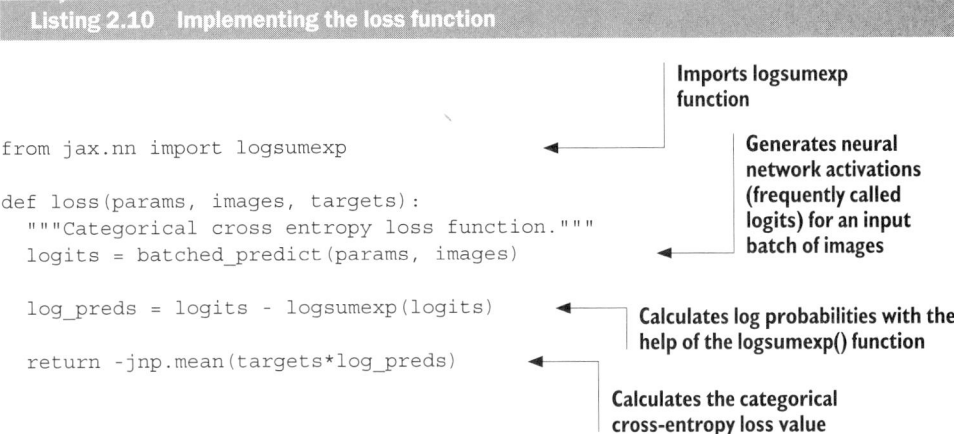

Listing 2.10 Implementing the loss function

```
from jax.nn import logsumexp

def loss(params, images, targets):
    """Categorical cross entropy loss function."""
    logits = batched_predict(params, images)

    log_preds = logits - logsumexp(logits)

    return -jnp.mean(targets*log_preds)
```

Imports logsumexp function

Generates neural network activations (frequently called logits) for an input batch of images

Calculates log probabilities with the help of the logsumexp() function

Calculates the categorical cross-entropy loss value

Here, we use a `logsumexp()` function, a common trick in machine learning to normalize a vector of log probabilities without having under- or overflow numerical issues. If you want to learn more about this topic, see https://mng.bz/BdJq.

The `loss()` function needs ground truth values, or targets, to calculate the discrepancy between the model prediction and the ground truth. Model predictions are already in the form of class activations, where each output neuron produces some score for the corresponding class. The targets are originally just class numbers. For the class 0, it is the number 0; for the class 1, it is the number 1, and so on. We need to convert these numbers into activations, and in such cases, special one-hot encoding is used. The class "0" produces an array of activations with a number 1 being at position 0 and zeros at all the other positions. The class 1 produces a number 1 at position 1, and so on. This conversion will be done outside of the `loss()` function.

After the loss function is defined, step 5 is done. We are ready to implement the gradient descent update.

2.6.2 Obtaining gradients

The logic is simple. We have to calculate the gradients of the loss function with respect to the model parameters based on the current batch of data. Here comes the `grad()` transformation. The transformation takes in a function (here, the loss function). It creates a function that evaluates the gradient of the loss function with respect to a specific parameter, which is, by default, the first parameter of the function (here, the `params`). Step 6 is done this way.

2.6.3   *Gradient update step*

Gradient updating in JAX is distinct from other frameworks like TensorFlow and PyTorch. In those frameworks, you usually get gradients after performing the forward pass, and the framework tracks all the operations being done on the tensors of interest. JAX uses a different approach. It transforms your function and generates another function that calculates gradients. And then you calculate the gradients by providing all the relevant parameters, the neural network weights, and the data into this function.

Here, we calculate the gradients and then update all the parameters in the direction opposite to the gradient (hence, the minus sign in the weight update formulas). All the gradients are scaled with the learning rate parameter that depends on the number of epochs (one epoch is a complete pass through the training set). We made an exponentially decaying learning rate, so for later epochs, the learning rate will be lower than for the earlier ones.

Listing 2.11   Implementing the gradient update step

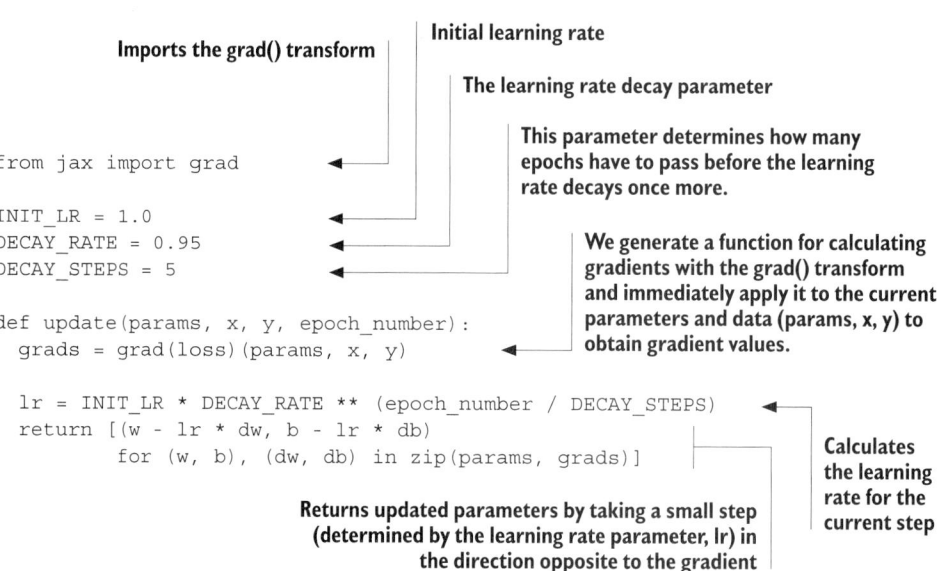

In this example, you do not calculate your loss function directly. You calculate only gradients. In many cases, you also want to track the loss values, and JAX provides another function, `value_and_grad()`, that calculates both the value and the gradient of a function. We can change the `update()` function accordingly.

Listing 2.12   Implementing the gradient update step with both loss value and gradient

```
from jax import value_and_grad

def update(params, x, y, epoch_number):
```
Importing value_and_grad function

```
loss_value, grads = value_and_grad(loss)(params, x, y)
lr = INIT_LR * DECAY_RATE ** (epoch_number / DECAY_STEPS)
return [(w - lr * dw, b - lr * db)
        for (w, b), (dw, db) in
        zip(params, grads)], loss_value
```

◀— **Calculating both the loss value and the gradient**

◀— **Returning both updated parameters and the loss value**

Step 7 is done.

2.6.4   *Training loop*

Now we need to run a training loop for a specified number of epochs. To do that, we need a few more utility functions to calculate accuracy and some logging to track all the relevant information during training.

Listing 2.13   Implementing gradient descent

```
from jax.nn import one_hot

num_epochs = 25

def batch_accuracy(params, images, targets):
  images = jnp.reshape(images, (len(images), NUM_PIXELS))
  predicted_class = jnp.argmax(batched_predict(params, images), axis=1)
  return jnp.mean(predicted_class == targets)

def accuracy(params, data):
  accs = []
  for images, targets in data:
    accs.append(batch_accuracy(params, images, targets))
  return jnp.mean(jnp.array(accs))

import time

for epoch in range(num_epochs):
  start_time = time.time()
  losses = []
  for x, y in train_data:
    x = jnp.reshape(x, (len(x), NUM_PIXELS))
    y = one_hot(y, NUM_LABELS)
    params, loss_value = update(params, x, y, epoch)
    losses.append(loss_value)
  epoch_time = time.time() - start_time

  start_time = time.time()
  train_acc = accuracy(params, train_data)
  test_acc = accuracy(params, test_data)
  eval_time = time.time() - start_time
  print("Epoch {} in {:0.2f} sec".format(epoch, epoch_time))
  print("Eval in {:0.2f} sec".format(eval_time))
  print("Training set loss {}".format(jnp.mean(jnp.array(losses))))
  print("Training set accuracy {}".format(train_acc))
  print("Test set accuracy {}".format(test_acc))
```

◀— **One more helper function to generate one-hot encoding for the class label**

◀— **Defines the number of epochs to train**

◀— **Calculates accuracy (the percentage of correct answers) for a batch**

◀— **Calculates accuracy for a whole dataset with many batches**

◀— **Flattens an input image into a ID array**

◀— **Converts a class label into one-hot encoding**

◀— **Updates parameters by a single step of the gradient descent procedure**

◀— **Stores the loss value for training statistics**

◀— **Logs time for training statistics**

Once per epoch calculates accuracy on the train and test data

We are ready to run our first training loop:

```
Epoch 0 in 36.39 sec
Eval in 8.06 sec
Training set loss 0.41040700674057007
Training set accuracy 0.9299499988555908
Test set accuracy 0.931010365486145
Epoch 1 in 32.82 sec
Eval in 6.47 sec
Training set loss 0.37730318307876587
Training set accuracy 0.9500166773796082
Test set accuracy 0.9497803449630737
Epoch 2 in 32.91 sec
Eval in 6.35 sec
Training set loss 0.3708733022212982
Training set accuracy 0.9603500366210938
Test set accuracy 0.9593650102615356
Epoch 3 in 32.88 sec
...
Epoch 23 in 32.63 sec
Eval in 6.32 sec
Training set loss 0.35422590374946594
Training set accuracy 0.9921666979789734
Test set accuracy 0.9811301827430725
Epoch 24 in 32.60 sec
Eval in 6.37 sec
Training set loss 0.354021817445755
Training set accuracy 0.9924833178520203
Test set accuracy 0.9812300205230713
```

Step 8 is done, and we trained our first neural network with JAX! It seems everything works, and it solves the problem of handwritten digit classification on the MNIST dataset with an accuracy of 98.12%. Not bad.

Our solution takes more than 30 seconds per epoch and an additional 6 seconds for the evaluation run each epoch. Is that fast or not? Let's check what improvements can be made with the JIT compilation, step 9 in our procedure.

2.7 JIT: Compiling your code to make it faster

We have already implemented an entire neural network for handwritten digit classification. It may even use GPU if you run it on a GPU machine, as all the tensors are placed by default on GPU in that case. However, we can make our solution even faster! The previous solution did not use JIT compilation and acceleration provided by XLA. Let's do it.

Compiling your functions is easy. You can use either `jit()` function transformation or `@jit` annotation. We will use the latter.

Here, we compile the two most resource-heavy functions, the `update()` and `batch_accuracy()` functions. All that you need is to add the `@jit` annotation before the function definitions.

Listing 2.14 Adding JIT compilation to the code

Imports the jit() transform

```
from jax import jit
```

Uses the jit() transform as a
function annotation

```
@jit
def update(params, x, y, epoch_number):
  loss_value, grads = value_and_grad(loss)(params, x, y)
  lr = INIT_LR * DECAY_RATE ** (epoch_number / DECAY_STEPS)
  return [(w - lr * dw, b - lr * db)
          for (w, b), (dw, db) in zip(params, grads)], loss_value


@jit
def batch_accuracy(params, images, targets):
  images = jnp.reshape(images, (len(images), NUM_PIXELS))
  predicted_class = jnp.argmax(batched_predict(params, images), axis=1)
  return jnp.mean(predicted_class == targets)
```

Step 9 is done now.

We omit step 10 here as we do not need distributed training for such a simple problem. There are many ways to distribute your computations in JAX, and I dedicate chapters 7 and 8 to these topics.

After reinitializing neural network parameters and rerunning the training loop, we get the following results:

```
Epoch 0 in 2.15 sec
Eval in 2.52 sec
Training set loss 0.41040700674057007
Training set accuracy 0.9299499988555908
Test set accuracy 0.931010365486145
Epoch 1 in 1.68 sec
Eval in 2.06 sec
Training set loss 0.37730318307876587
Training set accuracy 0.9500166773796082
Test set accuracy 0.9497803449630737
Epoch 2 in 1.69 sec
Eval in 2.01 sec
Training set loss 0.3708733022212982
Training set accuracy 0.9603500366210938
Test set accuracy 0.9593650102615356
Epoch 3 in 1.67 sec
...
Epoch 23 in 1.69 sec
Eval in 2.07 sec
Training set loss 0.35422590374946594
Training set accuracy 0.9921666979789734
Test set accuracy 0.9811301827430725
Epoch 24 in 1.69 sec
Eval in 2.06 sec
Training set loss 0.3540217876434326
Training set accuracy 0.9924833178520203
Test set accuracy 0.9812300205230713
```

Quality is the same, but the speed improved significantly. An epoch takes nearly 1.7 seconds instead of 32.6, and an evaluation run takes close to 2 seconds instead of 6.3 seconds. That's a pretty significant improvement!

You might also notice that the first iterations take longer than the subsequent ones. Because compilation happens during the first run of a function, the first run is slower. Subsequent runs use the compiled function and are faster. We will dive deeper into JIT compilation in chapter 5.

Step 11 is done, and we are almost done with our machine learning problem.

2.8   *Saving and deploying the model*

When you are done with your model, you first need to save it, and then, depending on your case, you may either want to deploy it somewhere or just occasionally load it and use it for some ad hoc calculations without the need to have production infrastructure.

JAX does not provide any special tool for saving a model because, technically speaking, JAX does not know anything about a model. It's just a framework for high-performance tensor calculations. The simplest way to save the model is by using standard Python tools like `pickle`. However, using `pickle` is not a good practice from a security standpoint, so it's better to use safer options. The `safetensors` package (https://github.com/huggingface/safetensors) provides a good replacement.

In the following listing, we save and restore model parameters stored as a nested Python data structure called a *pytree*. I dedicate chapter 10 to pytrees.

Listing 2.15   Saving and loading model parameters

```
import pickle                                        ◄──── Imports pickle module

model_weights_file = 'mlp_weights.pickle'            ◄──── File name for saved parameters

with open(model_weights_file, 'wb') as file:         │ Saves model parameters
    pickle.dump(params, file)

with open(model_weights_file, 'rb') as file:         │ Restores model parameters
    restored_params = pickle.load(file)
```

To use a restored model for inference in a separate program, we need to duplicate the code for the `predict()` or `batched_predict()` functions as well, as the saved file contains only the structure with model weights.

Higher-level neural network libraries on top of JAX, like Flax or Equinox, have their own concepts of a model and provide their own tools for model serialization/ deserialization. I touch on this topic in chapter 11, where we use Flax.

So, step 12 is done.

For step 13, we only showed model loading from a saved checkpoint. If you need a production infrastructure, that's a separate topic, and I'd recommend starting with the JAX2TF tool (https://www.tensorflow.org/guide/jax2tf), which provides an easy way to convert a JAX model into a TensorFlow SavedModel. Then you can do many different things, for example:

- Running *inference* on a server using TensorFlow (TF) Serving, on a device using TFLite, or on the web using TensorFlow.js
- Performing *fine-tuning* by continuing to train a JAX-trained model in TensorFlow with your existing training data and setup
- Doing *fusion* by combining parts of models that were trained using JAX with those trained using TensorFlow

Another project by Google, called Saxml or Sax (https://github.com/google/saxml), is an experimental system that serves JAX, Paxml (a JAX-based machine learning framework for training large-scale models, say, LLMs; see chapter 11), and PyTorch models for inference. A Sax cell (aka Sax cluster) consists of an admin server and a group of model servers. The admin server keeps track of model servers, assigns published models to model servers to serve, and helps clients locate model servers serving specific published models. This project just reached its 1.0.0 release.

Some tools work in the opposite direction, allowing the use of JAX with models created in other frameworks.

First, there is an experimental TF2JAX library by DeepMind (https://github.com/deepmind/tf2jax) for converting TensorFlow functions/graphs to JAX functions, allowing existing TF models to be reused and fine-tuned in JAX codebases.

There is a toolchain called JAX ONNX Runtime (https://github.com/google/jaxonnxruntime) that enables the seamless execution of open neural network exchange models using JAX as the backend.

There are also frameworks that unify different backends, usually TensorFlow, JAX, PyTorch, and NumPy. I'd highlight Keras 3 (https://keras.io/) and Ivy (https://github.com/ivy-llc/ivy). For example, Ivy can transpile a model from PyTorch to JAX (https://mng.bz/d6Az).

Let's consider some more general thoughts about how JAX differs from other frameworks and why its pure functional approach with composable function transformations is essential.

2.9 *Pure functions and composable transformations: Why are they important?*

We have created and trained our first neural network with JAX. Along the way, we highlighted some significant differences between JAX and classical frameworks like PyTorch and TensorFlow. These differences are based on the functional approach JAX follows.

As I have said several times, JAX functions must be pure. This means that their behavior must be defined only by their inputs, and the same input must always produce the same output. No internal state that affects calculations is allowed. Side effects are not allowed, either.

There are many reasons why pure functions are beneficial. Among them are easy parallelization, caching, and the ability to make functional compositions like `jit(vmap(grad(some_function)))`. Debugging is also easier.

One crucial difference we noticed is related to random numbers. NumPy random number generators (RNG) are impure as they contain an internal state. JAX makes its RNG explicitly pure. A state is passed into a function that requires randomness. So, given the same state, you will always produce the same "random" numbers. So be careful. I will talk about RNG in chapter 9.

Another critical difference is that neural network parameters are not hidden inside some object but are always explicitly passed around. Many neural network computations are structured in the following way: first, you generate, or initialize, your parameters; then, you pass them into a function that uses them for calculations. We will see this pattern in high-level neural network libraries on top of JAX, like Flax or Equinox. Gradients are also calculated and applied explicitly, with no hidden magic involved.

The neural network parameters become an entity on their own. And such structure gives you much freedom in what you do. You can implement custom updates, save and restore them easily, and create various function compositions.

Having no side effects is especially important when compiling your functions with JIT. You can get unexpected results when ignoring purity as `jit()` compiles and caches a function. If the function behavior is influenced by some state or produces some side effects, then a compiled version might save computations that happened during its first run and reproduce them on the subsequent calls, which might not be what you want. I will talk about that more in chapter 5.

Congratulations! We're done! Different parts of the project can be replaced with modules from the ecosystem, even in this typical project. If you work with more advanced topics in machine learning, like reinforcement learning, graph neural networks, meta-learning, or evolutionary computations, then you will add more special modules from the JAX ecosystem and/or change some parts of this general scheme.

That's it! We are ready to dive into the core JAX.

Exercise 2.1

1 Modify the `predict()` function to accept a list of activation functions for the hidden layer.
2 Modify the neural network architecture and/or training process to improve classification quality. Hints: Change architecture, activation functions, learning rate, optimizer, anything else.
3 Implement a different machine learning pipeline, for example, working with different types of data (e.g., a tweet sentiment classifier based on this dataset: https://mng.bz/rV7E).

Summary

- JAX does not have its own data loader; you can use an external data loader from PyTorch or TensorFlow.
- In JAX, parameters of a neural network are typically passed as an external parameter to the function performing all the calculations, not stored inside an object as is usually done in TensorFlow/PyTorch.
- Model parameters are stored in a nested Python data structure called pytree.
- Random number generators in JAX are stateless, so you need to provide an external state (a PRNGKey) to them.
- The `vmap()` transformation converts a function for a single input into a function working on a batch.
- You can calculate a gradient of your function with the `grad()` function.
- If you need both a value and a gradient of the function, you can use the `value_and_grad()` function.
- The `jit()` transformation compiles your function with the XLA linear algebra compiler and produces optimized code able to run on a CPU, GPU, or TPU.
- You can easily save and load model weights using standard Python libraries like `pickle` or safer modules like `safetensors` from Hugging Face.
- You can use the TensorFlow ecosystem to deploy JAX models with the JAX2TF package.
- You need to use pure functions with no internal state and side effects for your transformations to work correctly.

Part 2

Core JAX

Dive deeper into the mechanics of JAX in part 2, where we explore the core features that make JAX a formidable tool for deep learning and scientific computing. Spanning eight chapters, this section provides a thorough examination of JAX's capabilities, from working with arrays and calculating gradients to compiling, vectorizing, and parallelizing your code. Each chapter focuses on a fundamental aspect of JAX, illustrated with practical examples and in-depth discussions to solidify your understanding and skills.

Chapters 3 through 10 are meticulously designed to guide you through the intricacies of JAX, ensuring a mastery of its most powerful features. You'll start by working with arrays (chapter 3), to understand the nuances that differentiate JAX from NumPy and learn how to use these differences to your advantage. As you progress, you'll delve into calculating gradients (chapter 4) using JAX's automatic differentiation capabilities to simplify and accelerate the training of neural networks. Chapters 5 and 6 introduce you to JAX's just-in-time compilation and auto-vectorization, revealing strategies to significantly boost performance.

The journey through Core JAX doesn't stop there. You'll explore parallelizing your computations and using tensor sharding (chapters 7 and 8) to scale your applications across multiple devices, a critical skill for handling large-scale models and datasets. The exploration of random numbers in JAX (chapter 9) unveils the functional approach to randomness, ensuring reproducibility and efficiency in stochastic operations. Finally, chapter 10, on working with pytrees, teaches you to manage complex data structures elegantly, further enhancing your ability to build sophisticated models and algorithms with JAX.

By the end of part 2, you'll have a solid grasp of JAX's core functionalities and be equipped with the knowledge to tackle advanced deep learning projects. This section is crucial for anyone looking to harness the full potential of JAX in research or industry applications.

Working with arrays 3

This chapter covers

- Working with NumPy arrays
- Working with JAX arrays on CPU/GPU/TPU
- Adapting code to differences between NumPy arrays and JAX arrays
- Using high-level and low-level interfaces: `jax.numpy` and `jax.lax`

In the previous chapter, we developed a simple neural network on JAX. With this chapter, we start diving deeper into the JAX core, beginning with arrays (or tensors—we will use these words interchangeably).

The tensor or multidimensional array is the basic data structure in deep learning and scientific computing frameworks. Every program relies on some form of tensor, be it a 1D array, a 2D matrix, or a higher-dimensional array. Handwritten digit images from the previous chapter, intermediate activations, and the resulting network predictions—everything is a tensor. NumPy provides you with the `numpy.ndarray` type; in JAX, there is an `Array` type (previously known as `DeviceArray`).

NumPy arrays (the `numpy.ndarray` type) and their API became the de facto industry standard many other frameworks respect. JAX provides you with a (mostly)

NumPy-compatible API, so the transition from NumPy to JAX should not be hard, and there are many cases when you don't need to change anything in your code except the import statement. However, some things are different, and we will highlight them.

This chapter covers arrays and their respective operations in NumPy and JAX. We will implement an image processing example using matrix filters. First, we will build it in pure NumPy using its abstraction for a multidimensional array, the `numpy` `.ndarray`. Then, we will switch to JAX, introduce the JAX `Array` data structure, and explain JAX-specific things, especially device-related operations. Finally, we'll highlight the differences between NumPy and JAX APIs.

In this chapter, you will find a lot of code, but I don't want you to feel overwhelmed by it, so it's short pieces and well annotated. The reason for all this code is that I want to demonstrate all the essential concepts. Having this code in front of your eyes says much more than having the text alone, and I believe programmers grasp ideas much faster when they are supported by code. I'd also like you to be able to follow the ideas in the text even without access to a computer (though, if you can experiment while reading the chapter, that's even better).

3.1 *Image processing with NumPy arrays*

Let's start with a real-life image processing task built using pure NumPy. Images are excellent visual examples of tensors or multidimensional arrays, so working on an image processing case provides you with intuition on tensors and some important tensor operations in an easy way.

Imagine you have a collection of photos you want to process. Some photos have an extra space to crop, others have noise artifacts you want to remove, and many are good, but you want to apply artistic effects to them. For simplicity, let's focus only on denoising images, as shown in figure 3.1.

noisy image   restored image

Figure 3.1   An example of image processing we want to implement

To implement such processing, you must load images into some data structure and write functions to process them. Suppose you have a photo (I've chosen one of the cat statues by Fernando Botero at the Yerevan Cascade complex in Armenia), and your camera produced some strange noise artifacts on it. You want to remove the noise and maybe apply some artistic filters to the image. Of course, many image processing tools exist, but we'd like to implement our pipeline for demonstration purposes. You may also want to add neural network processing to the pipeline in the future—for example, implementing super resolution or more artistic filters. With JAX, it's pretty straightforward.

Our image processing example will consist of several steps:

1 Load a photo from a file into a tensor in memory (here, a NumPy array).
2 Preprocess the image if necessary, and convert pixel values to float numbers.
3 Generate a noisy version of the photo to simulate camera noise.
4 Filter the image to reduce noise and increase sharpness.
5 Save a processed image into a file.

Each step involves different tensor operations and helps you develop basic tensor processing skills. They will help you later in your deep learning career as they are ubiquitous: whether you build a data processing and augmentation pipeline, initialize model weights, apply neural networks to data, save model weights or model outputs—tensors are everywhere.

First, we implement the example using pure NumPy. Then, we will switch to JAX (spoiler: by changing only a couple of import statements!). Let's start with image loading.

3.1.1 *Loading an image into a NumPy array*

First, we need to load images. Images arc good examples of multidimensional objects. They have two spatial dimensions (width and height) and usually have another dimension with color channels (typically red, green, blue, and sometimes alpha). Therefore, images are naturally represented with multidimensional arrays, and the NumPy array is a suitable structure to keep images in computer memory. This array is visualized in figure 3.2.

A corresponding image tensor also has three dimensions: width, height, and color channels. Black-and-white or grayscale images may lack the channel dimension. In NumPy indexing, the first dimension corresponds to rows, while the second corresponds to columns. The color dimension can be put before or after the spatial dimensions. Technically, it can also reside between the height and width dimensions, but that makes no sense. In the `scikit-image`, the channels are aligned as RGB (red is first, then green, then blue). Other libraries like OpenCV may use another layout, say, BGR, with the reverse order of the color channels.

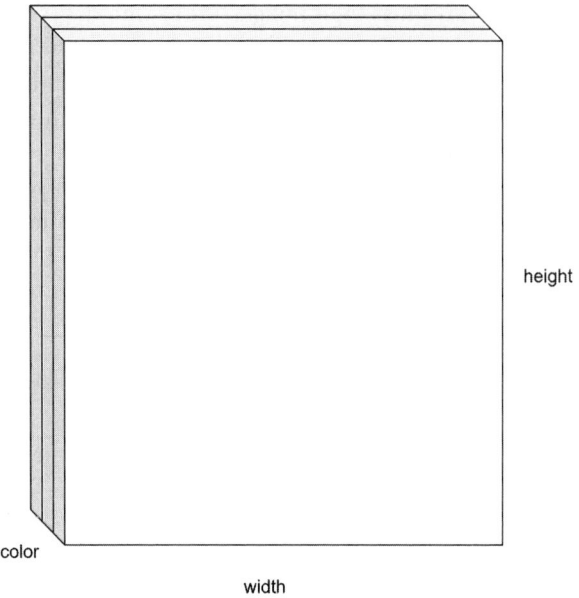

Figure 3.2   The image tensor has three dimensions: width, height, and color channels.

Let's load the image and look at its properties. I put my image named `The_Cat.jpg` into the current folder. You can put any other image instead, but do not forget to change the filename in the code.

We will use the well-known `scikit-image` library for loading and saving images. In Google Colab, it is preinstalled, but if you lack this library, install it according to the instructions at https://mng.bz/AdPE.

The following code for this section and the image can be found in the book code repository on GitHub: https://mng.bz/ZE8j. The code in the following listing loads the image.

Listing 3.1   Loading an image into the NumPy array

```
import numpy as np
from scipy.signal import convolve2d

from matplotlib import pyplot as plt            Imports all we need
from skimage.io import imread, imsave           here and later
from skimage.util import (img_as_float32,
  img_as_ubyte, random_noise)

img = imread('The_Cat.jpg')          ◄─── Loads the image

from matplotlib import pyplot as plt
plt.figure(figsize = (6, 10))               Displays the image
plt.imshow(img)
```

The image will be displayed as in figure 3.3. Depending on your screen resolution, you may want to change the image size. Feel free to do it using the `figsize` parameter. It is a `(width, height)` tuple where each value is in inches.

Figure 3.3 **The color image (shown in the print book in grayscale) is represented as a 3D array with height, width, and color dimensions.**

Step 1 is done, and we can check the type of the image tensor:

```
type(img)

>>> numpy.ndarray
```
This is a NumPy ndarray type.

Tensors are usually described by their shapes, a tuple with the number of elements equal to the tensor rank (or the number of dimensions). Each tuple element represents a number of index positions along the dimension. The `shape` property references it. The number of dimensions may be known with the `ndim` property.

For example, a 1024 × 768 color image might be represented by a shape: (768, 1024, 3) or (3, 768, 1024).

When you work with a batch of images, a new batch dimension is added, typically the first one with index 0.

A batch of 32 1024 × 768 color images may be represented with a shape (32, 768, 1024, 3) or (32, 3, 768, 1024):

```
img.ndim
>>> 3
```
**The image tensor has
three dimensions.**

```
img.shape
>>> (667, 500, 3)
```
**Their size is 667 (height), 500
(width), and 3 (color channels).**

As you see, the image is represented by a 3D array, with the first dimension being height (667 pixels), the second being width (500 pixels), and the third being color channels (3 channels).

Tensor layouts in memory: NCHW vs. NHWC

Image tensors are usually represented in memory in two common formats: NCHW or NHWC. These uppercase letters encode tensor axis semantics, where N stands for batch dimension, C for channel dimension, H for height, and W for width. A tensor described this way contains a batch composed of N images of C color channels, each with height H and width W. It's problematic to have objects of different sizes in a batch, but special data structures, such as ragged tensors, can do it. Another option is to pad different objects to the same size with some placeholder element.

Different frameworks and libraries prefer different formats. JAX (https://mng.bz/RZYn) and PyTorch (https://mng.bz/2K8N) use NCHW by default. TensorFlow (https://mng.bz/1GWZ), Flax (https://mng.bz/DpKn), and Haiku (https://mng.bz/JZXp) use NHWC, and almost any library has some function to convert between these formats or a parameter specifying what type of an image tensor is being passed to a function.

From the mathematical point of view, these representations are equivalent, but from the practical point of view, there may be a difference. For example, convolutions implemented in NVIDIA Tensor Cores require NHWC layout and work faster when input tensors are laid out in the NHWC format (https://mng.bz/wx77).

Grappler, the default graph optimization system in the TF runtime (https://mng.bz/qO7K), can convert NHWC into NCHW automatically during layout optimization (https://research.google/pubs/pub48051/).

There are also two useful properties related to size. The `size` property returns the number of elements in the tensor. It is equal to the product of the array's dimensions. The `nbytes` property returns the total bytes consumed by the elements of the array. It does not include memory consumed by nonelement attributes of the array object. For a tensor comprising `uint8` values, these properties return the same number, as each element requires only a single byte.

```
img.size
>>> 1000500
```
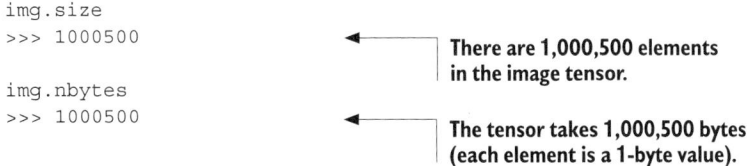
There are 1,000,500 elements
in the image tensor.

```
img.nbytes
>>> 1000500
```
The tensor takes 1,000,500 bytes
(each element is a 1-byte value).

For `float32` values, there will be four times more bytes than the number of elements. So, step 1 is done, and the image is loaded. Now, we need to do some preprocessing.

3.1.2 *Performing basic preprocessing operations with an image*

We are in step 2, where we preprocess the image. Why might we need this step?

First, you may want to crop the image to eliminate some irrelevant details near the border. Here, we do not need this (the image is perfect enough), but I just want to let you know about a powerful feature called *slicing*, which we can directly use for cropping. With slicing, you can select specific tensor elements along each axis. For example, you can select a specific rectangular image subregion or take only chosen color channels.

Listing 3.2 Slicing NumPy arrays

```
cat_face = img[80:220, 190:330, 1]
cat_face.shape

>>> (140, 140)

plt.figure(figsize = (3,4))
plt.imshow(cat_face, cmap='gray')
```

We slice the pixels from line 80 to line 220
(non-inclusive) by height, columns from 190
to 330, and the second color channel (with an
index of 1, as indices start from zero).

The resulting tensor is 140 pixels in
height and 140 pixels in width.

This code selects pixels related to the cat's face only from the image's green channel (the middle one with an index of 1). We displayed the image as grayscale as it contains only single-color channel information. You may choose another color palette if you want. The resulting image is shown in figure 3.4. You can also easily implement other basic transformations like image flipping with array slicing.

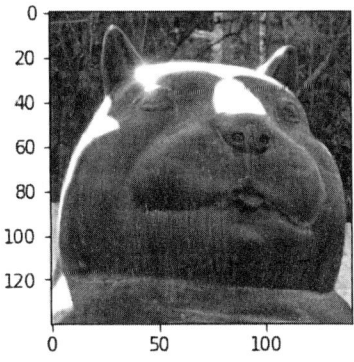

**Figure 3.4
Cropped image
with a single-color
channel**

The code `img = img[:,::-1,:]` reverses the order of pixels along the horizontal dimension while preserving the vertical and channel axes. You can also use the `flip()` function from NumPy. Rotation can be performed with the `rot90()` function for a given number of rotations (parameter `k=2`) as in the code `img = np.rot90(img, k=2, axes=(0, 1))`.

The second thing important to preprocessing is related to data types. Each tensor has a data type associated with all the elements. It is referenced as `dtype`. Images are usually represented either with float values in the range of [0, 1] or unsigned integers in the range of [0, 255]. The values inside our tensor are unsigned 8-bit integers (`uint8`).

Here, we want to convert our image from the `uint8` data type to `float32`. It will be easier for us to work with floating-point values in the [0.0, 1.0] range. We use the `img_as_float()` function from `scikit-image`.

Listing 3.3   Converting image pixel values to float numbers

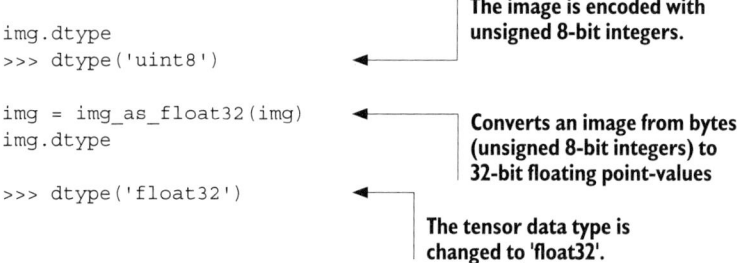

```
img.dtype
>>> dtype('uint8')                          The image is encoded with
                                            unsigned 8-bit integers.

img = img_as_float32(img)                   Converts an image from bytes
img.dtype                                   (unsigned 8-bit integers) to
                                            32-bit floating point-values
>>> dtype('float32')
                                            The tensor data type is
                                            changed to 'float32'.
```

Step 2 is done.

3.1.3   *Adding noise to the image*

Step 3 is only required for demonstration purposes. To simulate a noisy image, we use the Gaussian noise, which frequently appears in digital cameras with low-light conditions and high ISO light sensitivities. We use a `random_noise` function from the same `scikit-image` library.

Listing 3.4   Generating a noisy version of the image

```
img_noised = random_noise(img, mode='gaussian')      We use a function from
                                                     scikit-image to add random
plt.figure(figsize = (6, 10))                        noise with the specified type.
plt.imshow(img_noised)
```

The code generates a noisy version of the image displayed in figure 3.5. You may also experiment with other interesting noise types, such as salt-and-pepper or impulse noise, occurring as sparse minimum and maximum value pixels.

Figure 3.5   The noisy version of the image

Step 3 is done. We are now ready to implement some more advanced image processing.

3.1.4   Implementing image filtering

Step 4 is the core of our image processing example. This step consists of two substeps: (1) creating a filter kernel (more on kernels in the following sidebar) and (2) applying the filter kernel to an image (or performing the filtering step itself).

CREATING A FILTER KERNEL

Gaussian blur filters typically remove the type of noise we have. Gaussian blur filters belong to a large family of matrix filters, also called *finite impulse response* (FIR) filters, in the digital signal processing (DSP) field. You may also have seen matrix filters in image processing applications like Photoshop or GIMP.

FIR filters and convolution

An FIR filter is described by its matrix, also called the *kernel*. The matrix contains weights with which image pixels are taken when the filter slides along the image. During each step, all the pixels of a window through which the kernel "looks" at part of the image get multiplied by the corresponding weights of the kernel. Then, the products are summed into a single number, which is the resulting pixel intensity for a pixel in the output (filtered) image. This operation that takes in a signal and a kernel (another signal) and produces a filtered signal called *convolution*. This process is visualized in the following figure.

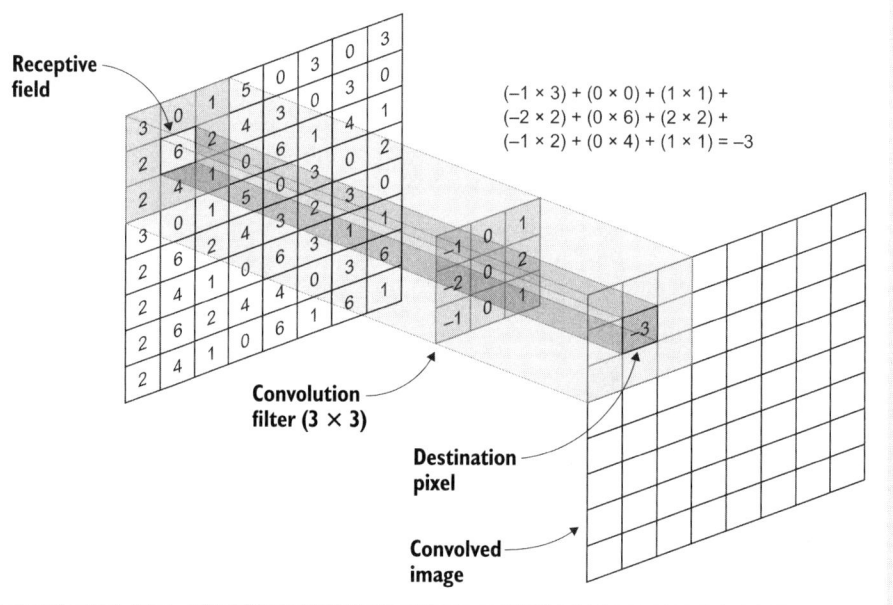

An FIR filter is implemented by convolution (image from the book *Deep Learning for Vision Systems* by Mohamed Elgendy; Manning, 2020).

The convolution can be any-dimensional. For 1D inputs, it is a 1D convolution; for 2D inputs (like images), it's a 2D convolution, and so on. This operation is heavily used in convolutional neural networks (CNNs). We will apply a 2D convolution to each image channel separately. In CNNs, all the image channels are usually processed at once with a kernel of the same channel dimension as the image.

If you want to learn more about these digital filters and convolutions, I recommend the excellent book on digital signal processing: https://dspguide.com/.

We start with a simple blur (not Gaussian blur) filter to demonstrate the process of creating a kernel. Then, we create a kernel for the Gaussian blur filter, which we use for image denoising.

The blur filter comprises a matrix of equal values, meaning that each pixel in the neighborhood of the target pixel is taken with an equal weight. This is equivalent to averaging all values inside the receptive field of the kernel. You may have heard about such a filter as a simple, moving average filter. The following code demonstrates how to create a blur filter kernel of the size 5×5 pixels.

Listing 3.5 Matrix (or kernel) for a simple blur filter

```
kernel_blur = np.ones((5,5))
kernel_blur /= np.sum(kernel_blur)
kernel_blur

>>> array([[0.04, 0.04, 0.04, 0.04, 0.04],
>>>         [0.04, 0.04, 0.04, 0.04, 0.04],
>>>         [0.04, 0.04, 0.04, 0.04, 0.04],
>>>         [0.04, 0.04, 0.04, 0.04, 0.04],
>>>         [0.04, 0.04, 0.04, 0.04, 0.04]])
```

Generates a 5×5 matrix of ones

Divides each element of the matrix by the sum of elements

The resulting array contains the same numbers that together sum to 1.

Gaussian blur is a more involved version of the blur filter; its matrix contains different values that tend to have higher values closer to the center. The well-known Gaussian function produces the Gaussian kernel.

Listing 3.6 Gaussian blur kernel

```
def gaussian_kernel(kernel_size, sigma=1.0, mu=0.0):
    """ A function to generate Gaussian 2D kernel """
    center = kernel_size // 2
    x, y = np.mgrid[
        -center : kernel_size - center,
        -center : kernel_size - center]
    d = np.sqrt(np.square(x) + np.square(y))
    koeff = 1 / (2 * np.pi * np.square(sigma))
    kernel = koeff * np.exp(-np.square(d-mu) /
      (2 * np.square(sigma)))
    return kernel

kernel_gauss = gaussian_kernel(5)
kernel_gauss

>>> array([[0.00291502, 0.01306423, 0.02153928,
0.01306423, 0.00291502],
>>>         [0.01306423, 0.05854983, 0.09653235,
0.05854983, 0.01306423],
>>>         [0.02153928, 0.09653235, 0.15915494,
0.09653235, 0.02153928],
>>>         [0.01306423, 0.05854983, 0.09653235,
0.05854983, 0.01306423],
>>>         [0.00291502, 0.01306423, 0.02153928,
0.01306423, 0.00291502]])
```

Finds the center position of the kernel

Generates the X and Y grid values

Generates the kernel coefficients according to the formula

The resulting kernel

We now must implement the function to apply the filter to an image.

APPLYING THE FILTER KERNEL TO AN IMAGE

This is the most complicated part of the chapter. Figure 3.6 describes the process of applying a filter to an image.

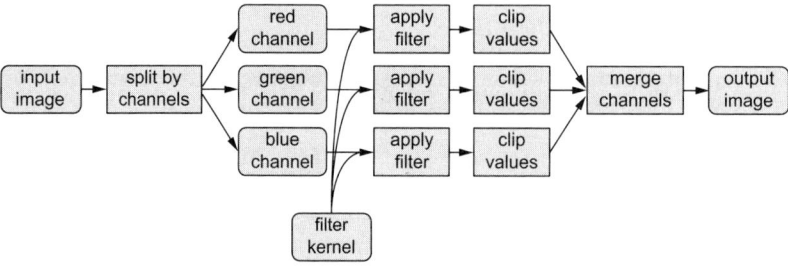

Figure 3.6   The process of applying a filter to an image

We apply a filter to each color channel separately. The function must apply a 2D convolution with the filter kernel inside each color channel. We also clip the resulting values to restrict the range to [0.0, 1.0]. Then, we merge the processed color channels together to form a processed image. The function assumes the channel dimension is the last one in the image tensor. The translation of the scheme depicted in figure 3.6 to the code is now straightforward.

Listing 3.7   Function to apply a filter to an image

```
def color_convolution(image, kernel):
""" A function to apply a filter to an image"""
    channels = []
    for i in range(3):
        color_channel = image[:,:,i]
        filtered_channel = convolve2d(
            color_channel, kernel, mode="same")
        filtered_channel = np.clip(
            filtered_channel, 0.0, 1.0)
        channels.append(filtered_channel)
    final_image = np.stack(channels, axis=2)
    return final_image
```

Extracts a channel with slicing

Applies the filter to the extracted channel

Clips the values to the range of [0.0, 1.0]

Generates the final image by concatenating filtered channels

We are ready to apply our filter to the image.

Listing 3.8   Filtering the noised image

```
img_blur = color_convolution(img_noised, kernel_gauss)
plt.figure(figsize = (12,10))
plt.imshow(np.hstack((img_blur, img_noised)))
```

Apply the Gaussian blur filter to the noised image

The resulting denoised image is shown in figure 3.7. It is better to look at the images on a computer, but you can see that the amount of noise is significantly reduced but the image becomes blurry. While it is expected (we applied a blur filter, after all!), we would like to make the image sharper if possible.

Figure 3.7 Denoised (left) and noised (right) image versions

Not surprisingly, there is another matrix filter for sharpening images. Its kernel contains a large positive number in the center and negative numbers in the neighborhood. This filter aims to improve the contrast between the central point and its neighborhood.

We normalize the kernel values by dividing each one by the sum of all values. This restricts the resulting values to the allowed range after filter application. We have a clip() function inside our filter application function, but that's the last resort that cuts every value outside the range to its boundary. The finer normalizing approach would preserve more information in the signal.

Listing 3.9 Sharpening filter kernel

```
kernel_sharpen = np.array(
    [[-1, -1, -1, -1, -1],
     [-1, -1, -1, -1, -1],          Creates a kernel with a
     [-1, -1, 50, -1, -1],          large positive value in
     [-1, -1, -1, -1, -1],          the middle and small
     [-1, -1, -1, -1, -1]], dtype=np.float32    negative values around
)

kernel_sharpen /= np.sum(kernel_sharpen)    ◄──── Normalizes the kernel
kernel_sharpen

>>> array([[-0.03846154, -0.03846154, -0.03846154, -0.03846154, -0.03846154],
>>>        [-0.03846154, -0.03846154, -0.03846154, -0.03846154, -0.03846154],
>>>        [-0.03846154, -0.03846154,  1.9230769 , -0.03846154, -0.03846154],
>>>        [-0.03846154, -0.03846154, -0.03846154, -0.03846154, -0.03846154],
```

```
>>>         [-0.03846154, -0.03846154, -0.03846154, -0.03846154, -0.03846154]],
>>>         dtype=float32)
```

Let's apply our sharpening filter to the blurred image.

```
img_restored = color_convolution(
    img_blur, kernel_sharpen)
plt.figure(figsize = (12,20))
plt.imshow(np.vstack(
    (np.hstack((img, img_noised)),
     np.hstack((img_restored, img_blur)))
))
```

Applies sharpening filter to the blurred image

Displays four images together (clockwise): the original photo, noised version, blurred image, sharpened or restored image

In figure 3.8, four different images are shown (in the clockwise direction): the original image at the top left, a noisy version at the top right, a denoised blurry version at the bottom right, and finally, a sharpened version at the bottom left. We restored some sharpness in the image while successfully removing some original noise!

Figure 3.8   Original image (top left), noised (top right), denoised but blurred (bottom right), and sharpened (bottom left) versions of the image

Step 4 is done, and we are almost finished!

3.1.5 Saving a tensor as an image file

The final step, 5, is to save the resulting image. Before saving a file, we need to "undo" some of the preprocessings we did in step 2 regarding the conversion of data types. There, we converted a tensor of bytes to a tensor of floating-point numbers, making working with them easier. Now, to save the image, we need to convert the tensor back to bytes, so here we do it.

Listing 3.11   Saving an image from a NumPy array

```
image_modified = img_as_ubyte(img_restored)
imsave('The_Cat_modified.jpg', arr=image_modified)
```

Converts float32 values
back to 8-bit integers

Saves the array
as a JPEG image

We are done with our image processing example. You can try many other exciting filters—for example, emboss, edge detection, or a custom filter. I put some filters into the corresponding Colab notebook. You can also combine several filter kernels into a single kernel. But we will stop here for now and review what we did.

We started with image loading and learned how to implement basic image processing operations like a crop and flipping with slicing. Then, we made a noisy version of the image and learned about matrix filters. We did some noise filtering and image sharpening with matrix filters.

We implemented everything with NumPy, and now it's time to look at what has changed with JAX.

3.2   Arrays in JAX

We will rewrite our image processing program to work on top of JAX instead of NumPy. This section is a model case for migrating your NumPy program to JAX.

We already have a working code for our solution that loads an image, adds random noise, creates a digital filter, applies it to the noisy image, and then saves the processed result. The loading and saving parts will remain the same, and the changes mostly affect the core part with digital filters. But there will be a few of them!

3.2.1 Switching to JAX NumPy-like API

The beautiful thing is that you can replace a couple of import statements, and all the rest of the code will work with JAX! Try it yourself.

Listing 3.12   Replacing imports from NumPy to JAX

```
## NumPy
#import numpy as np
#from scipy.signal import convolve2d
```

NumPy and SciPy imports

```
## JAX
import jax.numpy as np
from jax.scipy.signal import convolve2d
```

JAX imports

JAX has a NumPy-like API imported from the `jax.numpy` module. There are also some higher-level functions from SciPy reimplemented in JAX. This `jax.scipy` module is less rich than the entire SciPy library, yet the function we used (the `convolve2d()` function) is present there.

Sometimes, you find there is no corresponding function in JAX. For example, we might use the `gaussian_filter()` function from `scipy.ndimage` for Gaussian filtering. There is no such function in `jax.scipy.ndimage`.

In such a case, you might still use the NumPy function with JAX and have two imports, one from NumPy and another for the JAX NumPy interface. It is usually done as shown in the following listing.

Listing 3.13   Using both NumPy and JAX

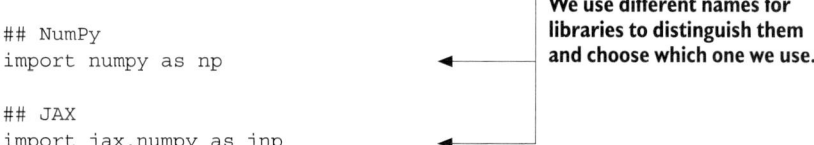

```
## NumPy
import numpy as np

## JAX
import jax.numpy as jnp
```

We use different names for libraries to distinguish them and choose which one we use.

You use a function from NumPy with the prefix `np`, and a function from JAX with the prefix `jnp`. It might prevent you from using some JAX features on NumPy functions, either because they are implemented in C++ (Python only provides bindings) or are not functionally pure. Another option is that you might implement new functions on your own, as we did with Gaussian filtering.

If you run our image filtering example, changing imports to JAX, you will see that all the code works well thanks to the JAX NumPy-compatible API. The only thing you might notice is that in places where we create arrays, the `numpy.ndarray` type will be replaced with the JAX `Array` (or, more specifically, the `jaxlib.xla_extension.ArrayImpl` type), as is the case with filter kernel creation.

Listing 3.14   Matrix (or kernel) for a simple blur filter when using JAX

```
kernel_blur = np.ones((5,5))
kernel_blur /= np.sum(kernel_blur)
kernel_blur
```

```
>>> Array([[0.04, 0.04, 0.04, 0.04, 0.04],
>>>        [0.04, 0.04, 0.04, 0.04, 0.04],
>>>        [0.04, 0.04, 0.04, 0.04, 0.04],
>>>        [0.04, 0.04, 0.04, 0.04, 0.04],
>>>        [0.04, 0.04, 0.04, 0.04, 0.04]], dtype=float32)
```

NumPy array is replaced with a JAX Array.

The data is now explicitly marked with the float32 type.

```
type(kernel_blur)
```

```
>>> jaxlib.xla_extension.ArrayImpl
```

The full name of the Array type

We also see that the data type is now `float32`. With NumPy, it will be `float64` in most cases. Everything else works as usual. We will discuss floating-point data types later in section 3.3.2.

Let's keep our image processing example aside and focus on what an `Array` is. The `jax.Array` type (along with its alias, `jax.numpy.ndarray`) is the core type for storing tensors or multidimensional arrays in JAX. You will constantly work with `Array`s in JAX the same as in NumPy. Understanding its properties and differences from NumPy arrays is worth spending some time on.

3.2.2 *What is Array?*

`Array` is the default type for representing arrays in JAX. It can use different backends—CPU, GPU, and TPU. It is equivalent to the `numpy.ndarray` backed by a memory buffer on a single device as well as on multiple devices (see chapter 8). In general, a *device* is something used by JAX to perform computations.

> ### DeviceArray and Array
>
> In JAX, before version 0.4.1, the default array implementation was the `DeviceArray`. Since version 0.4.1, JAX switched its default array implementation to the new `jax.Array` type.
>
> In the future, `jax.Array` will be the only type of array in JAX. It is a unified array type that subsumes `DeviceArray`, `ShardedDeviceArray`, and `GlobalDeviceArray` types in JAX. This new type helps make parallelism a core feature of JAX, simplifies and unifies JAX internals, and allows unifying JIT (the topic of chapter 5) and `pjit()` (appendix D). `jax.Array` provides distributed arrays out of the box and allows easy automatic parallelization (see chapter 8).
>
> If your code uses the older types, you must migrate to `jax.Array` according to the instructions here: https://mng.bz/7dBx.

You often do not need to instantiate `Array` objects manually (and we didn't). You will create them via `jax.numpy` functions like `array()`, `linspace()`, etc.

A noticeable difference from NumPy here is that NumPy usually accepts Python lists or tuples as inputs to its API functions (not including the `array()` constructor). JAX deliberately chooses not to accept lists or tuples as inputs to its functions because that can lead to silent performance degradation, which is hard to detect.

If you want to pass a Python list to a JAX function, you must explicitly convert it into an array. The following code demonstrates working with Python lists in JAX functions. The code for this and the following sections is located in the book's repository: https://mng.bz/ma7n.

Listing 3.15   Using Python lists or tuples in functions

```
import numpy as np
import jax.numpy as jnp

np.array([1, 42, 31337])

>>> array([    1,    42, 31337])

jnp.array([1, 42, 31337])

>>> Array([    1,    42, 31337], dtype=int32)

np.sum([1, 42, 31337])

>>> 31380

try:
  jnp.sum([1, 42, 31337])
except TypeError as e:
  print(e)

>>> sum requires ndarray or scalar arguments, got <class 'list'> at position
0.

jnp.sum(jnp.array([1, 42, 31337]))

>>> Array(31380, dtype=int32)
```

◄——— **NumPy nparray can be created from a Python list.**

◄——— **JAX Array can also be created from a Python list.**

◄——— **NumPy sum() function can work with Python lists.**

◄——— **jax.numpy sum() function does not accept Python lists.**

◄——— **You have to create an Array first in order to use jax.numpy sum() function.**

Notice from the return type of the `jnp.sum()` call that scalars are also packed into the Array type.

The JAX `Array` has a list of properties similar to the NumPy array. The official documentation shows the complete list of methods and properties (https://mng.bz/5l54).

Listing 3.16   Using standard NumPy-like properties

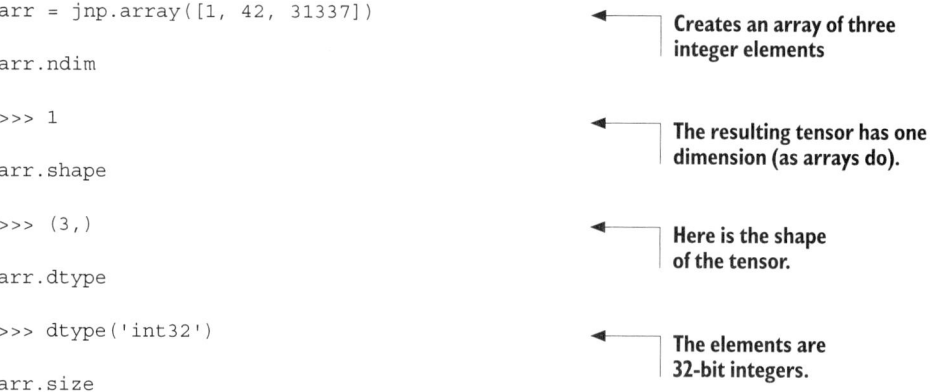

```
arr = jnp.array([1, 42, 31337])

arr.ndim

>>> 1

arr.shape

>>> (3,)

arr.dtype

>>> dtype('int32')

arr.size
```

◄——— **Creates an array of three integer elements**

◄——— **The resulting tensor has one dimension (as arrays do).**

◄——— **Here is the shape of the tensor.**

◄——— **The elements are 32-bit integers.**

```
>>> 3
```
◄─── **The tensor has 3 elements.**

```
arr.nbytes
```

```
>>> 12
```
◄─── **These 3 elements require 12 bytes to store (as each element is 4 bytes long).**

Array objects are designed to work seamlessly with Python standard library tools where appropriate. For example, when `copy.copy()` or `copy.deepcopy()` from the built-in Python `copy` module encounters an `Array`, it is equivalent to calling the `copy()` method, which will create a copy of the buffer on the *same* device as the original array.

`Arrays` can also be serialized or translated into a format stored in a file via the built-in `pickle` module. In a manner similar to `numpy.ndarray` objects, `Array` will be serialized via a compact bit representation. When you do the reverse operation, deserializing or unpickling, the result will be a new `Array` object on the *default* device. This is because unpickling may occur in a different environment with different devices.

3.2.3 *Device-related operations*

Special computing devices like GPU or TPU help make your code run faster. Sometimes, the difference may be of orders of magnitude. This is especially important for training large neural networks or performing large-scale simulations. So, you should know how to use this hardware acceleration power. To use accelerated computations, an accelerator (GPU or TPU) needs all the data participating in the computations (the tensors themselves) to reside in a device's memory. So, the first step to using hardware acceleration is to learn how to transfer data between devices.

Not surprisingly, there are a bunch of methods dedicated to tensor device placement. There might be plenty of devices available. I will use a Colab with GPU runtime in the following examples to demonstrate some device-related operations.

Types of hardware: CPU, GPU, TPU

A CPU is a central processing unit, a typical processor from Intel, AMD, or Apple (which now uses their own ARM processors). It is a universal general-purpose computing device, yet many new processors have special instructions to improve performance on machine learning workloads.

A GPU is a graphics processing unit, a special highly parallel processor originally created for computer graphics tasks. Modern GPUs contain a lot (thousands) of simple processors (cores) and are highly parallel, which makes them very effective in running some algorithms. Matrix multiplications, the core of deep learning, are among these. The most famous and best supported are NVIDIA GPUs, yet AMD and Intel have their own GPUs.

A TPU is a tensor processing unit from Google, the most well-known example of an application-specific integrated circuit (ASIC). ASIC is an integrated circuit customized for a particular use rather than intended for general-purpose use like a CPU. ASICs are more specialized than GPUs because a GPU is still a massively parallel processor with thousands of computational units capable of executing many different algorithms, while an

(continued)

ASIC is a processor designed to be capable of doing a very small set of computations (say, only matrix multiplications). But it does so extremely well. There are many other ASICs for deep learning and AI, but for now, their support is very limited among deep learning frameworks.

More on ASICs is available here: https://mng.bz/676G.

As I use a system with GPU, I will have an additional device available. The following examples will use both CPU and GPU devices. If your system has no device besides the CPU, try using Google Colab. It provides cloud GPUs even in the free tier.

LOCAL AND GLOBAL DEVICES

First of all, there is a host. A host is the CPU that manages several devices. A single host can manage several devices (usually up to eight), so a multihost configuration is needed to use more devices (it will also be multiprocess, as in this case, there will be many JAX Python processes run independently on each host).

JAX distinguishes between local and global devices. A local device for a process is a device that the process can directly address and launch computations on. It is a device attached directly to the host (or computer) where the JAX program runs, for example, a CPU, a local GPU, or eight TPU cores directly attached to the host. The `jax.local_devices()` function shows a process's local devices. The `jax.local_device_count()` function returns the number of devices addressable by this process. Both functions receive a parameter for the XLA backend that could be `'cpu'`, `'gpu'`, or `'tpu'`. By default, this parameter is `None,` which means the default backend (GPU or TPU if available).

A global device is a device across all processes. It is relevant to multihost and multiprocess environments. As long as each process launches the computation on its local devices, a computation can span devices across processes and use collective operations (the topic of chapters 6 and 7) via direct communication links between the devices (usually, the high-speed interconnects between Cloud TPUs or GPUs). The `jax.devices()` function shows all available global devices, and `jax.device_count()` returns the total number of devices across all processes.

We will talk about multihost and multiprocess environments later in chapter 7. For now, let's concentrate on single-host environments only; in our case, the global device list will be equal to the local one. The following code demonstrates how to get information about local and global devices.

Listing 3.17   Getting info about devices

```
import jax
jax.devices()
```
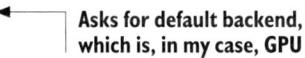
Asks for default backend, which is, in my case, GPU

```
>>> [gpu(id=0)]
```
◄———— **There is one GPU device.**

```
jax.local_devices()
```
◄———— **Asks only for local devices**

```
>>> [gpu(id=0)]
```

```
jax.devices('cpu')
```
◄——┐
　　　Asks directly about
```
>>> [CpuDevice(id=0)]
```
　　　CPU backends

```
jax.device_count('gpu')
```
◄——┐
　　　Asks for the number
```
>>> 1
```
　　　of GPU devices

For some non-CPU devices, you may also see a `process_index` attribute. This is the case for TPU now (we will see it later in the chapter), and for previous versions of JAX, this was also the case for GPU. Each JAX process can obtain its process index with the `jax.process_index()` function. In most cases, it will be equal to 0, but for multiprocess configurations, this will vary.

COMMITTED AND UNCOMMITTED DATA

In JAX, the computation follows data placement. There are two different placement properties:

- The device where the data resides.
- Whether the data is committed to the device or not. When the data is committed, it is sometimes referred to as being *sticky* to the device.

You can know where the data is located with the help of the `device()` method.

By default, JAX `Array` objects are placed *uncommitted* on the default device. The default device is the first item of the list returned by the `jax.devices()` function call (`jax.devices()[0]`). It is the first GPU or TPU if it is present; otherwise, it is the CPU:

```
arr = jnp.array([1, 42, 31337])
arr.device()
```
　　　　　　　　　　　　　　　│ **The original tensor is on GPU,**
　　　　　　　　　　　　　　　│ **but it's not committed.**
```
>>> gpu(id=0)
```
◄————

You can use `jax.default_device()` context manager to temporarily override the default device for JAX operations if you want to. You can also use the `JAX PLATFORMS` environment variable or the `--jax_platforms` command-line flag. It is also possible to set a priority order when providing a list of platforms in the `JAX_PLATFORMS` variable.

Computations involving uncommitted data are performed on the default device, and the results are also uncommitted on the default device. Say you want a specific GPU to run computations with a specific tensor. You can explicitly put data on a specific device using the `jax.device_put()` function call with a `device` parameter. In this case, the data becomes *committed* to the device. If you pass `None` as the `device` parameter, the operation will behave like the identity function if the operand is already on any device. Otherwise, it will transfer the data to the default device uncommitted:

```
arr_cpu = jax.device_put(arr, jax.devices('cpu')[0])
arr_cpu.device()
```
◄ **We put a copy of the tensor on the first CPU device.**

```
>>> CpuDevice(id=0)
```
◄ **Checks that the new tensor is on the CPU**

```
arr.device()
```

```
>>> gpu(id=0)
```
◄ **The original tensor location is still GPU.**

Remember the functional nature of JAX. The `jax.device_put()` function creates a copy of your data on the specified device and returns it. The original data is unchanged.

There is a reverse operation, `jax.device_get()`, to transfer data from a device to the Python process on your host. The returned data is a NumPy `ndarray`:

```
arr_host = jax.device_get(arr)
type(arr_host)
```
◄ **Takes the original tensor from GPU to the host in the form of NumPy ndarray**

```
>>> numpy.ndarray
```

```
arr_host
```

```
>>> array([   1,   42, 31337], dtype=int32)
```

Computations involving committed data are performed on the committed device, and the results will be committed to the same device. You will get an error when you invoke an operation on arguments committed to different devices (but no error if some arguments are uncommitted). The code in the following listing demonstrates device placement.

Listing 3.18   Placing data to a device

```
arr = jnp.array([1, 42, 31337])
arr.device()
```
The original tensor is on GPU, but it's not committed.

```
>>> gpu(id=0)
```
◄

```
arr_cpu = jax.device_put(arr, jax.devices('cpu')[0])
arr_cpu.device()
```
◄ **We put a copy of the tensor on the first CPU device.**

```
>>> CpuDevice(id=0)
```
◄ **Checks that the new tensor is on the CPU**

```
arr + arr_cpu
```
◄

```
>>> Array([   2,   84, 62674], dtype=int32)
```
◄ **Calls a binary operation for uncommitted and committed tensors on different devices (OK)**

```
arr_gpu = jax.device_put(arr, jax.devices('gpu')[0])
```
◄ **Commits a new tensor to a different device**

```
try:
  arr_gpu + arr_cpu
except ValueError as e:
  print(e)
```
◄ **Now calls a binary operation for two tensors committed to different devices (not OK)**

```
>>> Received incompatible devices for jitted computation.
Got argument x1 of jax.numpy.add with shape int32[3] and
device ids [0] on platform GPU and argument x2 of
jax.numpy.add with shape int32[3] and device ids [0]
on platform CPU
```

In older JAX versions before the pull request #6002 (https://github.com/google/jax/pull/6002), there was some laziness in array creation, which held for all the constant creation operations (zeros, ones, eye, etc.). This meant that if you made a call like jax.device_put(jnp.ones(...), jax.devices()[1]), then this call created an array with zeros on the device corresponding to jax.devices()[1], not on the default device and then copying to the jax.devices()[1]. In modern JAX versions, this optimization is removed so as to simplify the implementation.

Pallas: A JAX kernel language

JAX has an extension called Pallas. It enables writing custom kernels for GPU and TPU using a model similar to Triton (https://triton-lang.org/main/index.html), a GPU compiler built and maintained by OpenAI.

Please refer to Pallas documentation on its design (https://jax.readthedocs.io/en/latest/pallas/design.html) and examples (https://mng.bz/oezN).

Among real-life examples of using Pallas, you may find RecurrentGemma code (https://github.com/google-deepmind/recurrentgemma), which includes a specialized Pallas kernel to perform the linear recurrence on TPU (https://mng.bz/ngGv).

Now, you have an easy way to have NumPy-like computations on GPU. Just remember that this is only part of the whole story regarding increasing performance. Chapter 5 will talk about JIT, which provides more performance improvements. Chapter 8 will describe distributed arrays and automatic parallelization.

3.2.4 *Asynchronous dispatch*

An important thing to know about how JAX works is that it uses asynchronous dispatch. This means that when an operation is executed, JAX does not wait for operation completion and returns control to the Python program. JAX returns an Array, which is technically a "future." In the future, a value is not available immediately and, as the name suggests, will be produced in the future on an accelerator device. Yet the future already contains the shape and type; you can also pass it to the subsequent JAX computation.

We did not notice it before because when you inspect the result by printing or converting to a NumPy array, JAX automatically forces Python to wait for the computation to complete. If you want to wait for the result explicitly, you can use the block_until_ready() method of an Array.

Asynchronous dispatch is very useful as it allows Python to run ahead and not wait for an accelerator, helping the Python code not be on the critical path. If the Python code enqueues computations on a device faster than they can be executed, and if it does not need to inspect values in between, then the Python program can use an accelerator most efficiently without the accelerator having to wait.

Not knowing about asynchronous dispatch may mislead you when doing benchmarks, and you might obtain overly optimistic results. This is why we used the `block_until_ready()` method in section 1.1.1 when we benchmarked a function computation on different backends with and without JIT compilation.

In the following example, we highlight the difference in time when measuring with and without blocking. Without blocking, we measure only the time to dispatch the work, not counting the computation. Additionally, we measure the computation time on a GPU and CPU. We do it by committing the data tensors to the corresponding devices.

Listing 3.19   Working with asynchronous dispatch

```
a = jnp.array(range(1000000)).reshape((1000,1000))
a.device()

>>> gpu(id=0)

%time x = jnp.dot(a,a)                                      ◄──── Only measures time
                                                                  to dispatch the work
>>> CPU times: user 757 µs, sys: 0 ns, total: 757 µs
>>> Wall time: 770 µs

%time x = jnp.dot(a,a).block_until_ready()                 ◄──── Measures the full
                                                                  computation on GPU
>>> CPU times: user 1.34 ms, sys: 65 µs, total: 1.41 ms
>>> Wall time: 4.33 ms

a_cpu = jax.device_put(a, jax.devices('cpu')[0])
a_cpu.device()

>>> CpuDevice(id=0)
                                                           ◄──── Measures the full
%time x = jnp.dot(a_cpu,a_cpu).block_until_ready()                computation on CPU

>>> CPU times: user 272 ms, sys: 0 ns, total: 272 ms
>>> Wall time: 150 ms
```

As you can see, GPU computation is 30 times faster than CPU computation (4.33 milliseconds vs. 150 milliseconds).

When reading the documentation, you may notice some functions are explicitly described as asynchronous. For example, for the `device_put()`, it is said that "This function is always asynchronous, i.e. returns immediately" (https://mng.bz/v8Ex). So now you know what that means.

Last but not least, let me show you how to prepare a Cloud TPU and run JAX code on this accelerator. We have already changed our code to work with JAX, and our code works on a GPU. We did nothing special to transfer computations to the GPU, but the default device became the GPU device when we ran this code on a system with a GPU. Magic! Everything worked out of the box.

Let's do one more thing: run our code on TPU. Why? Because we can!

3.2.5 *Running computations on TPU*

Running our code on TPU is unnecessary for our image processing example, but it might be beneficial for training your large neural networks. So, it's the right time to demonstrate how to connect to TPU and run JAX there. Anytime later in the book, you can easily switch from local CPU or GPU to TPU.

This configuration assumes you still run the code in Google Colab (or your local Jupyter) but do not use Colab TPU runtimes. Instead, you deploy your host with Cloud TPUs in Google Cloud and connect Colab to this in what is called *local runtime*, meaning a runtime provided by yourself.

Using Cloud TPU will cost you some money (you can check the actual pricing here: https://cloud.google.com/tpu/pricing), so feel free to skip this section if you are not interested in this option.

> ### Colab TPU vs. Cloud TPU
>
> There are two types of TPU systems you may face with. It's not about the TPU version but rather about how such a system is organized:
>
> First, there is *Colab TPU* runtime, which is available in Colab and *is no longer supported by JAX since version 0.4*. This architecture connects Cloud TPUs remotely over the network using gRPC to a host machine running Colab. You have no access to the TPU host, a machine attached to TPU accelerators.
>
> Colab TPU needs a setup step to be called before any JAX operation:
>
> ```
> import jax.tools.colab_tpu
> jax.tools.colab_tpu.setup_tpu()
> ```
>
> Second, there is *Cloud TPU,* available in Google Cloud. It's a new architecture with Cloud TPU Virtual Machines (VMs) running on the TPU host machines directly attached to TPU accelerators. This new Cloud TPU system architecture is simpler and more flexible. In addition to major usability benefits, you may achieve performance gains because your code no longer needs to make round trips across the datacenter network to reach the TPUs.
>
> You may find more details on the new Cloud TPU architecture here: https://mng.bz/4JwB.
>
> In this book, we will use Cloud TPUs, which require running separate VMs and connecting them to Google Colab manually using Colab local runtime.

Now we need to know how to run Cloud TPU VMs.

TPU PREPARATIONS

To start with, you must prepare a Cloud TPU. Appendix C contains all the details of this process, and here we highlight the important steps.

Here, we run a machine with a TPU v2-8 accelerator (you may want to choose a different option) and connect to it using Colab local runtime:

```
$gcloud compute tpus tpu-vm create node-jax \
--zone us-central1-b --accelerator-type v2-8 \
--version tpu-vm-base
$gcloud compute tpus tpu-vm list --zone us-central1-b

$gcloud compute tpus tpu-vm ssh \
--zone us-central1-b node-jax -- \
-L 8888:localhost:8888
```

An SSH shell is opened with an SSH tunnel forwarding traffic from your local port 8888 to the same port at the remote machine where we will run Jupyter. We can do all the required installation on this machine (see appendix C).

We skip installing JAX, as we will do that from the notebook, and install everything required to run the Jupyter server:

```
$pip install -U jinja2
$pip install notebook

# modify this path according to your username
$export PATH=$PATH:/home/grigo/.local/bin

$pip install jupyter_http_over_ws
$jupyter notebook \
  --NotebookApp.allow_origin='https://colab.research.google.com' \
  --port=8888 \
  --NotebookApp.port_retries=0
```

Jupyter server runs and gives us a link to connect to the notebook (something like http://localhost:8888/?token=ac7ca95a1a2ebc0239a17f07dd4b8cb469d56ea1d1f51b 36). Copy that link and use it to connect Colab to a local runtime (see appendix C for the detailed instructions with screenshots).

Our Colab notebook is ready to use a Cloud TPU! You can delete the Cloud TPU machine when you no longer need it *(don't forget to do it; otherwise, you will pay for it even if you do not use it!)*:

```
$gcloud compute tpus tpu-vm delete node-jax --zone us-central1-b
```

RUNNING COMPUTATIONS ON TPU

With a Cloud TPU attached to the Colab notebook, we can now use hardware acceleration provided by TPUs. Listing 3.20 reproduces listing 3.19 but with computations performed on TPU. The book repo also contains a copy of the notebook with `jax. Array` examples but with a TPU backend instead of a GPU.

Listing 3.20 Working with Cloud TPU

```
!pip install jax[tpu] -f https://storage.googleapis.com/jax-releases/libtpu_
releases.html
```
◄ **Installs JAX with TPU support**

```
from jax.lib import xla_bridge
print(xla_bridge.get_backend().platform)
```
Checks what backend JAX uses

```
>>> tpu
```

```
import jax
jax.local_devices()
```

```
>>> [TpuDevice(id=0, process_index=0,
coords=(0,0,0), core_on_chip=0),
>>>  TpuDevice(id=1, process_index=0,
coords=(0,0,0), core_on_chip=1),
>>>  TpuDevice(id=2, process_index=0,
coords=(1,0,0), core_on_chip=0),
>>>  TpuDevice(id=3, process_index=0,
coords=(1,0,0), core_on_chip=1),
>>>  TpuDevice(id=4, process_index=0,
coords=(0,1,0), core_on_chip=0),
>>>  TpuDevice(id=5, process_index=0,
coords=(0,1,0), core_on_chip=1),
>>>  TpuDevice(id=6, process_index=0,
coords=(1,1,0), core_on_chip=0),
>>>  TpuDevice(id=7, process_index=0,
coords=(1,1,0), core_on_chip=1)]
```
◄ **We see there are eight TPU devices available.**

```
import jax.numpy as jnp
a = jnp.array(range(1000000)).reshape((1000,1000))
a.device()
```

```
>>> TpuDevice(id=0, process_index=0,
coords=(0,0,0), core_on_chip=0)
```
◄ **The array resides on a single TPU core (out of eight).**

```
%time x = jnp.dot(a,a)
```
◄ **Only measures time to dispatch the work**

```
>>> CPU times: user 1.07 ms, sys: 674 µs, total: 1.74 ms
>>> Wall time: 953 µs
```

```
%time x = jnp.dot(a,a).block_until_ready()
```
◄ **Measures the time for a large operation on TPU**

```
>>> CPU times: user 1.85 ms, sys: 1.17 ms, total: 3.02 ms
>>> Wall time: 2.07 ms
```

Here, you see that there are eight TPU devices with IDs from 0 to 7, as each Cloud TPU is a TPU board with four TPU chips, each containing two cores. The coords tuple contains the binary TPU chip coordinates on the TPU board, and the core_on_chip attribute marks the TPU core number inside the two-core TPU chip.

You can see that the device where our tensor resides is now a TPU. More interesting, it is one particular TPU core out of eight cores (the first device, which was the default device). The dot product calculation took place on this particular core as well.

You may also see the `process_index` attribute. All the TPUs here are connected to a single JAX process with an index of 0. For multiprocess configurations, you may see more diversity here. Each JAX process can obtain its process index with the `jax.process_index()` function.

> **WARNING**   Remember to stop and delete your Cloud GPU or TPU machines when you do not use them. Otherwise, it may lead to significant expenses.

We are done with TPU. You see, it is relatively easy to start using it; usually, only the first preparation takes time.

Now we know how JAX works with tensors and how to adapt a NumPy program to JAX. You can even move our image processing to TPU, though it doesn't bring us significant benefits for such a simple example.

Next, I want to highlight the differences between JAX and NumPy.

3.3   Differences from NumPy

You may still want to use pure NumPy for cases where you do not need any benefits from JAX, especially when running small one-off calculations. If that's not the case, and you want to use the benefits JAX provides, you may switch from NumPy to JAX. However, you might also need to make some changes to the code.

Even though the JAX NumPy-like API tries to follow the original NumPy API as closely as possible, several important distinctions exist. An obvious distinction we already know about is accelerator support. Tensors can reside on different backends (CPU, GPU, TPU), and you can manage tensor device placement precisely. Asynchronous dispatch also belongs in this category, as it was designed to use accelerated computations efficiently.

Another difference we already mentioned is the behavior with nonarray inputs, discussed in section 3.2.2. Remember that many JAX functions do not accept lists or tuples as their inputs, to prevent performance degradation. Other differences include immutability and special topics related to supported data types and type promotion. Let's discuss these topics in depth.

3.3.1   Immutability

JAX arrays are immutable. We might not have noticed it before, but try to change any tensor, and you will see an error. Why is the error? Let's change a tensor and see what happens.

Listing 3.21   Updating an element of a tensor

```
a_jnp = jnp.array(range(10))
a_np  = np.array(range(10))
a_np[5], a_jnp[5]

>>> (5, Array(5, dtype=int32))

a_np[5] = 100                                    ◄──────   In-place element
a_np[5]                                                    assignment in NumPy (OK)

>>> 100

try:
  a_jnp[5] = 100                                 ◄──────   In-place element assignment
except TypeError as e:                                     in JAX (not allowed)
  print(e)

>>> '<class 'jaxlib.xla_extension.ArrayImpl'>'
object does not support item assignment. JAX
arrays are immutable. Instead of ``x[idx] = y``,
use ``x = x.at[idx].set(y)`` or another .at[] method: ...
```

Remember, JAX is designed to follow the functional programming paradigm. This is why JAX transformations are so powerful. There are beautiful books on functional programming, such as *Grokking Functional Programming* (https://www.manning.com/books/grokking-functional-programming), *Grokking Simplicity* (https://www.manning.com/books/grokking-simplicity), and others, and I do not pretend to cover this topic fully in this book. But remember the basics of functional purity: the code must not have side effects. The code that modifies the original arguments is not functionally pure. The only way to create a modified tensor is to create another tensor based on the original one. You may have seen such behavior in other systems and languages that follow the functional paradigm, for example, in Spark.

This contradicts some of the NumPy programming practices. A typical operation in NumPy is index update, which is when you change a value inside a tensor by index, say, changing the value of the fifth element of an array. That's perfectly fine in NumPy, yet it raises an error in JAX.

Thanks to JAX, the error message is very informative and suggests a solution to the problem. Let's see how to solve the error in listing 3.21.

INDEX UPDATE FUNCTIONALITY

For all the typical in-place expressions used to update the value of an element of a tensor, there is a corresponding functionally pure equivalent you can use in JAX. In table 3.1, you will find the list of JAX functional operations equivalent to NumPy-style in-place expressions.

Table 3.1   Index update functionality in JAX

NumPy-style in-place expression	Equivalent JAX syntax
`x[idx] = y`	`x = x.at[idx].set(y)`
`x[idx] += y`	`x = x.at[idx].add(y)`
`x[idx] *= y`	`x = x.at[idx].multiply(y)`
`x[idx] /= y`	`x = x.at[idx].divide(y)`
`x[idx] **= y`	`x = x.at[idx].power(y)`
`x[idx] = minimum(x[idx], y)`	`x = x.at[idx].min(y)`
`x[idx] = maximum(x[idx], y)`	`x = x.at[idx].max(y)`
`ufunc.at(x, idx)`	`x = x.at[idx].apply(ufunc)`
`x = x[idx]`	`x = x.at[idx].get()`

All of these `x.at` expressions return a modified copy of x, not changing the original. It could be less efficient than the original in-place modifying code, but, thanks to JIT compilation, low-level expressions like `x = x.at[idx].set(y)` are guaranteed to be applied in place (if the original copy is not used anymore), making the computation efficient. So, you don't have to worry about efficiency when using index update functionality.

WARNING   There are older `jax.ops.index_*` functions that are now deprecated since JAX 0.2.22.

Now we can change the code to fix the error by replacing the NumPy-style element update with the JAX-provided index update functionality.

Listing 3.22   Updating an element of a tensor in JAX

```
a_jnp = a_jnp.at[5].set(100)
a_jnp[5]

>>> Array(100, dtype=int32)
```

Creates a copy of the original tensor with a specific element changed

This sums up immutability; the code changes required are pretty straightforward, and JAX will let you know how to fix it if you miss something.

OUT-OF-BOUNDS INDEXING

A common type of bug is to index arrays outside of their bounds. In NumPy, relying on Python exceptions to handle such situations is pretty straightforward. However, when the code runs on an accelerator, it may be difficult or even impossible. Therefore, we need some non-error behavior for out-of-bounds indexing. For index-update out-of-bound operations, we'd like to skip such updates, and for index-retrieval out-of-bound operations, the index is clamped to the bound of the array as we need something to return. It resembles handling errors with floating-point calculations with special values like NaN.

By default, JAX assumes that all indices are in-bounds. There is experimental support for giving more precise semantics to out-of-bounds indexed accesses via the `mode` parameter of the index update functions. The possible options are

- `"promise_in_bounds"` (*default*)—The user promises that all indexes are in-bounds, so no additional checking is performed. In practice, it means that all out-of-bound indices are clipped in `get()` and are dropped in `set()`, `add()`, and other modifying functions.
- `"clip"`—Clamps out-of-bounds indices into valid range.
- `"drop"`—Ignores out-of-bound indices.
- `"fill"`—An alias for `"drop"`, but for `get()`, it will return the value specified in the optional `fill_value` argument.

The following listing shows an example of using different options.

Listing 3.23 Out-of-bounds indexing

```
a_jnp = jnp.array(range(10))
a_jnp

>>> Array([0, 1, 2, 3, 4, 5, 6, 7, 8, 9], dtype=int32)

a_jnp[42]                                          ◀——————  Default out-of-bounds behavior
                                                            (clip for 'get' operation)
>>> Array(9, dtype=int32)

a_jnp.at[42].get(mode='drop')                      ◀——————  Uses drop behavior

>>> Array(-2147483648, dtype=int32)

a_jnp.at[42].get(mode='fill', fill_value=-1)       ◀——————  Uses fill behavior with a
                                                            specified fill value
>>> Array(-1, dtype=int32)

a_jnp = a_jnp.at[42].set(100)                      ◀——————  Default out-of-bounds behavior
a_jnp                                                        (drop for 'set' operation)

>>> Array([0, 1, 2, 3, 4, 5, 6, 7, 8, 9], dtype=int32)

a_jnp = a_jnp.at[42].set(100, mode='clip')         ◀——————  Uses clip behavior
a_jnp

>>> Array([  0,   1,   2,   3,   4,   5,   6,   7,   8, 100], dtype=int32)
```

As you can see, out-of-bounds indexing does not produce errors; it always returns some value, and you can control the behavior for such cases.

That's it for immutability for now. Let's look at another big topic with many differences compared to NumPy.

3.3.2 *Types*

There are several differences with NumPy regarding data types. These include low- and high-precision floating-point format support and type promotion semantics, which govern what type will have an operation result if its operands are of specific (possibly different) types.

FLOAT64 SUPPORT

While NumPy aggressively promotes operands to double precision (or `float64`) type, JAX, by default, enforces single-precision (or `float32`) numbers. You may be surprised when you create a `float64` array directly, but JAX silently makes it `float32`. For many machine learning (and especially deep learning) workloads, that's perfectly fine. For some high-precision scientific calculations, it may not be desired.

Floating-point types: float64, float32, float16, bfloat16

There are many floating-point types used in scientific computing and deep learning. The IEEE Standard for Floating-Point Arithmetic (IEEE 754) defines several formats of different precision, which are widely used.

The default floating-point data type for scientific computing is a double-precision float, or `float64`, as the size of this float is 64 bits. The IEEE 754 double-precision binary floating-point format has a 1-bit sign, 11-bit exponent, and 52-bit fraction part. It has a range of ~2.23e-308 to ~1.80e308 with full 15–17 decimal digits precision.

There are higher precision types for some cases, like long double or extended precision float, which is typically an 80-bit float on x86 platforms (however, there are many caveats). NumPy supports the `np.longdouble` type for extended precision, while JAX has no support for this type.

Deep learning applications tend to be robust to lower precision, so single-precision float or `float32` became the default data type for such applications and is the default floating-point data type in JAX. The 32-bit IEEE 754 float has a 1-bit sign, 8-bit exponent, and 23-bit fraction. Its range is ~1.18e-38 to ~3.40e38 with 6–9 significant decimal digits precision.

For many deep learning cases, even 32-bit float is too much, and during recent years, lower precision training and inference have become popular. It is usually easier to do lower precision inference than training, and some tricky schemes of mixed float16/32 precision training are present.

Among the lower-precision floating-point formats are two 16-bit floats: `float16` and `bfloat16`. The IEEE 754 half-precision float or `float16` has a 1-bit sign, 5-bit exponent, and 10-bit fraction. Its range is ~5.96e−8 to 65504 with four significant decimal digits. Another 16-bit format originally developed by Google is called "Brain Floating Point Format," or `bfloat16` for short. The original IEEE `float16` was not designed with deep learning applications in mind, and its dynamic range is too narrow. The `bfloat16` type solves this, providing a dynamic range identical to that of `float32`. It has a 1-bit sign, 8-bit exponent, and 7-bit fraction. Its range is ~1.18e-38 to ~3.40e38 with three significant decimal digits.

The `bfloat16` format, being a truncated IEEE 754 `float32`, allows for fast conversion to and from an IEEE 754 `float32`. In conversion to the `bfloat16` format, the exponent bits are preserved while the significand field can be reduced by truncation.

There are some other special formats, and you can read more about them in my article here: https://mng.bz/QZBm.

To force `float64` computations, you need to set the `jax_enable_x64` configuration variable at startup. The code in the following listing demonstrates this.

Listing 3.24 Forcing `float64` computations

```
# this only works on startup!
from jax.config import config
config.update("jax_enable_x64", True)          ◀——  We need to
import jax.numpy as jnp                               enable float64.

# this may not work on TPU backend. Try using CPU or GPU.
x = jnp.array(range(10), dtype=jnp.float64)    ◀——  Creates an array
x.dtype                                               with float64 type

>>> dtype('float64')        ◀——  Should be 'float64' if we enabled it on
                                  startup. Otherwise, it will be 'float32'.
```

However, 64-bit data types are not supported on every backend. For example, TPU does not support it.

You may also want to go the opposite direction, to lower precision formats.

FLOAT16/BFLOAT16 SUPPORT

In deep learning, there is a tendency to use lower precision formats, most frequently, half-precision or `float16`, or a more special `bfloat16`, which is not supported in vanilla NumPy. With JAX, you can easily switch to using these lower-precision 16-bit types.

Listing 3.25 Using 16-bit floating-point types

```
xb16 = jnp.array(range(10), dtype=jnp.bfloat16)
xb16.dtype

>>> dtype(bfloat16)            ◀———  Uses bfloat16 type

xb16.nbytes

>>> 20

x16 = jnp.array(range(10), dtype=jnp.float16)
x16.dtype

>>> dtype('float16')           ◀———  Uses float16 type
```

Again, there may be limitations on specific backends.

TYPE PROMOTION SEMANTICS

For binary operations, JAX's type promotion rules differ somewhat from NumPy's.

Obviously, it is different for the `bfloat16` type, as NumPy does not support this type. Yet, it also differs in some other cases.

Interestingly, when you add two 16-bit floats, one being an ordinary `float16` and another one being `bfloat16`, you get a `float32` type.

Listing 3.26   Type promotion semantics

```
xb16+x16                                    ◄──────  Sums bfloat16 with float16 values

>>> Array([ 0.,  2.,  4.,  6.,  8., 10., 12., 14., 16., 18.], dtype=float32)

xb16+xb16                                   ◄──────  Sums two bfloat16 values

>>> Array([0, 2, 4, 6, 8, 10, 12, 14, 16, 18], dtype=bfloat16)
```

The table highlighting differences between NumPy and JAX NumPy type promotion semantics for binary operations is located here: https://mng.bz/X1RY. There is also a more thorough comparison between NumPy/TensorFlow/PyTorch/JAX NumPy, and JAX lax (see the next section about lax): https://mng.bz/y8mJ.

SPECIAL TENSOR TYPES

We dealt with so-called *dense* tensors up to now. Dense tensors explicitly contain all the values. Yet there are many cases where you have *sparse* data, meaning there are many zero-valued elements and some (usually orders of magnitude less) non-zero ones.

Sparse tensors explicitly contain only non-zero values and may save a lot of memory. Still, to efficiently use them, you need special linear algebra routines with sparsity support. JAX has an experimental API related to sparse tensors and sparse matrix operations located in the `jax.experimental.sparse` module. Things will probably change when this book is out, and we will not discuss this experimental module here.

Another use case is a collection of tensors with different shapes—say, speech recordings of different lengths. To make a batch with such tensors, there are special data structures in modern frameworks—for example, the *ragged tensor* in TensorFlow.

JAX has no special structure like a ragged tensor, yet you are not prohibited from working with such data. Auto-batching with `vmap()` can help in many ways, and we will see examples of that in chapter 6. Another big difference between JAX and the original NumPy is that, in JAX, there is another lower-level API, which we will discuss.

3.4   *High-level and low-level interfaces: jax.numpy and jax.lax*

During the development of the image processing example, we got familiar with the `jax.numpy` API. It is designed to provide a familiar interface for those who know NumPy. For our image processing example, the NumPy API was enough, and we didn't need any other API.

However, you should know that there is another `jax.lax` lower-level API that underpins libraries such as `jax.numpy`. The `jax.numpy` API is a higher-level wrapper with all the operations expressed in terms of `jax.lax` primitives. Many of the `jax.lax` primitives themselves are thin wrappers around equivalent XLA operations (https://mng .bz/MZE2). In figure 3.9, a diagram of the JAX API layers is shown.

The higher-level `jax.numpy` API is more stable and less likely to change than the `jax.lax` API. The JAX authors recommend using libraries such as `jax.numpy` instead of `jax.lax` directly when possible.

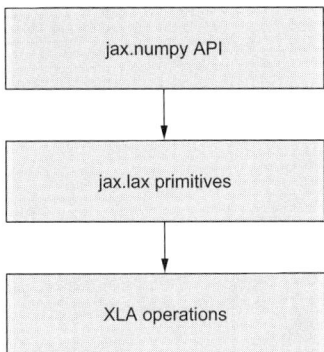

Figure 3.9   Diagram of the JAX API layers

`jax.lax` provides a vast set of mathematical operators. Some of them are more general and provide features absent in `jax.numpy`. For example, when you do a 1D convolution in `jax.numpy`, you use the `jnp.convolve` function (https://mng.bz/ aEnJ). This function uses a more general `conv_general_dilated` function from `jax.lax` (https://mng.bz/gvMR).

There are also other groups of operators: control flow operators, custom gradient operators, operators for parallelism support, and linear algebra operators. The full list of `jax.lax` operators is available at https://mng.bz/eoXJ.

I will talk about some gradient operators in chapter 4 and about parallelism support in chapter 7. Now, I briefly describe control flow primitives.

3.4.1   *Control flow primitives*

The set of structured control flow primitives in `jax.lax` includes `lax.cond` to conditionally apply one of two functions (analog of an `if` statement), `lax.switch` for many branches, `lax.while_loop` and `lax.fori_loop` for repeatedly calling a function in a loop, `lax.scan` and `lax.associative_scan` for scanning a function over an array while carrying along with state, and a `lax.map` function to apply a function over leading array axes. These primitives are JIT-able and differentiable, helping to avoid unrolling large loops.

In JAX, you can still use Python control structures, and in most cases, they work (in section 5.2, I discuss the internals of this process and its limitations). Yet, these solutions might be suboptimal, either because there is a more performant solution or because they produce less efficient differentiation code.

We will use some of these and other `jax.lax` primitives throughout the book, and I will describe them in later chapters at first use. Right now, I will give you one example with `lax.switch`.

Let's consider the case quite the opposite of image filtering. In deep learning for computer vision, you often want to make your neural network robust to different image distortions. For example, you want your neural network to be robust to noise. In order to do that, you provide noisy versions of images in the dataset, and you need to create such noisy images. You may also want to use image augmentations to effectively increase your training dataset with variations of an original image: some rotations, left–right (and sometimes up–down) flips, color distortions, etc.

Suppose you have a set of functions for image augmentation:

```
augmentations = [
    add_noise_func,
    horizontal_flip_func,
    rotate_func,
    adjust_colors_func
]
```

A list of four stub functions for image processing (it is only an example, code for these functions is not provided)

We will not provide the code for these functions; they are just for demonstration purposes. You may implement them on your own as an exercise.

In in listing 3.27, we use `lax.switch` to choose a random image augmentation among multiple options. The value of the first parameter, here, the `augmentation_index` variable, determines which particular branch among several ones will be applied. The second parameter, here, the `augmentations` list, provides a sequence of functions (or branches) to choose from. We use a list of image augmentation functions, each one performing its own image processing, be it noise addition, making a horizontal flip, rotation, and so on. If the `augmentation_index` variable is 0, then the first element of the `augmentations` list is called; if the `augmentation_index` variable is 1, then the second element is called; and so on. The rest of the parameters, here, only one called `image`, are passed to the chosen function, and the value returned by the chosen function, here, an augmented image, is the resulting value of the `lax.switch` operator.

Listing 3.27 Control flow example with `lax.switch`

Imports module for random numbers in JAX (more on this in chapter 9)

```
from jax import random

def random_augmentation(image, augmentations, rng_key):
    '''A function that applies a random transformation to an image'''
    augmentation_index = random.randint(
        key=rng_key, minval=0,
        maxval=len(augmentations), shape=())
    augmented_image = lax.switch(
```

Generates a random integer value to index the augmentations list

```
        augmentation_index, augmentations, image)    ◄──┐
    return augmented_image
```

**Uses lax.switch() function
to choose between
multiple options**

```
new_image = random_augmentation(image, augmentations, random.PRNGKey(42))
```

In chapter 5 we will understand the reasons why the code that uses `jax.lax` control flow primitives may result in more efficient computations. In chapter 9, we will build this function's final version, discussing the right ways of working with random numbers.

3.4.2 *Type promotion*

The `jax.lax` API is stricter than `jax.numpy`. It does not implicitly promote arguments for operations with mixed data types. With `jax.lax`, you have to do type promotion in such cases manually.

> **Listing 3.28   Type promotion in `jax.numpy` and `jax.lax`**

```
import jax.numpy as jnp
jnp.add(42, 42.0)
```
**Adds integer and floating-point
value in jax.numpy (OK)**

```
>>> Array(84., dtype=float32, weak_type=True)
```
**The result is promoted
to the float32 value.**

```
from jax import lax
try:
    lax.add(42, 42.0)
except TypeError as e:
  print(e)
```
**Adds integer and floating-point
value in jax.lax (not OK)**

```
>>> lax.add requires arguments to have the same
dtypes, got int32, float32. (Tip: jnp.add is a
similar function that does automatic type
promotion on inputs).
```

```
lax.add(jnp.float32(42), 42.0)
```
**Manually performs type conversion
to have two float32 values and adds
them with jax.lax (OK)**

```
>>> Array(84., dtype=float32)
```

In this example, you see a `weak_type` property in the `Array` value. This property means there was a value with no explicitly user-specified type, such as Python scalar literals. You can read more about weakly typed values in JAX here: https://mng .bz/pp0P.

We will not dive deeply into the `jax.lax` API here, as most of its benefits will be clear only after chapters 4 through 6. Right now, it's important to highlight that the `jax.numpy` API is not the only one in JAX.

Exercise 3.1

1 Implement your digital filter of choice.

2 Implement the image augmentation functions we proposed in section 3.4.

3 Implement other image processing operations: crop, resize, rotate, and anything else you need.

Summary

- Tensor or multidimensional arrays are the basic data structure in deep learning and scientific computing frameworks.

- For representing tensors, NumPy provides you with the `numpy.ndarray` type; in JAX, there is a `jax.Array` type (previously known as `DeviceArray`).

- JAX has a NumPy-like API imported from the `jax.numpy` module that tries to follow the original NumPy API as closely as possible, but some differences exist.

- You can precisely manage device placement for `Array` data, committing it to the device of choice, be it a CPU, GPU, or TPU.

- In JAX, the computation follows data placement.

- JAX distinguishes between local and global devices. Local devices are devices connected to the local host. Global devices are devices available across all JAX processes across multiple hosts.

- JAX uses asynchronous dispatch for computations.

- You can use the `block_until_ready()` method of an `Array` to wait for the result explicitly.

- To use TPUs, you need to deploy your own host with Cloud TPUs in Google Cloud and connect it to Colab using a local runtime.

- JAX arrays are immutable, so you must use the functionally pure equivalent of NumPy-style in-place expressions.

- JAX provides different modes for controlling non-error behavior for out-of-bounds indexing.

- JAX default floating-point data type is `float32`. If you want, you can use `float64`/`float16`/`bfloat16`, but some limitations on specific backends might exist.

- For binary operations, JAX's type promotion rules differ somewhat from NumPy's.

- The lower-level `jax.lax` API is stricter and often provides more powerful features than the high-level `jax.numpy` API.

- The `jax.lax` API includes structured control flow primitives, which are JIT-able and differentiable, helping to avoid unrolling large loops.

- The `jax.lax` API does not implicitly promote arguments for operations with mixed data types.

Calculating gradients

This chapter covers

- Calculating derivatives in different ways
- Using automatic differentiation (autodiff) in JAX to calculate gradients of your functions (and neural networks)
- Using forward and reverse modes of autodiff

In chapter 2, we trained a simple neural network for handwritten digit classification. The crucial thing for training any neural network is the ability to calculate a derivative of a loss function with respect to neural network weights.

In case you need a reminder, neural networks are typically trained by gradient descent procedure (usually some advanced version of it, like Adam). A neural network is a complicated mathematical function defined by its weights (sometimes billions of weights, as is the case for GPT-3 and other large models). Given weights, you can calculate an output value of the neural network, and given a loss function, you evaluate this result and how far it is from the ideal. So, you want to update the neural network weights to decrease the loss function value. The gradient descent procedure takes a function (a neural network with its weights) and a loss function, calculates the loss function derivative with respect to the weights, and obtains a gradient, which is the direction and rate of the fastest increase of the function. Then, going opposite to the gradient, you update the neural network weights and reduce the loss function value. As you can see, calculating gradients is a crucial step here, and having a way of getting them is a must.

There are several ways of getting the derivatives of your functions (or *differentiating* them), but automatic differentiation (or autodiff, for short) is the main one used in modern deep learning frameworks. Autodiff is also one of the JAX framework pillars (remember, JAX is frequently referred to as "Autograd and XLA"). It lets you write your Python and NumPy-like code, leaving the hard and tricky part of getting derivatives to the framework. This chapter teaches you how to work with autodiff efficiently; we will go over its essentials and go deeply into how autodiff works in JAX.

We will start by comparing the different ways of getting derivatives: manual, symbolic, numerical, and automatic differentiation. It is very helpful to understand the difference between these methods as it will be much clearer why autodiff is such a great thing. If you already know this, feel free to jump to the next section.

In the second section, we will compare how to take gradients in PyTorch, TensorFlow, and JAX and explore all the basics of gradient transformations in JAX. This is the main part of the chapter, and all the basics of how to use JAX for calculating derivatives are here. To start using JAX, this is the most important part.

The final section is for those who want to understand the machinery behind autodiff. I will describe the forward and reverse modes of autodiff and two corresponding JAX transformations called `jvp()` and `vjp()`. It is the hardest part of the book, I think. If you want, you may safely skip it, as you can still use JAX without understanding autodiff internals in many cases. However, this knowledge will reward you with a better understanding of how to use JAX efficiently.

4.1   *Different ways of getting derivatives*

There are many tasks where you need to get derivatives. In neural network training, you need derivatives (actually, gradients) to train a network, which means minimizing a loss function by making consecutive steps in the direction opposite to the gradient. There are simpler cases familiar from the calculus classes when you need to find the minima (or maxima) of the function. There are many other cases in physics, engineering, biology, and other disciplines.

Let's start with an easily digestible teaching example of finding a function minima (which is exactly the essence of a training procedure in deep learning). You have a simple mathematical function, say, $f(x) = x^4 + 12x + 1/x$. Let's implement it as code. The code for this part is available on GitHub in this notebook: https://mng.bz/9dv8.

> **Listing 4.1   A simple function we will use as a model**

```
def f(x):
    return x**4 + 12*x + 1/x
```
◄——— **A simple mathematical function implemented as Python code**

You are searching for the local minima of the function. You need to find the points where a derivative of this function is zero; and then check each point found to be a minimum, not a maximum, or a saddle point.

Minimum, maximum, and saddle points

There are three types of points at which a real-valued function has a zero derivative:

- *Maxima* (the plural of *maximum*) are the points at which a function has a value larger than or equal to any neighboring point. *Local (or relative) maxima* are the points at which a function has the largest value in the interval. A local maximum is additionally called *global* (or *absolute*) *maximum* if it also has the largest value on a domain (a set of accepted inputs) of the function.
- *Minima* (the plural of *minimum*) are the points at which a function has a value smaller than or equal to any neighboring point. *Local minima* are the points at which a function has the smallest value in the interval. A local minimum is additionally called a *global minimum* if it also has the smallest value on a function domain.

  Both minima and maxima are called *extrema* (the plural of *extremum*).
- A *saddle point (or minimax point)* is a point with a zero derivative but which is not a local extremum of the function.

We can visualize these types of points in the following.

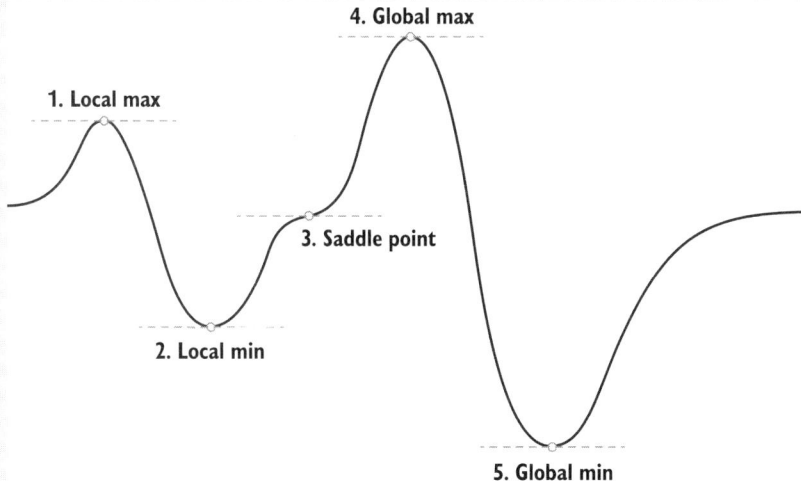

Visualizing local and global minima, maxima, and a saddle point of some function (not the same as we use in the text). The dashed line displays a tangent line to the function at these specific points. Its slope is equal to the function's derivative at these points; at all these points, the derivative is zero.

Point 1 is a maximum, as it is higher than its neighboring points, but it is a local and not the global maximum of the function, as there is another maximum with a higher value, point 4. Points 2 and 5 are minima, as they are lower than their neighboring points, and point 5 is a global minimum (the lowest one) while point 2 is a local one. Finally, point 3 is a saddle point, a point with a zero derivative of the function that is neither minimum nor maximum because there are both higher and lower points in its neighborhood.

You need to be able to calculate a function derivative. We will not go through the full procedure of finding a function minima but only discuss the part on calculating derivatives.

There are different ways of calculating derivatives. I will discuss how they work, compare them, and show why autodiff is so useful. It is essential to know about these different methods as several are sometimes negligently called autodiff, while only one is truly autodiff.

4.1.1   Manual differentiation

The good, old method known by many from calculus classes in school is taking derivatives by hand. Technically speaking, the function domain is non-zero real numbers, and we calculate the derivative only on the domain.

For this particular function, the derivative will be $f'(x) = 4x^3 + 12 - 1/x^2$ and can be easily calculated by hand (because a derivative of a sum is a sum of derivatives, and the derivative for x^4 is $4x^3$, for $12x$ is 12, and for $1/x$ is $-1/x^2$) if you remember differentiation rules and derivatives for some basic functions. If we need this result in code, we can implement it directly after we obtain a derivative by hand.

Listing 4.2   A closed-form expression for a derivative calculated manually

```
def df(x):
    return 4*x**3 + 12 - 1/x**2          Manually calculated derivative
                                         of our model function
x = 11.0

print(f(x))

>>> 14773.09090909091

print(df(x))

>>> 5335.99173553719
```

Here you have a so-called closed-form expression that can be evaluated at any point of interest. In the previous example, we calculated the derivative at the point $x = 11.0$.

Things get harder for not-so-simple functions—for example, functions that are products of other functions or functions being a composition of other functions. Say, for a function $f(x) = (2x + 7)(17x^2 - 3x)(x^2 - 1/x)(x^3 + 21x)/(17x - 5/x^2)$, I do not even want to try doing this manually. I used WolframAlpha (https://www.wolframalpha.com/) to get the derivative of this function and got a huge expression of $(x^2(-6615 + 47460\,x + 17325\,x^2 + 16620\,x^3 - 122206\,x^4 - 51282\,x^5 - 33339\,x^6 + 157352\,x^7 + 58905\,x^8 + 11526\,x^9 + 4046\,x^{10}))/(5 - 17\,x^3)^2$. I'd use a couple of sheets of paper to perform all the differentiation steps, and I won't be sure about the final results. It's easy to make a mistake along the way.

It is helpful to understand how to take a derivative manually, as it is always great to know the fundamental things. However, for real neural networks, it's a pain to do everything with manual differentiation. It would be quite time consuming and error prone to implement a neural network without autodiff (as you had to do if you worked on neural networks 10 or more years ago). You must calculate all the layer derivatives by hand and implement them as a separate code for backpropagation calculations. With this process, you cannot iterate your code quickly.

4.1.2 Symbolic differentiation

In the previous section, I used WolframAlpha to get the derivative of a function, and its engine does symbolic differentiation, performing all the steps you'd do by hand in an automatic way. You can program all the differentiation rules, and a computer can follow these rules much faster than a human can. It also does it more reliably, without any chances of occasional errors (unless someone introduces bugs into the engine or you have buggy and unreliable hardware).

There are different options for using symbolic differentiation. In Python, you can use symbolic differentiation with a library called SymPy (https://www.sympy.org/en/index.html). It is installed by default in Google Colab, but you can install it on your particular system according to the instructions from the site (https://mng.bz/jXe9).

Listing 4.3 SymPy example of getting symbolic derivative

```
import sympy

x = 11.0                                    Defines a variable x

x_sym = sympy.symbols('x')                  Creates a symbolic
                                            expression passing a
f_sym = f(x_sym)                            variable into our function

df_sym = sympy.diff(f_sym)                  Calculates symbolic derivative

print(f_sym)                                Displays our functions
                                            in symbolic form
>>> x**4 + 12*x + 1/x

print(df_sym)

>>> 4*x**3 + 12 - 1/x**2

f = sympy.lambdify(x_sym, f_sym)            Converts SymPy
                                            expressions into
print(f(x))                  Numerically evaluates   expressions that
                             the original function   can be evaluated
>>> 14773.09090909091        and its derivative      numerically

df = sympy.lambdify(x_sym, df_sym)

print(df(x))

>>> 5335.99173553719
```

As with manual differentiation, the result of symbolic differentiation is also a closed-form expression, which is actually a separate function. You can apply this function to any point you are interested in. In the previous example, we evaluate the derivative at the same point, $x = 11.0$.

It's beautiful when you can do calculations in symbolic form. Symbolic differentiation is great, yet things still get hard in some cases.

First, you have to express all your calculations as a closed-form expression. It could be harder to have a closed-form expression if you implement your calculations as an algorithm, especially when using some control flow logic with if statements and for loops.

Second, symbolic expressions tend to grow bigger if you do subsequent differentiation—for example, when getting higher-order derivatives. This is called *expression swell*. Sometimes, they get exponentially bigger.

4.1.3   *Numerical differentiation*

With manual or symbolic differentiation, you have a closed-form expression with a function of interest and obtain a closed-form expression for its derivative, which you can use to calculate the derivative at any given point. The problem is that expressing your original function in this form is not always easy. Moreover, there are many cases where you are interested in derivative values at one specific point, not at any possible point. This is precisely the case for deep learning, where you want gradients for the current set of weights.

A method called *numerical differentiation* is frequently used in science and engineering to estimate the derivative of a function. Numerical differentiation is a way of getting an approximate value of a mathematical derivative. There are many techniques for numerical differentiation. One of the most well-known ones uses a method of finite differences based upon the limit definition of a derivative. It estimates a derivative of the function $f(x)$ by computing the slope of a nearby secant line through the points $(x, f(x))$ and $(x + \Delta x, f(x + \Delta x))$:

$$f'(x) \cong \frac{f(x + \Delta x) - f(x)}{\Delta x}$$

This method uses two evaluations of the function at nearby points, denoted by x and $(x+\Delta x)$, where Δx, or step size, is a small value, say 10^{-6}.

Listing 4.4   **Finding a derivative with numeric differentiation**

```
x = 11.0
dx = 1e-6                                          ◄──────  Chooses the step size

df_x_numeric = (f(x+dx)-f(x))/dx                   ◄────┐  Does numeric differentiation
                                                        └  for our model function
print(df_x_numeric)

>>> 5335.992456821259
```

The result is an approximated value of the gradient at specific point x (here, at the point $x = 11.0$). Because it is an approximation, the result is not exact, and we see that it differs from manual or symbolic differentiation results in the third decimal place.

Compared to manual and symbolic differentiation, which return a closed-form solution that can be used at any point, numeric differentiation does not know anything about it. It just calculates an approximated derivative at a specific point.

This method has several issues with speed, accuracy, and numerical stability. Let's start with speed. You need two function evaluations for a function with a single scalar input, which might be costly for heavy functions. Moreover, you need two evaluations per scalar input for a function with many inputs, which leads to $O(N)$ computational complexity. Almost all neural networks are functions of many variables (remember, they might have millions, billions, or even trillions of trainable weights that we optimize with gradient descent). So, this process scales poorly.

Accuracy is not perfect by definition, as we use approximation. Still, two types of errors lead to inaccuracy: *approximation error* and *round-off error*, both related to the step size.

You should choose the step size wisely. You want this step size to be small enough to approximate the derivative better. So, you start reducing the step size, and the approximation error (sometimes also called a *truncation error*, the error originating from the fact that the step size is not infinitesimal) reduces. But at some point, you become limited by the numerical precision of floating-point arithmetic, and the error tends to increase after some point if you continue reducing the step size. It is called a *round-off error*, originating from the fact that valuable low-order bits of the final answer compete for machine-word space with high-order bits of $f(x + \Delta x)$ and $f(x)$ values, as these values are stored just until they cancel each other in the subtraction at the end. You also might get unstable results for noisy functions because small changes in the input (data or weight values) may result in large changes in the derivative.

In practice, you cannot use numeric differentiation as the main method of getting derivatives in gradient-based learning methods. It would be too slow. In the good old days, when you had to calculate all your layer derivatives manually, numeric differentiation was used as a sanity check by comparing with the manually calculated derivatives. If they were close enough to each other (another meta-parameter, which you had to determine on your own, say, they should not differ more than 10^{-8}), then you probably were right with your manual differentiation and may use it further. If not, there is an error somewhere, and you must redo your manual derivative calculation work.

4.1.4 *Automatic differentiation*

Finally, autodiff came on the scene. The idea behind autodiff is clever. A differentiable function comprises primitives (additions, divisions, exponentiations, and so on) whose derivatives are known. During the computation of a function, autodiff tracks computations and propagates derivatives with the help of the chain rule (a rule for taking the derivative of a composite function) as the computation unfolds. This is very relevant to deep learning, as a neural network is a composition of functions of this form:

$f_L(f_{L-1}....f_1(f_0(x)))$, where f_i (i belongs to $[0, L]$) is a function that calculates ith layer, and x is the input data. This is a deeply nested composite function.

Autodiff allows obtaining derivatives for very complex computer programs, including control structures, branching, loops, and recursion that might be hard to express as a closed-form expression. That's a big deal!

Previously, if you had a Python function and wanted to calculate the derivative of this function, you had two options. The first option is to express it as a closed-form expression and then take a manual or symbolic derivative. For many practical functions with nontrivial control flow inside, it could be time consuming and hard or even impossible just to get a closed-form expression.

The second option is to use a numerical derivative, but that is slow and scales poorly with the number of scalar inputs. Say, for a neural network for classifying MNIST images from chapter 2, there are $28 \times 28 = 784$ scalar inputs. You need to perform two function evaluations for each one, so there are more than 1,500 neural network forward propagations to estimate all the gradients. That's a lot.

Autodiff provides a new alternative. (To be precise, autodiff is a pretty old topic starting at least in the 1960s. Unfortunately, it was long unknown—and still is—for many practitioners in the deep learning field.) It can be applied to regular code with minimal change, and you can focus on writing code for the computation you want while autodiff takes care of calculating derivatives.

All the major modern deep learning frameworks, including TensorFlow, PyTorch, and JAX, implement autodiff. We have already used it in the example in chapter 2, and you know that `grad()` transformation produces a function that calculates a derivative of the original function. In the next section, we will compare the JAX approach with TensorFlow and PyTorch approaches. The following example demonstrates using autodiff in JAX. The result here is slightly different compared to the manual and symbolic differentiation as JAX by default uses lower precision float numbers, `float32` instead of `float64`. You learned how to change that in chapter 3.

Listing 4.5   Finding derivative with autodiff in JAX

```
df = jax.grad(f)          ◄──────────┐
                                     │  Gets function derivative
print(df(x))              ◄──────────┤  with autodiff in JAX
                                     │
>>> 5335.9917               Calculates derivative
                            at the specific point
```

There are two modes for autodiff: the *forward mode* and the *reverse mode*. We will dive deeper into these later in the chapter.

If you started your neural network journey 10 or more years ago, you remember how things were done back then. You had some programming language with matrix support (and it was better to have MATLAB than C++), and you implemented your neural network architecture as a sequence of basic matrix operations (similarly, you can do that right now with NumPy). Then you had to implement backpropagation (backprop, for short). You had to calculate derivatives for your neural network layers by hand, implement them as another set of matrix operations, and then implement numerical differentiation only to check that your calculations were correct (you cannot use numerical differentiation instead of backprop as it is too slow, so you can use it only to check the results during development). It took a lot of time, and the process was highly error prone. You iterated very slowly, and that limited your research speed significantly.

Then frameworks came. Some major frameworks (say, Caffe) still required manual differentiation to implement your custom layers with both forward and backward functions. Some other frameworks (say, Theano, followed by TensorFlow and PyTorch) started to use autodiff to take care of calculating derivatives and allowed a user to focus on writing the forward computation logic only. That helped a lot. The speed of development iterations increased significantly, and (with the help of more powerful hardware) you could test different modifications in minutes instead of hours or days. I believe these frameworks were the biggest democratizer for the deep learning field itself.

JAX continues this beautiful tradition of calculating derivatives of your functions, adding the possibility of calculating gradients even for custom Python code with control logic. It was not the first framework with such a capability. (The Autograd library emerged before TensorFlow, and Chainer and DyNet were among the first supporting dynamic computational graphs; then came PyTorch. TensorFlow 1 had some very limited options to do it with the Fold library, but generally, TensorFlow started calculating derivatives for dynamic computation graphs with version 2.)

JAX gives you much more flexibility because it's not just calculating gradients for you, but it transforms functions into other functions that calculate gradients of the original function. You may choose not to stop here and generate a function for higher-order differentiation similarly. This is particularly important in scientific areas other than deep learning, which explains why JAX is also popular outside of deep learning.

We have discussed several approaches to differentiation and will dive deeper into how to use autodiff in modern frameworks.

4.2   Calculating gradients with autodiff

Now let's choose another practical example. We take a simple yet useful example of linear regression. Imagine you have a noisy dataset of temperature measurements you obtained from your brand-new Raspberry Pi with a temperature sensor. You want to calculate a linear trend that describes your data (a more complicated function with both a trend and a periodic component would be a better fit, but I leave that to you as an exercise).

This example can also be seen as a model case for almost any neural network training—for example, the image classification from chapter 2. Here, we will dive into how things work at the lower level.

I used an algorithmic procedure to generate noisy data. You may use any data you want—any other temperature or humidity measurements, number of meteors, stock prices, or anything else. The code for this part is available on GitHub in the notebook found here: https://mng.bz/WEZX.

I use the following procedure: generate some evenly spaced samples for the time measurement (let it be *x*); and then for each time measurement, generate a value that is a sum or a constant (65.0), a linear growing trend (1.8*x*), a periodic process (cosine function), and some random error (from normal distribution).

Listing 4.6 Generating data for our regression problem

```
import numpy as np
import matplotlib.pyplot as plt

x = np.linspace(0, 10*np.pi, num=1000)
e = np.random.normal(scale=10.0, size=x.size)
y = 65.0 + 1.8*x + 40*np.cos(x) + e

plt.scatter(x, y)
```

Generates 1,000 points in the range from 0 to 10π

Generates random Gaussian noise

Generates the data consisting of bias, linear trend, sinusoidal wave, and noise

This code generates and displays the data, and you can see the result in figure 4.1.

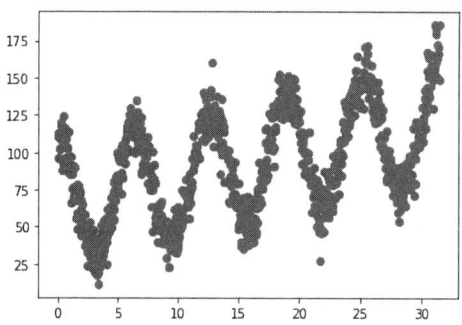

Figure 4.1 Visualized temperature measurements from our synthetic data

The structure of the problem is very similar to the image classification problem from chapter 2: we have training data consisting of *x* and *y* values, a function $y = f(x)$ to predict the *y* value from *x*, a loss function to evaluate the prediction error, and a gradient procedure to adapt model weights in the direction opposite to gradient of the loss function with respect to the model weights. On a high level, the model function (here, $f(x)$) and the loss function are linked, as shown in figure 4.2.

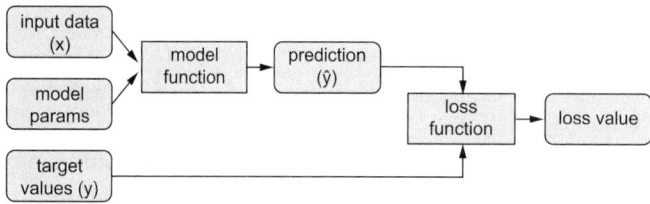

Figure 4.2 Calculating a value of the loss function

Now, y contains real-valued numbers instead of classes. The prediction model is now a simple linear function (instead of a multilayer neural network) of the form $y = wx + b$, where x and y are the data and w and b are the learned weights (model parameters). We call here the result of applying the model function as $\hat{y}$ to distinguish it from the true value of y. The loss function that evaluates how far your predictions ($\hat{y}$) are from true data (y) is now the mean squared error (MSE) frequently used for regression problems.

Finally, you have a training loop that iteratively performs gradient update steps. It is mostly the same loop we used for the image classification example from chapter 2; this is the part we are most interested in right now.

Let's look at gradient computation differently and compare how things are done in TensorFlow/PyTorch and JAX. If you do not work with TensorFlow or PyTorch and are not interested in how they work with gradients, you can jump to section 4.2.3.

4.2.1 *Working with gradients in TensorFlow*

In TensorFlow (as in many other frameworks), you must let the framework know which tensors it needs to track computations to collect gradients. You do so by using `trainable=True` for variables in TensorFlow.

Then you perform calculations with the tensors, and the framework keeps tracking what computations are being done. In TensorFlow, you need to use *gradient tapes* to track that (you will learn more about gradient tapes at the end of the chapter when we dive into forward and reverse modes).

In the case of neural network training, you have some final value, a prediction error, or, more generally, a loss function. Finally, you want to calculate the derivatives of the loss function with respect to the computation parameters (your tensors of interest). In TensorFlow, you use a function `gradient()`, passing the loss function and parameters of interest. Autograd then calculates the gradients for each model parameter, returning them as a result of the `gradient()` function.

With these gradients, you can perform a gradient descent step if needed. In our examples, we implement only a single gradient step. You might want to expand the example to have a complete training loop, so treat it as an exercise.

Listing 4.7   Calculating gradients in TensorFlow

```
import tensorflow as tf                        ◄─── Imports TensorFlow

xt = tf.constant(x, dtype=tf.float32)          │ Converts the training data
yt = tf.constant(y, dtype=tf.float32)          │ into TensorFlow tensors

learning_rate = 1e-2

w = tf.Variable(1.0, trainable=True)           │ Tensors with model weights marked
b = tf.Variable(1.0, trainable=True)           │ with a flag to track gradients

def model(x):                                  ◄─── The function implements
    return w * x + b                           │ a simple linear model.
```

```
def loss_fn(prediction, y):                          ◀──── MSE loss function
    return tf.reduce_mean(tf.square(prediction-y))

with tf.GradientTape() as tape:                      Does computations inside
    prediction = model(x)                            GradientTape context
    loss = loss_fn(prediction, y)

dw, db = tape.gradient(loss, [w, b])      ◀──── Extracts gradients from the gradient tape

w.assign_sub(learning_rate * dw)                     Makes a single step
b.assign_sub(learning_rate * db)                     of gradient update
```

As you see, things are not particularly hard, especially when you are already used to it. But it's not intuitive when you first face it, and you have to remember a recipe: mark tensors with a special parameter, create a gradient tape, and call a special function to get the gradients. It's very far from mathematical notation.

Now we will look at PyTorch's way of getting gradients.

4.2.2 *Working with gradients in PyTorch*

In PyTorch, you also need to mark the tensors you want to track gradients for using a special parameter called `requires_grad=True` for PyTorch tensors. PyTorch builds a directed acyclic graph (DAG) to track operations during computations involving marked tensors. After computations, you calculate gradients by calling a special function `backward()` on the loss tensor. Autograd then calculates the gradients for each model parameter, storing them in a special attribute of a tensor called `grad`.

Listing 4.8 Calculating gradients in PyTorch

```
import torch                                         ◀──── Imports PyTorch

xt = torch.tensor(x)                                 Converts the training data
yt = torch.tensor(y)                                 into PyTorch tensors

learning_rate = 1e-2

w = torch.tensor(1.0, requires_grad=True)            Tensors with model weights marked
b = torch.tensor(1.0, requires_grad=True)            with a flag to track gradients

def model(x):                                        ◀──── The function implements a
    return w * x + b                                       simple linear model.

def loss_fn(prediction, y):                          ◀──── MSE loss function
    return ((prediction-y)**2).mean()

prediction = model(xt)                               Does model and loss computations
loss = loss_fn(prediction, yt)

loss.backward()                                      ◀──── Calculates gradients

with torch.no_grad():                                Uses context manager to disable
                                                     gradient calculations (we do not want
                                                     parameter updates to affect gradients)
```

```
w -= w.grad * learning_rate
b -= b.grad * learning_rate
w.grad.zero_()
b.grad.zero_()
```

Makes a single step of gradient update

Sets the gradients to zero before the next gradient computation

The structure is basically the same as that of TensorFlow. You still mark tensors with a special attribute, you need to know about a special scope to calculate (or not calculate) gradients (now with underlying DAG instead of a gradient tape), and you need to know special methods and attributes to get the gradients.

Because all the operations are tracked in a gradient tape or a DAG as they are executed, Python control flow is naturally handled, and you may use control flow statements (like `if` or `while`) in your model.

4.2.3 Working with gradients in JAX

JAX does autodiff in a functional programming-friendly way. A special transformation, `jax.grad()`, takes a numerical function written in Python and returns a new Python function that computes the gradient of the original function with respect to the first parameter of a function. Figure 4.3 depicts the process of calculating gradients in JAX.

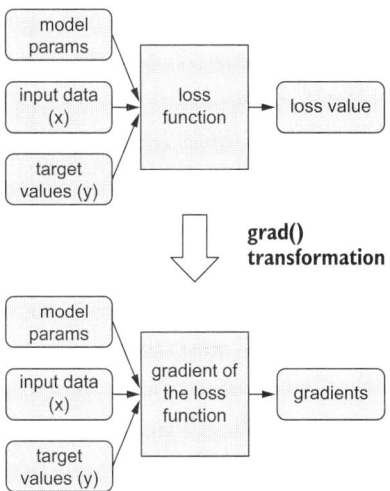

Figure 4.3   Obtaining function for calculating gradients

The important thing is that the `grad()` result is a function, not a gradient value. To calculate the gradient values, you have to pass the point at which you want the gradient.

Listing 4.9   Calculating gradients in JAX

```
import jax
import jax.numpy as jnp

xt = jnp.array(x)
yt = jnp.array(y)
```

Imports PyTorch

Converts the training data to JAX arrays

```
learning_rate = 1e-2

model_parameters = jnp.array([1., 1.])          ◀──── Tensors with model weights
                                                        without any special mark
def model(theta, x):                             ◀──── The function implements a
    w, b = theta                                         simple linear model.
    return w * x + b

def loss_fn(model_parameters, x, y):             ◀──── MSE loss function
    prediction = model(model_parameters, x)
    return jnp.mean((prediction-y)**2)           ◀──── Creates a function for
                                                        calculating gradients
grads_fn = jax.grad(loss_fn)                     ◀────
grads = grads_fn(model_parameters, xt, yt)       ◀──── Calculates gradients
model_parameters -= learning_rate * grads        ◀────
                                                        Makes a single step of
                                                        gradient update
```

This approach makes the JAX API quite different from other autodiff libraries like TensorFlow and PyTorch. In JAX, you work directly with functions, staying closer to the underlying math, and in some sense, it is more natural: your loss function is a function of model parameters and the data, so you find its gradient the same way you would in math.

You do not need to mark tensors in a special way, you do not need to know about underlying machinery regarding gradient tapes or DAGs, and you do not need to remember any particular way of getting gradients with special functions and attributes. You just use a function (the grad() transformation) to create a function that calculates gradients. Then, you directly use that second function.

As you see, in frameworks like PyTorch or TensorFlow, a large part of this magic is usually hidden behind high-level APIs and objects with internal states. This is also the case for optimizers we didn't use in our examples.

WHEN DIFFERENTIATING WITH RESPECT TO THE FIRST PARAMETER IS NOT ENOUGH

We mentioned that the jax.grad() transformation computes the gradient of the original function with respect to the first parameter of a function. What if you need to differentiate with respect to more than one parameter or not the first one? There are ways to do that!

Let's examine the case when the parameter of interest is not the first one (the code from this point up until the end of the chapter is located in the the notebook here: https://mng.bz/8wng). We create a generalized function for calculating the distance between two points, called the Minkowski distance. This function takes in an additional parameter that determines the order. We do not want to differentiate with respect to this parameter. We want to differentiate with respect to the parameter called x:

A function with an additional parameter at the first position. We want to differentiate with respect to the second parameter.

```
def dist(order, x, y):                ◀────
    return jnp.power(jnp.sum(jnp.abs(x-y)**order), 1.0/order)
```

There are several ways of rewriting your original function to use the default behavior of the grad() function and differentiate it with respect to the first parameter. You can either rewrite your original function and move the order parameter to the end, or you can use an adapter function to change the order of parameters.

But suppose you do not want to do this for some reason. For such a case, there is an additional parameter in the grad() function called argnums. This parameter determines which positional argument to differentiate with respect to:

```
dist_d_x = jax.grad(dist, argnums=1)
```

We want to differentiate with respect to the second parameter, x.

```
dist_d_x(1, jnp.array([1.0,1.0,1.0]), jnp.array([2.0,2.0,2.0]))

>>> Array([-1., -1., -1.], dtype=float32)
```

The argnums parameter can do more.

DIFFERENTIATING WITH RESPECT TO MULTIPLE PARAMETERS

The argnums parameter allows differentiating with respect to more than one parameter. If we want to differentiate with respect to both x and y parameters, we can pass a tuple specifying their positions:

```
dist_d_xy = jax.grad(dist, argnums=(1,2))
```

We want to differentiate with respect to the x and y parameters.

```
dist_d_xy(1, jnp.array([1.0,1.0,1.0]), jnp.array([2.0,2.0,2.0]))

>>> (Array([-1., -1., -1.], dtype=float32), Array([1., 1., 1.],
dtype=float32))
```

The argnums parameter can be an integer (if you specify a single parameter to differentiate with respect to) or a sequence of integers (if you specify multiple parameters).

When argnums is an integer, the gradient returned has the same shape and type as the positional argument indicated by this integer. When argnums is a sequence (say, tuple), the gradient is a tuple of values with the same shapes and types as the corresponding arguments.

In addition to manually specifying with respect to which parameters of the original function we want to differentiate and using the argnums parameter, there is also an option to pack multiple values into a single parameter of the function, and we have already silently used this possibility in listing 4.9. We packed two values into a single array and passed this array to a function.

JAX allows the user to differentiate with respect to different data structures, not only arrays and tuples. You can, for example, differentiate with respect to dictionaries (dicts). There is a more general data structure called *pytree*, a tree-like structure built from container-like Python objects. We will dive deeper into this topic in chapter 10.

Listing 4.10 is an example of how to differentiate with respect to Python dicts. It is the core part of listing 4.9, changed to work with dicts.

Listing 4.10   Differentiating with respect to dicts

```
model_parameters = {
    'w': jnp.array([1.]),
    'b': jnp.array([1.])
}

def model(param_dict, x):
    w, b = param_dict['w'], param_dict['b']
    return w * x + b

def loss_fn(model_parameters, x, y):
    prediction = model(model_parameters, x)
    return jnp.mean((prediction-y)**2)

grads_fn = jax.grad(loss_fn)
grads = grads_fn(model_parameters, xt, yt)

grads

>>> {'b': Array([-153.29868], dtype=float32),
'w': Array([-2533.0576], dtype=float32)}
```

◄——— **Now model parameters are a dict, not an array.**

◄——— **The model function changed to work with dicts**

◄——— **Gradients are now a dict.**

You see that differentiating with respect to standard Python containers works perfectly.

RETURNING AUXILIARY DATA FROM A FUNCTION

The function you pass to a grad() transformation should return a scalar, as this transformation is only defined on scalar functions. Sometimes, you want to return intermediate results, but in this case, your function returns a tuple, and grad() does not work.

Suppose, in our linear regression example from listing 4.9, we wanted to return the prediction results for logging purposes. Figure 4.4 visualizes it.

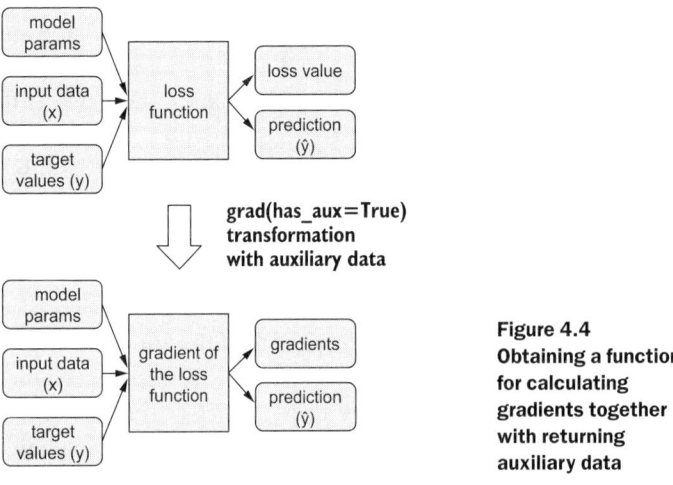

Figure 4.4
Obtaining a function for calculating gradients together with returning auxiliary data

Changing the loss_fn() function to return some additional data will cause the grad() transform to return an error. To fix it, we let the grad() transform know that the function returns some auxiliary data.

Listing 4.11 Returning auxiliary data from a function

```
model_parameters = jnp.array([1., 1.])

def model(theta, x):
    w, b = theta
    return w * x + b

def loss_fn(model_parameters, x, y):
    prediction = model(model_parameters, x)
    return jnp.mean((prediction-y)**2), prediction

grads_fn = jax.grad(loss_fn, has_aux=True)
grads, preds = grads_fn(model_parameters, xt, yt)
model_parameters -= learning_rate * grads
```

The original loss function from listing 4.9 also returns prediction results.

has_aux parameter says that the function now returns a pair (out, aux)

Now the gradient function returns both gradients and auxiliary data, predictions, in our case.

The has_aux parameter informs the grad() transformation that the function returns a pair (out, auxiliary_data). It makes grad() ignore the additional returning parameter (auxiliary_data), passing it through to the user, and differentiate the loss_fn() function as if its only first (out) parameter was returned. If has_aux is set to True, then a pair of (gradient, auxiliary_data) is returned.

For neural networks, this is useful if your model has some internal state you need to maintain, for example, running statistics in the case of BatchNorm.

OBTAINING BOTH THE GRADIENT AND VALUE OF THE FUNCTION

Another frequent situation you face is when you want to get loss function values to track learning progress. It is nice to have gradients for the gradient descent algorithm, but knowing how good the current set of weights is and how loss values behave is important. Surely, you can calculate the quality of the current solution separately, calculating loss and any other metrics after a training update. However, we already calculated loss during the training update, and doing this calculation twice will be suboptimal (especially for large neural networks). The process is depicted in the figure 4.5.

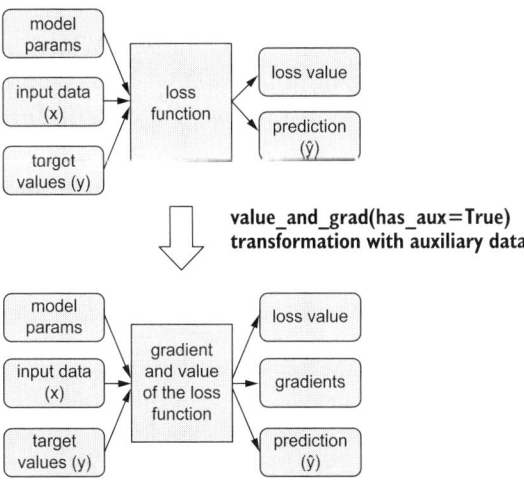

value_and_grad(has_aux=True) transformation with auxiliary data

Figure 4.5 Obtaining function for calculating gradients together with loss function value and auxiliary data

For such a case, there is a `value_and_grad()` function, which we already used in chapter 2.

Listing 4.12   Returning gradients, values, and auxiliary data

```
model_parameters = jnp.array([1., 1.])

def model(theta, x):                                    Now we want
    w, b = theta                                        both values and
    return w * x + b                                    gradients.

def loss_fn(model_parameters, x, y):                    In addition to
    prediction = model(model_parameters, x)             gradients and
    return jnp.mean((prediction-y)**2), prediction      auxiliary data,
                                                        we now return
grads_fn = jax.value_and_grad(loss_fn, has_aux=True)    the loss values.
(loss, preds), grads  = grads_fn(model_parameters, xt, yt)
model_parameters -= learning_rate * grads
```

In this example, we combined values, gradients, and auxiliary data. In such a case, a tuple of `((value, auxiliary_data), gradient)` is returned. It is a tuple of `(value, gradient)` without auxiliary data.

PER-SAMPLE GRADIENTS

In a typical machine learning setup, you usually train your model with a gradient descent procedure using batches of data. You get a gradient for the whole batch and update the model parameters accordingly.

In most cases, that level of granularity is okay, but in some situations, you want sample-level gradients. One way of doing this is by setting the batch size to 1. But it's not computationally efficient, as modern hardware such as GPU or TPU prefers to perform massive computations to fully load all the underlying computing units.

One interesting use case for per-sample gradients is when you want to estimate the importance of separate data samples and choose those with higher gradient magnitude as more important ones to use in a special training algorithm for prioritized sampling; do hard sample mining; or highlight data points for further analysis. While these numbers exist inside the gradient computations, many libraries directly accumulate gradients over a batch, so you have no easy way to get this information.

In JAX, it is pretty straightforward. Remember the chapter 2 example of MNIST digits classification. There, we wrote a function to make a single prediction, then created its batched version with `vmap()`, and finally, in the loss function, aggregated individual losses. If we wanted these individual losses, we could easily get them.

So, the recipe for obtaining per-sample gradients is as follows:

1 Create a function for making a per-sample prediction, say, `predict(x)`.

2 Create a function for calculating gradients for per-sample prediction with the `grad()` transformation, getting `grad(predict)(x)`.

3 Make a batched version of the gradient calculating function with the `vmap()` transformation, obtaining `vmap(grad(predict))(x_batch)`. This is the reverse

order of transformations we did in chapter 2 when we trained a neural network. There, we basically did `grad(vmap(predict))`, which gives us a gradient for the batch. Here, we obtain a batch of gradients.

4   Optionally, compile the resulting function with the `jit()` transformation to make it more efficient on the underlying hardware, finally obtaining `jit(vmap(grad(predict)))(x_batch)`.

STOPPING GRADIENTS

Sometimes you do not want the gradients to flow through some subset of the computation graph. There might be different reasons for this: maybe there are some auxiliary computations you want to perform but do not want to influence your gradient computations. For example, this might be some additional metrics or logging data, which is not functionally pure. Or you might want to update variables of your model with other losses, so while calculating one of your losses, you want to exclude variables you update with another loss (this can also be done from the optimizer side; there are ways to specify which parameters to update and which not to update). You frequently need this functionality in reinforcement learning.

In the following simple example, the computations for a function `f(x,y) = x**2 + y**2` form a computational graph (a directed graph resembling the order of computations) with two branches, calculating `x**2` in one branch and `y**2` in another. Each one is independent of the other (see figure 4.6).

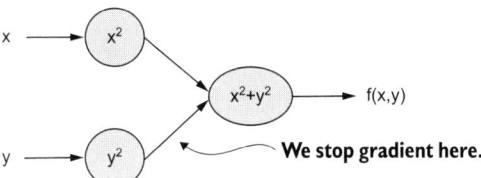

Figure 4.6   Computational graph of example $f(x,y) = x^2 + y^2$. **The branches for** x^2 **and** y^2 **do not depend on each other, and in our example, we want gradients to flow only through one of them.**

Say you do not want the second branch to influence your gradients. There is a function for such cases. The `jax.lax.stop_gradient()` function applied for some input variable works as an identity transformation, returning the argument unchanged. At the same time, it prevents the flow of gradients during forward-or reverse-mode autodiff. It is similar to PyTorch's `detach()` method.

Listing 4.13   Stopping gradient flow

```
def f(x, y):
    return x**2 + jax.lax.stop_gradient(y**2)     ←   Uses stop_gradient() to prevent
                                                       gradient calculation for y

jax.grad(f, argnums=(0,1))(1.0, 1.0)     ←   Calculates gradients at
                                              a particular point
```

```
>>> (Array(2., dtype=float32, weak_type=True),
    Array(0., dtype=float32, weak_type=True))
```
The resulting gradients show that they were calculated only to the first variable.

We marked a part of the calculations related to the second function parameter with the `stop_gradient()` function. The subsequent gradient calculation gives us zero gradients with respect to the second function parameter. Without the `stop_gradient()` call, the result would be 2.0.

4.2.4   *Higher-order derivatives*

You can compute higher-order derivatives in JAX. Thanks to the functional nature of JAX, `grad()` transformation transforms a function into another function that calculates the derivative of the original function. As a `grad()` result is also a function, you can run this process several times to obtain higher-order derivatives.

Let's return to a simple function we differentiated at the beginning of the chapter. We used a function $f(x) = x^4 + 12x + 1/x$. We know its derivative is $f'(x) = 4x^3 + 12 - 1/x^2$. The second derivative is $f''(x) = 12x^2 + 2/x^3$. Its third derivative is $f'''(x) = 24x - 6/x^4$, and so on. Let's calculate these derivatives in JAX.

Listing 4.14   Finding higher-order derivatives

```
def f(x):
    return x**4 + 12*x + 1/x

f_d1 = jax.grad(f)
f_d2 = jax.grad(f_d1)
f_d3 = jax.grad(f_d2)

x = 11.0

print(f_d1(x))
print(f_d2(x))
print(f_d3(x))

>>> 5335.9917
>>> 1452.0015
>>> 263.9996
```

Taking a first derivative of the function

Second derivative

Third derivative

You can stack (or combine) these transformations together:

```
f_d3 = jax.grad(jax.grad(jax.grad(f)))
```

We calculated the derivatives at a given point ($x = 11.0$), but remember, JAX returns a function you can apply anywhere it is valid. In the following example, we take several consecutive derivatives of another function and draw them on a graph.

Listing 4.15   Drawing higher-order derivatives

```
def f(x):
    return x**3 + 12*x + 7*x*jnp.sin(x)

x = np.linspace(-10, 10, num=500)
```

Another function to differentiate

```
fig, ax = plt.subplots(figsize=(10,10))
ax.plot(x, f(x), label = r"$y = x^3 + 12x + 7x*sin(x)$")

df = f
for d in range(3):
  df = jax.grad(df)
  ax.plot(x, jax.vmap(df)(x),
      label=f"{['1st','2nd','3rd'][d]} derivative")
  ax.legend()
```

Consequently takes derivatives

Uses vmap to apply a derivative function to a vector of values

Here we used `vmap` to make a derivative function applicable to a vector of values. We can apply the original function to a vector of values thanks to NumPy broadcasting and vectorization. Functions obtained through the `grad()` transformation are only defined for scalar output functions, so we use `vmap()` to vectorize this function along the array dimension. We will discuss `vmap()` more in chapter 6. Figure 4.7 shows the result of these calculations.

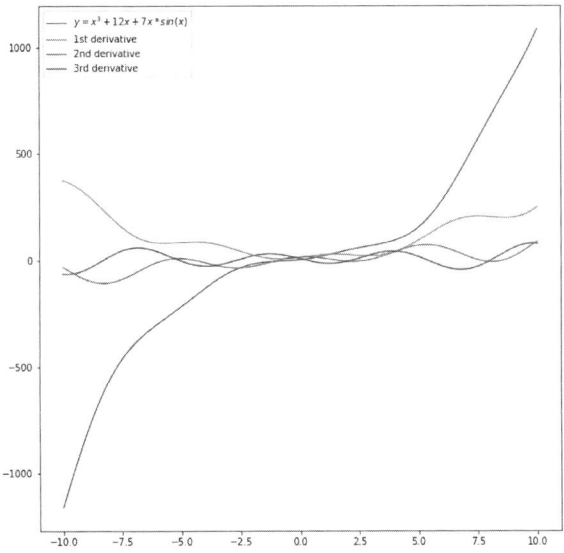

Figure 4.7   Calculating a function f(x) = x^3 + 12x + 7x × sin(x) and its three derivatives

In JAX, you can also do higher-order optimization, such as learned optimization or meta-learning, where you must differentiate through gradient updates. One interesting resource for learned optimization is Google's repository: https://github.com/google/learned_optimization. Here you will find a set of interesting examples, starting from an optimizer with learnable parameters.

Another interesting example is model-agnostic meta-learning (MAML) (https://arxiv.org/abs/1703.03400), which tries to learn an initial set of model weights that can be quickly adapted to new tasks. One good tutorial on meta-learning can be found here: https://blog.evjang.com/2019/02/maml-jax.html.

4.2.5 *Multivariable case*

We have started with a simple function for linear regression with a single scalar input (a single number) and a single scalar output. There was only one derivative, and we calculated it using a function obtained with the `grad()` transformation.

Then, we saw a more general case of having multiple input parameters but still a single scalar output. We calculated partial derivatives with respect to multiple input variables with the help of the `argnums` parameter of the `grad()` transformation. There is an even more general case when your function inputs and outputs are vectors (multiple values).

JACOBIAN MATRIX

To calculate many partial derivatives with respect to many input variables, you might need a *Jacobian matrix*. A Jacobian matrix, or just Jacobian, is a matrix containing all partial derivatives for a vector-valued function of several variables:

$$\mathbf{J} = \left[\frac{\partial f}{\partial x_1} \quad \cdots \quad \frac{\partial f}{\partial x_n} \right] = \begin{bmatrix} \nabla^T f_1 \\ \vdots \\ \nabla^T f_m \end{bmatrix} = \begin{bmatrix} \frac{\partial f_1}{\partial x_1} & \cdots & \frac{\partial f_1}{\partial x_n} \\ \vdots & \ddots & \vdots \\ \frac{\partial f_m}{\partial x_1} & \cdots & \frac{\partial f_m}{\partial x_n} \end{bmatrix}$$

In the context of deep learning, the Jacobian for a neural network model would contain the partial derivatives of the loss function with respect to the parameters of the model. The chain rule allows us to express this in terms of a product of Jacobian matrices that contain the partial derivatives of the output of each layer with respect to the outputs of the previous layer.

There are two functions to compute full Jacobian matrices, `jacfwd()` and `jacrev()`. They compute the same values, but their implementations are different, based on forward- and reverse-mode autodiff, respectively (I will discuss these later in section 4.3). The first one, `jacfwd()`, is more efficient for "tall" Jacobian matrices, where the number of outputs (rows in the Jacobian matrix) is significantly larger than the number of input variables (columns in the Jacobian matrix). The `jacrev()` is more efficient for "wide" Jacobian matrices where the number of input variables is significantly larger than the number of outputs. For near-square matrices, `jacfwd()` is probably better (as we will see in the following example).

Let's create a simple vector-valued function with two outputs and three input variables.

Listing 4.16   Calculating Jacobian of a vector-valued function

```
def f(x):
  return [
      x[0]**2 + x[1]**2 - x[1]*x[2],
      x[0]**2 - x[1]**2 + 3*x[0]*x[2]
  ]
```

First output of the function

Second output of the function

```
print(jax.jacrev(f)(jnp.array([3.0, 4.0, 5.0])))         ◄──────── Uses jacrev()

>>> [Array([ 6.,   3.,  -4.], dtype=float32),
Array([21.,  -8.,   9.], dtype=float32)]

print(jax.jacfwd(f)(jnp.array([3.0, 4.0, 5.0])))         ◄──────── Uses jacfwd()

>>> [Array([ 6.,   3.,  -4.], dtype=float32),
Array([21.,  -8.,   9.], dtype=float32)]

%timeit -n 100 jax.jacrev(f)(jnp.array([3.0, 4.0, 5.0]))

>>> 29.9 ms ± 2.5 ms per loop (mean ± std. dev. of 7 runs, 100 loops each)

%timeit -n 100 jax.jacfwd(f)(jnp.array([3.0, 4.0, 5.0]))

>>> 17.8 ms ± 336 µs per loop (mean ± std. dev. of 7 runs, 100 loops each)
```

As you see, both functions produce the same result, yet jacfwd() is slightly faster than jacrev(), with three inputs and two outputs, is. If the number of inputs is significantly larger than the number of outputs, jacrev() will be faster, but here, the numbers are comparable, so jacfwd() is the winner.

By default, both functions for calculating Jacobian differentiate with respect to the first parameter of a function. In our case, we passed all the parameters in a single vector, but you might want to use a function with several separate parameters instead of this. In such a case, you can use the already familiar argnums parameter.

HESSIAN MATRIX

In the case of the second-order derivative of a function of multiple inputs, we obtain a *Hessian matrix* or just Hessian. Hessian is a square matrix that contains all the second derivatives:

$$(\mathbf{H}_f)_{i,j} = \frac{\partial^2 f}{\partial x_i \partial x_j}$$

$$\mathbf{H}_f = \begin{bmatrix} \frac{\partial^2 f}{\partial x_1^2} & \frac{\partial^2 f}{\partial x_1 \partial x_2} & \cdots & \frac{\partial^2 f}{\partial x_1 \partial x_n} \\ \frac{\partial^2 f}{\partial x_2 \partial x_1} & \frac{\partial^2 f}{\partial x_2^2} & \cdots & \frac{\partial^2 f}{\partial x_2 \partial x_n} \\ \vdots & \vdots & \ddots & \vdots \\ \frac{\partial^2 f}{\partial x_n \partial x_1} & \frac{\partial^2 f}{\partial x_n \partial x_2} & \cdots & \frac{\partial^2 f}{\partial x_n^2} \end{bmatrix}$$

You can use a hessian() function to compute dense Hessian matrices.

Listing 4.17 Calculating the Hessian of a function

```
def f(x):
  return x[0]**2 - x[1]**2 + 3*x[0]*x[2]      ◀── A function with three parameters

jax.hessian(f)(jnp.array([3.0, 4.0, 5.0]))    ◀── Calculates Hessian in a specific point
```

The Hessian of a function f is a Jacobian of the gradient of f, so it can be implemented this way:

```
def hessian(f):
    return jacfwd(grad(f))
```

In JAX, it is implemented the following way, which suggests that the grad() is implemented using reverse mode:

```
def hessian(f):
    return jacfwd(jacrev(f))
```

This function is a generalization of the usual definition of the Hessian that supports nested Python containers (and pytrees) as inputs and outputs.

In many cases, we do not need the full Hessian. Instead, a Hessian-vector product can be used for some calculations without materializing the whole Hessian matrix.

Now we have already met several things that require an understanding of the forward and reverse modes, so it's time to dive deeper into the internals of autodiff and learn about it.

4.3   *Forward- and reverse-mode autodiff*

This section is for those who want to understand the basics of the machinery behind autodiff. I will describe the forward and reverse modes of autodiff and two corresponding JAX transformations called jvp() and vjp().

To understand them, you need some calculus knowledge. You need to know a derivative, partial derivative, and directional derivative. You also need to know differentiating rules.

This is the hardest part of the book, I think. So, to get it, you might have to read it several times and solve the examples independently. Do not be upset if it's hard. It's really hard. You can still use JAX without understanding autodiff internals in many cases. However, this knowledge will reward you with a better understanding of using JAX efficiently.

Reading about autodiff

Several resources will help you along the way.

First is a great short video tutorial called "What Is Automatic Differentiation?" by Ari Seff (https://www.youtube.com/watch?v=wG_nF1awSSY). Ari explains these things visually and with simple words, which is very helpful.

Second, there is an in-depth article, "Automatic Differentiation in Machine Learning: A Survey," by Atilim Gunes Baydin, Barak A. Pearlmutter, Alexey Andreyevich Radul, and Jeffrey Mark Siskind (https://arxiv.org/abs/1502.05767). This article gives you a much broader context and helps you understand deeper details of autodiff.

In case you want to understand the internals of autodiff even deeper, there are seminal books like *Evaluating Derivatives* by Andreas Griewank and Andrea Walther (https://epubs.siam.org/doi/book/10.1137/1.9780898717761) and *The Art of Differentiating Computer Programs* by Uwe Naumann (https://epubs.siam.org/doi/book/10.1137/1.9781611972078).

Let's return to the idea of autodiff. The numerical computations we perform are ultimately compositions of a finite set of elementary operations like addition, multiplication, exponentiation, trigonometric functions, and so on. For these elementary operations, derivatives are known. For a computation consisting of such operations, we can combine derivatives of constituent operations through the chain rule for differentiation, so obtaining the derivative of the overall composition. Baydin et al. (https://arxiv.org/abs/1502.05767) state in their paper, "Automatic differentiation can be thought of as performing a non-standard interpretation of a computer program where this interpretation involves augmenting the standard computation with the calculation of various derivatives."

4.3.1 Evaluation trace

A computation can be represented as an *evaluation trace* of elementary operations, also called the *Wengert list* (now also called a *tape*; from R. E. Wengert's article in 1964; https://dl.acm.org/doi/10.1145/355586.364791), with specific input values. The computation (or a function) is decomposed into a series of elementary functional steps, introducing *intermediary variables*. The Wengert list abstracts away from all control-flow considerations, which means autodiff is blind to any operation, including control-flow statements, which do not directly alter numeric values. The taken branch replaces all conditional statements, all the loops are unrolled, and all the function calls are inlined.

Let us have a specific real-valued function with two variables $f(x_1, x_2) = x_1 \times x_2 + sin$ $(x_1 \times x_2)$ to compute a derivative and an evaluation trace for that function (table 4.1). We will use this example to illustrate forward- and reverse-mode autodiff.

Table 4.1. Evaluation trace (Wengert list) for the function $f(x_1, x_2) = x_1 \times x_2 + sin(x_1 \times x_2)$

Evaluation trace
Input variables
$v_{-1} = x_1$
$v_0 = x_2$
Intermediate variables
$v_1 = v_{-1} \times v_0$
$v_2 = sin(v_1)$
$v_3 = v_1 + v_2$
Output variables
$y = v_3$

This computation can also be expressed as a computational graph (see figure 4.8).

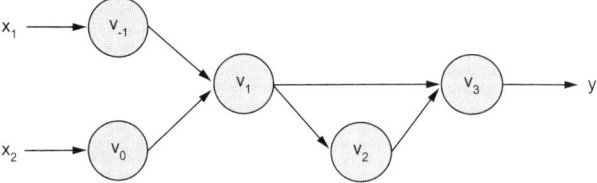

Figure 4.8   Computational graph of the example $f(x_1, x_2) = x_1 \times x_2 + sin(x_1 \times x_2)$

Suppose we want to compute a partial derivative of the function with respect to the first variable x_1 at some point, say $(x_1, x_2) = (7.0, 2.0)$. Let's start with the forward-mode autodiff.

4.3.2   *Forward mode and jvp()*

The forward accumulation mode autodiff (or tangent linear mode) is conceptually the simplest.

FORWARD-MODE CALCULATIONS

To compute a derivative of the function with respect to the first variable x_1, we start to associate with each intermediate variable v_i its derivative dv_i/dx_1 (in the following example, denoted as v_i' for short). Instead of a single value for each v_i, we have a tuple (v_i, v_i'). Original intermediate values are called *primals*, and derivatives are called *tangents*. This is called a *dual numbers approach*. We apply the chain rule to each elementary operation in the forward tangent trace (table 4.2).

Table 4.2.   Forward mode autodiff example with $f(x_1, x_2) = x_1 \times x_2 + sin(x_1 \times x_2)$ evaluated at the point (7.0, 2.0) with respect to the first variable x_1

Forward primal trace	Forward tangent (derivative) trace
$v_{-1} = x_1\ \ = 7.0$ (start)	$v'_{-1} = x'_1\ \ \ \ \ = 1.0$ (start)
$v_0\ = x_2\ \ = 2.0$	$v'_0\ = x'_2\ \ \ \ \ = 0.0$
$v_1\ = v_{-1} \times v_0 = 14.0$	$v'_1\ = v'_{-1} \times v_0 + v_{-1} \times v'_0\ = 1.0 \times 2.0 + 7.0 \times 0.0$
$v_2\ = sin(v_1) = 0.99$	$v'_2\ = v'_1 \times cos(v_1)\ \ \ \ = 2.0 \times 0.137$
$v_3\ = v_1 + v_2 = 14.99$	$v'_3\ = v'_1 + v'_2\ \ \ \ \ \ \ = 2.0 + 0.274$
$y\ \ = v_3\ \ \ \ = 14.99$ (end)	$y'\ \ = v'_3\ \ \ \ \ \ \ \ \ \ \ = 2.274$ (end)

The single pass through the function now produces not only the function result (the original output, here 14.99) but also its derivative with respect to x_1 (here 2.274). We can check our manual calculations using JAX.

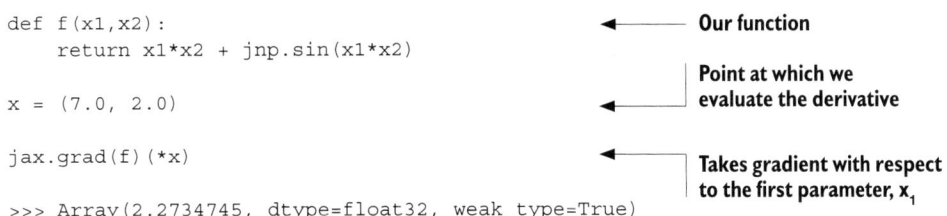

Listing 4.18 Checking manual forward-mode calculations

```
def f(x1,x2):                              ◄─────── Our function
    return x1*x2 + jnp.sin(x1*x2)
                                           ┌ Point at which we
x = (7.0, 2.0)                             ◄─┘ evaluate the derivative

jax.grad(f)(*x)                            ◄──────┐ Takes gradient with respect
                                                  └ to the first parameter, x₁
>>> Array(2.2734745, dtype=float32, weak_type=True)
```

The numbers almost match. Manually we get a value of 2.274; JAX returns a more precise answer of 2.2734745. The manually obtained value is less precise, as I rounded some results during the calculation.

Autodiff systems use an operator overloading or source code transformation approach to implement such calculations. JAX uses operator overloading. The topic of autodiff systems implementation is out of the book's scope.

Now, suppose the function has several outputs. We can compute partial derivatives for each output in a single forward pass. But you need to run a separate forward pass for each input variable. As you can see, in the preceding example, we only got a derivative with respect to x_1. For x_2, we need to perform a separate forward pass.

For a general function $f: R^n \rightarrow R^m$, a forward pass for a single input variable produces one column of the corresponding function Jacobian (partial derivatives for each output with respect to the specific input variable). The full Jacobian can be computed in n evaluations. The previously mentioned $jacfwd()$ function does exactly this.

So, it should be intuitive that the forward mode is preferred when the number of outputs is significantly larger than the number of input variables, or $m \gg n$, or so-called tall Jacobians.

DIRECTIONAL DERIVATIVE AND JVP()

A *directional derivative* generalizes the notion of partial derivatives. Partial derivatives calculate the slope in the positive direction of an axis represented by a specific variable. We used an input tangent vector $(v_{-1}, v_0) = (1.0, 0.0)$ for the partial derivative with respect to the first variable. But we can calculate the slope in any direction. To do so, we must specify the direction. You specify direction with a vector (u_1, u_2) that points in the direction we want to compute the slope. The directional derivative is the same as the partial derivative when this vector points in the positive x_1 or x_2 direction and looks like $(1.0, 0.0)$ or $(0.0, 1.0)$.

Calculating directional derivatives is easy with autodiff. Just pass the direction vector as an initial value for your tangents. And that's it. The result is a directional derivative value at a specific point.

Even more generally, we can compute a Jacobian-vector product (JVP) without computing the Jacobian itself in just a single forward pass. We set the input tangent vector (v_{-1}, v_0) to the vector of interest and proceed with the forward-mode autodiff. This operation is called $jvp()$ for the Jacobian-vector product.

`jvp()` takes in

- A function `fun` to be differentiated
- The `primals` values at which the Jacobian of the function `fun` should be evaluated
- A vector of `tangents` for which the Jacobian-vector product should be evaluated

The result is a (`primals_out`, `tangents_out`) pair, where `primals_out` is the function `fun` applied to `primals` (a value of the original function at the specific point), and `tangents_out` is the Jacobian-vector product of the function evaluated at `primals` with given `tangents`. For example, it could be a directional derivative in a given direction or a partial derivative with respect to a particular variable.

We can say that for the given function f, an input vector x, and a tangent vector v, `jvp()` produces both an output of the function $f(x)$, and a directional derivative $\partial f(x)v$:

$$(x, v) \rightarrow (f(x), \partial f(x)v)$$

If you are familiar with Haskell-like type signatures, this function could be written as

```
jvp :: (a -> b) -> a -> T a -> (b, T b)
```

which means `jvp` is a function name. The function's first parameter is another function with a signature (`a -> b`) that transforms the value of type `a` into type `b`. The second parameter has type `a`; here, it is a vector of primals. The third parameter, denoted as `T a`, is a type of tangents for type `a`. The last type is the return value type (`b`, `T b`). It consists of two items: the type for output primals `b` and the corresponding tangents type `T b`.

TIP   Some good basic introductions to Haskell type signatures can be found at https://mng.bz/XVW9, https://mng.bz/7dEy, and https://mng.bz/d6Qz.

In the following listing, we calculate the JVP for the function from the Jacobian example in listing 4.16.

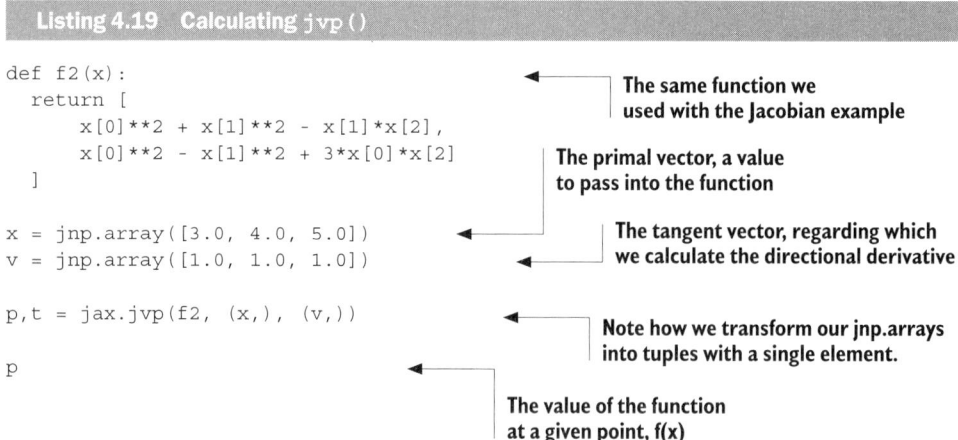

Listing 4.19   Calculating `jvp()`

```
def f2(x):
  return [
      x[0]**2 + x[1]**2 - x[1]*x[2],
      x[0]**2 - x[1]**2 + 3*x[0]*x[2]
  ]

x = jnp.array([3.0, 4.0, 5.0])
v = jnp.array([1.0, 1.0, 1.0])

p,t = jax.jvp(f2, (x,), (v,))

p
```

The same function we used with the Jacobian example

The primal vector, a value to pass into the function

The tangent vector, regarding which we calculate the directional derivative

Note how we transform our jnp.arrays into tuples with a single element.

The value of the function at a given point, f(x)

```
>>> [Array(5., dtype=float32), Array(38., dtype=float32)]

t
```

The directional
derivative in
the direction of
vector v

```
>>> [Array(5., dtype=float32), Array(22., dtype=float32)]
```

`jvp()` expects primals and tangents to be either a tuple or a list of arguments; it doesn't work with `Array` here, so we manually pack our `jnp.arrays` into a tuple.

In this example, we calculated the value of the function $f(x)$ and the directional derivative during the same pass. We can recover all the partial derivatives (the Jacobian) in three passes by passing vectors [1.0, 0.0, 0.0], [0.0, 1.0, 0.0], and [0.0, 0.0, 1.0] as tangents.

Listing 4.20   Recovering Jacobian columns with `jvp()`

```
p,t = jax.jvp(f2, (x,), (jnp.array([1.0, 0.0, 0.0]),))
t
```

Passing unit
vectors to
recover separate
Jacobian
columns

```
>>> [Array(6., dtype=float32), Array(21., dtype=float32)]

p,t = jax.jvp(f2, (x,), (jnp.array([0.0, 1.0, 0.0]),))
t

>>> [Array(3., dtype=float32), Array(-8., dtype=float32)]

p,t = jax.jvp(f2, (x,), (jnp.array([0.0, 0.0, 1.0]),))
t

>>> [Array(-4., dtype=float32), Array(9., dtype=float32)]
```

Now that we know what the JVP is, we can use the `jvp()` function to verify our manual forward-mode computations.

Listing 4.21   Checking manual forward-mode calculations with JVP

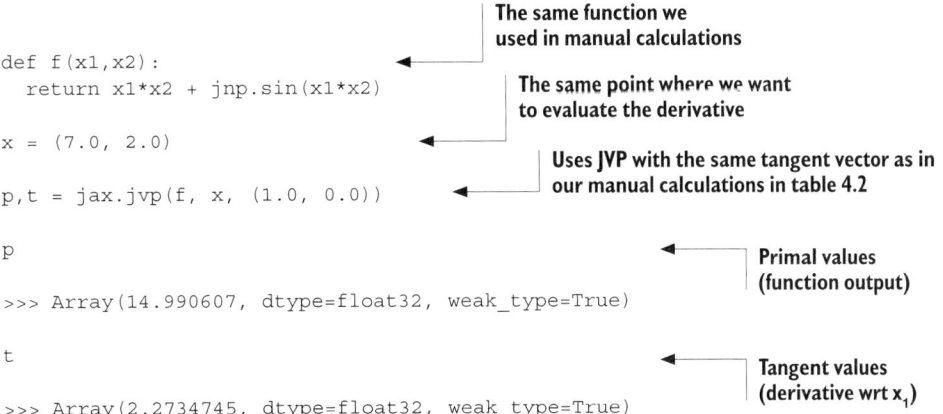

The same function we
used in manual calculations

```
def f(x1,x2):
  return x1*x2 + jnp.sin(x1*x2)
```

The same point where we want
to evaluate the derivative

```
x = (7.0, 2.0)

p,t = jax.jvp(f, x, (1.0, 0.0))
```

Uses JVP with the same tangent vector as in
our manual calculations in table 4.2

```
p

>>> Array(14.990607, dtype=float32, weak_type=True)
```

Primal values
(function output)

```
t

>>> Array(2.2734745, dtype=float32, weak_type=True)
```

Tangent values
(derivative wrt x_1)

Now that we are familiar with the JVP, our manual example directly translates to the code using the `jvp()` function. Here, our primal and tangent values are already tuples, so we didn't have to convert them and pass them directly into the `jvp()` function.

4.3.3   Reverse mode and vjp()

Forward mode is efficient when the number of inputs is much smaller than the number of outputs. In machine learning, we typically have the opposite situation: the number of inputs is large, yet there are only a few outputs. Reverse-mode autodiff solves this problem: it propagates derivatives back from the output and corresponds to a generalized backpropagation algorithm.

REVERSE-MODE CALCULATIONS

In reverse-mode autodiff, the process consists of two phases. In the first phase, the original function is run forward. Intermediate variables (the values we get when building an evaluation trace) are populated during this process, and all the dependencies in the computation graph are recorded. These calculations are in the left column of table 4.3 and go from top to bottom.

Table 4.3   Reverse mode autodiff example with $f(x_1, x_2) = x_1 \times x_2 + sin(x_1 \times x_2)$ evaluated at the point (7.0, 2.0)

Forward primal trace	Reverse adjoint (derivative) trace
$v_{-1} = x_1$ $\quad = 7.0 \quad$ (start)	$x'_1 = v'_{-1}$ $\qquad = 2.274 \qquad$ (end)
$v_0 = x_2$ $\quad = 2.0$	$x'_2 = v'_0$ $\qquad = 7.959$
$v_1 = v_{-1} \times v_0 = 14.0$	$v'_{-1} = v'_1 \, dv_1/dv_{-1} = v'_1 \times v_0 = 1.137 \times 2.0 = 2.274$
	$v'_0 = v'_1 \, dv_1/dv_0 = v'_1 \times v_{-1} = 1.137 \times 7.0 = 7.959$
$v_2 = sin(v_1) = 0.99$	$v'_1 = v'_1 + v'_2 \, dv_2/dv_1 = v'_1 + v'_2 \times cos(v_1) = 1.0 + 1.0 \times 0.137 = 1.137$
	$v'_1 = v'_3 \, dv_3/dv_1 = v'_3 \times 1 = 1.0$
$v_3 = v_1 + v_2 = 14.99$	$v'_2 = v'_3 \, dv_3/dv_2 = v'_3 \times 1 = 1.0$
$y = v_3$ $\quad = 14.99 \quad$ (end)	$v'_3 = y'$ $\qquad = 1.0 \qquad$ (start)

In the second phase, each intermediate variable v_i is complemented with an *adjoint* (or *cotangent*) $v'_i = dy_j / dv_i$. It's a derivative of the *j*th output y_j with respect to v_i that represents the sensitivity of an output y_j with respect to changes in v_i. Derivatives are calculated backward by propagating adjoints v'_i in reverse, from outputs to inputs. These calculations are in the right column of table 4.3 and go from bottom to top, calculating derivatives as we reversedly traverse the graph. So, for example, when you see the variable v'_i is updated twice in the right column, you should read it as two sequential updates, first the update at the bottom of the cell, then the next update on top of it.

In our example, after the forward pass (which is the same as in forward mode), we run the reverse pass, starting with $v'_3 = y' = 1.0$. If some variable affects the output in multiple ways, we sum its contributions on these different paths, as in the example for v'_1. At the end of the procedure, we get all the derivatives $dy/dx_1 = x'_1$ and $dy/dx_2 = x'_2$ in a single backward pass.

Remember, we can calculate the derivatives with respect to both function variables using the `argnums` parameter to check out calculations.

Listing 4.22 Checking manual reverse-mode calculations

```
def f(x1,x2):                                    ◄─────── The same function
    return x1*x2 + jnp.sin(x1*x2)

x = (7.0, 2.0)                                   ◄─────── The same point

jax.grad(f, argnums=(0,1))(*x)                   ◄─────┐ Now we are taking
                                                       │ gradients with
>>> (Array(2.2734745, dtype=float32, weak_type=True),  │ respect to the
 Array(7.9571605, dtype=float32, weak_type=True))      │ parameters, x₁ and x₂.
```

Again, the numbers almost match; manually, we get a value of 2.274 for the derivative with respect to x_1 and 7.595 with respect to x_2. JAX returns more precise values of 2.2734745 and 7.9571605.

As you can see, we calculated derivatives for both input variables simultaneously in a single backward pass. So, the advantage of the reverse mode is that it is computationally cheaper than the forward mode for functions with many inputs when $n \gg m$. However, storage requirements are higher for reverse mode. In an extreme case of a function with n input variables and a single output, reverse mode calculates all the derivatives in a single pass, while forward mode needs n passes. In machine learning, multiple parameters and a single scalar output are typical, so the reverse mode (and backpropagation) is prevalent for such settings. However, there are experimental approaches to use forward-mode autodiff for gradient descent (see "Gradients Without Backpropagation," https://arxiv.org/abs/2202.08587).

REVERSE MODE GENERALIZATION AND VJP()

In a way similar to the matrix-free computation of the Jacobian-vector product with the forward mode, the reverse mode can be used to compute the transposed Jacobian-vector product or, equivalently, vector-Jacobian product (the VJP), initializing the reverse phase with a given adjoint (or cotangent). It can be used to build Jacobian matrices one row at a time and is efficient for so-called wide Jacobians. This operation is called `vjp()` for the vector-Jacobian product.

`vjp()` takes in

- A function `fun` to be differentiated
- The `primals` values at which the Jacobian of the function `fun` should be evaluated

The result is a (`primals_out`, `vjpfun`) pair, where `primals_out` is the function `fun` applied to primals (a value of the original function at the specific point), and `vjpfun` is a function from an adjoint (cotangent) vector with the same shape as `primals_out` to a tuple of adjoint (cotangent) vectors with the same shape as `primals`, representing the vector-Jacobian product of `fun` evaluated at `primals`.

This description is a bit hard to understand. Let's describe it another way and look at the code. It means that for the given function *f* and an input vector *x*, the JAX `vjp()` transform produces both an output of the function *f(x)* and a function to evaluate VJP with a given adjoint (cotangent) for the backward phase.

With Haskell-like type signatures, we can write the `vjp()` type as

```
vjp :: (a -> b) -> a -> (b, CT b -> CT a)
```

which means that, as with JVP, you still pass the original function with a type `(a -> b)` and an input value `x` of the type `a`. You do not pass an adjoint value to this function. The output is also different. The first returning value is still a primal output, the result of calculating the *f(x)* with type `b`. The second value is a function for the backward pass that takes in an adjoint value for type `b` and returns an adjoint value for type `a`.

Now, look at the code using `vjp()` for the same function we used in table 4.3 to verify our manual reverse-mode computations.

Listing 4.23   Checking manual reverse-mode calculations with VJP

```
def f(x1,x2):                              ◀── The same function we used
  return x1*x2 + jnp.sin(x1*x2)               in manual calculations

x = (7.0, 2.0)                             ◀── The same point where we want
                                              to evaluate the derivative

p,vjp_func = jax.vjp(f, *x)                ◀── We pass the original function
                                              parameters as separate parameters.

p
                                           ◀──
>>> Array(14.990607, dtype=float32, weak_type=True)     Primal values
                                                        (function output)

vjp_func(1.0)                              ◀──
                                                        Passes the same
>>> (Array(2.2734745, dtype=float32, weak_type=True),   adjoint we used in the
 Array(7.9571605, dtype=float32, weak_type=True))        manual example to
                                                        backward computation
```

We obtained derivatives with respect to both function parameters in a single reverse pass.

For a more complicated function with two outputs, let's use the same function we used in the Jacobian example and restore the full Jacobian.

Listing 4.24   Recovering Jacobian rows with `vjp()`

```
def f2(x):
  return [
      x[0]**2 + x[1]**2 - x[1]*x[2],
      x[0]**2 - x[1]**2 + 3*x[0]*x[2]
```

```
      ]

x = jnp.array([3.0, 4.0, 5.0])

p,vjp_func = jax.vjp(f2, x)

p

>>> [Array(5., dtype=float32), Array(38., dtype=float32)]

vjp_func([1.0, 0.0])

>>> (Array([ 6.,   3., -4.], dtype=float32),)

vjp_func([0.0, 1.0])

>>> (Array([21., -8.,  9.], dtype=float32),)
```

Passes unit vectors to recover separate Jacobian columns

Here we had to call the `vjp_func()` obtained from the `vjp()` transformation twice, as there are two outputs of the function.

4.3.4 *Going deeper*

There is much more on autodiff in JAX. And there are several things worth your attention if you want to go deeper. First, there is a beautiful "Autodiff Cookbook" (https://mng.bz/x2Dq) in the original JAX documentation. If you want to know more about mathematical and implementation details on JVP and VJP, how to calculate Hessian-vector products, differentiate for complex numbers, and so on, start with this great source of information.

To define custom differentiation rules in JAX, read "Custom Derivative Rules for JAX-Transformable Python Functions" (https://mng.bz/AdeE). Here, you will learn about using `jax.custom_jvp()` and `jax.custom_vjp()` to define custom differentiation rules for Python functions that are already JAX transformable.

Another useful tutorial is "How JAX Primitives Work" (https://mng.bz/ZE1j). This document explains the interface a JAX primitive must support to allow JAX to perform all its transformations. It can help if you want to define new `core.Primitive` instances, along with all their transformation rules.

The "Autodidax: JAX Core From Scratch" (https://mng.bz/RZdn) tutorial explains the ideas in JAX's core system, including how autodiff works. There is also a great autodiff (and Autograd, the predecessor of JAX) tutorial by Matt Johnson here: https://mng.bz/2KPN.

Finally, do not forget to look into the autodiff section for the JAX package (https://mng.bz/1G1Z) in the public API documentation.

Summary

- There are different ways of getting derivatives: manual differentiation, symbolic differentiation, numeric differentiation, and autodiff.

- Automatic differentiation (autodiff, or simply AD) is a clever technique to compute gradients of the computations expressed as code.

- Autodiff can calculate gradients of even very complex computer programs, including control structures and branching, loops, and recursion that might be hard to express as closed-form expressions.

- In JAX, you compute gradients with the help of `grad()` transformation.

- By default, `grad()` computes the derivative with respect to the function's first parameter, but you can control this behavior with the `argnums` parameter.

- If you need to return additional auxiliary data from your function, use the `has_aux` parameter in the `grad()` and other related transformations.

- You can obtain a gradient and a function value with the `value_and_grad()` transformation.

- To calculate higher-order derivatives, you may use subsequent `grad()` transformations.

- The `jacfwd()` and `jacrev()` functions calculate Jacobian matrices, and the `hessian()` function calculates Hessian matrices.

- Autodiff has two modes: forward and reverse.

- Forward mode calculates gradients of all the function outputs with respect to one function input in a single pass. It is efficient when the number of outputs is significantly larger than the number of input variables.

- Reverse mode calculates the gradient of one function output with respect to all the function inputs in a single pass and is more efficient for functions with many inputs and few outputs.

- The `jvp()` function computes a Jacobian-vector product (JVP) without computing the Jacobian itself in a single forward pass.

- The `vjp()` function computes the transposed Jacobian-vector product (equivalently, vector-Jacobian product or VJP) in a single run of reverse-mode autodiff.

Compiling your code 5

This chapter covers

- Just-in-time (JIT) compilation to produce performant code for CPU, GPU, or TPU
- JIT internals: intermediate representations and accelerated linear algebra compilers
- JIT limitations

In chapter 1, we compared the performance of a simple JAX function on a CPU and GPU, with and without JIT. In chapter 2, we used JIT to compile two functions in a training loop for a simple neural network. So you basically know what JIT does. It compiles your function for a target hardware platform and makes it faster.

Beginning in chapter 4, we started learning JAX transformations (remember, JAX is about composable function transformations!). That chapter taught us about auto-diff and the grad() transformation. This chapter will discuss compilation and the corresponding jit() transformation. In the following chapters, we will learn more transformations related to auto-vectorization and parallelization.

In the landscape of numerical computing, JAX emerged as a compelling framework rooted in the foundational strength of Google's XLA compiler. The XLA compiler is not just another tool in the computational toolkit; it is specifically tailored to produce efficient code for high-performance computing tasks. Think of it as an

119

architect meticulously designing blueprints to build structures optimized for their purpose.

The significance of JAX's reliance on XLA is profound. XLA has a well-established legacy of powering machine learning frameworks, notably, TensorFlow. Its versatility is underscored by its compatibility with a range of devices: CPUs, the bedrock of general-purpose computing; GPUs, specialized units adept at parallel computations; and TPUs, Google's dedicated accelerators crafted for machine learning workloads. This compatibility spectrum signifies JAX's adaptability, indicating that it's optimized for varied hardware environments. In computational domains, uniform code doesn't always translate to uniform performance across platforms, but with XLA's expertise, JAX aspires to maintain consistent efficiency.

Beyond mere integration with XLA, JAX offers a proactive approach to compilation: enter the `jit()` function transformation for JIT compilation and the recently added means for ahead-of-time (AOT) compilation. Envision a strategist charting out the most efficient routes on a map, ensuring that every journey is optimized for time and resources. The JIT compilation serves a similar purpose for computational graphs. It streamlines, refines, and consolidates (or fuses) operations where feasible, morphing a series of computations into a singular, more efficient procedure. This capability not only enhances the speed but also refines the overall computational process by identifying and negating superfluous calculations. You don't need to have a GPU or a TPU to gain benefits from JIT. It improves performance even on the CPU.

The overarching importance of this lies in performance optimization. Whether one's computations are executed on a CPU or more advanced hardware, JIT ensures maximal efficiency. Through the synergistic integration of JAX, XLA, and JIT, the developer isn't merely coding; they are engineering a pathway to computational excellence.

In this chapter, we will cover the mechanics of JIT and AOT compilation, discuss how to use it efficiently, and explain its limitations.

5.1   Using compilation

This chapter is dedicated to compilation and explains how to use it to make your code run faster. We will use simple teaching examples to understand compilation in JAX and highlight its features. It will be especially applicable for massive and long computations—be it a large neural network training, a climate model, or another large-scale computation task. It can be as valuable for not-so-massive tasks as well. For example, speeding up an image filter might have tremendous value for your application's user.

Let's start with a well-known activation function called *scaled exponential linear unit* or *SELU* (https://arxiv.org/abs/1706.02515), which we mentioned in chapter 2. We will use this function to demonstrate JIT:

$$\text{Selu}(x) = scale * \begin{cases} x, & x > 0 \\ \alpha e^x - \alpha, & x \leq 0 \end{cases}$$

We implement this function with the code in the following listing, with alpha and scale constants having values from the SELU paper.

Listing 5.1 SELU activation function

```
def selu(x,
         alpha=1.6732632423543772848170429916717,
         scale=1.0507009873554804934193349852946):
  '''Scaled exponential linear unit activation function.'''
  return scale * jnp.where(x > 0, x, alpha * jnp.exp(x) - alpha)
```

The core of the
SELU function

This function contains two branches. When the argument x is positive, it returns the value of x scaled by a `scale` factor. Otherwise, it is a more complicated formula of *scale*(alpha*e^x-alpha)*. This function is frequently used in neural networks as a nonlinear activation.

5.1.1 Using JIT compilation

Suppose we have a million activations for which we have to apply the SELU function. While in a single forward run of a typical neural network, you hardly get a million computations of the function, you still have many forward runs during training, so the example might not be too far from reality. Let's use JIT and compare the performance of the function with and without JIT.

USING JAX.JIT AS A TRANSFORMATION OR ANNOTATION

From chapters 1 and 2, you already know that there is a `jit()` transformation and a corresponding `@jit` annotation to compile a function of your choice.

> ## JIT and AOT
>
> There are two types of compilation: just-in-time (JIT) and ahead-of-time (AOT) compilation.
>
> JIT compilation performs compilation during the execution of the program at a run time. Code gets compiled when it's needed. In JAX, it happens when the code marked to be compiled is executed for the first time. It is traced using abstract values representing the input arrays and compiled, and then the actual arrays are passed to the compiled function for execution. So the first run is slower than the subsequent calls.
>
> AOT compilation, or static compilation, converts a program in a high-level language into a lower-level language before the program is executed. All the code is compiled in advance, irrespective of whether it will be needed. It reduces the total workload required during execution and moves heavy compilation into the build stage.
>
> JAX was originally known for its JIT compilation. However, JAX provides some options for AOT compilation now (more on that in section 5.2.3).

The `jax.jit()` transformation takes in a pure function and returns a wrapped version of the function set up for JIT compilation.

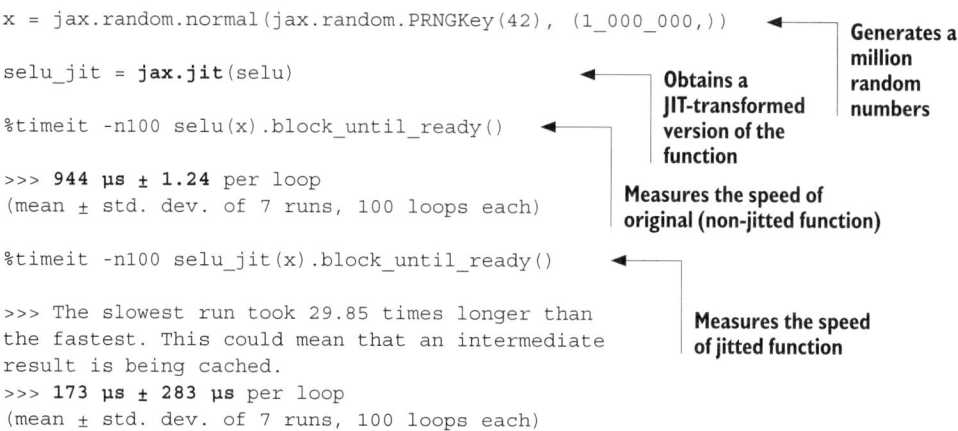

Listing 5.2   Comparing SELU performance with and without JIT

```
x = jax.random.normal(jax.random.PRNGKey(42), (1_000_000,))
```
Generates a million random numbers

```
selu_jit = jax.jit(selu)
```
Obtains a JIT-transformed version of the function

```
%timeit -n100 selu(x).block_until_ready()
```
Measures the speed of original (non-jitted function)

```
>>> 944 µs ± 1.24 per loop
(mean ± std. dev. of 7 runs, 100 loops each)
```

```
%timeit -n100 selu_jit(x).block_until_ready()
```
Measures the speed of jitted function

```
>>> The slowest run took 29.85 times longer than
the fastest. This could mean that an intermediate
result is being cached.
>>> 173 µs ± 283 µs per loop
(mean ± std. dev. of 7 runs, 100 loops each)
```

In the preceding example, you can see that the JIT-compiled version of the function is more than five times faster than the non-compiled one. At the same time, both still use GPU (in my case, NVIDIA A100-SXM4-40GB).

> **TIP** To get maximum performance from JAX, apply jax.jit() on your outer-most function calls.

I want to emphasize that calling jax.jit() will not compile the function immediately. It performs all the necessary preparations for the function to be JIT-compiled, which will take place during the first call to the function. We will discuss the details of the process in sections 5.1.2 and 5.2. As a result, benchmarking here is slightly incorrect; the first run of the function is slower than the subsequent ones, as compilation happens during the first call. The warning also highlights that this might be the case, as the slowest run is almost 30 times slower than the fastest. We ignored it here as, even with this inaccuracy, the results are great; in reality, the compiled version of the function is even faster than these averaged numbers.

You can also use a @jit annotation before the function. In the following code, we compile the same selu() function with the help of a @jit annotation. We also benchmark the right way here, with a warm-up call to trigger the compilation, and then benchmark the already compiled function. We will skip the warm-up for many upcoming examples to make the code shorter and also because, in many cases, it's okay to do compilation during the first run of the function. But remember it when you do benchmarking.

Listing 5.3   Using JIT with an annotation

```
@jax.jit
def selu(x,
         alpha=1.6732632423543772848170429916717,
         scale=1.0507009873554804934193349852946):
```
Uses annotation to JIT-compile the function

```
        '''Scaled exponential linear unit activation function.'''
        return scale * jnp.where(x > 0, x, alpha * jnp.exp(x) - alpha)

z = selu(x)                                          ◄──── Warms up the function

%timeit -n100 selu(x).block_until_ready()    ◄──── Measures speed of jitted function

>>> 60.6 µs ± 7.34 µs per loop (mean ± std. dev. of 7 runs, 100 loops each)
```

This way, you do not need a separate wrapped function; this magic is hidden from you, and you get your original function already wrapped. With the warm-up and the correct measurement, we see that the real numbers are much better, and the function is 15 times faster than the non-compiled one from the previous run.

The jit() transformation has several parameters; we next discuss some of them.

COMPILING AND RUNNING ON SPECIFIC HARDWARE

Two parameters are related to the hardware you wish to use. Beware: both are experimental features, and the API is likely to change.

The backend parameter is a string representing the XLA backend: 'cpu', 'gpu', or 'tpu'. If there is a GPU or TPU available in the system, JAX will use this backend instead of a CPU.

The device parameter specifies the device on which the jitted function will run. You may pass the specific device obtained from the jax.devices() call. Usually, by default, it is the first element of the resulting array. If you have more than one GPU or TPU in the system, this parameter allows you to control precisely where to run the computations.

In the following example, we deliberately compile the function for the CPU and GPU. Here, we compile separate versions of our function for CPU and GPU, and we can see the almost 10-fold difference in speed between the selu_jit_cpu() and selu_jit_gpu() functions.

Listing 5.4   Controlling which backend to use

```
def selu(x,
         alpha=1.6732632423543772848170429916717,
         scale=1.0507009873554804934193349852946):     Recreates the same
    '''Scaled exponential linear unit activation function.'''   function to not
    return scale * jnp.where(                           interfere with the
        x > 0, x, alpha * jnp.exp(x) - alpha)           @jit-annotated
                                                         version

selu_jit_cpu = jax.jit(selu, backend='cpu')   ◄────┐
selu_jit_gpu = jax.jit(selu, backend='gpu')   ◄────┤   CPU-targeted version

%timeit -n100 selu(x).block_until_ready()      ◄────┤   GPU-targeted version
```

Calls the original, non-JIT-compiled version. This version still may use GPU/TPU if available.

```
>>> 791 μs ± 66.8 μs per loop (mean ± std. dev. of 7 runs, 100 loops each)

%timeit -n100 selu_jit_cpu(x).block_until_ready()          ◀── Calls the function on the CPU

>>> 1.81 ms ± 178 μs per loop (mean ± std. dev. of 7 runs, 100 loops each)

%timeit -n100 selu_jit_gpu(x).block_until_ready()          ◀──┐ Calls the function on the
                                                              │ GPU (remember the
>>> The slowest run took 12.60 times longer                   │ slowest first run)
than the fastest. This could mean that an
intermediate result is being cached.
>>> 165 μs ± 247 μs per loop (mean ± std. dev. of 7 runs, 100 loops each)
```

The selu() call measurement may be misleading, as JAX may still use GPU or TPU if available in the system. The only difference is the function will not be compiled with XLA. My system has a GPU available, and the tensor x with data resides on the GPU, so computations also happen there.

To have a correct benchmark, we have to put the data tensors on the corresponding devices with the device_put() method (as we did in chapter 3) and then run the original function.

Listing 5.5   Controlling both backend and tensor device placement

```
                                                        ┌─ Places data tensor on CPU
                                                        │
                                                        │  Places data tensor on GPU
x_cpu = jax.device_put(x, jax.devices('cpu')[0])   ◀────┘  │
x_gpu = jax.device_put(x, jax.devices('gpu')[0])   ◀───────┘

%timeit -n100 selu(x_cpu).block_until_ready()      ◀──┤ Measures the non-compiled
                                                      │ function on the CPU
>>> 2.74 ms ± 95.8 μs per loop (mean ± std. dev. of 7 runs, 100 loops each)

%timeit -n100 selu(x_gpu).block_until_ready()      ◀──┤ Measures the non-compiled
                                                      │ function on the GPU
>>> 872 μs ± 80.8 μs per loop (mean ± std. dev. of 7 runs, 100 loops each)

%timeit -n100 selu_jit_cpu(x_cpu).block_until_ready()  ◀─┤ Measures the JIT-compiled
                                                         │ function on the CPU
>>> 437 μs ± 4.29 μs per loop (mean ± std. dev. of 7 runs, 100 loops each)

%timeit -n100 selu_jit_gpu(x_gpu).block_until_ready()  ◀─┤ Measures the JIT-compiled
                                                         │ function on the GPU
>>> 27.1 μs ± 4.94 μs per loop (mean ± std. dev. of 7 runs, 100 loops each)
```

Here, I have run these measurements on the same system I used before. You can see that the GPU-based data produces results at approximately the same time as a simple non-compiled function call, while the CPU-based data produces results more than three times slower. Both JIT-compiled versions are faster than the corresponding non-compiled calls. For the CPU, it is 6x faster; for the GPU, it is 32x faster. Note that JAX (at least my current version, 0.3.17) does not prohibit you from using a GPU-compiled function with CPU-based data or vice versa.

USING STATIC ARGUMENTS

In JAX, a mechanism of *static arguments* may be useful in different cases. You will learn more about the mechanics behind it later in section 5.2 when we discuss tracing.

One simple example of when you might need to use static arguments is when you want to compile a function with parameters that are not arrays but, for example, an instance of some class or a function. Say you want to compile a neural network layer with an activation function passed as a parameter. In this case, JIT will fail, as the arguments and return value of the function you want to compile should be arrays, scalars, or standard Python containers (like `tuple`, `list`, or `dict`, respectively, possibly nested). Static arguments may solve this problem, as arguments indicated as static can be anything, provided they are hashable and have an equality operation defined.

So you can mark some arguments as static or compile-time constants. You can do this with either the `static_argnums` or `static_argnames` parameters. Both are optional. The `static_argnums` parameter is an integer or collection of integers that specifies which positional arguments to treat as static. The `static_argnames` is a string or collection of strings specifying which named arguments to treat as static. No arguments are treated as static if neither `static_argnums` nor `static_argnames` is provided.

Technically, this means that operations that depend only on static arguments will be constant-folded in Python during tracing. Constant folding is an optimization technique that eliminates expressions that calculate a value that can already be determined before code execution. The following listing implements this example.

Listing 5.6   Fixing a JIT compilation error with static arguments

```
def dense_layer(x, w, b, activation_func):        ◀──  A function parameterized
    return activation_func(x*w+b)                        by another function

x = jnp.array([1.0, 2.0, 3.0])
w = jnp.ones((3,3))                               │    Some test data
b = jnp.ones(3)

dense_layer_jit = jax.jit(dense_layer)            ◀──  Creating the JIT-compiled
                                                        version of the function
dense_layer_jit(x, w, b, selu)                    ◀──
                                                      The compilation fails because
>>> ...                                               the fourth argument is a
>>>      > 3 dense_layer_jit(x, w, b, selu)           function, not a valid JAX type
>>> ...
>>> TypeError: Cannot interpret value of type
<class 'function'> as an abstract array; it does
not have a dtype attribute
                                                       Marking the fourth
dense_layer_jit = jax.jit(dense_layer, static_argnums=3)  ◀──┘  argument as static

dense_layer_jit(x, w, b, selu)                    ◀──── JIT now succeeds.

>>> Array([[2.101402, 3.152103, 4.202804],
>>>        [2.101402, 3.152103, 4.202804],
>>>        [2.101402, 3.152103, 4.202804]], dtype=float32)
```

Here, we passed an activation function as a parameter for our `dense_layer()` function. Because a function is not an allowed type for input and output values for a jitted function, we get an error. And because the real compilation happens during the first call of the jitted function, the error will appear only during the first call, not when you call `jit()`. To eliminate this error, we marked this specific parameter as static. After specifying the activation function to be static, JAX knows to compile one version of this function for different activation functions and to create compiled functions that accept variables for x, w, and b.

In another example, we create a function to calculate the Minkowski distance between two vectors. The function has a parameter called `order`. `order=1` calculates the Manhattan distance. `order=2` calculates the Euclidean distance. This function perfectly compiles without any static parameters, but if the order parameter is static, it allows the creation of specialized compiled versions of the function. So when you call this function with `order=1`, a version of the function with this parameter constantly set to 1 is compiled. When you call this function with `order=2`, another version is compiled for which this parameter is constantly set to 2.

Listing 5.7 Marking an argument as static

A function of three parameters; the first one should have only a limited number of values.

A side effect that will be visible on each compilation

```
def dist(order, x, y):
  print("Compiling")
  return jnp.power(jnp.sum(jnp.abs(x-y)**order), 1.0/order)

dist_jit = jax.jit(dist, static_argnums=0)

dist_jit(1, jnp.array([0.0, 0.0]), jnp.array([2.0, 2.0]))

>>> Compiling
>>> Array(4., dtype=float32)

dist_jit(2, jnp.array([0.0, 0.0]), jnp.array([2.0, 2.0]))

>>> Compiling
>>> Array(2.828427, dtype=float32)

dist_jit(1, jnp.array([10.0, 10.0]),
    jnp.array([2.0, 2.0]))

>>> Array(16., dtype=float32)
```

JIT-ting the function and declaring that the first parameter is static

Compile function for the given parameter value and run.

Compile function for another parameter value and run.

For this parameter value, the function is already compiled.

Calling the jitted function with different values for static parameters will trigger recompilation. Here, the function was compiled twice: for the value of 1 of the first parameter and for the value of 2 of this parameter. We deliberately use a side effect that will only be visible during the first run of the function. We discuss why this is happening later in section 5.2.

Such specialized compiled versions may simplify the resulting compiled code. Say you don't need to square numbers and calculate a square root for the `order=1`, then the resulting code is simpler. Such code may also be faster (because it is simpler and more specialized). This approach makes sense when the set of possible static parameter values is limited.

In the book, we will face other cases when using static parameters makes sense. One such case is later in listing 5.15.

If you want to specify static arguments when using `jit` as a decorator (or annotation), you can use Python's `functools.partial`.

Listing 5.8 Using `functools.partial` with `jit` as a decorator

```
from functools import partial

@partial(jax.jit, static_argnums=0)          ◄─── Creates a partially applied jax.jit() function
def dist(order, x, y):                             with an argument static_argnums=0
  return jnp.power(jnp.sum(jnp.abs(x-y)**order), 1.0/order)
```

The `partial()` function creates a functional object, which, when called, will behave like the original function with the given parameters. Here it creates a partially applied `jax.jit()` function with the fixed `static_argnums=0` parameter. This partial function is applied to our `dist()` function as an annotation, compiling it with its first argument (the `order`) being static.

OPTIMIZATION-RELATED ARGUMENTS

There are also special parameters in the `jit` transformation that could be used for different optimizations. I don't dive into the details here; I just briefly mention them so you won't be surprised when you see them.

First, there is the `jit` function argument called `donate_argnums`. It marks specific positional arguments that can be "donated" to the computation. The rationale behind this is as follows. Input arguments use some memory buffers to store their values. During the function execution, they might no longer be needed at some point after they were used in the computation. You can donate these memory buffers, and XLA may use them to reduce the amount of memory needed for the computation—for example, to store the result. Of course, you should not reuse the buffers you are donating. If you do, JAX raises an error. By default, no argument buffers are donated. For named arguments there is a similar `donate_argnames` parameter. You can read more about it here: https://mng.bz/eorz.

Second, the `keep_unused` argument (which is `False` by default) controls how JAX treats arguments it determines to be unused. By default, it drops such arguments from the resulting compiled XLA code. They will not be transferred to the device and will not be provided to the underlying executable. You can turn off this logic if you do not want to prune such parameters.

There is also an option to inline your function into enclosing Jaxprs (an intermediate representation to which Python code is converted; more on Jaxpr in section 5.2), removing overhead for function calls. You can use the `inline=True` parameter to do this. By default, it is `False`, and the function call is represented as an application of the `xla_call` primitive with its own sub-Jaxpr. With inlining, there are no separate function calls. The function code is inserted in the place where it is called, removing overhead from calling a function and returning values from it.

5.1.2   *Pure functions and compilation process*

JIT compilation works with JAX-compatible functions. JAX is designed to work with functionally pure code without global state and side effects. You can still write and run impure functions, but JAX does not guarantee they'll work correctly.

JAX transforms Python functions by first converting them into a simple, intermediate language called Jaxpr using a process called *tracing* (we will discuss Jaxpr and tracing in section 5.2). Then the transformations work on the Jaxpr representation. With compilation, the Jaxpr representation is being compiled further with XLA (there are more steps at this stage; we will also discuss them in section 5.2). This high-level scheme is depicted in figure 5.1.

Figure 5.1   High-level scheme of how JAX compiles the code

Compilation happens during the first call of a function (thus the name *just-in-time* compilation). JAX traces the function by running it; then it creates a Jaxpr representation, compiles it with XLA, and caches the compiled code.

There are several consequences of such a process. First, the first run of a function is slower than subsequent runs. So to correctly measure function performance, you must warm up the function by running it the first time to make compilation happen. Then measure the function performance with an already compiled code, not counting compilation overhead in your measurements.

Second, everything that happened during the first run of the function gets stored in the representation. If the function behavior differs during other runs (which might happen if the function is not pure), you will not see it in the compiled version.

Also, side effects are not logged in Jaxpr, so you see their results only during the first run of the function. Listing 5.9 shows an example of what happens if a function is not pure. Our example function has a side effect and uses a global state. We compile the function and look at its behavior.

Listing 5.9   Compiling an impure function

```
global_state = 1

def impure_function(x):
```
←── **Global state to be used in an impure function**

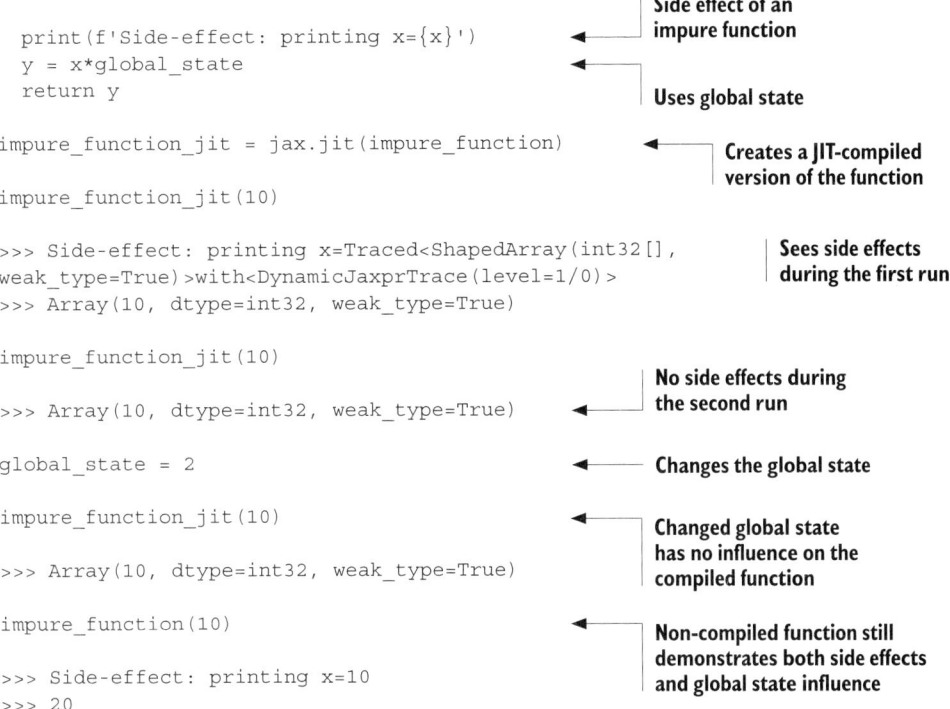

```
  print(f'Side-effect: printing x={x}')          ◄─── Side effect of an
  y = x*global_state                              ◄───   impure function
  return y                                        ◄─── Uses global state

impure_function_jit = jax.jit(impure_function)    ◄─── Creates a JIT-compiled
                                                        version of the function
impure_function_jit(10)

>>> Side-effect: printing x=Traced<ShapedArray(int32[],    Sees side effects
weak_type=True)>with<DynamicJaxprTrace(level=1/0)>         during the first run
>>> Array(10, dtype=int32, weak_type=True)

impure_function_jit(10)
                                                  ◄─── No side effects during
>>> Array(10, dtype=int32, weak_type=True)             the second run

global_state = 2                                  ◄─── Changes the global state

impure_function_jit(10)                           ◄─── Changed global state
                                                       has no influence on the
>>> Array(10, dtype=int32, weak_type=True)             compiled function

impure_function(10)                               ◄─── Non-compiled function still
                                                       demonstrates both side effects
>>> Side-effect: printing x=10                         and global state influence
>>> 20
```

In listing 5.9, we create an impure function with both a side effect (a print statement) and a global state (a variable global_state). Then we compile the function, but it actually creates a function wrapper, and the real compilation will take place later when we call the function for the first time. During the first call, JAX traces the function using abstract values representing the input arrays, and we see the side effect. But this side effect is not captured in the resulting Jaxpr representation and the compiled code (we will look at the internals soon), and during the second call of the function, we do not see the side effect. Moreover, the global state is also not present in the compiled code, so after changing the global state, the function behaves as if it still had an old value. The non-compiled original function behaves as expected, demonstrating both a side effect and global state influence.

We used print() statements here to analyze what is happening and when. However, it's just an implementation detail that the Python code is run at least once. You should not rely on it. Take care of your code, and remember that the proper way to use JAX is only on functionally pure Python functions.

To better understand why JIT works the way it works, it's worth diving into its internals. It is not strictly necessary if you want just to use JIT, but understanding internals will help you efficiently deal with JIT limitations (the topic of section 5.3), and it may help in debugging complicated cases, like slow compilation and inefficient code. I believe it is also valuable for those (like me) who love to look under the hood and understand how things work.

5.2   JIT internals

I have already mentioned Jaxpr and the JAX compilation workflow several times. It's time to dive deeper into these details and describe how different steps of this process work. I first describe the "Python to Jaxpr" conversion and then the "Jaxpr to native code" conversion.

5.2.1   Jaxpr, an intermediate representation for JAX programs

First, we focus on the first stage of compilation, converting Python code to Jaxpr (see figure 5.2).

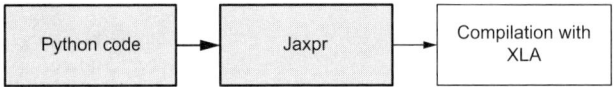

Figure 5.2   This section focuses on Python-to-Jaxpr conversion.

JAX converts code to an intermediate representation (IR) of a computation before doing transformations and sending the code to XLA. This IR is called *Jaxpr*, which is short for JAX Expression. The transformations then work on the Jaxpr representation.

JAXPR LANGUAGE

Jaxpr is essentially a simple functional language with very limited higher-order capabilities (a primitive is higher order if it is parameterized by a function). You can view the jaxpr using the jax.make_jaxpr() transformation.

Listing 5.10   Using `jax.make_jaxpr()`

```
def f1(x, y, z):                                    ◀─── The same simple function
  return jnp.sum(x + y * z)                              with a few operations

x = jnp.array([1.0, 1.0, 1.0])
y = jnp.ones((3,3))*2.0                              ─── Some test data
z = jnp.array([2.0, 1.0, 0.0]).T

jax.make_jaxpr(f1)(x,y,z)                            ◀─── Generates jaxpr for the function

>>> { lambda ; a:f32[3] b:f32[3,3] c:f32[3]. let
>>>     d:f32[1,3] = broadcast_in_dim[broadcast_dimensions=(1,) shape=(1, 3)]
c
>>>     e:f32[3,3] = mul b d
>>>     f:f32[1,3] = broadcast_in_dim[broadcast_dimensions=(1,) shape=(1, 3)]
a
>>>     g:f32[3,3] = add f e
>>>     h:f32[] = reduce_sum[axes=(0, 1)] g
>>>   in (h,) }
```

Here, you see our function is converted into Jaxpr. The Jaxpr is printed using the following grammar:

```
jaxpr ::= { lambda Var* ; Var+.
            let Eqn*
            in  [Expr+] }
```

Jaxpr contains one or more input parameters comprising two lists appearing after the word `lambda` and separated by a semicolon: a list of constants (`Var*` in the grammar, which is empty in listing 5.10) and a list of input variables to the Python function (`Var+` in the grammar, which is `a:f32[3]  b:f32[3,3]  c:f32[3]` in the listing). Any variables used by the function that are not input parameters will be treated as constant values and will be in the list of constants. There is a list of output atomic expressions (represented as `in  [Expr+]` in the grammar, and `(h,)` in the listing—actually a tuple). A list of equations (`let Eqn*`) defining intermediate variables refers to intermediate expressions. Each equation defines one or more variables as the result of applying a primitive on some atomic expressions (for example, `g:f32[3,3] = add f e` for addition). Each equation uses only input variables and intermediate variables defined by previous equations. Jaxpr is explicitly typed; here, you can see both types and shapes for each variable.

Most Jaxpr primitives take just one or more `Expr` as arguments and are documented in the `jax.lax` module (https://mng.bz/ppMG). These are the primitives like `add`, `sub`, `sin`, `mul`, and `reduce_sum`. Jaxpr also includes several higher-order primitives that include sub-Jaxprs. Among them are `switch` and `cond` conditionals, `while` and `fori` loops, `scan` (we mentioned them in chapter 3), and a special `xla_call` primitive that encapsulates a sub-Jaxpr along with parameters that specify the backend and the device on which the computation should run (we mentioned the `xla_call` primitive when discussed inlining in the "Optimization-related arguments" subsection of section 5.1). If you are interested in a thorough description of the Jaxpr language, see https://jax .readthedocs.io/en/latest/jaxpr.html.

The `make_jaxpr()` transformation creates another function that takes in parameters of the original function and returns Jaxpr in the value of the `jax.core.ClosedJaxpr` type (https://mng.bz/OZdn). The `jax.core.ClosedJaxpr` type contains both Jaxpr and constants. The Jaxpr resides in the `jaxpr` attribute and has a `jax.core.Jaxpr` type (https://mng.bz/Y7QN). Constants are in the `consts` attribute, which is a list.

TRACING

JAX performs the conversion to Jaxpr using tracing. During tracing, JAX wraps each argument with a special tracer object. It is an object of the `jax.core.Tracer` class and is used as a substitute for a JAX `Array` to determine the sequence of operations performed by a Python function.

The tracer records all JAX operations performed on it during the function call. Then, JAX reconstructs the function using the tracer records. The output of that reconstruction is the Jaxpr. The Python side effects still happen during the tracing, but the tracers do not record them, and they do not appear in the Jaxpr. In the following listing, we change our function to contain a side effect (the `print()` statement) and use a global variable (variable `z`).

Listing 5.11   Looking at `jaxpr` for a function with side effects

```
x = jnp.array([1.0, 1.0, 1.0])
y = jnp.ones((3,3))*2.0
z = jnp.array([2.0, 1.0, 0.0]).T

def f2(x, y):                                    ┐  Side effect
  print(f'x={x}, y={y}, z={z}')          ◄──────┘
  return jnp.sum(x + y * z)              ◄────── Uses global variable z

f2_jaxpr = jax.make_jaxpr(f2)(x,y)       ◄────── Generates jaxpr for the function

>>> x=Traced<ShapedArray(float32[3])>with<
DynamicJaxprTrace(level=1/0)>,
y=Traced<ShapedArray(float32[3,3])>with<
DynamicJaxprTrace(level=1/0)>, z=[2. 1. 0.]   ◄────── Side effect result

f2_jaxpr.jaxpr                                ◄────── Checks the resulting jaxpr

>>> { lambda a:f32[3]; b:f32[3] c:f32[3,3]. let
>>>     d:f32[1,3] = broadcast_in_dim[broadcast_dimensions=(1,) shape=(1, 3)]
a
>>>     e:f32[3,3] = mul c d
>>>     f:f32[1,3] = broadcast_in_dim[broadcast_dimensions=(1,) shape=(1, 3)]
b
>>>     g:f32[3,3] = add f e
>>>     h:f32[] = reduce_sum[axes=(0, 1)] g
>>>   in (h,) }

f2_jaxpr.consts                               ◄────── Checks the list of constants

>>> [Array([2., 1., 0.], dtype=float32)]    ◄────── Our global variable is now a constant.
```

The side effect emerges during tracing so that we can see its result during the call of the function obtained with the `make_jaxpr()` function transformation. The resulting `jaxpr` does not contain anything related to the print statement. The global variable is now saved in the list of constants accompanying the resulting `jaxpr`, so if you later change the global variable, the compiled function will still use the old value stored as a constant.

By default, `jax.jit` uses the `ShapedArray` tracer for tracing. It has a concrete shape but no concrete value. Because of this, the compiled function works on all possible inputs with the same shape, which is a typical case in machine learning. For example, suppose we create a function to calculate the dot product of two vectors, and we want to JIT-compile the function. In the first call, we pass two vectors of shape [100,1] that consist of floating-point numbers. The shapes and data types will be saved to the cache during the first call. Now, the compiled version of the function is available to reuse for different instantiations of the vectors of the same size and type.

The idea is that we want our compiled (or more generally transformed) code to work with different input values, so JAX traces on abstract values representing sets of possible inputs. There are different levels of abstraction (https://mng.bz/GZpq), and different transformations use different levels. Higher levels of abstraction give a more general view of the Python code and reduce the number of recompilations but impose more constraints on the Python code to be able to be traced. Tracing with the highest level of abstraction using the UnshapedArray tracer is not currently a default for any transformation.

In the case of JIT, this means tracing has no problems with control flow statements if they do not depend on any input parameter value (but it is allowable for control flow statements to use input parameter shapes). The code in the following listing uses a fixed value independent of any input parameter and an input parameter shape to make a loop.

Listing 5.12   Tracing with control structures

```
def f3(x):
  y = x
  for i in range(5):          ◄──────  The loop does not depend
    y += i                            on an input parameter.
  return y


jax.make_jaxpr(f3)(0)

>>> { lambda ; a:i32[]. let
>>>     b:i32[] = add a 0
>>>     c:i32[] = add b 1
>>>     d:i32[] = add c 2         The loop is unrolled.
>>>     e:i32[] = add d 3
>>>     f:i32[] = add e 4
>>>   in (f,) }


jax.jit(f3)(0)                  ◄──────  JIT compilation succeeded.

>>> Array(10, dtype=int32, weak_type=True)

def f4(x):
  y = 0
  for i in range(x.shape[0]):   ◄──────  The loop depends on an
    y += x[i]                            input parameter shape.
  return y

jax.make_jaxpr(f4)(jnp.array([1.0, 2.0, 3.0]))
                                         The loop is unrolled.
>>> { lambda ; a:f32[3]. let        ◄──────
>>>     b:f32[1] = slice[limit_indices=(1,) start_indices=(0,) strides=(1,)]
a
>>>     c:f32[] = squeeze[dimensions=(0,)] b
>>>     d:f32[] = add 0.0 c
>>>     e:f32[1] = slice[limit_indices=(2,) start_indices=(1,) strides=(1,)]
a
>>>     f:f32[] = squeeze[dimensions=(0,)] e
>>>     g:f32[] = add d f
>>>     h:f32[1] = slice[limit_indices=(3,) start_indices=(2,) strides=(1,)]
a
```

```
>>>     i:f32[] = squeeze[dimensions=(0,)] h
>>>     j:f32[] = add g i
>>>   in (j,) }

jax.jit(f4)(jnp.array([1.0, 2.0, 3.0]))
```
◄——— **JIT compilation succeeded.**

```
>>> Array(6., dtype=float32)
```

JAX successfully traced both cases, unrolling the loops and JIT-compiling the functions. However, if you try to use an input parameter value in a control structure, you will fail.

Listing 5.13   Tracing with a `for` loop depending on the input parameter value

```
def f5(x):
  y = 0
  for i in range(x):
    y += i
  return y
```
◄—— **The loop depends on an input parameter.**

```
f5(5)
```
◄—— **It is a perfectly normal Python function that works.**

```
>>> 10

jax.make_jaxpr(f5)(5)
```
◄—— **JAX has problems tracing the function.**

```
>>> ...
>>> The above exception was the direct cause of the following exception:
>>>
>>> TracerIntegerConversionError               Traceback (most recent call
last)
>>> <ipython-input-54-626705d2393b> in f5(x)
>>>       1 def f5(x):
>>>       2   y = 0
>>> ----> 3   for i in range(x):
>>>       4     y += i
>>>       5   return y
>>>
>>> /usr/local/lib/python3.10/dist-packages/jax/_src/core.py in __index__
(self)
>>>     617
>>>     618   def __index__(self):
>>> --> 619     raise TracerIntegerConversionError(self)
>>>     620
>>>     621   def tolist(self):
>>>
>>> TracerIntegerConversionError: The __index__() method was called on traced
array with shape int32[].
>>> The error occurred while tracing the function
f5 at <ipython-input-77-626705d2393b>:1 for make_jaxpr.
This concrete value was not available in Python because
it depends on the value of the argument x.
>>> See https://jax.readthedocs.io/en/latest/errors.html#jax.errors.
TracerIntegerConversionError
```
◄——| **JIT fails because the tracing fails.**

Here, we used an input parameter value as a parameter for the loop, and tracing has problems doing its work because it is unable to deal with the parameter value. The same would happen if we used an `if` statement.

Listing 5.14 Tracing with an `if` statement depending on the input parameter value

```
def relu(x):
  if x > 0:                                    ◄───┐ If statement depends
    return x                                        │ on an input parameter
  return 0.0


relu(10.0)                                     ◄───┐ It is a perfectly normal
                                                    │ Python function that works.
>>> 10.0


jax.make_jaxpr(relu)(10.0)                     ◄─── Tracing fails

>>> The above exception was the direct cause of the following exception:
>>>
>>> ConcretizationTypeError                    Traceback (most recent call
last)
>>> <ipython-input-58-5bd36ce502aa> in relu(x)
>>>       1 def relu(x):
>>> ----> 2   if x > 0:
>>>       3     return x
>>>       4   return 0.0
>>>
>>>
>>> /usr/local/lib/python3.10/dist-packages/jax/_src/core.py in error(self,
arg)
>>>    1394   if fun is bool:
>>>    1395     def error(self, arg):
>>> -> 1396       raise TracerBoolConversionError(arg)
>>>    1397   else:
>>>    1398     def error(self, arg):
>>>
>>> TracerBoolConversionError: Attempted boolean conversion of traced array
with shape bool[]..
>>> The error occurred while tracing the function
relu at <ipython-input-83-5064d3aeee39>:1 for make_jaxpr.
This concrete value was not available in Python because
it depends on the value of the argument x.
>>> See https://jax.readthedocs.io/en/latest/errors.html#jax.errors.
TracerBoolConversionError
```

Here, we used an input parameter value in the `if` statement, and tracing failed. However, the function is a normal Python function that works.

You have control over the tracing process and can use the mechanism of static parameters you are already familiar with (see section 5.1.1). Specifying a particular parameter as static (both `jax.jit()` and `jax.make_jaxpr()` functions support it) makes tracing use of concrete values and the compilation works.

Listing 5.15   Using static values to trace with concrete values

```
def f5(x):
  y = 0
  for i in range(x):                              ◄─── Dependency on an
    y += i                                              input parameter
  return y

def relu(x):
  if x > 0:                                       ◄───
    return x
  return 0.0

jax.make_jaxpr(f5, static_argnums=0)(5)          ◄───                    Marks the
                                                                          first
>>> { lambda ; . let  in (10,) }         ◄───    The resulting          parameter
                                                  expression is          as static
jax.jit(f5, static_argnums=0)(5)                  effectively a       ◄───
                                                  precalculated
>>> Array(10, dtype=int32, weak_type=True)  ◄─┐   constant.
                                              │
jax.make_jaxpr(relu, static_argnums=0)(12.3)  │                      ◄───
                                              │
>>> { lambda ; . let  in (12.3,) }       ◄────┤
                                              │
jax.jit(relu, static_argnums=0)(12.3)         │                      ◄───
                                              │
>>> Array(12.3, dtype=float32, weak_type=True) ◄┘  Compilation
                                                   also succeeded.
```

Here is the tradeoff. Your function is now being compiled on any call with a new input parameter value. This might be okay for a function with a small set of possible values (as might be for our f5() function). Still, it is definitely not okay for functions with many possible values (which is definitely the case for the relu() activation function, which may take in almost any value during neural network training).

Another way to solve this problem more efficiently is to use the structured control flow primitives we mentioned in section 3.4. Let's first replace our Python for-loop from Listing 5.13 with a jax.lax.fori_loop() primitive (https://jax.readthedocs.io/en/latest/_autosummary/jax.lax.fori_loop.html). The fori_loop(lower, upper, body_fun, init_val) is equivalent to the following Python code:

```
def fori_loop(lower, upper, body_fun, init_val):
  val = init_val
  for i in range(lower, upper):
    val = body_fun(i, val)
  return val
```

The changed code looks like the following listing.

```
def f5(x):
  return jax.lax.fori_loop(0, x, lambda i,v: v+i, 0)

f5(5)
```
◀— Uses jax.lax.fori_loop to replace a for loop of Listing 5.12

```
>>> Array(10, dtype=int32, weak_type=True)
```
◀— The result is still the same.

```
jax.make_jaxpr(f5)(5)
```
◀— Jaxpr is now more complex.

```
>>> { lambda ; a:i32[]. let
>>>     _:i32[] _:i32[] b:i32[] = while[
>>>       body_jaxpr={ lambda ; c:i32[] d:i32[] e:i32[]. let
>>>         f:i32[] = add c 1
>>>         g:i32[] = add e c
>>>       in (f, d, g) }
>>>       body_nconsts=0
>>>       cond_jaxpr={ lambda ; h:i32[] i:i32[] j:i32[]. let
>>>         k:bool[] = lt h i
>>>       in (k,) }
>>>       cond_nconsts=0
>>>     ] 0 a 0
>>>   in (b,) }

jax.jit(f5)(5)
```
◀— The function now compiles.

```
>>> Array(10, dtype=int32, weak_type=True)
```

Here, we replaced a for-loop dependent on an input parameter from listing 5.13 with the jax.lax.fori_loop() primitive, and tracing succeeds now.

Now, let's replace the if statement from listing 5.14 with the jax.lax.cond() primitive (https://mng.bz/z8da). The cond() primitive is equivalent to the following Python implementation:

```
def cond(pred, true_fun, false_fun, *operands):
  if pred:
    return true_fun(*operands)
  else:
    return false_fun(*operands)
```

Both true_fun() and false_fun() must be callable objects and return exactly the same types.

It is straightforward to apply the cond() primitive to our code.

```
def relu(x):
  return jax.lax.cond(x>0, lambda x: x, lambda x: 0.0, x)

relu(12.3)
```
◀— Uses jax.lax.cond to replace an if statement of listing 5.14

```
>>> Array(12.3, dtype=float32, weak_type=True)        ◄──┐  The result is
                                                          │  still the same.
jax.make_jaxpr(relu)(12.3)                     ◄──────┐
                                                      │   jaxpr is now
>>> { lambda ; a:f32[]. let                           │   more complex.
>>>     b:bool[] = gt a 0.0
>>>     c:i32[] = convert_element_type[new_dtype=int32 weak_type=False] b
>>>     d:f32[] = cond[
>>>       branches=(
>>>         { lambda ; e:f32[]. let  in (0.0,) }
>>>         { lambda ; f:f32[]. let  in (f,) }
>>>       )
>>>       linear=(False,)
>>>     ] c a
>>>   in (d,) }
                                                      The function
jax.jit(relu)(12.3)                          ◄──────┘  now compiles.

>>> Array(12.3, dtype=float32, weak_type=True)
```

We replaced the Python if statement with jax.lax.cond(), and tracing now succeeds.

Actually, not every JAX transformation materializes a Jaxpr, as discussed before. Some transformations, like taking gradients or batching, apply transformations incrementally during tracing (not taking a Jaxpr first and then processing it to obtain a modified Jaxpr).

We have finished with the first stage of compilation, converting Python code to an intermediate representation, Jaxpr. Next, the second stage happens: compiling Jaxpr to native code with XLA.

5.2.2   XLA

XLA stands for Accelerated Linear Algebra (https://www.tensorflow.org/xla), a domain-specific compiler for linear algebra, originally developed to accelerate Tensor-Flow models, potentially with no source code changes (see figure 5.3).

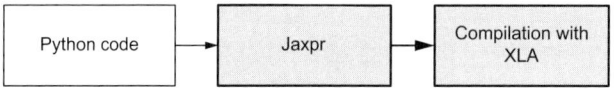

Figure 5.3   Jaxpr-to-native code conversion

XLA ORIGINS AND ARCHITECTURE

XLA was created because, though each separate operation in a computation graph may be highly optimized, a user may compose more complex operations out of simpler ones or create a large composition that is not guaranteed to run efficiently. So Google developed XLA, which used JIT-compilation techniques to analyze the TensorFlow graph, specialize it for the actual run-time dimensions and types, and, most importantly, fuse multiple operations. It can exploit model-specific information for optimization and compile the TensorFlow graph into a sequence of computation kernels generated specifically for the given model.

For example, let's take an operation we had in listing 5.10 that takes three tensors at its input and calculates output:

```
def f(x, y, z):
  return jnp.sum(x + y * z)
```
◄──── **Performs three operations:**
      multiplication, addition, and sum

Without XLA, such computation may result in three different operations implemented with different computation kernels, say, on the GPU: one for multiplication, one for addition, and one for the final summation. XLA can optimize the computation to produce the result in a single kernel launch. It can fuse multiplication, addition, and summation into a single GPU kernel. Moreover, the fused operation does not produce intermediate variables containing $y \times z$ and $x + y \times z$ in memory. It may feed them directly to subsequent computations, keeping data in the same memory location or GPU registers. Removing unnecessary memory transfers is a big deal, as memory bandwidth can be a bottleneck for your computation.

XLA emits efficient native machine code for devices like CPUs, GPUs, and custom accelerators like Google's TPU. The XLA subsystem that performs target device–specific optimization and code generation is called the *backend*.

The system that sends data to XLA is called the *frontend*. The original frontend for XLA was TensorFlow, but now XLA programs can also be generated by PyTorch, JAX, Julia, and Nx (the numerical computing library for the Elixir programming language).

OpenXLA

OpenXLA (https://github.com/openxla) is an open source ML compiler ecosystem co-developed by AI/ML industry leaders, including Alibaba, Amazon Web Services, AMD, Anyscale, Apple, Arm, Cerebras, Google, Graphcore, Hugging Face, Intel, Meta, and NVIDIA. It was created to provide a home for a community-driven, open source ML compiler ecosystem.

The XLA compiler was decoupled from TensorFlow and passed to the OpenXLA project, so the community started by collaboratively evolving it. The project also includes StableHLO (more on that later) and IREE repositories. All of this enhances MLIR: a compiler infrastructure that enables machine learning models to be consistently represented, optimized, and executed on hardware (more on that later as well).

OpenXLA provides a modular toolchain that is supported by all leading frameworks through a common compiler interface, enhances standardized model representations that are portable, and provides a domain-specific compiler with powerful target-independent and hardware-specific optimizations.

You can read more about OpenXLA in the Google Open Source Blog: https://mng .bz/0Gax.

XLA uses a special input language called *high-level operations intermediate representation* (HLO IR, or just HLO). XLA takes in computations defined in HLO and compiles them into special machine instructions for target hardware architecture.

There are many basic operations in HLO. You can see the whole list at https://www.tensorflow.org/xla/operation_semantics.

Figure 5.4 shows the two optimization steps: target-independent and target-dependent. On the target-independent step, XLA makes optimizations independent of the hardware that will execute computations. This includes common subexpression elimination, target-independent operation fusion, and buffer analysis for allocating run-time memory for the computation.

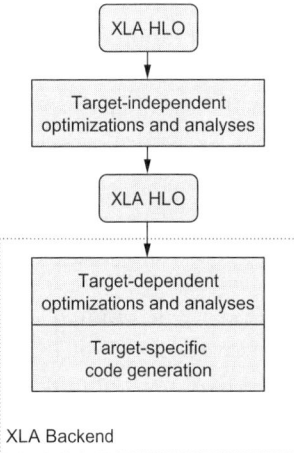

Figure 5.4   The compilation process in XLA

On the target-dependent step, the XLA backend can perform further HLO-level optimizations. For example, it may determine how to better partition computation into GPU streams and perform other fusions specifically for the particular GPU. It may also perform special pattern matching to replace certain operation combinations with optimized library calls.

After the target-dependent optimization and analysis, the XLA backend generates target-specific code. The CPU and GPU backends use LLVM (https://llvm.org/) for low-level intermediate representation, optimization, and code generation. These backends output LLVM IR representing XLA HLO IR and then invoke LLVM to generate native code from this LLVM IR.

The CPU backend supports x64 and ARM64; the GPU backend supports NVIDIA GPUs and, to some extent, GPUs from AMD (https://mng.bz/KZjK), Apple, and Intel (https://mng.bz/9dBl). Of course, there is a TPU backend supporting Google Cloud TPUs. There is also a way to develop your own XLA backends (https://mng.bz/jXwx), which presents a real opportunity for having all recent deep learning hardware supported soon.

XLA AND JAX

JAX uses XLA to generate efficient code for specific backends. But that is not the whole story. Since January 2022, JAX has used the *MHLO* MLIR dialect as its primary target compiler IR by default, and the backend was switched from XLA/HLO to MLIR/MHLO. Then the workflow was as follows (https://github.com/google/jax/issues/10715):

1 You write a Python function.
2 JAX converts the Python function to Jaxpr.
3 JAX converts the Jaxpr to MHLO for MLIR.
4 MLIR converts MHLO to optimized MHLO.
5 JAX converts optimized MHLO to HLO.
6 XLA converts HLO to optimized HLO.
7 XLA converts optimized HLO to the native code for CPU/GPU/TPU (for CPU and GPU it uses LLVM).

Then, at the end of 2022, JAX transitioned to *StableHLO* instead of MHLO (https://mng.bz/WEo0). You can still generate the MHLO dialect if needed; the lowering functions support both MHLO and StableHLO, although compatibility guarantees will only be provided for StableHLO and not for MHLO.

StableHLO (https://github.com/openxla/stablehlo) was created to provide a solid portability layer between different ML frameworks and ML compilers: ML frameworks that produce StableHLO programs are compatible with ML compilers that consume StableHLO programs. StableHLO is based on the MHLO dialect and enhances it with additional functionality, including serialization and versioning. It is a part of the OpenXLA project.

MLIR

MLIR (https://mlir.llvm.org/), or Multi-Level Intermediate Representation, is a successor of LLVM, also inspired by Chris Lattner (https://www.youtube.com/watch?v=qzljG6DKgic).

MLIR aims to build reusable and extensible compiler infrastructure suitable for the heterogeneous hardware world. In particular, it has great perspectives on building an optimizing compiler infrastructure for deep learning applications.

MLIR is intended to be a hybrid IR that can support multiple different requirements in a unified infrastructure, including but not limited to

- Representing dataflow graphs such as in TensorFlow
- Optimizations and transformations typically done on such graphs
- Ability to host high-performance-computing-style loop optimizations across kernels (fusion, loop interchange, tiling, etc.) and to transform memory layouts of data

(continued)

- Code generation "lowering" transformations such as DMA insertion, explicit cache management, memory tiling, and vectorization for 1D and 2D register architectures
- Ability to represent target-specific operations, e.g., accelerator-specific high-level operations
- Quantization and other graph transformations done on a deep learning graph
- Polyhedral primitives
- Hardware synthesis tools/high-level synthesis

MLIR is a powerful representation, but it also has non-goals. It does not try to support low-level machine code generation algorithms (like register allocation and instruction scheduling), as there are better fits for lower-level optimizers (such as LLVM). Also, MLIR is not intended to be a source language that end users would themselves write kernels in (analogous to CUDA C++).

MLIR supports different *dialects* (https://www.tensorflow.org/mlir/dialects) for its IR. JAX used the MLIR MHLO dialect ("meta"-HLO dialect; https://mng.bz/8wDP). The list of its operations can be viewed at https://www.tensorflow.org/mlir/hlo_ops.

There was a movement to build a standalone "HLO" MLIR-based compiler called MLIR-HLO (https://github.com/tensorflow/mlir-hlo). Currently, the team is sunsetting the MLIR-HLO repository (https://mng.bz/EZMJ) in favor of the StableHLO (https://github.com/openxla/stablehlo) project.

In the code in listing 5.18, we see how the Python function is converted first to Stable-HLO (or MHLO if you use an older JAX version) and then to lower-level HLO. We take the same function we used in sections on Jaxpr and XLA. It contains multiplication, addition, and summation. We provide some test data to calculate the function.

Then, exciting things begin. We JIT-compile our function. For the jitted function, we can create a lowered function. *Lowering* is a process of converting a higher-level representation to a lower-level representation. Here, we create a StableHLO IR code consisting of basic StableHLO operations. This code is pretty straightforward and almost resembles the original calculations. Then we move further, compiling this StableHLO code to HLO optimized for the target backend. This HLO code contains fused computation. The full code is available in the book's repository; here, I highlight only the StableHLO and HLO parts.

Listing 5.18   Compiling Python code to StableHLO and HLO

```
def f(x, y, z):
  return jnp.sum(x + y * z)

x = jnp.array([1.0, 1.0, 1.0])
y = jnp.ones((3,3))*2.0
z = jnp.array([2.0, 1.0, 0.0]).T
```

A simple function with a few operations

Some test data

```
f_jitted = jax.jit(f)
```
← **JITs the function**

```
f_lowered = f_jitted.lower(x,y,z)
print(f_lowered.as_text())
```
← **Lowers the function (generating StableHLO code)**

```
>>> ...
>>>    %5 = stablehlo.add %4, %2 : tensor<3x3xf32>
>>>    %6 = stablehlo.constant dense<0.000000e+00> : tensor<f32>
>>> ...
```
StableHLO representation

```
f_compiled = f_jitted.lower(x,y,z).compile()
print(f_compiled.as_text())
```
← **Compiles the lowered function for the specific backend (generating HLO code)**

```
>>> ...
>>>    %multiply.1 = f32[3,3]{1,0} multiply(f32[3,3]{1,0}
%param_0.4, f32[3,3]{1,0} %broadcast.4),
metadata={op_name="jit(f)/jit(main)/mul"
source_file="<ipython-input-99-95d48614b981>"
source_line=2}
>>>    %add.2 = f32[3,3]{1,0} add(f32[3,3]{1,0}
%broadcast.5, f32[3,3]{1,0} %multiply.1),
metadata={op_name="jit(f)/jit(main)/add"
source_file="<ipython-input-99-95d48614b981>" source_line=2}
>>> ...
```
HLO representation

Analyzing the StableHLO and HLO code and diving deeper into XLA and MLIR are outside the book's scope; yet you now understand the stages of the compilation process and what happens there.

Here, to obtain StableHLO and HLO, we used special functions for lowering and compiling code. These functions actually compose the new AOT compilation API.

5.2.3 *Using AOT compilation*

Since September 2022 and the release of JAX version 0.3.18, AOT compilation has been introduced (https://mng.bz/NRlD). AOT compilation might help if you want control over when different parts of the compilation process happen or if you want to compile fully before execution time. For example, this can save function startup time by doing the compilation stage in advance and avoids spending the first function run doing JIT compilation.

Say you have some Python function f(x) where x is an array. You apply the jit() transformation to the function and obtain a wrapped version f_jit = jit(f). Then, at some point, you invoke the jitted function with arguments f_jit(x). Here, compilation happens. We can depict the process this way, as shown in figure 5.5.

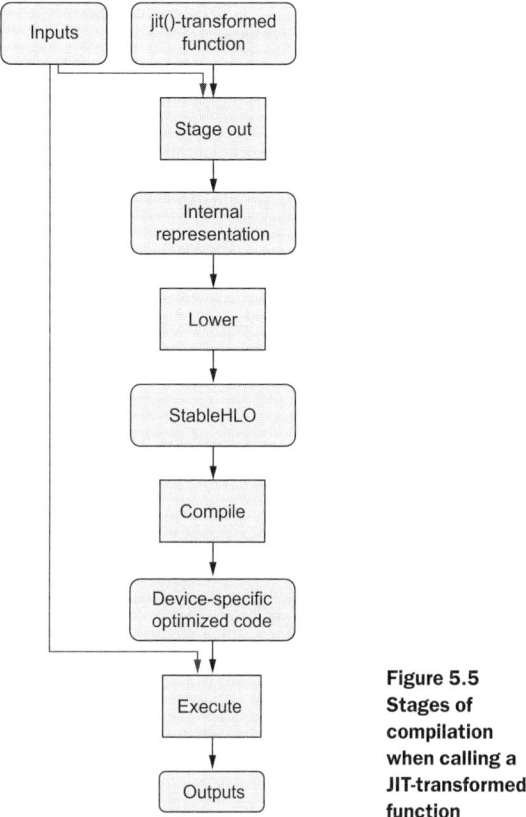

**Figure 5.5
Stages of
compilation
when calling a
JIT-transformed
function**

The compilation has several stages:

- *Stage out* the original function f to an internal representation. This specialized version of the function reflects restrictions to input types inferred from properties of arguments (here, only x).
- *Lower* the specialized staged-out representation to the input language of MLIR and XLA (here, StableHLO).
- *Compile* the lowered HLO program into device-specific optimized code for CPU, GPU, or TPU.
- *Execute* the compiled code with given arguments (here, x).

AOT API gives you control over the last three stages. There is a special `jax.stages` API (https://mng.bz/DdXE) to represent stages of the compiled execution process.

In listing 5.19, we use the same `selu()` activation function from the beginning of the chapter. Still, we deliberately add a side effect to understand where tracing and compilation happen. We create a JIT-compiled version and an AOT-compiled version.

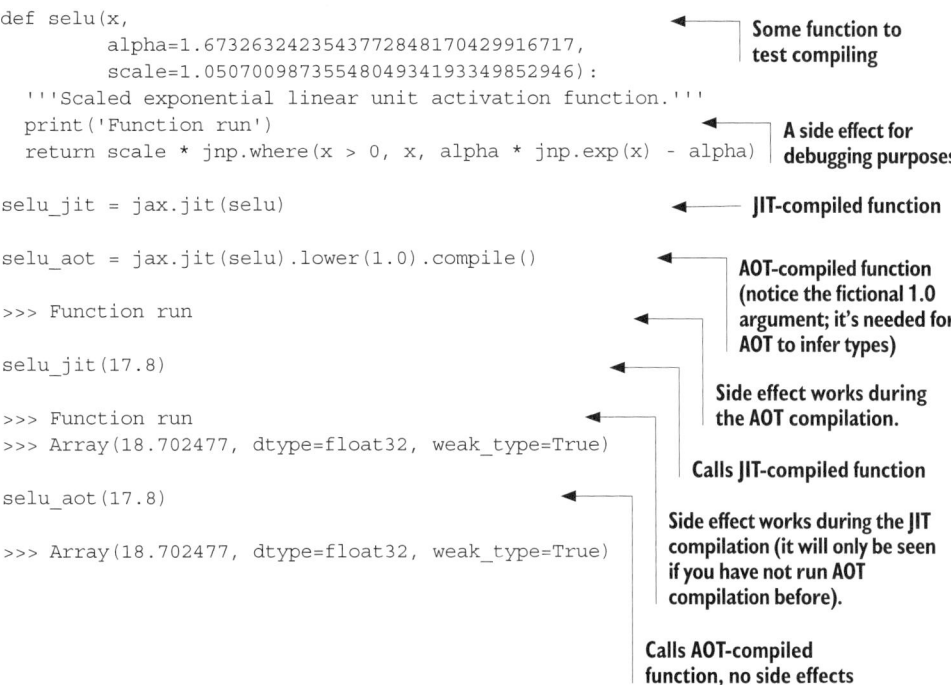

Listing 5.19 Compiling with JIT and AOT

```
def selu(x,
         alpha=1.6732632423543772848170429916717,
         scale=1.0507009873554804934193349852946):
  '''Scaled exponential linear unit activation function.'''
  print('Function run')
  return scale * jnp.where(x > 0, x, alpha * jnp.exp(x) - alpha)

selu_jit = jax.jit(selu)

selu_aot = jax.jit(selu).lower(1.0).compile()

>>> Function run

selu_jit(17.8)

>>> Function run
>>> Array(18.702477, dtype=float32, weak_type=True)

selu_aot(17.8)

>>> Array(18.702477, dtype=float32, weak_type=True)
```

Some function to test compiling

A side effect for debugging purposes

JIT-compiled function

AOT-compiled function (notice the fictional 1.0 argument; it's needed for AOT to infer types)

Side effect works during the AOT compilation.

Calls JIT-compiled function

Side effect works during the JIT compilation (it will only be seen if you have not run AOT compilation before).

Calls AOT-compiled function, no side effects

Both functions produce the same results. However, the AOT-compiled one does not require a warm-up, and at the moment of its invocation, we have already compiled the code. We see it by the time the side effect works. The AOT-compiled function works during the direct compilation; the JIT-compiled function happens during the first function invocation, when the compilation really happens.

Both lowering and compilation happen for a fixed type signature, and the AOT-compiled function can only be called with arguments of the fixed type signature. If you invoke the AOT-compiled function with arguments that are incompatible with its lowering (say, float32 instead of int32), you will get an error.

AOT-compiled functions cannot be transformed with transformations such as jit, grad, jvp, vmap. This is done because, internally, many transformations alter the type signature of functions. Though jit does not modify its arguments' type signature, it is disallowed as well.

The code in listing 5.20 applies both compiled functions from the previous example to a different data type—now for 32-bit integers instead of 32-bit floats. For the JIT-compiled function, this is not a problem; the function is recompiled. The AOT-compiled function cannot be recompiled, so an error is returned.

Then we apply a second transformation, vmap(), that creates a batched version of the function (more on this transformation in the next chapter; however, we have already used it in chapter 2). The JIT-compiled function combines with the new transformation well, but the AOT-compiled function cannot do it, and an error is returned.

Listing 5.20   Differences in behavior between JIT and AOT

```
selu_jit(17)
```
◄—— **Calls a JIT-compiled function on integer data; runs recompilation**

```
>>> Function run
>>> Array(17.861917, dtype=float32, weak_type=True)
```

```
selu_aot(17)
```
◄—— **Calls an AOT-compiled function on integer data; cannot run recompilation and returns an error**

```
>>> ...
>>> TypeError: Argument types differ from the types
for which this computation was compiled.
The mismatches are:
>>> Argument 'x' compiled with float32[] and called with int32[]
```

```
selu_jit_batched = jax.vmap(selu_jit)
selu_aot_batched = jax.vmap(selu_aot)
```
Creates batched versions of the function (on vmap; see the next chapter)

```
selu_jit_batched(jnp.array([42.0, 78.0, -12.3]))
```
◄—— **The JIT-compiled function can be transformed, and compilation happens again.**

```
>>> Function run
>>> Array([44.129444 , 81.95468  , -1.7580913], dtype=float32)
```

```
selu_aot_batched(jnp.array([42.0, 78.0, -12.3]))
```
◄—— **The AOT-compiled function cannot be transformed, and an error is returned.**

```
>>> ...
>>> TypeError: Cannot apply JAX transformations to
a function lowered and compiled for a particular
signature. Detected argument of Tracer type <class
'jax._src.interpreters.batching.BatchTracer'>.
```

The AOT stages also offer some additional features for debugging purposes. We used this functionality in listing 5.18 to obtain StableHLO and HLO representations. For compiled functions, you can also get cost and memory analyses via `cost_analysis()` and `memory_analysis()` functions. Both are intended for visualization and debugging purposes. They provide some simple data structures that can easily be printed or serialized, but it may be inconsistent across JAX and `jaxlib` versions or even invocations.

JAX and jaxlib

JAX is published as two separate Python packages:

- `jax`, a pure Python package
- `jaxlib`, a mostly-C++ package that contains libraries such as XLA, pieces of LLVM used by XLA, MLIR infrastructure with MHLO Python bindings, and JAX-specific C++ libraries for fast JIT and pytree manipulation

The JAX distribution is structured this way because most changes to JAX touch only Python code, and it makes it easy to work on the Python part of JAX without building C++ code. So the Python pieces can be updated independently of the C++ pieces, which improves development velocity.

Both `jax` and `jaxlib` share the same version number but are released separately. When installed, the `jax` package version must be greater than or equal to `jaxlib`'s version, and `jaxlib`'s version must be greater than or equal to the minimum `jaxlib` version specified by `jax`.

You can read more about JAX and jaxlib versioning at https://mng.bz/lM6y.

We have covered a lot of ground on how to use JIT and AOT compilation and how JAX works internally. It will help us in dealing with JIT limitations, and it is important to summarize the JIT limitations.

5.3   JIT limitations

JIT is a powerful mechanism. However, it has limitations and does not work everywhere. We have already discussed some of them; here we gather them together. Now that you understand the JIT internals, it will be much easier to understand the nature of these limitations, and we have tools to overcome them.

5.3.1   Pure and impure functions

First, as we have already discussed in section 5.1.2, JIT correctly works only with pure functions. So JIT can change the behavior of your function if you rely on its impurity, use of side effects, or global state. For example, a compiled function that uses some global value will not reflect changes in this value, as the compiled version will use the value from the moment of compilation (and tracing).

5.3.2   Exact numerics

Second, JIT can change the exact numerics of function outputs. This may happen because of optimizations along the way. For example, XLA may rearrange floating-point operations or get rid of some redundant computations that should not have any effect from the mathematical point of view (say, first dividing a value by some number and then multiplying the result with the same number) but may have an effect because of accumulating arithmetical errors due to floating-point arithmetic problems.

5.3.3   Conditioning on input parameter values

Third, there are limitations related to having control flow and conditioning on input parameter values. For example, a loop that depends on the input parameter value cannot be traced, but it can be replaced by a solution with structured control flow primitives from the `jax.lax` API. We discussed these in section 5.2.1.

5.3.4   Slow compilation

Fourth, jitted functions could sometimes be very slow to compile—even 10 or more seconds. This can happen when your code generates a very large internal representation, the Jaxpr. A long Jaxpr could arise from long loops that are unrolled during tracing and heavy use of control flow. This problem can be diagnosed by generating a Jaxpr for your function. If the Jaxpr contains hundreds or thousands of lines, you can expect slow compilation, as XLA compilation time scales to roughly the square of the number of operations sent to it.

You should remove such loops from your program. There are many ways to do this, including vectorizing the calculations (typical advice for any NumPy-like computations) and replacing Python loops with structured control flow primitives from `jax.lax`. Changing the algorithm may also be an option (but do not mix compilation time with execution time; the latter usually matters much more). You might also avoid wrapping such loops with `jit`. However, you may use `jit` for functions inside the loop.

Consider an illustrative example of calculating a cumulative sum (or running total). You have an array of elements, and the goal is to produce another array where each element is a sum of all elements from the original array before it and including it. A naive Python implementation may look like the following listing.

Listing 5.21 Cumulative sum naive implementation

```
def cumulative_sum(x):                    ◄─── The function for calculating
  acc = 0.0                                      the cumulative sum
  y = []
  for i in range(x.shape[0]):
    acc += x[i]
    y.append(acc)
  return y

j = jax.make_jaxpr(cumulative_sum)(jnp.ones(10000))

len(j.jaxpr.eqns)                         ◄─── The resulting jaxpr contains
                                                thousands of lines
>>> 30000

%time jax.jit(cumulative_sum)(jnp.ones(10000))

>>> CPU times: user 2min 16s, sys: 1.47 s, total: 2min 18s    │ Compilation takes
>>> Wall time: 2min 23s                                        │ pretty long.
```

Here, our simple one-level loop produced a lot of intermediate Jaxpr equations as the loop was unrolled. There are 30,000 equations in the Jaxpr, and the compilation takes more than 2 minutes.

We can easily replace the solution with a long `for` loop with the `lax.scan` primitive (https://mng.bz/BdnJ). The `jax.lax.scan()` primitive goes (scans) along the array and calculates a given function for each element and an accumulated state (called carry). We use `carry` for storing accumulated sums. The function returns a new value for the accumulated state and a corresponding element of the output array. It is equivalent to the following Python code:

```
def scan(f, init, xs, length=None):
  if xs is None:
    xs = [None] * length
```

```
carry = init
ys = []
for x in xs:
  carry, y = f(carry, x)
  ys.append(y)
return carry, np.stack(ys)
```

The updated code looks like the following listing.

Listing 5.22 Cumulative sum implementation with `lax.scan`

```
def cumulative_sum_fast(x):
  result, array = jax.lax.scan(
    lambda carry, elem: (carry+elem, carry+elem), 1.0, x)
  return array

j = jax.make_jaxpr(cumulative_sum_fast)(jnp.ones(10000))

len(j.jaxpr.eqns)                                      ◀─── The resulting jaxpr contains only
                                                            one line (yet, pretty complex).
>>> 1

%time cs = jax.jit(cumulative_sum_fast)(jnp.ones(10000))

>>> CPU times: user 145 ms, sys: 6.02 ms, total: 151 ms   │ Compilation is
>>> Wall time: 213 ms                                     │ very fast.
```

Here, we significantly reduced the intermediate representation, and the compilation time is now significantly less. The `lax.scan` is a JAX primitive, so the resulting representation is tiny.

5.3.5 Class methods

Another tricky thing is that we previously used `@jit` annotations only with standalone functions. However, you might want to use `@jit` for class methods. Simply annotating a class method with a `@jit` annotation will produce an error.

Listing 5.23 Annotating a class method

```
class ScaleClass:
  def __init__(self, scale: jnp.array):
    self.scale = scale

  @jax.jit                                              A class method we want to JIT
  def apply(self, x: jnp.array):                      ◀─┘
    return self.scale * x
                                                        Creates a class instance
scale_double = ScaleClass(2)                         ◀─┘
                                                        Calls the jitted function
scale_double.apply(10)                               ◀─── and gets an error

>>> TypeError: Cannot interpret value of type <class '__main__.ScaleClass'>
as an abstract array; it does not have a dtype attribute
```

We get an exception here because the class function has a first parameter, which is the instance of the class (here, ScaleClass). JAX does not know how to handle this type; it does not implement an abstract array interface. There are several ways to deal with this. First, you may use a helper function.

Listing 5.24   Using a helper function for a class method

```
from functools import partial

class ScaleClass:
  def __init__(self, scale: jnp.array):
    self.scale = scale

  def apply(self, x: jnp.array):
    return _apply_helper(self.scale, x)

@partial(jax.jit, static_argnums=0)
def _apply_helper(scale, x):
  return scale*x

scale_double = ScaleClass(2)

scale_double.apply(10)

>>> Array(20, dtype=int32, weak_type=True)
```

Now the method does not use JIT but uses a helper function.

Uses JIT annotation with the scale parameter being static

The helper function outside of the class

Now everything works correctly.

Here, we removed @jit annotation from the class method, created a helper function outside of the class, and used this function in the class method. The helper function is annotated with jit annotation, but we used functools.partial to specify a static parameter. We marked the first parameter of the helper function as static because we assume it will not frequently change as it initializes a class instance. The same value will be applied to many different arguments.

You can also make the self parameter static in the original code, but you need more changes in the code to avoid unexpected things. This method is described at https://mng.bz/d6BQ.

Another, more flexible approach is to make our ScaleClass class a pytree. We will talk about pytrees in chapter 10, but if you are interested in this approach, see https://mng.bz/rVpX.

5.3.6   *Simple functions*

There might be cases where a function is already small, and using JIT does not provide any significant boost. Moreover, it takes additional time to compile, and all the overhead of using MLIR/XLA and even the time to copy data to a hardware accelerator may not be worth it. Measure what you get from JIT and try to compile the largest possible chunk of the computation. This gives the compiler the freedom to optimize better.

In this chapter, we covered speeding up your code with compilation and the corresponding jit() transformation. In the following chapters, we will learn how to make your code even more performant with vectorization and parallelization and the corresponding `vmap()` and `pmap()` transformations. Appendix D contains information on `pjit()`, an experimental parallelization technique that was finally unified with the `jit()` transformation.

Exercise 5.1

Implement a JIT-compiled function that takes a time series and a window and calculates a moving average.

Summary

- JAX uses JIT compilation to produce efficient code for CPUs, GPUs, and TPUs with the `jit()` transformation or a corresponding `@jit` annotation.
- JIT compilation happens when a JIT-transformed function is executed for the first time.
- JAX is designed to work with functionally pure code without global state and side effects. You can still write and run impure functions, but JAX does not guarantee they will work correctly.
- JAX transformations first convert Python functions into a simple intermediate language called Jaxpr (short for JAX Expression) using tracing.
- By default, `jit()` uses the `ShapedArray` tracer for tracing, which has a concrete shape but no concrete value. Because of this, the compiled function works on all possible inputs with the same shape.
- You can use Python control flow and loops inside functions if they do not depend on input parameter values (but may depend on their shape).
- You can mark specific arguments as static to use concrete values for tracing. When a function is called with a different value, recompilation happens.
- You can also use `jax.lax` structured control flow primitives when you need to condition on an input parameter value.
- JAX uses MLIR and XLA to perform target-independent and target-dependent optimizations and generate target-specific code for CPUs, GPUs, and TPUs.
- XLA and MLIR use their special input languages, or intermediate representations, called HLO and StableHLO (or MHLO in older versions), respectively.
- In addition to JIT compilation, JAX provides an AOT compilation API to control when different parts of the compilation process happen.
- JIT can change the exact numerics of function outputs because of optimizations along the way.
- Jitted functions can sometimes be very slow to compile when your code generates a large internal representation, the `jaxpr`.
- Class methods require special approaches to work with JIT.

Vectorizing your code

This chapter covers

- Approaches to vectorizing your code
- Controlling `vmap()` behavior using its parameters
- Analyzing typical cases where you might benefit
  from auto-vectorization

In chapter 3, you learned how to speed up your calculations by running them on GPUs and TPUs. Then, in chapter 5, you learned another option to speed up your code with compilation and XLA. Now it's time to learn two more ways to make computations faster: automatic vectorization and parallelization. This chapter is dedicated to auto-vectorization, while chapters 7 and 8 look at parallelizing your computations.

Auto-vectorization provides you with several benefits. First, it simplifies the programming process by allowing you to write simpler functions for processing a single element and then automatically transform them into more complex functions working on batches (or arrays) of elements. Second, it can speed up your computations if your hardware resources and program logic allow you to perform computations for many items simultaneously. This is typically much faster than processing the same array item by item. It won't usually be faster than a manually vectorized version (though it won't be significantly slower either). Still, it will be much faster in another dimension: the developer's productivity and time to vectorize a function by hand.

In high-performance computing and deep learning, it is typical to have batches of elements you want to process simultaneously. Mini-batch gradient descent is built upon this idea. All the matrix multiplications inside the neural networks' forward and backward passes are organized so that multiple elements can be processed at once. Otherwise, processing would be too inefficient. So it is essential to use vectorization.

We start with a few concrete examples with simple functions to demonstrate auto-vectorization so you can obtain the intuition behind it. In the second section, we look deeper at different aspects of auto-vectorization. Finally, the third section contains several real-life examples where auto-vectorization helps.

6.1 Different ways to vectorize a function

We have already touched on the topic of auto-vectorization and using `vmap()` in chapter 2. Let me remind you of the idea behind it.

You frequently have a function to process a single element—to process a single data point, to apply a filter to an image, to apply a neural network for a single element of data, and so on. Figure 6.1 depicts the case of a dot product function processing a pair of vectors. Numbers in parentheses are tuples with data shapes.

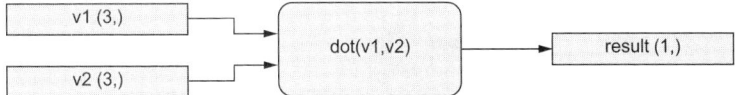

Figure 6.1 Function for processing a single pair of vectors

In all of these cases, you might want to apply the same function to an array of elements or a batch—to process many data points in a data loader, apply a filter to multiple images at once, or apply a neural network to a batch of data. Figure 6.2 depicts a function processing arrays of vectors.

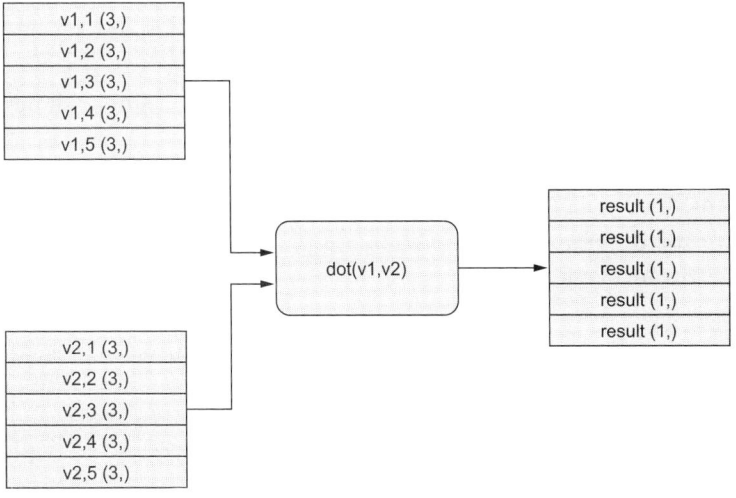

Figure 6.2 Function for processing arrays of vectors

Here we will discuss how to transition from a function applied to a single element to a function applied to an array (or batch) of elements. Let's start with a simple function calculating a dot product between two vectors (or rank-1 tensors with the type of `Array`, to be precise).

Listing 6.1   A function for calculating a dot product between two vectors

```
def dot(v1, v2):
  return jnp.vdot(v1, v2)          ◄────── Uses the vdot() function

dot(jnp.array([1., 1., 1.]), jnp.array([1., 2., -1]))    ◄─── Calculates the dot
                                                              product between
>>> Array(2., dtype=float32)                                  two vectors
```

The function is elementary; it just calculates a dot product between a pair of vectors.

Now suppose instead of two vectors, you have two lists of vectors (JAX functions do not work with Python lists, so here we actually assume an `Array` that contains a "list" of vectors; technically, it's an `Array` with an additional dimension or a rank-2 tensor in our case), and you need to calculate a `list` of dot products between the corresponding elements of these two input lists.

Listing 6.2   Generating two lists of vectors

```
                                        Creates a random number
                                        generator key (more on          Generates a
                                        that in chapter 9)              two-dimensional
rng_key = random.PRNGKey(42)    ◄───┘                                   array of random
                                                                       numbers
vs = random.normal(rng_key, shape=(20,3))    ◄─────────────────────┘

v1s = vs[:10,:]          │ Splits this array into two parts; the first 10 go to the
v2s = vs[10:,:]          │ first list, and the second 10 go to the second list.
```

There are different ways to get what you want. You can apply what I call the naive approaches that may (or may not) work, which are usually inefficient. You can manually rewrite the function to work on arrays (to vectorize it). Or you can rely on automatic vectorization that converts a function working on a single element into a function working on an array of elements. Let's cover all these approaches.

6.1.1   *Naive approaches*

First, there are two different naive approaches; they are the most straightforward but not necessarily the most efficient.

FIRST NAIVE APPROACH

The first naive approach is to pass arrays to the original function without changing anything. Broadly speaking, there are three possible outcomes:

- You may get what you want. This happens because NumPy may use broadcasting (https://mng.bz/o04M) and universal functions (ufuncs) (https://mng.bz/n0EK) to vectorize array operations. If you used the `selu()` activation function from the previous chapter (or almost any other activation function), you had a good chance that a function designed to work on a single element would automatically work on an array of elements. This is a good case, and it happens, but you cannot depend on that happening every time.

- You may get an error if your function is designed in a way that broadcasting and ufuncs (universal functions) cannot help you. This is also a good case, even if it returns an error. At least you know immediately that something is wrong, and you can fix it.

- You may get some result (I mean without any error) that is incorrect and is not what you want. This is really bad, because you may think that everything is okay and your program works, but the results are not what they should be. If the result is used for other calculations, which also use broadcasting and automatic type conversions, it might go unnoticed for a long time until you (hopefully) finally understand that you are getting strange results.

With our function, we are in the third (bad) case. We may detect that something is wrong with the result's shape, as it is just a single number instead of an array of dot products.

Listing 6.3 Naively applying the function to two lists of vectors

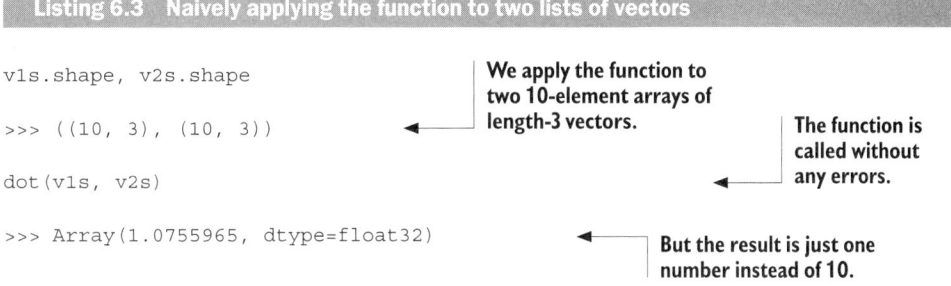

```
v1s.shape, v2s.shape
>>> ((10, 3), (10, 3))
dot(v1s, v2s)
>>> Array(1.0755965, dtype=float32)
```

We apply the function to two 10-element arrays of length-3 vectors.

The function is called without any errors.

But the result is just one number instead of 10.

Here, we got one number instead of 10 pairwise dot products. The error may go unnoticed if we use this result in subsequent calculations without any checks. For example, you might use dot products as weights to scale some other items, and with broadcasting, all the subsequent multiplications may go without errors as well, so you might think that everything is okay.

These types of errors are particularly hard to notice; they may manifest only in the lower-than-expected quality of your algorithm. So I prefer not to use this error-prone approach or at least have additional checks that the result seems to be correct (at least by shape).

Second naive approach

The second naive approach is to apply the function to each input element from the array and then gather all the results into a new array.

Listing 6.4   Naively generating results one item at a time

```
[dot(v1s[i],v2s[i]) for i in range(v1s.shape[0])]
```

We apply the function elementwise in a Python list comprehension.

```
>>> [Array(-0.9443626, dtype=float32),
>>>  Array(0.8561607, dtype=float32),
>>>  Array(-0.45202938, dtype=float32),
>>>  Array(0.7629303, dtype=float32),
>>>  Array(-2.06525, dtype=float32),
>>>  Array(0.5056444, dtype=float32),
>>>  Array(-0.5623387, dtype=float32),
>>>  Array(1.5973439, dtype=float32),
>>>  Array(1.7121218, dtype=float32),
>>>  Array(-0.33462408, dtype=float32)]
```

The result has an (almost) expected shape of 10 items.

Here, we get almost the expected result. But there are two caveats: a fairly insignificant one and a significant one.

The fairly insignificant caveat is that you get a Python list of `Arrays`, not a single `Array` with a multidimensional array inside. You likely want to use it in another computation. Still, as you might remember from section 3.2.2, JAX deliberately chooses not to accept lists or tuples as inputs to its functions because that can lead to silent performance degradation, which is hard to detect. So you will need to convert this list to some other structure.

The significant caveat is the same as the reason for not accepting lists in JAX functions: performance degradation. This approach is simple but usually inefficient. We will compare its speed with the speed of vectorized approaches soon.

6.1.2 *Manual vectorization*

The standard way to overcome the inefficiencies of the naive approach is to rewrite and manually vectorize your single-element function to accept batches of data at its input. This usually means our input tensors will have an additional batch dimension, and we need to rewrite the calculations to use it. It is straightforward for simple calculations, but it can be complicated for sophisticated functions.

Here we will use a very powerful function from the NumPy interface called `einsum()`. We touch on it in appendix D when talking about `xmap()`. For now, just consider it an option to make our function vectorized.

Listing 6.5   Manually vectorizing the function

```
def dot_vectorized(v1s, v2s):
    return jnp.einsum('ij,ij->i',v1s, v2s)

dot_vectorized(v1s, v2s)
```

We have rewritten our function to support arrays as inputs.

```
>>> Array([-0.9443626 ,  0.8561607 , -0.45202938,  0.7629303 ,
>>>        -2.06525   ,  0.5056444 , -0.5623387 ,  1.5973439 ,
>>>         1.7121218 , -0.33462408], dtype=float32)
```

The result is as expected.

Here, the approach worked perfectly well, and we got the result with the shape we needed. The einsum() solution is not the only one, and we could use other approaches to write a vectorized version of our function. But the common basis for all these approaches is that we usually have to rewrite the function to support it. For more complex functions, it might be much harder, and in many cases, this process is error prone.

6.1.3 *Automatic vectorization*

JAX provides an alternative called *automatic vectorization*. The vmap() transformation transforms a function able to work with a single element into a function able to work on batches (see figure 6.3).

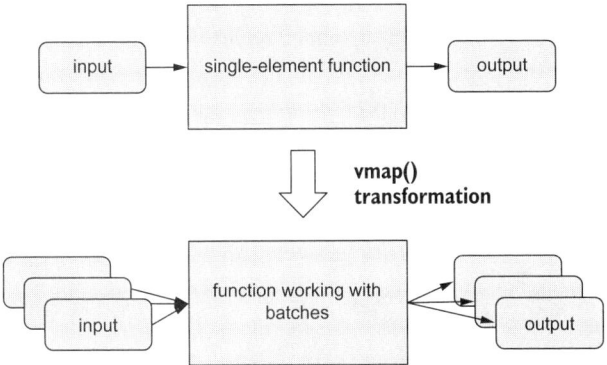

Figure 6.3 **Transforming a function for a single element into a function for batches of elements with the** vmap() **transformation**

In code, it is very straightforward.

Listing 6.6 Automatically vectorizing the function

```
dot_vmapped = jax.vmap(dot)

dot_vmapped(v1s, v2s)
```

The vmap() transformation has created another function that supports arrays as inputs.

```
>>> Array([-0.9443626 ,  0.8561607 , -0.45202938,  0.7629303 ,
>>>          2.06525   ,  0.5056444 , -0.5623387 ,  1.5973439 ,
>>>          1.7121218 , -0.33462408], dtype=float32)
```

The result is as expected.

The beauty of this approach is that we didn't change the original function and got the desired result.

The benefit I particularly like is that your code is typically more straightforward and easier to understand. That's a big deal in computer science because most code requires maintenance, and others must read and understand it. The code for processing a single element is typically intuitive to understand, while manually vectorized code is frequently heavily optimized and hard to grasp. So other people maintaining your code either spend more time trying to understand it or make errors while changing it because they misunderstood it.

Our example with `einsum()` is not hard to understand unless you have no idea about this function. And you may face really beautiful examples of manual vectorization, but I bet that is not typical.

Now that we have several implementations, let's compare how they behave and perform.

6.1.4   Speed comparisons

As we mentioned, naive approaches may provide a straightforward solution. However, this solution might have some drawbacks.

Here, we have two time-related metrics important to us: the time to develop a solution and the time to execute the computation. With the time to develop a solution, it's almost clear: automatic vectorization is simpler than arranging a loop and also, in our case, is simpler than even keeping the function unchanged; in this case, we need much more time to understand what is wrong and finally write a correct solution. Compared to manual vectorization, it is also much faster to develop.

Let's check the second time-related metric, the speed of all the approaches.

Listing 6.7   Comparing the speed of different approaches

```
                                                          Don't forget about
                                                          asynchronous dispatch!

%timeit [dot(v1s[i],v2s[i]).block_until_ready() for i in range(v1s.shape[0])] ◄

>>> 4.58 ms ± 152 µs per loop                    The naive approach is
(mean ± std. dev. of 7 runs, 100 loops each)     the slowest one.

%timeit dot_vectorized(v1s, v2s).block_until_ready()

>>> 91.9 µs ± 20 µs per loop                     The manually vectorized function
(mean ± std. dev. of 7 runs, 10000 loops each)   has great performance.

%timeit dot_vmapped(v1s, v2s).block_until_ready()

>>> 831 µs ± 7.7 µs per loop                      The automatically vectorized
(mean ± std. dev. of 7 runs, 1000 loops each)     function is slower but still very fast.

dot_vectorized_jitted = jax.jit(dot_vectorized)   JIT-ting both
dot_vmapped_jitted = jax.jit(dot_vmapped)          vectorized functions

# warm-up
dot_vectorized_jitted(v1s, v2s);
dot_vmapped_jitted(v1s, v2s);

%timeit dot_vectorized_jitted(v1s, v2s).block_until_ready()
```

```
>>> 6.93 µs ± 194 ns per loop
(mean ± std. dev. of 7 runs, 100000 loops each)

%timeit dot_vmapped_jitted(v1s, v2s).block_until_ready()

>>> 7.6 µs ± 1.42 µs per loop
(mean ± std. dev. of 7 runs, 100000 loops each)
```

After JIT-ting, the speeds of manually and automatically vectorized solutions are much closer.

As you can see, the naive approach is very slow and inefficient. The manually vectorized function delivers the best performance, and the automatically vectorized function is a bit slower yet still an order of magnitude faster than the naive approach. After JIT-compiling both solutions, their speeds become similar, with the automatically vectorized one slightly slower (however, their confidence intervals intersect, so we cannot say for sure).

Let's look at the internals and generate `jaxprs` of these functions.

Listing 6.8 The resulting `jaxprs`

```
jax.make_jaxpr(dot)(jnp.array([1., 1., 1.]

      jnp.array([1., 1., -1]))
>>> { lambda ; a:f32[3] b:f32[3]. let
>>>     c:f32[] = dot_general[
>>>        dimension_numbers=(([0], [0]), ([], []))
>>>        preferred_element_type=float32
>>>     ] a b
>>>   in (c,) }
```

Jaxpr of the original non-vectorized function

```
jax.make_jaxpr(dot_vectorized)(v1s, v2s)

>>> { lambda ; a:f32[10,3] b:f32[10,3]. let
>>>     c:f32[10] = dot_general[
>>>        dimension_numbers=(([1], [1]), ([0], [0]))
>>>        preferred_element_type=float32
>>>     ] a b
>>>   in (c,) }
```

The manually vectorized function

```
jax.make_jaxpr(dot_vmapped)(v1s, v2s)

>>> { lambda ; a:f32[10,3] b:f32[10,3]. let
>>>     c:f32[10] = dot_general[
>>>        dimension_numbers=(([1], [1]), ([0], [0]))
>>>        preferred_element_type=float32
>>>     ] a b
>>>   in (c,) }
```

The automatically vectorized function

As you can see, the original non-vectorized function uses the `dot_general()` function from `jax.lax` (https://mng.bz/vJrM).

Both `einsum()` and `vmap()`-ped versions have the same code calling the `dot_general()` function. This solution has no loops, and the generated code is efficient.

6.2 Controlling vmap() behavior

While basic use of the `vmap()` transformation is pretty straightforward, there are many cases when you need more fine-grained control. For example, your arrays might be arranged differently, with a batch dimension not being the first. Or you may use more complex structures as function parameters—for example, a `dict`. The `vmap()` provides useful ways to deal with different tensor structures.

6.2.1 Controlling array axes to map over

You can control which array axes to map over. For this, the `vmap()` function has a parameter called `in_axes`. This parameter can be an integer, `None`, or a (possibly nested) standard Python container such as a `tuple`, `list`, or `dict`.

If the `in_axes` parameter is an integer (the default value is 0), then the array axis specified by this number is used to map over all the function arguments. In our example in listing 6.6, we did not explicitly use this parameter, so the function was mapped over the first axis (with index 0) for each argument, and the batch dimension was the dimension with index 0.

Suppose you need to use a different index for different parameters. In that case, you can use a tuple of integers and `None`s with a length equal to the number of positional arguments of the original function. The `None` value means we do not map over this particular parameter. The general rule is the `in_axes` structure should correspond to the structure of the associated inputs.

The `vmap()` call from listing 6.6 is equivalent to the following listing.

Listing 6.9 Using the `in_axes` parameter

```
dot_vmapped = jax.vmap(dot, in_axes=(0,0))
```
◄——— This is equivalent to skipping the in_axes parameter in our example.

Figure 6.4 depicts two transposed arrays where vectors are arranged across the horizontal dimension of the tensor.

If you want to map over transposed arrays, as depicted in figure 6.4, you might use the `in_axes=(1,1)` value.

Let's consider an even more complex case with different axes and axes that do not have to be mapped over. We added a new parameter called `koeff` to our dot product function. It calculates the same dot product as before, but now it is multiplied by a factor passed as a separate parameter. The arrays you want this function to apply to are structured differently: the first one is the same as before, but the second is a transposed version of the original one, with the batch dimension now being with index 1. This may happen naturally if you process different data sources with the data arranged differently.

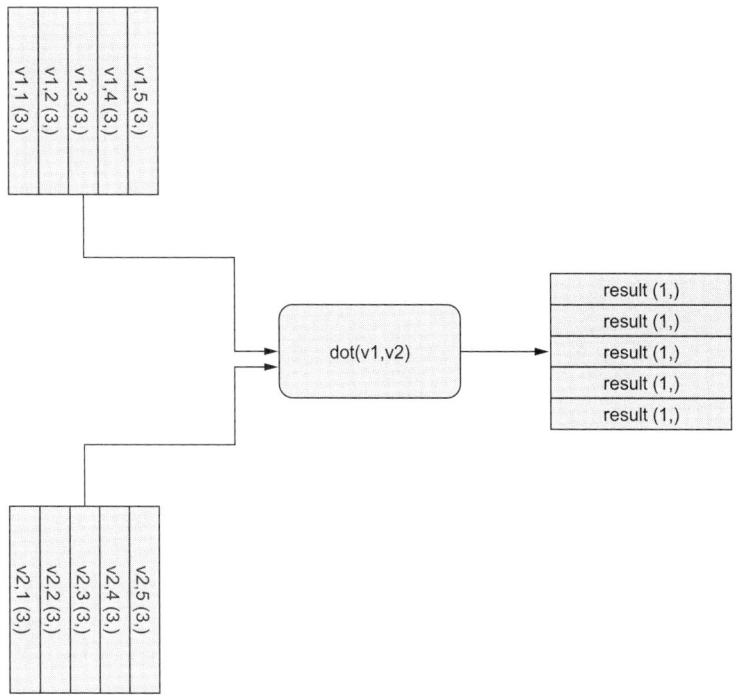

Figure 6.4 Function for processing transposed arrays of vectors

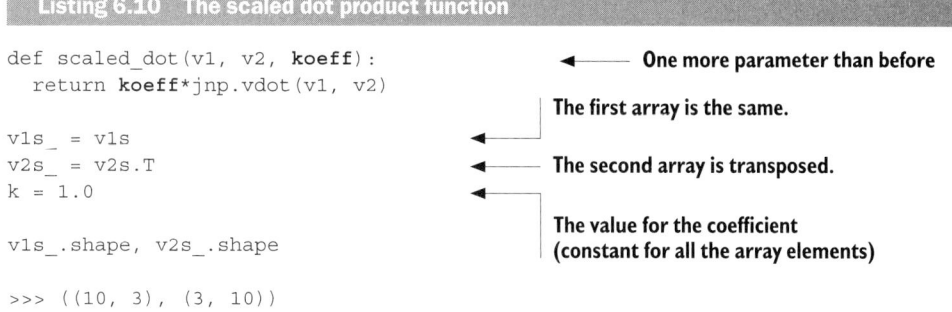

```
def scaled_dot(v1, v2, koeff):          ◄──── One more parameter than before
  return koeff*jnp.vdot(v1, v2)

                                        The first array is the same.
v1s_ = v1s                              ◄───┘
v2s_ = v2s.T                            ◄──── The second array is transposed.
k = 1.0                                 ◄───
                                        The value for the coefficient
v1s_.shape, v2s_.shape                  (constant for all the array elements)

>>> ((10, 3), (3, 10))
```

In such a case, you may want to transform the data to have everything in the same lay-out. Alternatively, you may skip this step (and possibly reduce the number of compu-tations, though hardly significantly) and let the batched function know that the input arrays are organized differently. This new array structure and the scaled_dot() func-tion can be depicted as shown in figure 6.5.

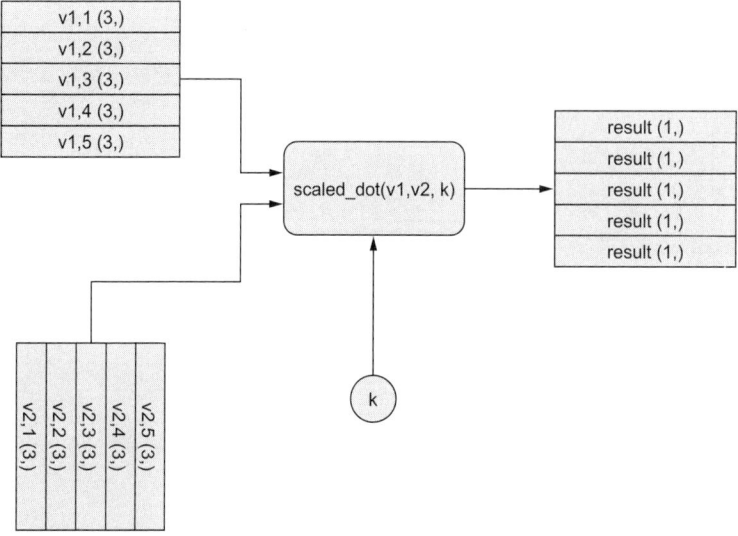

Figure 6.5   Function for the scaled dot product

Now, you want to apply this function to the arrays with the help of vmap(). To deal with this argument's structure, you have to pass the in_axes parameter with a tuple describing what axis to map over for each argument.

Listing 6.11   Using the `in_axes` parameter for dissimilar arguments

```
scaled_dot_batched = jax.vmap(scaled_dot, in_axes=(0,1,None))    ◄───┐ Passing in_axes
                                                                     │ parameter with
scaled_dot_batched(v1s_, v2s_, k)                                    │ a tuple

>>> Array([-0.9443626 ,   0.8561607 , -0.45202938,   0.7629303 ,
>>>             -2.06525   ,   0.5056444 , -0.5623387 ,   1.5973439 ,
>>>            1.7121218 , -0.33462408], dtype=float32)
```

Here we have asked the vmap() transformation to iterate over the axis with index 0 for the first parameter, to iterate over the axis with index 1 for the second one, and not to iterate over the third parameter, which contains just a scalar, not an array.

The in_axes parameter may also be a standard Python container, possibly nested.

Listing 6.12   Using the `in_axes` parameter with a Python container

```
def scaled_dot(data, koeff):                      ◄───┐ Now the function consumes
  return koeff*jnp.vdot(data['a'], data['b'])         │ a dict and a scalar.

scaled_dot_batched=jax.vmap(scaled_dot,
  in_axes=({'a':0,'b':1},None))                   ◄───┐ Marks axes for the dict
                                                       │ and the scalar parameters
scaled_dot_batched({'a':v1s_, 'b': v2s_}, k)
```

```
>>> Array([-0.9443626 ,  0.8561607 , -0.45202938,  0.7629303 ,
>>>          -2.06525   ,  0.5056444 , -0.5623387 ,  1.5973439 ,
>>>           1.7121218 , -0.33462408], dtype=float32)
```

Here, we have passed a tuple with a `dict` and a scalar, which match the function parameters. The `dict` specifies mapping axes for each element and corresponds to the first function parameter, and the scalar (here, `None`) specifies mapping for the second function parameter.

6.2.2 Controlling output array axes

You can also control the output layout if it has more than one dimension and you need your batch dimension to be not the leading one. Maybe it's just because the next function in the pipeline wants its input data in this format.

Say we have a function to scale a vector with a coefficient, and we want the output to be transposed compared to the input vector layout, as depicted in the figure 6.6.

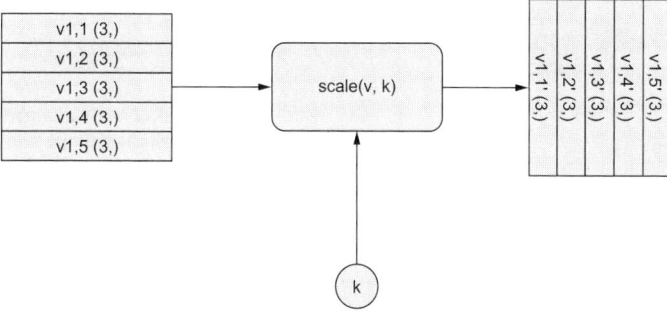

Figure 6.6 **Function to scale and transpose vectors**

There is an `out_axes` parameter for this.

> **Listing 6.13   Using the `out_axes` parameter**

```
def scale(v, koeff):              ◀──── A simple function to scale a vector
  return koeff*v

scale_batched = jax.vmap(scale,        Specifies batch
                  in_axes=(0,None),  ◀── dimensions for the input
                  out_axes=(1))      ◀──
                                       Specifies batch dimension
scale_batched(v1s, 2.0)                for the output

>>> Array([[-1.4672383 , -1.6510035 ,  3.5308602 , -2.2189112 ,  0.3024418 ,
>>>          0.7649379 , -4.028754  , -3.0968533 ,  0.34476107, -2.9087348 ],
>>>        [-1.5357308 , -0.7061183 ,  4.0082793 , -0.69232166, -3.2186441 ,
>>>          2.0812016 ,  3.585087  ,  0.15288436,  2.0001278 ,  2.0246687 ],
>>>        [-1.6228952 ,  1.5497094 , -3.2013843 ,  0.50127184, -0.2000112 ,
>>>          1.6244346 ,  0.17156784, -1.3113307 , -2.532448  , -1.60574   ]],
>>>        dtype=float32)
```

Here, our function returns a scaled vector, and the batched version returns an array of scaled vectors. Note that we want the returned array to be transposed, and the batch dimension should be the dimension with the index 1, not 0. Sometimes it might help you avoid additional transformations and achieve your needs with just vmap().

6.2.3   *Using named arguments*

Sometimes your functions use named arguments instead of purely positional ones. Functions with named arguments are easier to read, and it's harder to make an error calling such functions by mixing up values from different parameters.

There is an important thing to know about arguments passed as keywords: they are always mapped over their leading axis (with index 0). Otherwise, you may get unexpected error messages.

Let's use the same scale() function from the previous example but make its second parameter the named argument, which is natural for this particular function. After this change, the preceding code will fail.

```
Listing 6.14   Using named arguments

def scale(v, koeff=1.0):          ◄────┐ Makes koeff a named argument
  return koeff*v                        │ with the default value

scale_batched = jax.vmap(scale,
                         in_axes=(0,None),
                         out_axes=(1))
                                       ┌─ Calls the function with the
scale_batched(v1s, koeff=2.0)     ◄────┘ named parameter

>>> …                             ◄──── Gets some strange error
>>> ValueError: vmap in_axes specification must be
a tree prefix of the corresponding value, got
specification (0, None) for value tree PyTreeDef((*,)).
>>> …

scale_batched = jax.vmap(scale,
                         in_axes=(0),      ◄────┐ Fixes in_axes as it works for
                         out_axes=(1))           │ positional arguments only

scale_batched(v1s, koeff=2.0)

>>> …                             ◄──── Gets some new strange error
>>> ValueError: vmap was requested to map its argument
along axis 0, which implies that its rank should be
at least 1, but is only 0 (its shape is ())
>>> …
```

We get some strange error because the in_axes parameter is made for positional arguments, not named (or keyword) arguments. It seems an easy fix to change the in_axes parameter from (0,None) to (0) to reflect the change in positional and named arguments. However, it does not help, and we get another strange error. In this case, `vmap()` tried to map over the parameter that does not have a dimension to map. It is precisely the `koeff` parameter, and, as we mentioned, named parameters are always mapped over their leading axis.

There are several ways to deal with it. You can switch back to positional parameters. You can also make a wrapper function that hides this parameter. Or you can broadcast the named parameter into an array with the required dimension to map over. We will demonstrate the last two approaches.

Listing 6.15 Changing code to work with named arguments

```
from functools import partial

scale2 = partial(scale, koeff=2.0)           Makes a partial function with a
                                             fixed koeff parameter value

scale_batched = jax.vmap(scale2,
                         in_axes=(0),         We map over one
                         out_axes=(1))        positional parameter.


scale_batched(v1s)

>>> Array([[-1.4672383 , -1.6510035 ,  3.5308602 , -2.2189112 ,  0.3024418 ,
>>>          0.7649379 , -4.028754  , -3.0968533 ,  0.34476107, -2.9087348 ],
>>>        [-1.5357308 , -0.7061183 ,  4.0082793 , -0.69232166, -3.2186441 ,
>>>          2.0812016 ,  3.585087  ,  0.15288436,  2.0001278 ,  2.0246687 ],
>>>        [-1.6228952 ,  1.5497094 , -3.2013843 ,  0.50127184, -0.2000112 ,
>>>          1.6244346 ,  0.17156784, -1.3113307 , -2.532448  , -1.60574   ]],
>>>        dtype=float32)                      Now it works and produces
                                               correct results.

scale_batched = jax.vmap(scale,               Uses the old function with a
                         in_axes=(0),          positional and named parameter
                         out_axes=(1))


scale_batched(v1s, koeff=jnp.broadcast_to(2.0, (v1s.shape[0],)))

>>> Array([[-1.4672383 , -1.6510035 ,  3.5308602 , -2.2189112 ,  0.3024418 ,
>>>          0.7649379 , -4.028754  , -3.0968533 ,  0.34476107, -2.9087348 ],
>>>        [-1.5357308 , -0.7061183 ,  4.0082793 , -0.69232166, -3.2186441 ,
>>>          2.0812016 ,  3.585087  ,  0.15288436,  2.0001278 ,  2.0246687 ],
>>>        [-1.6228952 ,  1.5497094 , -3.2013843 ,  0.50127184, -0.2000112 ,
>>>          1.6244346 ,  0.17156784, -1.3113307 , -2.532448  , -1.60574   ]],
>>>        dtype=float32)
```

It works and produces correct results.

Before calling the function, we change the named parameter to have an axis to map.

Here, we made a new function with the help of the standard Python partial object, which gives us a function with the fixed `koeff` parameter value (alternatively, we can write a function wrapper ourselves). With this function, everything now works.

In another approach, we kept an old function and made the keyword parameter an array with an axis to map over. We fill this array with the same value of the coefficient we want to use (using the standard `broadcast_to()` function from the NumPy API). With this approach, we also get correct results.

6.2.4   *Using decorator style*

As with many other functional transformations, you can use `vmap()` with decorators. Depending on the situation, it may give you clearer code without temporary functions.

Here, we rewrite the `scale()` function from listing 6.13 using a decorator.

Listing 6.16   Using a decorator

```
from functools import partial                          ◄─── Imports standard Python
                                                             functools module
@partial(jax.vmap, in_axes=(0,None), out_axes=(1))    ◄─┐  Moves vmap call to
def scale(v, koeff):                                     │  the decorator
  return koeff*v

scale(vls, 2.0)

>>> Array([[-1.4672383 , -1.6510035 ,  3.5308602 , -2.2189112 ,  0.3024418 ,
>>>          0.7649379 , -4.028754  , -3.0968533 ,  0.34476107, -2.9087348 ],
>>>        [-1.5357308 , -0.7061183 ,  4.0082793 , -0.69232166, -3.2186441 ,
>>>          2.0812016 ,  3.585087  ,  0.15288436,  2.0001278 ,  2.0246687 ],
>>>        [-1.6228952 ,  1.5497094 , -3.2013843 ,  0.50127184, -0.2000112 ,
>>>          1.6244346 ,  0.17156784, -1.3113307 , -2.532448  , -1.60574   ]],
>>>       dtype=float32)                               ◄─── It works and produces
                                                            correct results.
```

Here, we moved a separate `vmap()` call with its parameters into a decorator and removed an extra functional object.

It is useful if you do not need the function working with a single element alone, and the bached function is the only thing you care about. This way, decorators help you write simple code for processing a single element and automatically transform it into code suitable for batches of elements.

6.2.5   *Using collective operations*

Suppose you write code that needs communication between different elements of a batch (this is the same as when you parallel your computations across devices and need to pass information between the devices). In that case, JAX provides collective operations (or collective ops) (https://mng.bz/4pqV). These are typically the operations with the prefix `jax.lax.p*`.

These ops are mainly used for parallelization (which is the topic of the next chapter) for communicating across devices and were designed for `pmap()`. However, they also work with `vmap()`, and they may be a very handy solution if you implement something like batch normalization when you need to calculate batch statistics and modify batch elements.

Collective ops work the following way:

- When you vectorize calculations with `vmap()` along some axis, you may specify the name of this axis using the `axis_name` argument. Here, you may pass any name you want to use, and that helps you to distinguish this axis from possibly other axes. It is just a string label.

- You may refer to the named axis inside a collective op using the same `axis_name` argument. The operation will be performed across the named axis.

Let's consider a simple case of normalizing array values so they sum to 1. We can do it as shown in the following listing.

Listing 6.17 Using collective ops and `axis_name`

```
arr = jnp.array(range(50))          ◄──  Generates an array
arr                                        for illustration

>>> Array([ 0,  1,  2,  3,  4,  5,  6,  7,  8,  9, 10,
>>>        11, 12, 13, 14, 15, 16, 17, 18, 19, 20,
>>>        21, 22, 23, 24, 25, 26, 27, 28, 29, 30,
>>>        31, 32, 33, 34, 35, 36, 37, 38, 39, 40,
>>>        41, 42, 43, 44, 45, 46, 47, 48, 49],       ◄── Uses psum() op with
>>>        dtype=int32)                                    axis_name='batch'

norm = jax.vmap(                                       ◄── Uses axis_name='batch'
    lambda x: x/jax.lax.psum(x, axis_name='batch'),  ◄──    in vmap()
    axis_name='batch')                               ◄──

norm(arr)                            ◄──  Applies our normalization function

>>> Array([0.      , 0.00081633, 0.00163265, 0.00244898, 0.00326531,
>>>        0.00408163, 0.00489796, 0.00571429, 0.00653061, 0.00734694,
>>>        0.00816326, 0.00897959, 0.00979592, 0.01061224, 0.01142857,
>>>        0.0122449 , 0.01306122, 0.01387755, 0.01469388, 0.0155102 ,
>>>        0.01632653, 0.01714286, 0.01795918, 0.01877551, 0.01959184,
>>>        0.02040816, 0.02122449, 0.02204082, 0.02285714, 0.02367347,
>>>        0.0244898 , 0.02530612, 0.02612245, 0.02693878, 0.0277551 ,
>>>        0.02857143, 0.02938776, 0.03020408, 0.03102041, 0.03183673,
>>>        0.03265306, 0.03346939, 0.03428571, 0.03510204, 0.03591837,
>>>        0.03673469, 0.03755102, 0.03836735, 0.03918367, 0.04      ],
>>>        dtype=float32)

jnp.sum(norm(arr))                   ◄──  Checks normalized
                                          values
>>> Array(1., dtype=float32)
```

Here we have marked the axis across which we vectorized our calculations with `axis_name='batch'` in the `vmap()` arguments.

Inside the vectorized function, we use a simple expression `x/jax.lax.psum(x, axis_name='batch')`, where x is the current element of a batch being processed, and `jax.lax.psum(x, axis_name='batch')` performs an all-reduce sum over the mapped axis `axis_name`. So `psum()` returns the sum of the values across the batch dimension, and the function divides the current element by this sum. This effectively normalizes each element so that its sum is 1.0.

There are other collective ops like `pmin()` and `pmax()` for minimum and maximum, `pmean()` for calculating mean value, `all_gather()` for gathering values across all replicas, and some other useful ops (https://mng.bz/XVWM) you may want to use.

With an understanding of auto-vectorization basics, let's apply our knowledge to a couple of already-known real-life cases.

6.3   *Real-life use cases for vmap()*

There are many cases where you might want to use auto-vectorization. I highlight several typical cases where you might benefit from `vmap()`.

The previous examples mainly targeted the batch data processing case to process a batch of elements with a function designed to process a single element. However, many cases can be reduced to this general pattern at some level; there are semantically different cases you will face for which `vmap()` can be very helpful. Let's start with the already known case, extend it a bit, and then cover some other use cases for `vmap()`.

6.3.1   *Batch data processing*

This is probably the most straightforward case. You have a function to process a single element of anything (say, one image), and then you want to apply this function to a batch of elements. If you are not getting each item separately but receive (or at least can receive) them in batches, using `vmap()` is a no-brainer.

The only caveat here is that items should not communicate with each other, which is indeed a frequent case. It might not easily work when you have some sort of normalization that requires batch statistics or any running calculations beyond each separate element.

This case applies to data augmentations as well. You may have several functions for performing different augmentations and may decide which one (or any combination) to apply to any particular element. The `jax.lax` control flow primitives can be helpful here.

Consider the model case of applying random augmentations from chapter 3.

Listing 6.18   Augmenting a single element of data

```
add_noise_func = lambda x: x+10
horizontal_flip_func = lambda x: x+1
rotate_func = lambda x: x+2
adjust_colors_func = lambda x: x+3

augmentations = [
```

A list of four stub functions for image processing (just for illustration purposes)

```
    add_noise_func,
    horizontal_flip_func,
    rotate_func,
    adjust_colors_func
]
```

A list of four stub functions for image processing (just for illustration purposes)

A function to apply a random transformation from the set of available ones

```
def random_augmentation(image, augmentations, rng_key):
    '''A function that applies a random transformation to an image'''
    augmentation_index = random.randint(
      key=rng_key, minval=0, maxval=len(augmentations), shape=())
    augmented_image = lax.switch(augmentation_index, augmentations, image)
    return augmented_image
```

Some stub data

```
image = jnp.array(range(100))
augmented_image = random_augmentation(image, augmentations, random.PRNGKey(211))
```

Applies a random transformation

Here, a function `random_augmentation()` accepts an image to augment, a list of augmentation functions to choose from, and a key (or state) for the random number generator (more on random numbers in chapter 9). The function uses `lax.switch` for choosing a random image augmentation among multiple options.

To apply this function for a batch of images, we need to use a different random number generator key for each call (otherwise, each call will use the same key, generate the same random number, and apply the same transformation). Besides that, the application of the `vmap()` is pretty straightforward, and you only have to take care of the `in_axes` argument to mark arrays that contain a batch dimension.

Listing 6.19   Augmenting multiple elements of data

```
images = jnp.repeat(
  jnp.reshape(image, (1,len(image))),
  10, axis=0)

images.shape

>>> (10, 100)

rng_keys = random.split(random.PRNGKey(211), num=len(images))

random_augmentation_batch = jax.vmap(
  random_augmentation, in_axes=(0,None,0))

augmented_images = random_augmentation_batch(
  images, augmentations, rng_keys)
```

Generates a batch of stub data

Generates an array of random number generator keys

Auto-vectorizes the function

Applies the vectorized function to a batch

Here, we let `vmap()` know that images are batched along the first dimension of the image tensor, the list of augmentations is not batched and remains the same for every call, and random number generator keys are also provided in a batch. This might not be the most efficient implementation as it makes sense to move random number generation outside of the function and provide just an array of random numbers instead of keys. Still, I'll leave it for your exercise to rewrite the function and measure its performance. This way, you can further build a pipeline for data augmentation, adding meaningful functions and making augmentation logic more complex.

6.3.2 *Batching neural network models*

This is another straightforward case analogous to the previous one in many aspects. But first I highlight a couple of things.

There is a huge advantage for developers: they may write simpler code and not worry about the batch dimension. Such code is usually much easier to understand (and modify) than manually vectorized code. And you still have almost all the benefits of fully vectorized code, including its high performance.

We have already used `vmap()` for such neural network training in section 2.4. Here, I reproduce the relevant code from chapter 2.

Listing 6.20   Batching neural network predictions

```python
import jax.numpy as jnp
from jax.nn import swish
from jax import vmap

def predict(params, image):                          ◄─────  Function for per-example
  """Function for per-example predictions."""                predictions
  activations = image
  for w, b in params[:-1]:
    outputs = jnp.dot(w, activations) + b
    activations = swish(outputs)

  final_w, final_b = params[-1]
  logits = jnp.dot(final_w, activations) + final_b
  return logits                                              Creates a function that
                                                             works with batches of
batched_predict = vmap(predict, in_axes=(None, 0))  ◄──┘    images
```

We have an easily understandable function for a single-item prediction; then, we create a batched version of the function using the `vmap()` transformation. It is easy to write a batched function for such a simple example manually, but it can be impractical for more complex cases.

But there is a caveat. Many modern models use batch statistics and/or state inside a model. For example, that's the case for the well-known batch norm (or batch normalization). In such cases, you are not in the mode "write a single-item function; then apply `vmap` to it." And it might not be so straightforward to use `vmap()` with your models.

We will return to more complex neural networks later in the book when we dive into the Flax high-level neural network framework. Suppose you build complex neural networks from scratch using pure JAX. In that case, you may want to use collective ops from section 6.2.3 to implement interaction between batch elements or vectorize your code manually.

6.3.3 *Per-sample gradients*

The case related to neural network training is obtaining per-sample gradients, as discussed in section 4.2.3. In cases when you need per-sample gradients and at the same time do not want to lose the performance of batch processing, JAX provides an easy way to do it:

1 Create a function for making a per-sample prediction, say, `predict(model_params, x)`.

2 Create a loss function to evaluate a single prediction, say, `loss_fn(model_parameters, x, y)`.

3 Create a function for calculating gradients for per-sample prediction with the `grad()` transformation using `grad(loss_fn)`.

4 Make a batched version of the gradient calculating function with the `vmap()` transformation, obtaining `vmap(grad(loss_fn))`. You couldn't do it the other way—first getting a vectorized loss function and then taking the gradient of it—because the loss is always a scalar value, and `grad()` will return an error if you apply it to a vector-valued function. We actually did it previously, but back then, we didn't need per-item losses and aggregated them inside the loss-calculating function, so it returned a single value for a batch, and taking the gradient of it worked.

5 Optionally, compile the resulting function with the `jit()` transformation to make it more efficient on the underlying hardware, finally obtaining `jit(vmap(grad(loss_fn)))(model_params, batch_x, batch_y)`.

This might be hard to achieve in other frameworks when gradient descent updates use batch-aggregated gradients and provide no easy way to extract per-sample gradients from the internals of the procedure. The following listing shows a tiny example of per-sample gradients for a linear regression problem we used in chapter 4.

Listing 6.21 Calculating per-sample gradients

```
from jax import grad, vmap, jit

x = jnp.linspace(0, 10*jnp.pi, num=1000)
e = 10.0*random.normal(random.PRNGKey(42), shape=x.shape)     Some noisy data for a
y = 65.0 + 1.8*x + 40*jnp.cos(x) + e                          regression problem

model_parameters = jnp.array([1., 1.])        A simple linear
def predict(theta, x):                        regression model
    w, b = theta
    return w * x + b
```

```
def loss_fn(model_parameters, x, y):
    prediction = predict(model_parameters, x)
    return (prediction-y)**2
```
Function to compute prediction error on a single example

```
grads_fn = jit(vmap(grad(loss_fn), in_axes=(None, 0, 0)))
```
Making a JIT-compiled batched version of the gradient calculating function

```
batch_x, batch_y = x[:32], y[:32]

grads_fn(model_parameters, batch_x, batch_y)
```

```
>>> Array([[    0.      , -213.84189 ],
>>>        [  -5.541931, -176.22874 ],
>>>        [ -11.923036, -189.57124 ],
>>> …
>>>        [-177.83148 , -182.41585 ]], dtype=float32)
```

We used a simple loss function applicable to a single example (previous versions of this loss function in chapter 4 used loss aggregation). Then we applied a sequence of transformations, first getting a gradien-calculating function, then auto-vectorizing it to be applicable for batches of data, and finally JIT-compiling it. Note how easy it is to combine transformations in JAX!

6.3.4   *Vectorizing loops*

Let's return to our example of image filters from chapter 3. We had the code in the following listing for the image processing functions there.

Listing 6.22   Applying matrix filters to an image

```
import jax.numpy as jnp
from jax.scipy.signal import convolve2d
from skimage.io import imread
from skimage.util import img_as_float32
from matplotlib import pyplot as plt
```
Imports everything we need

```
kernel_blur = jnp.ones((5,5))
kernel_blur /= jnp.sum(kernel_blur)
```
Prepares a kernel for the blur filter

```
def color_convolution(image, kernel):
  channels = []
  for i in range(3):
    color_channel = image[:,:,i]
    filtered_channel = convolve2d(color_channel, kernel, mode="same")
    filtered_channel = jnp.clip(filtered_channel, 0.0, 1.0)
    channels.append(filtered_channel)
  final_image = jnp.stack(channels, axis=2)
  return final_image
```
The function to apply a filter kernel to a color image

```
img = img_as_float32(imread('The_Cat.jpg'))
```
Loads a test image from the book's repo (or replaces it with your own image)

```
img_blur = color_convolution(img, kernel_blur)
```
Applies the filter to the image

```
plt.figure(figsize = (12,10))
plt.imshow(jnp.hstack((img_blur, img)))
```
Shows the result

The core of the example was the `color_convolution()` function, which applies a filter kernel to an image. A filter kernel is just a rectangular matrix of weights—in our case, a matrix of equal elements. This means that to produce a new pixel in the output image, every pixel of the neighborhood should be taken with the same weight. If you forgot the idea behind this image processing, refer to chapter 3.

The result is a filtered image—in our case, a blurred one at the left in figure 6.7. We used the same file from chapter 3, which is also available in the book's GitHub repository. Feel free to replace this image file with your own if you cannot access the repository.

Figure 6.7   Filtered and original images

Let's see where we can apply auto-vectorization for such image processing. If you think on a high level, there is an obvious use case of batch image processing—you may want to apply the same filter to many images. Or you may want to apply different filters to the same image. Obviously, you can also combine both. It is the most straightforward way of applying the `vmap()`, and we have already discussed it in section 6.3.1.

If you look deeper into the code, you will also notice another interesting place to apply `vmap()`: the internal loop along color channels inside the `color_convolution()` function. This loop is perfectly suited for automatic vectorization as it is already processing a tensor with a dedicated batch-like dimension—here, the color channel dimension—and each channel processing is done independently of any other channel.

Let's rewrite the `color_convolution()` function using `vmap()` instead of a loop.

Listing 6.23 Vectorizing the function

```
import jax.numpy as jnp
from jax.scipy.signal import convolve2d
from skimage.io import imread
from skimage.util import img_as_float32
from matplotlib import pyplot as plt

kernel_blur = jnp.ones((5,5))
kernel_blur /= jnp.sum(kernel_blur)

def matrix_filter(channel, kernel):
    filtered_channel = convolve2d(channel, kernel, mode="same")
    filtered_channel = jnp.clip(filtered_channel, 0.0, 1.0)
    return filtered_channel

color_convolution_vmap = jax.vmap(
  matrix_filter, in_axes=(2, None), out_axes=2)

img = img_as_float32(imread('The_Cat.jpg'))

img_blur = color_convolution_vmap(img, kernel_blur)

plt.figure(figsize = (12,10))
plt.imshow(jnp.hstack((img_blur, img)))
```

We extracted the loop as a separate function.

Replaces the loop with vmap

Here, we replaced the loop inside the `color_convolution()` function with a simpler function and an auto-vectorized call of it. The code has actually become simpler, and if we measure its performance, we will see that it is also faster.

Listing 6.24 Benchmarking our changes

```
%timeit color_convolution(
  img, kernel_blur).block_until_ready()
```

Original function with a loop

```
>>> 405 ms ± 2.68 ms per loop (mean ± std. dev. of 7 runs, 1 loop each)
```

```
%timeit color_convolution_vmap(
  img, kernel_blur).block_until_ready()
```

Auto-vectorized function with vmap

```
>>> 184 ms ± 12.8 ms per loop (mean ± std. dev. of 7 runs, 10 loops each)
```

We can see that the function becomes more than twice as fast while also being simpler and easier to read. And we can make it even faster if we apply `jit()`.

Listing 6.25 Adding `jit` to the mix

```
color_convolution_jit = jax.jit(color_convolution)
color_convolution_vmap_jit = jax.jit(color_convolution_vmap)
```

JIT-ting the functions

```
color_convolution_jit(img, kernel_blur);
color_convolution_vmap_jit(img, kernel_blur);
```

Warm-up to make compilation happen

```
%timeit color_convolution_jit(
```

```
 img, kernel_blur).block_until_ready()
```

→ **Original function + JIT**

```
>>> 337 ms ± 1.33s per loop (mean ± std. dev. of 7 runs, 1 loop each)

%timeit color_convolution_vmap_jit(
 img, kernel_blur).block_until_ready()
```

→ **Auto-vectorized function + JIT**

```
>>> 143 ms ± 588 µs per loop (mean ± std. dev. of 7 runs, 10 loops each)
```

As you can see, JIT-compiling the original function gives a slower function than just auto-vectorizing it without any JIT. With JIT and auto-vectorization, the resulting function becomes even faster.

You can also use another `vmap()` call to make this function work on batches of images and/or filters, and the resulting combination will be

```
jit(vmap(vmap(matrix_filter(...))))
```

This example and the example on per-sample gradients both highlight the beauty of composable transformations you can do with JAX.

Summary

- There are several ways to vectorize your code: calling a function multiple times and manually gathering results (not really a vectorization), manual vectorization, and automatic vectorization.
- Automatic vectorization transforms a function processing one element to a function processing multiple elements simultaneously.
- Automatic vectorization with `vmap()` allows the speed benefits of manual vectorization while making your code simple and easily understandable.
- You can control which axis to map over using the `in_axes` parameter.
- You can control the output layout with the `out_axes` parameter.
- Using the decorator style can help you write less code if you care only about functions that process batches.
- The `axis_name` parameter allows you to use collective operations if your code needs communication between different batch elements.
- Batch data processing is the most straightforward case for applying auto-vectorization.
- The `vmap()` is also frequently used to batch neural network models. However, it might not be as straightforward if you use any functions to operate on batch statistics.
- You can easily get per-sample gradients by combining `grad()` and `vmap()` transforms.
- Vectorizing loops is another fruitful case for applying `vmap()`.

7
Parallelizing your computations

This chapter covers

- Using parallel evaluation to parallelize your calculations with pmap()
- Controlling pmap() behavior using its parameters
- Implementing data-parallel neural network training
- Running code in multihost configurations

In this chapter, we continue our exploration of JAX transformations. Here, we start diving into *parallelization* or running your computations on multiple devices simultaneously in parallel. This is especially relevant when you are doing large-scale neural network training, weather or ocean simulation, and any other task where at least part of the computations do not depend on each other and may be done in parallel. If that's the case, you can perform the whole computation faster in terms of time spent.

There are several mechanisms to parallelize your computations in JAX. The pmap() is the most straightforward, as here you explicitly control how your computation is done; we'll discuss it in this chapter. In the next chapter, we'll look at tensor sharding, the new and easy way of achieving parallelization implicitly, letting the compiler automatically partition your functions over devices. In appendix D, we additionally cover two experimental and partly outdated mechanisms, xmap(), and `pjit()`, for those who either are interested in the historical development of parallelization techniques in JAX or need to work with legacy code, which uses these techniques.

The `pmap()` transformation, or the parallel map, has an interface similar to the `vmap()`, so it is natural to start with it. The `pmap()` uses a so-called single-program multiple-data (SPMD) parallelism. In SPMD, you run the same program on multiple devices. The idea is that you split your data into chunks, and each device processes its own chunk of data simultaneously using the same code. This way, you can process more data at the same time, just adding more devices (however, the scaling is usually sublinear because of the communication overhead).

In this chapter, we will start with setting a problem that can be parallelized across multiple devices (a Cloud TPU with eight TPU cores) and get a basic understanding of how parallelization with `pmap()` works. Then we will dive deeper into `pmap()` parameters and use collective ops. Finally, we will apply all this knowledge and the acquired skills to the real-world task of neural network training. We will develop a data-parallel training of an image classification neural network from chapter 2. While the MNIST example may look too simple and repetitive, it's a good model example, and you can easily spot the changes in the code when other nonessential parts (like dataset and tensor sizes) are the same. I deliberately chose to use the same MNIST image classification example here and in the following chapter to highlight changes in the code and let you easily compare the different approaches.

Finally, we will learn how to run code in larger multihost environments like TPU Pods. Sometimes your functions (or neural networks) may be so large that they do not fit into a single GPU/TPU, and running computations on a cluster is required. This is a common situation with large language model (LLM) training and inference. Modern LLMs, like GPT-4, PaLM 2, Gemini, the largest versions of LLaMa 2, Falcon, and many others, require multi-GPU systems. JAX allows you to not only distribute (or split, or shard) data processing across different machines (called *data parallelism*) but also split large computations into parts performed across different machines (so-called *model parallelism*). You can use `pmap()` in a multihost configuration to manually distribute your computation across a cluster (though there are other ways of doing it; see chapter 8 and appendix D). If you do not have a GPU or TPU cluster and do not need large-scale training, you can safely skip this part.

7.1 Parallelizing computations with pmap()

Let's start with the simple problem of having multiple hardware acceleration devices (say, TPUs or GPUs) and a function whose work could be split across these devices in parallel.

The process is as follows:

1 Prepare a multidevice system.
2 Prepare the data you want to process; it is represented as some (possibly large) tensors.

3 Decide how the input tensor(s) can be split into independent chunks for processing separately.

4 Reshape each input tensor so that it has an additional axis with different chunks arranged along this axis.

5 Transform the function used for data processing with `pmap()` (and optionally with `vmap()` if the function is not vectorized but each chunk represents a batch of items).

6 Apply the transformed function to the reshaped tensor(s).

7 Reshape the resulting tensor to get rid of an additional dimension.

We will use a Cloud TPU with eight computing cores and the same function we used in the previous chapter for calculating a dot product between two vectors.

7.1.1 Setting up a problem

We start by setting up a system with multiple devices. Let's use a Cloud TPU that provides eight TPU cores in the cloud. This is the same setup we had in section 3.2.5, when we moved image processing to a TPU.

To use a Cloud TPU, follow the same procedure we used in chapter 3 or appendix C.

After creating a Cloud TPU and connecting Colab (or your local Jupyter notebook) to it, run the code in the following listing to check if TPU devices are available.

Listing 7.1   Setting up a Cloud TPU in Google Colab

```
from jax.lib import xla_bridge
print(xla_bridge.get_backend().platform)      Checks to determine which
                                               backend JAX uses
>>> tpu

import jax                                     ◀── Imports JAX, finally
jax.local_devices()

>>> [TpuDevice(id=0, process_index=0, coords=(0,0,0),
    core_on_chip=0),
>>>  TpuDevice(id=1, process_index=0, coords=(0,0,0),
    core_on_chip=1),
>>>  TpuDevice(id=2, process_index=0, coords=(1,0,0),
    core_on_chip=0),
>>>  TpuDevice(id=3, process_index=0, coords=(1,0,0),
    core_on_chip=1),                           Eight TPU devices
>>>  TpuDevice(id=4, process_index=0, coords=(0,1,0),   are available.
    core_on_chip=0),
>>>  TpuDevice(id=5, process_index=0, coords=(0,1,0),
    core_on_chip=1),
>>>  TpuDevice(id=6, process_index=0, coords=(1,1,0),
    core_on_chip=0),
>>>  TpuDevice(id=7, process_index=0, coords=(1,1,0),
    core_on_chip=1)]
```

Here you can see that in the current Python process with `process_index=0`, we have access to eight TPU cores located on four chips (the `coords` tuple marks the chip index in binarized format, and the `core_on_chip` value marks the core number on a chip; you can read more about TPUs at https://mng.bz/75Ve).

If you have no access to such a system, you can emulate a multidevice configuration with an arbitrary number of devices by using a special XLA flag, `--xla_force_host_platform_device_count`. You need to set this flag before importing JAX.

Listing 7.2   Emulating a multidevice system on a CPU

```
import os
os.environ['XLA_FLAGS'] = '--xla_force_host_platform_device_count=8'   ◄─────┐
                                                                            Sets the env variable with the
import jax                          ◄──────  Imports JAX                     desired number of devices
                                                                            before importing JAX
jax.devices("cpu")

WARNING:jax._src.lib.xla_bridge:No GPU/TPU found, falling back to CPU. (Set
TF_CPP_MIN_LOG_LEVEL=0 and rerun for more info.)
[CpuDevice(id=0),
 CpuDevice(id=1),
 CpuDevice(id=2),
 CpuDevice(id=3),                                        Eight CPU devices
 CpuDevice(id=4),                                        are available.
 CpuDevice(id=5),
 CpuDevice(id=6),
 CpuDevice(id=7)]
```

Using multiple CPU devices can help you prototype, debug, and test your multidevice code locally before running it on an expensive TPU or GPU system. Even in the case of using Google Colab, it can help you prototype faster because a CPU runtime is faster to restart.

Having a multicore CPU (a commodity now) is an easy way to parallelize your work across multiple cores. This option also works when the number of CPU devices in the XLA flag exceeds the number of CPUs in the system. It even works when a single physical device is available; in that case, you will not get any speed increase, but it is still useful for testing the semantics of your parallel implementation.

If you are lucky enough to have your own multi-GPU machine, you may use these multiple GPUs for parallelization.

> **NOTE**   `pmap()` requires that all participating devices be identical. This might be a problem for those with several different GPUs in their machine as it is impossible to use `pmap()` to parallelize a computation across different models of GPUs.

We use the same function we used in the previous chapter on `vmap()`—the function that calculates a dot product between two vectors.

Listing 7.3   A function for calculating the dot product between two vectors

```
import jax.numpy as jnp

def dot(v1, v2):                                    ◄─── Uses the vdot()
  return jnp.vdot(v1, v2)                                  function

dot(jnp.array([1., 1., 1.]), jnp.array([1., 2., -1]))   ◄─┐ Calculates the dot
                                                           │ product between
>>> Array(2., dtype=float32)                               │ two vectors
```

If instead of two vectors, as in the previous chapter, you have two lists of vectors, and you want to calculate dot products between the corresponding elements of the lists. Now these lists can be significantly larger to emulate the case when a single accelerator cannot efficiently perform all the multiplications in parallel. Splitting work between several accelerators may help.

Listing 7.4   Generating two large lists of vectors

```
from jax import random                              ◄─┐ Creates a random number
                                                       │ generator key (see more
rng_key = random.PRNGKey(42)                           │ details in chapter 9)

vs = random.normal(rng_key, shape=(20_000_000,3))   ◄─── Generates a two-dimensional
                                                         array of random numbers
v1s = vs[:10_000_000,:]
v2s = vs[10_000_000:,:]                              ──┐ Splits this array into two
                                                       │ parts, where the first 10 go to
v1s.shape, v2s.shape                                   │ the first list and the second 10
                                                       │ go to the second list
>>> ((10000000, 3), (10000000, 3))
```

Now we have all the required ingredients: a multidevice system, the data, and the function we want to apply. Our goal is to split the computation of all these dot products across the available devices.

7.1.2   Using pmap (almost) like vmap

What we didn't discuss in chapter 3 is that, although we have eight TPU devices, JAX runs computations on just a single one by default. If you want to use all the available devices, the simplest way of executing a computation is to map a function and have each device execute one index of the map. A straightforward way to split your computations across different devices is by using a parallel map, or pmap().

Like vmap(), pmap() maps a function over array axes. The difference is that vmap() vectorizes a function by adding a batch dimension to every primitive operation in the function (first into Jaxpr, which after compilation will be translated into corresponding HLO operations). At the same time, pmap() instead compiles the function with XLA (so you don't need a separate jit() transformation), replicates the function across devices, and executes each replica on its own device in parallel.

Single-program multiple-data

The purpose of `pmap()` is to express single-program multiple-data (SPMD) programs. SPMD stems from the taxonomy of computer architectures, proposed by Michael J. Flynn in 1966.

Flynn defined four initial classifications upon the number of concurrent instruction streams and data streams available in the architecture:

- *Single instruction single data* (SISD): This is a sequential computer with no data or instruction parallelism.
- *Single instruction multiple data* (SIMD): This is when a single instruction is simultaneously applied to multiple data streams. Modern processors have special vector instructions to achieve this type of parallelism—for example, MMX, SSE, and AVX in the x86 family. Later, in 1972, Flynn defined three additional subcategories of SIMD for array, pipelined, and vector processors.
- *Multiple instruction single data* (MISD): Multiple instructions operate on one data stream. This uncommon architecture is generally used for fault-tolerant applications, such as a flight control computer.
- *Multiple instruction multiple data* (MIMD): Multiple processors execute different instructions on different data.

You can find a more detailed explanation in the following video: https://www.youtube.com/watch?v=KVOc6369-Lo.

Originally not a part of Flynn's classification, the MIMD category is sometimes divided into further categories, including

- *Single program multiple data* (SPMD): In this type of parallelism, the same program (for example, some function or neural network) is executed simultaneously across multiple devices (such as several GPUs or TPUs), but the inputs to each of the running programs can differ (for example, it can be shards of an array or different batches), so there are multiple data streams. SPMD works on a higher level of abstraction compared to SIMD, and they are not mutually exclusive. An SPMD program can use SIMD instructions on each of the devices on which it is run if the devices provide such capabilities.
- *Multiple program multiple data* (MPMD): At least two different programs operate on multiple data streams.

Let's see examples of how `pmap()` behaves compared to `vmap()`. In listing 7.5, we try to create two versions of the function. One is auto-vectorized and compiled, and the other is a parallelized version of the function, obtained by just changing `vmap()` to `pmap()` and having no explicit `jit()` call.

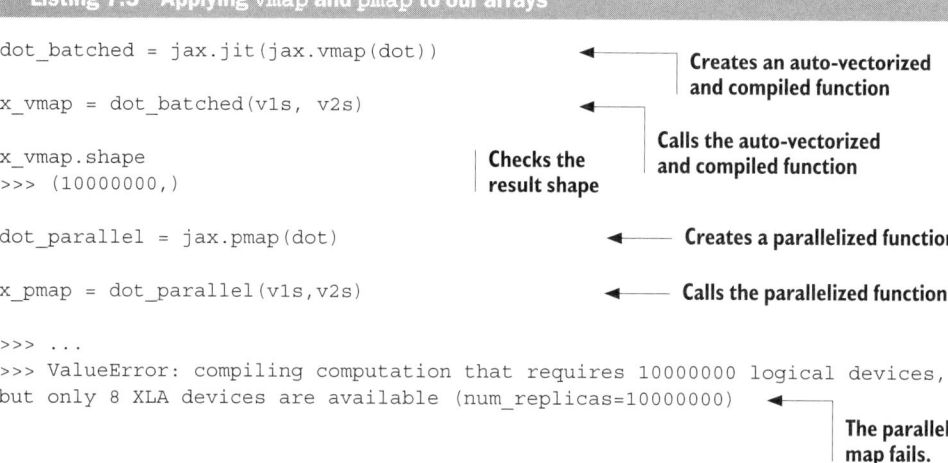

Listing 7.5   Applying `vmap` and `pmap` to our arrays

```
dot_batched = jax.jit(jax.vmap(dot))          ◄──── Creates an auto-vectorized
                                                     and compiled function
x_vmap = dot_batched(v1s, v2s)                ◄──┐
                                                 │   Calls the auto-vectorized
x_vmap.shape                    Checks the        │   and compiled function
>>> (10000000,)                 result shape

dot_parallel = jax.pmap(dot)                   ◄──── Creates a parallelized function

x_pmap = dot_parallel(v1s,v2s)                 ◄──── Calls the parallelized function

>>> ...
>>> ValueError: compiling computation that requires 10000000 logical devices,
but only 8 XLA devices are available (num_replicas=10000000)  ◄──┐
                                                                  The parallel
                                                                  map fails.
```

This listing features several interesting moments:

- The auto-vectorized and compiled version of the function, `dot_batched()`, is successfully applied to our arrays.
- The parallelized version of the function fails because it assumes that every element of the mapped axis is mapped to a separate device, and we do not have enough devices to do this mapping, so naively changing `vmap()` to `pmap()` does not work.

The important distinction between `vmap()` and `pmap()` is that the mapped axis size must be less than or equal to the number of local XLA devices available, as returned by `jax.local_device_count()`. We have only eight devices, whereas the mapped axis size is 10 million.

Here, we are doing steps 3 and 4 from the process description at the beginning of the chapter, namely, we decide how the input tensors should be split into independent chunks for separate processing. We reshape the tensors accordingly to have an additional axis with different chunks arranged along this axis.

We will split the array containing vectors into eight chunks and will not split the vector dimension (containing three elements) itself. We need to rearrange our arrays so that the dimension we parallelize matches the number of devices. We expect the parallelization to process across this axis and for each of the eight groups to be passed to a separate device.

Listing 7.6   Restructuring our arrays

```
v1s.shape

>>> (10000000, 3)          ◄──── We cannot pmap over the leading
                                  axis as we do not have an
                                  adequate number of devices.
```

```
v1sp = v1s.reshape((8, v1s.shape[0]//8, v1s.shape[1]))
v2sp = v2s.reshape((8, v2s.shape[0]//8, v2s.shape[1]))
```
Reshapes our arrays into eight chunks

```
v1sp.shape
```
Now our array contains eight chunks, 1.25 million elements each.
```
>>> (8, 1250000, 3)
```

Here, we restructured our arrays in such a way that the leading axis (which we want to use as the mapping axis) has eight elements, the number equal to the number of devices we have. Notice that we used integer division here (the `//` operation) because the ordinary division returns a floating-point number that cannot be used as a shape.

In many cases, the split dimension may not be divisible by the number of devices available. In this situation, you can use *padding*, or filling the array with some dummy value (say, 0) to make the dimension divisible. Then you need to remove dummy values (and the values resulting from them) after processing. Indeed, this only works if the dummy values do not influence the computation result. Otherwise, you may need to adjust the calculation as well.

We are almost ready to move to steps 5 and 6 from the process description at the beginning of the chapter—namely, transforming the function with `pmap()` and applying the transformed function to the reshaped tensor(s).

Let's apply the function transformed with `pmap()` to the reshaped array.

Listing 7.7   Applying `pmap` to the restructured arrays

```
x_pmap = dot_parallel(v1sp,v2sp)
```
Parallel map now succeeds.

```
x_pmap.shape
```
The resulting shape is not what we expected.
```
>>> (8,)
```

Now the function successfully finishes. But if we look at the resulting shape, we see that it is not what we expected. We expected to see a huge number of dot products inside each group, namely, 1.25 million. So we'd expect a shape like (8, 1250000), not (8,).

This is the same problem with vectorization as described in the previous chapter. The `dot()` function is designed to work with a single element, but it does not fail when we pass multiple elements; it just calculates the dot product for higher-rank tensors (which is not what we need).

As we split our arrays into eight chunks, each chunk is now a smaller array, and we need a vectorized function to process these inputs correctly. The recipe is already known: we may use `vmap()`! So we first vectorize the function with `vmap()`; then we parallelize it with `pmap()`.

Listing 7.8   Adding `vmap` to the mix

```
dot_parallel = jax.pmap(jax.vmap(dot))
```
Parallelizes the auto-vectorized function

```
x_pmap = dot_parallel(v1sp,v2sp)
```

```
x_pmap.shape
```

```
>>> (8, 1250000)
```

The resulting shape
is now correct.

```
type(x_pmap)
```

The result type is
an Array type.

```
>>> jaxlib.xla_extension.ArrayImpl
```

Here we have first created an auto-vectorized version of the function, and then we parallelized it across multiple devices. Now everything works correctly, and we get the result with the shape expected.

If you use an older version of JAX, you may have noticed a `ShardedDeviceArray` type. It was a special version of `DeviceArray`, which logically appears to be a single array, though it is physically split across the devices used in the computation. With newer versions of JAX, it is a `jaxlib.xla_extension.ArrayImpl` type, which is the familiar `Array` type.

Subsequent `pmap()` calls may proceed without moving data, depending on the computation. If you call a non-`pmap()` function on this data, communication happens behind the scenes to gather the values at one device.

One minor task remains—step 7 from our process: we need to restructure the resulting array to eliminate parallelization artifacts and then remove the extra axis if we do not want to do anything else with these results in a parallel fashion.

Listing 7.9   Getting rid of additional dimensions

```
x_pmap = x_pmap.reshape((x_pmap.shape[0]*x_pmap.shape[1]))
x_pmap.shape
```

Eliminates the
mapping axis

```
>>> (10000000,)
```

```
jax.numpy.all(x_pmap == x_vmap)
```

Checks to see that we got the same
result as we had with vmap()

```
>>> Array(True, dtype=bool)
```

Here we have flattened our array and removed the mapped axis because we no longer need it. When we compare our result with the result we got using `vmap()`, we can see that they are identical.

Let's summarize what we did:

1 We had an array (or several arrays) we wanted to process with a specific function.

2 We split our arrays into groups equal to the number of hardware devices available.

3 As each device needed to process a batch of data, we prepared a batched version of a function with `vmap()`.

4 The function was compiled and replicated across devices with `pmap()`.

5 `pmap()` ran computation on each device with the corresponding chunk of data, obtaining resulting arrays on each device.

6 We removed this partitioning, eliminating the dimension we mapped over. The output array now contains no artifacts of the parallelization process.

So, as you can see, the pmap() transformation is similar to the vmap() transformation, but they do different things, and you (usually) cannot replace one with another.

However, the pmap() and vmap() transformations can sometimes be interchangeable and equivalent from an external observer's point of view, for example, if we had a small number of elements to process, not larger than the number of devices available—say, up to eight in our case.

Listing 7.10   The case when vmap() and pmap() look the same

```
vs = random.normal(rng_key, shape=(16,3))      Generates small arrays with eight
v1s = vs[:8,:]                                  elements (the same as the
v2s = vs[8:,:]                                  number of devices available)


jax.vmap(dot)(v1s,v2s)                          ◄─── Auto-vectorizes the function

>>> Array([ 0.51048726, -0.7174605 , -0.20105815, -0.26437205, -1.3696793 ,
>>>         2.744793  ,  1.7936493 , -1.1743435 ], dtype=float32)

jax.pmap(dot)(v1s,v2s)                          ◄─── Parallelizes the function

>>> Array([ 0.51048726, -0.7174605 , -0.20105815, -0.26437205, -1.3696793 ,
>>>         2.744793  ,  1.7936493 , -1.1743435 ], dtype=float32)
```

Here we used both vmap() and pmap() identically. The result is the same. With the older JAX versions, you might see the only visible difference in the type of the resulting array, DeviceArray or ShardedDeviceArray.

Another not-so-obvious difference is speed because, for such small functions and arrays, it makes no sense to parallelize the computations. If everything can be computed on a single device, then parallelizing it over multiple devices will only add communication overhead and make the whole computation slower. Because a meaningful performance comparison should compare jitted versions of the code (otherwise, it might be suboptimal), we add explicit jit() calls to the following program.

Listing 7.11   Measuring the difference between vmap() and pmap()

```
dot_v = jax.jit(jax.vmap(dot))                  Compiles and warms
x = dot_v(v1s,v2s)                              up vmap() version

dot_pjo = jax.jit(jax.pmap(dot))                Compiles and warms up pmap()
x = dot_pjo(v1s,v2s)                            version with outer jit()
>>>… UserWarning: The jitted function dot includes
a pmap. Using jit-of-pmap can lead to inefficient
data movement, as the outer jit does not preserve
sharded data representations and instead collects
input and output arrays onto a single device. Consider
removing the outer jit unless you know what you're doing.
See https://github.com/google/jax/issues/2926.
```

```
    warnings.warn(
```

```
dot_pji = jax.pmap(jax.jit(dot))          Compiles and warms up pmap()
x = dot_pji(v1s,v2s)                        version with inner jit()
```

```
dot_p = jax.pmap(dot)                       Compiles and warms up pmap()
x = dot_p(v1s,v2s)                          version without explicit jit()
```

```
%timeit dot_v(v1s,v2s).block_until_ready()
```

```
>>> 122 µs ± 5.53 µs per loop (mean ± std. dev. of 7 runs, 100 loops each)
```

```
%timeit dot_pjo(v1s,v2s).block_until_ready()
```

```
>>> 2.08 ms ± 30.1 µs per loop (mean ± std. dev. of 7 runs, 10 loops each)
```

```
%timeit dot_pji(v1s,v2s).block_until_ready()
```

```
>>> 1.51 ms ± 43 µs per loop (mean ± std. dev. of 7 runs, 100 loops each)
```

```
%timeit dot_p(v1s,v2s).block_until_ready()
```

```
>>> 1.54 ms ± 51 µs per loop (mean ± std. dev. of 7 runs, 100 loops each)
```

Here we created compiled versions of

- The `vmap()`-transformed function
- The outer `jit()` above `pmap()`-transformed function
- `pmap()`-transformed, inner `jit()`-transformed function
- `pmap()`-transformed function without explicit `jit()`

Let me make a few interesting observations here:

- The `vmap()`-transformed version is the fastest one.
- The `pmap()`-transformed version, with and without explicit inner `jit()` transformation, produces the same results.
- The outer `jit()`-transformed, `pmap()`-transformed function is the slowest one, and JAX gives us an informative warning message that this combination may make performance worse because the outer `jit()` does not preserve sharded data representations and instead collects input and output arrays onto a single device.

With a basic understanding of what `pmap()` does, let's look closer at its parameters.

7.2   *Controlling pmap() behavior*

Because `pmap()` has an interface very similar to `vmap()`'s, it has the same ways of controlling input and output axes to map over. Your tensors may be organized in different ways when the dimension you want to map is not the leading one, and you might need to tell `pmap()` how they are organized. You may also use axis names and collective operations when you need to communicate between devices. Here we explore the relevant pmap() parameters for doing such things.

7.2.1 Controlling input and output mapping axes

Like with vmap(), you can control input and output mapping axes with special parameters. The cases here are the same as for controlling vmap() behavior in section 6.2. For example, your arrays might be arranged in a different way, with a dimension you want to parallelize that is not the first one. Or you may use more complex structures as function parameters—for example, a dict.

USING THE IN_AXES PARAMETER

By default, pmap() assumes all inputs to the function are being mapped over, and like with vmap(), you can use the in_axes parameter to specify which axes of positional arguments to map over. The arguments marked with None will be broadcasted (copied fully to each device), while integer values specify which axes of positional arguments to map over.

Older JAX versions only supported the leading axis (with index 0) to be mapped over, but now there are no such restrictions.

We can use all the same examples from the previous chapter with vmap(); the only change now is using pmap(). There is a limitation, as it will work this way only for cases where the mapping axis size is small enough to fit into a very limited number of hardware devices (say, eight). For more real-world cases, you may need to mix vmap() and pmap() to prepare batches for each device, as we did in the previous section.

We start with a simple example of using the in_axes parameter value equal to its default.

Listing 7.12 Explicitly using the `in_axes` parameter

```
vs = random.normal(rng_key, shape=(16,3))          Generates a small array for
v1s = vs[:8,:]                                      demonstration purposes
v2s = vs[8:,:]

def dot(v1, v2):                                    ◄──── The same dot function as before
  return jnp.vdot(v1, v2)

dot_pmapped = jax.pmap(dot, in_axes=(0,0))          ◄──── Creates a parallelized
                                                          function with explicitly passed
dot_pmapped(v1s, v2s)                                     in_axes parameter

>>> Array([ 0.51048726, -0.7174605 , -0.20105815,
    -0.26437205, -1.3696793 ,                       The resulting Array contains dot
>>>         2.744793 ,  1.7936493 , -1.1743435 ],   products calculated in parallel.
    dtype=float32)
```

Here, we have created a small array with the leading dimension of size 8 equal to the number of hardware devices we have. If you have a different setup, you might need to change the array sizes to match it.

As the `pmap()` default behavior is to use the leading axes for mapping all the function parameters, our example from listing 7.10 may use the explicitly passed `in_axes=(0,0)` value.

In the following listing, we transpose one or two input arrays, so the mapping should be done on their second axes (with index 1).

Listing 7.13   Using the `in_axes` parameter for non-leading axes

```
v1s.T.shape, v2s.shape

>>> ((3, 8), (8, 3))

jax.pmap(dot, in_axes=(1,0))(v1s.T, v2s)
```

> The mapping dimensions have indices 1 and 0 for the first and second array.

```
>>> Array([ 0.51048726, -0.7174605 , -0.20105815, -0.26437205, -1.3696793 ,
>>>         2.744793  ,  1.7936493 , -1.1743435 ], dtype=float32)

v1s.T.shape, v2s.T.shape

>>> ((3, 8), (3, 8))

jax.pmap(dot, in_axes=(1,1))(v1s.T, v2s.T)
```

> The mapping dimensions for both arrays now have index 1.

```
>>> Array([ 0.51048726, -0.7174605 , -0.20105815, -0.26437205, -1.3696793 ,
>>>         2.744793  ,  1.7936493 , -1.1743435 ], dtype=float32)
```

When we have a parameter that needs to be copied (or broadcasted) to each hardware device as is, without splitting, we may use the `None` value in the corresponding position of the `in_axes` parameter. Here, we use the already known function for the scaled dot product from the previous chapter where the last parameter of the function, `koeff`, should not be split.

Listing 7.14   Using the `in_axes` parameter for broadcasting

```
def scaled_dot(v1, v2, koeff):
  return koeff*jnp.vdot(v1, v2)
```
> The last parameter koeff needs to be copied to all devices.

```
v1s_ = v1s
v2s_ = v2s.T
k = 1.0
```
> This parameter will be mapped over axis number 0.
> This parameter will be mapped over axis number 1.
> This parameter will be broadcasted as is.

```
v1s_.shape, v2s_.shape

>>> ((8, 3), (3, 8))

scaled_dot_pmapped = jax.pmap(scaled_dot, in_axes=(0,1,None))
```
> Passes in_axes parameter

```
scaled_dot_pmapped(v1s_, v2s_, k)

>>> Array([ 0.51048726, -0.7174605 , -0.20105815, -0.26437205, -1.3696793 ,
>>>         2.744793  ,  1.7936493 , -1.1743435 ], dtype=float32)
```

> The function works as expected.

In this example, the function's last parameter, the scaling coefficient, is replicated across all the devices.

As with vmap(), you can also use more complex structures for the function parameters and the corresponding in_axes value. In the following example, we use Python dict.

Listing 7.15 Using the `in_axes` parameter with a Python container

```
def scaled_dot(data, koeff):
  return koeff*jnp.vdot(data['a'], data['b'])          ◄──  Now the function consumes
                                                            a dict and a scalar.

scaled_dot_pmapped = jax.pmap(scaled_dot, in_axes=({'a':0,'b':1},None))  ◄──

scaled_dot_pmapped({'a':v1s_, 'b': v2s_}, k)        Marks axes for the dict and
                                                    the scalar parameters

>>> Array([ 0.51048726, -0.7174605 , -0.20105815,
  -0.26437205, -1.3696793 ,                          The function
>>>         2.744793  ,  1.7936493 , -1.1743435 ],   works as expected.
  dtype=float32)
```

USING THE OUT_AXES PARAMETER

You can also control the output tensor layout with the out_axes parameter. In listing 7.16, we want a function to scale input vectors with a given coefficient and, for some reason, to return the result in a transposed way with the mapped axis in the output as index 1, not 0.

Listing 7.16 Using the `out_axes` parameter

```
def scale(v, koeff):                    A simple function
  return koeff*v                        to scale a vector

scale_pmapped = jax.pmap(scale,         Specifies batch
                in_axes=(0,None),   ◄── dimensions for the input
                out_axes=(1))       ◄── 
                                        Specifies batch
res = scale_pmapped(v1s, 2.0)           dimension for the output

v1s.shape, res.shape                    The output is now a
                                        transposed and scaled input.
>>> ((8, 3), (3, 8))
```

Here, the input dimension we map over is the dimension with index 0, indexing all the vectors we want to process, while the dimension with index 1 contains components of an individual vector. For the output tensor, we want a transposed tensor with the components of an individual vector to be located along the dimension with index 0, and scaled vector indices to be arranged along the dimension with index 1.

There is a special case with setting out_axes to None. This automatically returns the value on the first device and should be used only if you are confident the values arc the same on every device.

A LARGE ARRAY EXAMPLE

I have provided simple illustrative examples, but in real life, you will probably have arrays larger than the number of devices you want to use. As in the previous section, you will need to mix `pmap()` with `vmap()` to split work across multiple accelerators with the former and use batches on each accelerator with the latter.

Let's create large arrays for the dot product case and process them in a parallel fashion on our Cloud TPU setup (or any other setup you use). This time, we use arrays that are transposed (with rows and columns swapped) versions of the large arrays from the beginning of this chapter.

The following example is large and complicated. You must keep an eye on which dimensions you have and where and how to use them. Let's look carefully at all these details in figure 7.1.

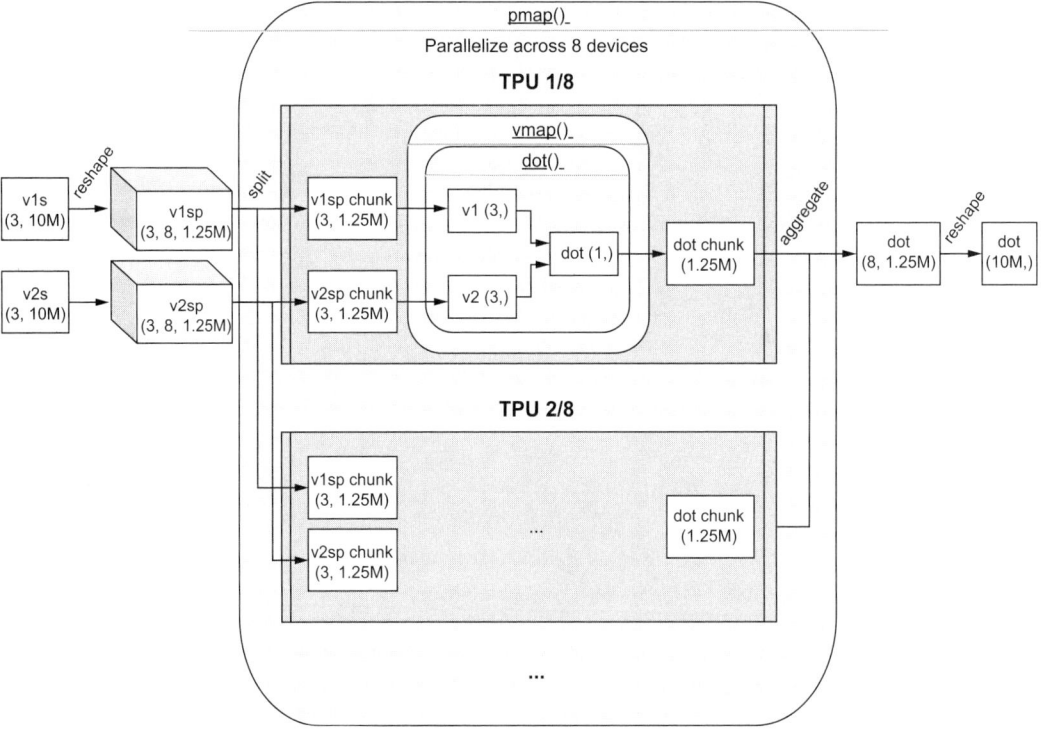

Figure 7.1   Scheme of data processing for the large transposed array example

First, we create two large arrays, and between their corresponding elements, we want to calculate dot products. These arrays are transposed versions of the arrays from the beginning of this chapter, and they have a shape of (3, 10000000). The first axis (with index 0) is the axis along which elements of an individual vector reside (three elements in each vector). The second axis (with index 1) is the axis that contains vectors themselves (10 million each), and the index along this axis marks a specific vector in the array of vectors.

We want to use the second axis for parallelization because it is pretty straightforward to split this axis into groups and calculate dot products for each group separately. If we used vmap() only, this would be the axis we map over. But for using pmap() we need to make groups first, so we reshape our arrays so that the second axis is split in two. The array shape after this transformation is (3, 8, 1250000), where the first axis remains unchanged (it still contains the components of a vector), and instead of the old second axis, we have two new axes: an axis for groups (the new axis with index 1) and the axis for vectors inside each group (the new axis with index 2).

Then we apply pmap(), passing it in_axes=(1,1), which says that both input tensors should be mapped over the second axis (with index 1) of the three axes. So the computation will be split into eight separate devices, each one taking in its own group.

Inside each group, there is still a smaller array (or batch) of vectors, so we use vmap() to map a single element function over these vectors. For vmap(), we also have to pass the in_axes parameter, and though it looks exactly the same as for pmap(), namely jax.vmap(dot, in_axes=(1,1)), its meaning is different. A vmap()-transformed function sees only a group of vectors that were sent to that particular device, so the array shape it gets is (3, 1250000). Mapping over the axis with index 1 here is mapping over an axis that contains 1,250,000 elements, not over an axis that contains eight groups.

The result of this computation is an array of shape (8, 1250000) where each of the eight groups that were calculated on their own device returned 1,250,000 dot products.

The final action is to get rid of this artificial group dimension and concatenate all these eight groups into a single array so that we finally get a resulting array with 10 million dot products that were calculated using eight devices in parallel.

Now, with an understanding of the process, let's look at the code.

Listing 7.17 Large array example

```
vs = random.normal(rng_key, shape=(20_000_000,3))
v1s = vs[:10_000_000,:].T          Now arrays are transposed
v2s = vs[10_000_000:,:].T          versions of the original arrays.


v1s.shape, v2s.shape               The first dimension contains
                                   components of a vector; the second
>>> ((3, 10000000), (3, 10000000))  dimension contains vectors.


v1sp = v1s.reshape((v1s.shape[0], 8, v1s.shape[1]//8))   Splits the second dimension,
v2sp = v2s.reshape((v2s.shape[0], 8, v2s.shape[1]//8))   which contains vectors,
v1sp.shape, v2sp.shape                                   into two dimensions:
                                                         groups and vectors
>>> ((3, 8, 1250000), (3, 8, 1250000))      Now we have eight groups of vectors.


dot_parallel = jax.pmap(
    jax.vmap(dot, in_axes=(1,1)),      Asks vmap to use the second dimension
                                       to map over (vmap does not see the
                                       group dimension, so its second
                                       dimension is the vector dimension)
```

```
        in_axes=(1,1)
)
```
◄────── **Asks pmap to use the second (group) dimension, which will not be visible to vmap**

```
x_pmap = dot_parallel(v1sp,v2sp)

x_pmap.shape
```
┌────── **Obtains eight groups of dot products**
```
>>> (8, 1250000)
```
◄─┘

```
x_pmap = x_pmap.reshape((x_pmap.shape[0]*x_pmap.shape[1]))
x_pmap.shape
```

```
>>> (10000000,)
```
◄─────── **Eliminates the group dimension**

```
jax.numpy.all(x_pmap == x_vmap)
```
│ **Checks to see that the result is correct (the same as for the purely vmap-calculated result**
```
>>> Array(True, dtype=bool)
```
│ **from the beginning of the chapter)**

This code straightforwardly implements the process from figure 7.1. Replace the constant 8 with a `jax.device_count()` function call to adapt the code for your own configuration.

I want to highlight again that you must track tensor dimensions carefully, and it might be confusing to operate only with axes indices. Remember this `in_axes=(1,1)` parameter means different things for `pmap()` and `vmap()` in the preceding code. It's pretty easy to introduce errors to such code. In the next chapter, we will see better and less error-prone ways to parallelize your code.

When working with tensor indices, it's easy to get confused and use the wrong indices or reshape an array incorrectly. For example, if we reshaped original arrays so that the group dimension would be the new tensor's last dimension, the vectors' semantics would change, and we would calculate dot products over different vectors. So take care when doing all these operations with indices, and double-check that everything is correct.

7.2.2   *Using named axes and collectives*

In all the earlier examples in this chapter, all calculations are independent of each other, and it is sufficient to perform simple parallel operations. But for more complicated data processing—for example, when doing global normalization or working with global minimum/maximum values—you may need to communicate and pass information between devices.

COMMUNICATING BETWEEN PROCESSES

From the previous chapter on auto-vectorization, you know that JAX provides collective operations (or collective ops). See table 7.1 (and https://mng.bz/mRg4) for the list of available operations.

Table 7.1 Collective operations

Operation	Description
`all_gather(x, axis_name, *[, ...])`	Gathers values of x across all replicas
`all_to_all(x, axis_name, split_axis, ...[, ...])`	Materializes the mapped axis and maps a different axis
`psum(x, axis_name, *[, axis_index_groups])`	Computes an all-reduce sum on x over the `pmapped` axis `axis_name`
`psum_scatter(x, axis_name, *[, ...])`	Like `psum(x, axis_name)` but each device retains only part of the result. It's like the first part of `psum` without gathering the result.
`pmax(x, axis_name, *[, axis_index_groups])`	Computes an all-reduce max on x over the `pmapped` axis `axis_name`
`pmin(x, axis_name, *[, axis_index_groups])`	Computes an all-reduce min on x over the `pmapped` axis `axis_name`
`pmean(x, axis_name, *[, axis_index_groups])`	Computes an all-reduce mean on x over the `pmapped` axis `axis_name`
`ppermute(x, axis_name, perm)`	Performs a collective permutation according to the permutation `perm`
`pshuffle(x, axis_name, perm)`	Serves as a convenience wrapper of `jax.lax.ppermute` with alternate permutation encoding
`pswapaxes(x, axis_name, axis, *[, ...])`	Swaps the `pmapped` axis `axis_name` with the unmapped axis `axis`
`axis_index(axis_name)`	Returns the index along the mapped axis `axis_name`

I omitted the `pdot()` operation from the original list because it is undocumented and its future is unclear (https://github.com/google/jax/discussions/13851).

These operations are performed along an axis specified using the `axis_name` parameter during a collective ops call. The same `axis_name` argument during the `pmap()` or `vmap()` call associates a name to the mapped axis so that collective ops can refer to it.

Collective operations

Collective operations are used in parallel programming to communicate between all processes in a process group (which is in contrast to point-to-point communication between specific processes). It comes from the Message Passing Interface (MPI) standard.

The MPI standard has three classes of operations: synchronization, data movement, and collective computation.

The following list describes some widely useful functions (or patterns). This is not the full list of possible operations, but it's enough to help you understand JAX collective ops:

(continued)

Broadcast: This function is used to distribute data from one processing unit to all processing units. In JAX, using `None` in `in_axes` indicates that an argument doesn't have an extra axis to map over and should be broadcasted. You can also use a special `static_broadcasted_argnums` parameter to specify which positional arguments to treat as static (compile-time constant) and broadcast to all devices.

Scatter: This pattern is used to distribute data from one processing unit to all the processing units, but unlike Broadcast, which sends the same message to each processing unit, Scatter splits the message and delivers one part of it to each processing unit. This is exactly what is done when we use mapping over an axis with `pmap()` or `vmap()`.

Reduce: This pattern is inverse to Broadcast and is used to collect data from various computing devices and combine them into global results with some given function (e.g., summation).

All-reduce: This is a special case of the Reduce pattern when the result of the Reduce operation must be distributed across all processing units. The `psum()`/`pmax()`/`pmin()`/`pmean()` functions perform all-reduce operations.

Gather: This pattern is used to store data from all processing units on a single processing unit.

All-gather: This pattern is used to collect data from all processing units and to store the collected data on all processing units.

All-to-all: This pattern, also called a *total exchange,* is used when each processing unit sends a message to every other processing unit.

If you want to dive deeper into the topic of MPI, you can start with this introduction: https://pdc-support.github.io/introduction-to-mpi. Or look at the "Designing and Building Applications for Extreme Scale Systems" course materials at https://wgropp.cs.illinois.edu/courses/cs598-s15/.

Listing 7.18 is a canonical example of parallel array normalization using the `psum()` collective op. We want to normalize an array so all its values sum to 1. We need to find a sum of all elements and divide each element by it.

Listing 7.18 Using collective ops and `axis_name`

```
arr = jnp.array(range(8))                              Generates an array for illustration

norm = jax.pmap(                                       Uses psum() op with
    lambda x: x/jax.lax.psum(x, axis_name='p'),        axis_name='p'
    axis_name='p')                                     Uses axis_name='p' in pmap()

norm(arr)                                              Applies our normalization function

>>> Array([0.       , 0.03571429, 0.07142857, 0.10714287, 0.14285715,
>>>        0.17857143, 0.21428573, 0.25      ], dtype=float32)
```

```
jnp.sum(norm(arr))                          ◀———— Checks normalized values

>>> Array(1., dtype=float32)
```

Here the `axis_name` argument inside the `pmap()` call gives a name to the axis that is being pmapped over. The axis to map over is defined by the `in_axes` argument, which is absent here and uses a default of axis with the index 0.

So we name the axis that we map over during the `pmap()` call, and inside the parallelized computation, we use `psum()`, which computes an all-reduce sum over the pmapped axis `axis_name='p'`. This results in calculating a sum of all elements along the named axis and dividing each element by this sum.

This was a toy example of working on a very small array when each element can be processed on its own device, but it's easy to expand the example to work with larger arrays for which you have to split the array into smaller parts and let each device process these subarrays.

The thing to remember here is that you need to use two different operations: one to aggregate the values inside a group on a single device and another, a collective op, to communicate between the devices and aggregate the values.

In the following listing, we do normalization for a larger array.

Listing 7.19 Normalization example for a larger array

```
arr = jnp.array(range(200))                 ◀———— Generates an array that has
                                                  more elements than you
arr = arr.reshape(8, 25)    ◀———————————————       have hardware devices
arr.shape
                                            Reshapes the array into
>>> (8, 25)                                 groups equal to the number
                                            of XLA devices available
norm = jax.pmap(
    lambda x: x/jax.lax.psum(jnp.sum(x), axis_name='p'),
    axis_name='p')                          ◀———— Aggregates values inside
                                                  each group as well
narr = norm(arr)            ◀————————————————
narr.shape
                                            Applies our
>>> (8, 25)                                 normalization function

jnp.sum(narr)                               ◀———— Checks for
                                                  normalized values
>>> Array(1., dtype=float32)
```

In listing 7.19, the only significant change is inside the `psum()` call. Using `jnp.sum()`, we take the sum of each array that each particular device has, and then, using `psum()`, we communicate these sums between all the devices and calculate the global sum. Finally, using NumPy-style broadcasting, we divide every element of the array by the global sum on each device to obtain a normalized array version. We did not reshape the resulting array into a flat one, which doesn't matter here, but you can easily check to ensure that all the elements now sum to 1.

Many all-reduce collective operations provide an optional `axis_index_groups` parameter that allows you to perform collective ops for groups that cover the axis, rather than the whole axis at once. This parameter is a list of lists containing axis indices; each list is a group that performs a collective operation over it.

NOTE Groups must cover all axis indices exactly once. Groups must also all be the same size.

Here, we have modified the previous normalization example to normalize the array across several groups. We specify four groups: a group for the devices with indexes 0 and 1, another group for devices with indices 2 and 3, and so on. The collective op will be performed for each group separately.

Listing 7.20   Normalization by groups

```
arr = jnp.array(range(200))

arr = arr.reshape(8, 25)
arr.shape

>>> (8, 25)

norm = jax.pmap(
    lambda x: x/jax.lax.psum(
        jnp.sum(x),
        axis_name='p',
        axis_index_groups=[[0,1], [2,3], [4,5], [6,7]]     ◄———  Provides indices
    ),                                                            for four groups
    axis_name='p')

narr = norm(arr)
narr.shape

>>> (8, 25)
```
Resulting array now sums to 4.

```
jnp.sum(narr)

>>> Array(4., dtype=float32)                                       ◄——— Examines each
                                                                         group separately

jnp.sum(narr[:2]), jnp.sum(narr[2:4]), jnp.sum(narr[4:6]), jnp.sum(narr[6:]) ◄—

>>> (Array(1., dtype=float32),
>>>  Array(1., dtype=float32),
>>>  Array(1.0000001, dtype=float32),          Each group sums to 1
>>>  Array(1., dtype=float32))                 (up to rounding error).
```

We provided the same `psum()` function with a list specifying which groups to calculate the function for. Four `psum()` operations were performed, and as a result, all the elements are now normalized according to the corresponding groups. Elements in the first two slices of the original array sum to 1, elements in the next two slices sum to 1, and so on. Elements in slices four and five sum to 1 up to the rounding error.

NESTED MAPS

Thanks to the functional nature of JAX, you can easily combine different JAX transformations—for example, making nested pmap() calls or mixing pmap() and vmap(). Mixing vmap() and pmap() is especially useful, as it is a typical situation when you parallelize batched processing across different machines. Doing nested pmap() calls is a rare case, especially with a small number of devices to parallelize, yet it still makes sense, especially if there are some nested loops.

We have already done the pmap() plus vmap() mix, but now we can extend this example to using different named axes to control an axis for collective operations. Here we create a mix of pmap() and vmap() with two different collective operations: one pmax() operation performed inside each array located on a separate device and another pmax() operation performed between different devices.

In the following listing, we create a function that calculates a ratio between the largest element across different batches (located on different devices) and the largest element inside a batch (located on a particular device).

Listing 7.21   Mixing collective ops

```
arr = jnp.array(range(200))

arr = arr.reshape(8, 25)
arr.shape

>>> (8, 25)

f = jax.pmap(                                          A function using two collective
    jax.vmap(                                          ops across different axes
        lambda x: jax.lax.pmax(x,
    axis_name='v')/jax.lax.pmax(x, axis_name='p'),
        axis_name='v'                                  ◀─── An axis for vmap
    ),
    axis_name='p')                                     ◀─── An axis for pmap

f(arr)

>>> Array([[0.13714285, 0.13636364, 0.1355932 , 0.13483146, 0.1340782 ,
>>>          0.13333334, 0.13259669, 0.13186814, 0.13114755, 0.13043478,
>>>          0.12972972, 0.12903225, 0.12834224, 0.12765957, 0.12690412,
>>>          0.12631579, 0.12565446, 0.125     , 0.12435233, 0.12371133,
>>>          0.12307693, 0.12244899, 0.12182741, 0.12121212, 0.12060301],
>>>
...
>>>          [1.1371429 , 1.1306819 , 1.1242937 , 1.1179775 , 1.1117318 ,
>>>           1.1055555 , 1.0994476 , 1.0934067 , 1.0874318 , 1.0815217 ,
>>>           1.0756756 , 1.0698925 , 1.0641712 , 1.0585107 , 1.05291   ,
>>>           1.0473684 , 1.0418848 , 1.0364584 , 1.0310881 , 1.0257732 ,
>>>           1.0205128 , 1.0153062 , 1.0101522 , 1.0050505 , 1.        ]],
>>>          dtype=float32)
```

Due to how we constructed our arrays, the largest value inside each batch is the last element of the batch, and the largest value across different batches is an element from the last batch. So the resulting array slices (or a resulting batch) start with a larger value that gradually gets smaller as we move across the array slice because the largest element in the batch is constant while the largest element across batches gradually becomes larger. The last value of the last resulting batch is 1 because both maximum values are the same here.

The `axis_name` parameter lets you easily control which axis you want to use with each collective op.

You can identify several mapped axes simultaneously when using a single collective. In such a case, you pass a tuple with all the named axes' names.

We can rewrite the global normalization example from listing 7.19 to get rid of the `jnp.sum()` call on each device by replacing it with a global sum, including the batch axis (introduced by `vmap()`) as well. We calculate a sum using a collective operation across both axes simultaneously by passing a tuple `axis_name=('p','v')` into the `psum()` function.

Listing 7.22   **Global normalization using two axes simultaneously**

```
arr = jnp.array(range(200))

arr = arr.reshape(8, 25)
arr.shape

>>> (8, 25)

norm = jax.pmap(
    jax.vmap(
        lambda x: x/jax.lax.psum(x, axis_name=('p','v')),     ◀──  Uses both axes
        axis_name='v'                                              simultaneously
    ),
    axis_name='p')

narr = norm(arr)                                               ◀──  Applies our
narr.shape                                                          normalization function

>>> (8, 25)

jnp.sum(narr)                                                  ◀──  Checks for normalized
                                                                    values
>>> Array(1., dtype=float32)
```

You can also nest `pmap()` transformations; *the only limitation is that the number of XLA devices should not be smaller than the product of the mapped axis sizes.* In the following simple example, we have a small matrix in which we map over its rows and columns. We use the same global normalization across two axes at one time, as in the previous example.

Listing 7.23 Nested `pmap()` example

```
arr = jnp.array(range(8)).reshape(2,4)          ◀──────┐ Generates a
arr                                                     │ small matrix

>>> Array([[0, 1, 2, 3],
        [4, 5, 6, 7]], dtype=int32)

n = jax.pmap(
    jax.pmap(
        lambda x: x/jax.lax.psum(x, axis_name=('rows','cols')),  ◀── Completes a
        axis_name='cols'                                             nested pmap
    ),                                                               over rows and
    axis_name='rows')                                               columns

jnp.sum(n(arr))
                                                ┌ Checks the
>>> Array(1., dtype=float32)          ◀─────────┘ normalization result
```

This function can also be expressed more clearly using the decorator style. Here we replace two nested `pmap()` calls with two decorators; this code typically is easier to read and understand.

Listing 7.24 Nested `pmap()` using the decorator style

```
from functools import partial          ◀─────── Imports the partial decorator

@partial(jax.pmap, axis_name='rows')   │ Uses two decorators
@partial(jax.pmap, axis_name='cols')
def n(x):
  return x/jax.lax.psum(x, axis_name=('rows','cols'))

jnp.sum(n(arr))
                                                ┌ Checks the
>>> Array(1., dtype=float32)          ◀─────────┘ normalization result
```

In the case of nested calls, axis names are resolved according to lexical scoping. The first decorator is responsible for the outer call; the second is for the inner.

Now we have all the required skills and knowledge for the real-world task of neural network training. In the next section, we develop a data-parallel training of an image classification neural network from chapter 2.

7.3   *Data-parallel neural network training example*

Here we build what I'd call the SPMD MNIST image classification example. There are different ways to parallelize neural network training, and here we will use data-parallel training.

Data parallelism and model parallelism

Data parallelism is a type of parallelism where the same operation is performed in parallel on elements of some data collection. Data is split into N chunks distributed across N nodes, and each node then processes its portion of the data.

In deep learning scenarios, a large dataset is typically split into chunks distributed across different nodes. Each node has the exact copy of the model and processes its chunk of data. The results of this processing (gradients) are communicated between nodes and aggregated, so each node updates the weights of its copy of the model to keep the processing function the same.

Model parallelism is a type of parallelism where a large model computation is split across different nodes—for example, calculating different layers of a neural network on different machines. It allows training large models that could not fit on any single machine.

Large neural networks can also be trained using *a combination of data and model parallelism*. For example, Google's LLM, called PaLM (https://arxiv.org/abs/2204.02311), which has 540B parameters, was trained in this way. Note PaLM used JAX.

In the next chapter, you will learn about other parallelization mechanisms that can be used for model parallel training.

7.3.1 *Preparing data and neural network structure*

Remember our image classification setting from chapter 2. We have handwritten images that represent numbers taken from the MNIST database. A few of them are presented in figure 7.2.

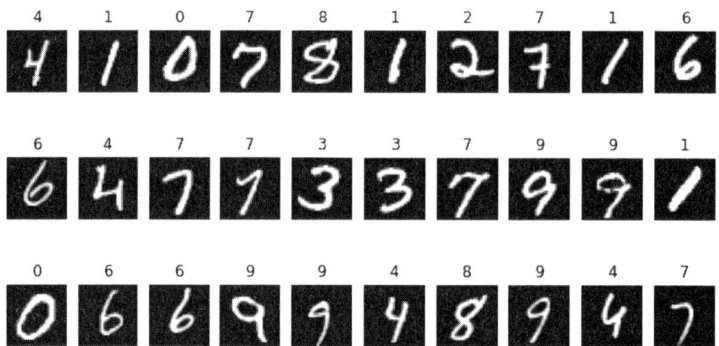

Figure 7.2   Handwritten images from the MNIST dataset

We built a simple MLP neural network with a few fully connected layers. Here, we reuse this network, but now we organize training to distribute it across many computational devices—in our case, eight TPU cores.

Loading and preparing the dataset is almost the same as it was before. The only difference is that we now get larger batches from the dataset that we can reshape later to a set of batches for multiple computing devices.

Listing 7.25 Loading the dataset

```
import tensorflow as tf
import tensorflow_datasets as tfds

data_dir = '/tmp/tfds'

data, info = tfds.load(name="mnist",
                       data_dir=data_dir,
                       as_supervised=True,
                       with_info=True)

data_train = data['train']
data_test  = data['test']

HEIGHT = 28
WIDTH  = 28
CHANNELS = 1
NUM_PIXELS = HEIGHT * WIDTH * CHANNELS
NUM_LABELS = info.features['label'].num_classes
NUM_DEVICES = jax.device_count()                       ◄─── A new constant for
BATCH_SIZE  = 32                                             the number of
                                                            computing devices
def preprocess(img, label):
  """Resize and preprocess images."""
  return (tf.cast(img, tf.float32)/255.0), label

train_data = tfds.as_numpy(
    data_train.map(preprocess).batch(
    NUM_DEVICES*BATCH_SIZE).prefetch(1)                ◄─── Asks for larger
)                                                           batches with the size
test_data  = tfds.as_numpy(                                 of 32*number of
    data_test.map(preprocess).batch(                        devices
    NUM_DEVICES*BATCH_SIZE).prefetch(1)                ◄───
)

len(train_data)
                                                       ┌─── There are 235 large
>>> 235                                            ◄───┘    batches in this dataset.
```

Here, we used the `jax.device_count()` function to get the number of available computing devices and increased the batch size accordingly to allow each device to have a batch size of 32.

The neural network structure is exactly the same as in chapter 2. The following listing provide its code for convenience.

Listing 7.26 MLP structure

```
import jax
import jax.numpy as jnp
from jax import grad, jit, vmap, value_and_grad
from jax import random
from jax.nn import swish, logsumexp, one_hot

LAYER_SIZES = [28*28, 512, 10]
PARAM_SCALE = 0.01

def init_network_params(sizes, key=random.PRNGKey(0), scale=1e-2):
  """Initialize all layers for a fully-connected neural network with given
sizes"""

  def random_layer_params(m, n, key, scale=1e-2):
    """A helper function to randomly initialize
weights and biases of a dense layer"""
    w_key, b_key = random.split(key)
    return (scale * random.normal(w_key, (n, m)),
        scale * random.normal(b_key, (n,)))

  keys = random.split(key, len(sizes))
  return [random_layer_params(m, n, k, scale)
    for m, n, k in zip(sizes[:-1], sizes[1:], keys)]

init_params = init_network_params(
  LAYER_SIZES, random.PRNGKey(0), scale=PARAM_SCALE)

def predict(params, image):
  """Function for per-example predictions."""
  activations = image
  for w, b in params[:-1]:
    outputs = jnp.dot(w, activations) + b
    activations = swish(outputs)

  final_w, final_b = params[-1]
  logits = jnp.dot(final_w, activations) + final_b
  return logits

batched_predict = vmap(predict, in_axes=(None, 0))
```

- **Specifies the number of neurons in each fully connected layer**
- **The function for random parameter initialization**
- **Prepares the initial parameters**
- **The forward-pass function**
- **Generates a batched forward-pass function**

Remember: the idea is to separate neural network parameters from the forward-pass function that uses them so the function will have no state and be functionally pure. We generate initial random parameters and store them in the `init_params` variable. We also prepare the `predict()` function that performs a forward pass and makes a batched version of this function using `vmap()`. The `in_axes=(None, 0)` statement here says that rather than map over the first parameter of the function (the neural network parameters), we map over the dimension number 0 for the second parameter (the data it processes).

Now that we have data and the neural network structure, we are ready to implement a parallelized training procedure. The procedure is as follows:

1   The data will be partitioned across all the available devices. Still, the model parameters will be replicated to each device, so each device will have its own full local copy of the model parameters to perform a gradient update step.

2   Change the `update()` function to aggregate the gradients across all the devices using the `jax.lax.psum()` collective op. In other parts, it remains unchanged, updating model parameters locally and returning both updated model parameters and the loss value

3   Transform the `update()` function with `pmap()`, saying that the data is mapped over (split across devices) but the model parameters are replicated.

4   Update the training loop so that after getting a batch of data from the dataloader, we can reshape it to add an additional axis to `pmap()` over.

5   Aggregate losses were obtained on each device.

That's it, and the changes are pretty localized. Let's take a closer look.

7.3.2   *Implementing data-parallel training*

Now we must prepare our loss function and the function for updating the neural network parameters. There are changes here to map the updating function over multiple computing devices. We need some significant changes compared to the chapter 2 model training to do it.

Let's start with a general idea. We want to have a large array of training examples and split the array across one chosen axis to multiple devices so that each device will have its part of the dataset (or, more specifically, the part of the current large batch). To run a training iteration, each device will also need a copy of the model parameters, and we need to replicate the initial neural network parameters across all the devices without splitting or any change. So each device will have its copy of the neural network parameters and a part of the dataset and can perform a gradient calculation step locally. Here, each device will have its gradients, and we need to aggregate (sum) all these gradients across all the devices and send the aggregated gradients to each device so the device can perform the parameter update step locally. After this step, each device will have the same parameter values again, and we can repeat the process.

Diving into the specific details, we assume that the `update()` function will work with

- A copy of neural network parameters (the function's first parameter, `params`). It will be the same for every device, but because we need it locally on each device, we have to copy it there. We can replicate the model parameters manually, or we can rely on `pmap()` itself, marking the first parameter of the `update()` function with `None` in the `in_axes` parameter. In the automatic case, the `pmap()`-transformed function replicates model parameters to each device before the computation runs. In the manual case, we must prepare a special version of the structure holding the neural network parameters with an additional axis and have replicated copies along this axis. Then `pmap()` would map over this additional dimension of the parameter value. In any case, each device will have its own copy of each layer's weight. We choose the automatic way.

- The data to train on, which comprises a batch of images (x parameter) and corresponding labels (y). Here, we just split a larger batch into groups of smaller batches (of size 32) with a separate axis to map over so that each device will get its own part of the larger batch.
- Some additional parameters—here, the epoch number (epoch_number)—allow a gradually decaying learning rate. This parameter will be broadcast to each device during the function call.

The update() function returns both model parameters and loss values; it will return many updated model parameters and loss values, one from each device. At the next iteration of the update, we will need to replicate model parameters once again, but before that, we need to choose the model parameters from one of the devices. This is an excellent place to rely on the special case with the out_axes parameter of the pmap() function by setting the value for the first returning parameter to None and receiving this value only from the first device. We are sure that the updated model parameters are the same on each device, as they were the same at the beginning of the update step (because they were replicated) and after we performed a gradient step, as the gradients were aggregated across all the devices. The second returning value contains loss, which is different across the devices because they work with different parts of the data, so the second value in the out_axes parameter is 0.

The following listing implements these changes.

Listing 7.27 Loss and update functions

```
from functools import partial

INIT_LR = 1.0
DECAY_RATE = 0.95
DECAY_STEPS = 5
NUM_EPOCHS  = 20

def loss(params, images, targets):                      # The same loss
    """Categorical cross entropy loss function."""      # function as before
    logits = batched_predict(params, images)
    log_preds = logits - logsumexp(logits)
    return -jnp.mean(targets*log_preds)

@partial(jax.pmap,                                      # Uses pmap to
    axis_name='devices',                                # parallelize function and
    in_axes=(None, 0, 0, None),                         # map over the data
    out_axes=(None,0))                                  # only; parameters are
def update(params, x, y, epoch_number):                 # replicated and not
    loss_value, grads = value_and_grad(loss)(params, x, y)  # mapped over
    grads = [(jax.lax.psum(dw, 'devices'),
        jax.lax.psum(db, 'devices'))                    # Accumulates gradients on
        for dw, db in grads]                            # each of the devices
```

```
lr = INIT_LR * DECAY_RATE ** (epoch_number / DECAY_STEPS)
return [(w - lr * dw, b - lr * db)
        for (w, b), (dw, db) in zip(params, grads)], loss_value
```

The `loss()` function is completely the same—no changes here—but the `update()` function has important changes.

We use a decorator to specify that the parameters related to the data have a dimension number 0 to map over, and the first and the fourth parameters are broadcasted to each device. The `in_axes=(None, 0, 0, None)` parameter describes this. In summary, each `update()` function call gets a part of the dataset to train on and a copy of neural network parameters and is able to calculate loss value and gradients locally on each device.

After calculating gradients locally on each device, we need to aggregate these gradients and send the aggregated gradients back to each of the devices so they will have the same results. We do this using the `psum()` collective for weights and biases of each layer.

Now every device has a sum of gradients across all the devices, and from this point, we are ready to perform a gradient update step. This is done locally on each device, and because the initial parameter values and the aggregated gradients are the same across every device, we get the same result on each device. We get the updated parameters from the first device and broadcast them on the next iteration to repeat the process. Suppose we used any stochasticity in the updating process; each device would obtain its own version of parameters. In that case, we'd also need to aggregate these parameters somehow, but that's not our case.

We can better understand what is happening inside by looking at tensor shapes.

Listing 7.28 Data tensor shapes

```
train_data_iter = iter(train_data)          Gets a batch of data from
x, y = next(train_data_iter)                the training dataset

x.shape, y.shape
                                            We have a 256-element
>>> ((256, 28, 28, 1), (256,))              batch here.

x = jnp.reshape(x, (NUM_DEVICES, BATCH_SIZE, NUM_PIXELS))    Reshapes data
y = jnp.reshape(                                             for our MLP and
    one_hot(y, NUM_LABELS),                                  adds a separate
    (NUM_DEVICES, BATCH_SIZE, NUM_LABELS))                   dimension for
                                                             parallelization
x.shape, y.shape                                             across eight
                                                             devices
>>> ((8, 32, 784), (8, 32, 10))

updated_params, loss_value = update(init_params, x, y, 0)    Makes one gradient
                                                             update step
loss_value

>>> Array([0.5771865 , 0.5766423 , 0.5766001 ,
```

```
     0.57689124, 0.57701343,
>>>         0.57676095, 0.57668227, 0.5764269 ],
     dtype=float32)
```

> ◀ **Each device has its own loss value**
> **because it was trained on a**
> **different portion of the dataset.**

Here, we do a lot of tensor reshaping.

The original version in chapter 2 obtained a 32-element batch of an image tensor (28 × 28 × 1) and a label tensor (with just a single scalar for each image). Then we flattened the image into 784 pixels each and one-hot encoded each label into a 10-element vector. Both tensors previously had a batch dimension of 32.

Now, in addition to these transformations, we split the batch dimension (now a larger batch of 256 elements) into two new dimensions: a device dimension (here, the size of 8, equal to the number of available devices) and a batch dimension (with the old size of 32). Here, the shape (8, 32, 784) means we have a batch of 32 flat 784-pixel images for each of the eight devices. It's the same for the shape (8, 32, 10), where we have a batch of 32 one-hot encoded 10-element vectors for each of the eight devices.

After running a single update step, we have the updated parameters (taken from the first device) and a list of losses from each device. The loss values are slightly different because each device calculated the loss and its gradients on a separate chunk of data. To get an aggregated loss, we can just sum all these losses.

Our approach performs two potentially large between-device communications regarding the model weights. First, we send the model parameters to each device at the beginning of each iteration. Second, we exchange gradients between all the devices, and the dimension of gradients is the same as the dimension of weights, as each learned weight will produce its own gradient.

The more efficient approach would be one that constantly stores a separate copy of model parameters on each device and updates them locally using aggregated gradients. We will implement this approach in the next chapter with the tensor sharding technique, and we will do the same using pmap() in section 10.2.

Finally, we have to implement the complete training loop. Here, almost everything is straightforward. We use the same functions to calculate accuracy as in chapter 2. The training loop is much the same, but we changed data reshaping as we described earlier. Now we have a device dimension to parallelize across and a batch dimension to use on each device. The only change is that we do not use the BATCH_SIZE constant; instead, we use the num_elements//NUM_DEVICES expression because the last large batch from the data generator might have fewer elements than is required for the entire batch, so we keep the device dimension unchanged, but the batch size on a device might be smaller for that case. You must adjust this part when you implement data-parallel training for your datasets. The dataset size might not allow splitting it into equal batches for all the devices available, and the last batch will need careful handling (or you might suddenly get an error).

Listing 7.29 The complete training loop

```
@jit
def batch_accuracy(params, images, targets):
  images = jnp.reshape(images, (len(images), NUM_PIXELS))
  predicted_class = jnp.argmax(batched_predict(params, images), axis=1)
  return jnp.mean(predicted_class == targets)

def accuracy(params, data):
  accs = []
  for images, targets in data:
    accs.append(batch_accuracy(params, images, targets))
  return jnp.mean(jnp.array(accs))

import time

params = init_params

for epoch in range(NUM_EPOCHS):
  start_time = time.time()
  losses = []
  for x, y in train_data:
    num_elements = len(y)
    x = jnp.reshape(x,
      (NUM_DEVICES, num_elements//NUM_DEVICES, NUM_PIXELS))
    y = jnp.reshape(one_hot(y, NUM_LABELS),
      (NUM_DEVICES, num_elements//NUM_DEVICES, NUM_LABELS))
    params, loss_value = update(params, x, y, epoch)
    losses.append(jnp.sum(loss_value))
  epoch_time = time.time() - start_time

  train_acc = accuracy(params, train_data)
  test_acc = accuracy(params, test_data)
  print("Epoch {} in {:0.2f} sec".format(epoch, epoch_time))
  print("Training set loss {}".format(jnp.mean(jnp.array(losses))))
  print("Training set accuracy {}".format(train_acc))
  print("Test set accuracy {}".format(test_acc))
```

Functions to calculate accuracy

The training loop begins.

Reshapes data for MLP and parallelization

Updates parameters in a data-parallel fashion

Aggregates losses for an epoch

```
>>> Epoch 0 in 16.44 sec
>>> Training set loss 3.3947665691375732
>>> Training set accuracy 0.9246563911437988
>>> Test set accuracy 0.9237304925918579
>>> Epoch 1 in 8.64 sec
>>> Training set loss 3.055901050567627
>>> Training set accuracy 0.9457446336746216
>>> Test set accuracy 0.946582019329071
...
>>> Epoch 19 in 9.53 sec
>>> Training set loss 2.8397674560546875
>>> Training set accuracy 0.9905917048454285
>>> Test set accuracy 0.98095703125
```

Notice how we calculate accuracy. We do it only on a single device; however, you might want to parallelize it as well (you may treat that as a separate exercise).

Also, you may notice that we aggregate losses by summing them. In addition, we did not use `jit()` for our update function as it is not required. Remember: `pmap()` JIT-compiles the function internally.

This data-parallel training example is also an example of one more function transformation combination, as it combines both `grad()`, `vmap()`, and `pmap()` transforms. Internally, it also uses `jit()`.

7.4   *Using multihost configurations*

We are almost finished, but another topic is worth discussing: running JAX in environments with multiple CPU hosts or JAX processes.

Previously, we limited our configurations to single-host systems with a maximum of one TPU card containing eight TPU cores. However, with TPUs, you may have much larger systems named TPU Pods or a subset of them called TPU Pod slices (https://mng .bz/5Oja).

JAX uses the multicontroller programming model. Each JAX Python process runs independently in this model, and the same JAX Python program runs in each process. This is unlike other distributed systems where a single controller manages many worker nodes.

It means you must manually run your JAX program on each host, and currently, there is no good way to manage multiple JAX Python processes from a single Colab notebook.

A few more things to know before we start include, first, you must instantiate and initialize a cluster. This is usually done using the `jax.distributed.initialize()` call. It is optional (but recommended) for TPU but required for GPU. This must be done before any JAX computations are executed. Later, you can get the index of a particular process by calling `jax.process_index()`.

Second, as you remember, there is a distinction between global and local devices, discussed in section 3.2.3:

- *Local devices* can be addressed locally by the JAX Python process. These are the GPUs directly connected to the host for a GPU system. For a Cloud TPU, these are all the TPU cores on a TPU board card connected to a host (maximum eight TPU cores per host). Previously, we only worked with local devices.
- *Global devices* are the devices across all JAX processes on different hosts. For example, for the v2-32 TPU Pod slice, 32 TPU v2 cores are connected to four hosts, each containing a TPU v2 board containing eight cores.

Each process can see only its local devices, though it can communicate across all the global devices using collective ops.

You can use `pmap()` to run computations across multiple processes. Each `pmap()` can see only its local devices, and you must prepare the data for each process separately. So each JAX process performs computation locally on its own piece of data.

However, when you call collective ops inside the function, they run across all global devices, so it looks like `pmap()` is running over an array sharded across different hosts. Each host sees and processes only its own shard, but they communicate using collective ops.

Here we write a program that performs parallelized dot product calculations across the cluster and then calculates a global sum of dot products. The program is run on all TPU hosts. Copy this code into a file called worker.py. Then we distribute it across the cluster and run it.

Listing 7.30 Program for TPU Pod slice

```
import jax
import jax.numpy as jnp
from jax import random

jax.distributed.initialize()              ◄── Initializes a cluster

print('== Running worker: ', jax.process_index())   ◄── Each worker prints a
                                                         message with its own id.
def dot(v1, v2):
  return jnp.vdot(v1, v2)

rng_key = random.PRNGKey(42 + 10*jax.process_index())    ── Generates a random tensor
vs = random.normal(rng_key, shape=(2_000_000,3))            unique on each host using
v1s = vs[:1_000_000,:]                                      different seeds for the
v2s = vs[1_000_000:,:]                                      random number generator

# The total number of TPU cores in the Pod
device_count = jax.device_count()          ◄── Gets global device
                                               count (here, 32)
# The number of TPU cores attached to this host
local_device_count = jax.local_device_count()   ◄── Gets local
                                                     device
if jax.process_index() == 0:                 ◄──     count (here,
    print('-- global device count:', jax.device_count())   eight)
    #print('global devices:', jax.devices())
    print('-- local device count:', jax.local_device_count())  Process 0 prints
    #print('local devices:', jax.local_devices())              information
    print('-- JAX version:', jax.__version__)

v1sp = v1s.reshape(
  (local_device_count,
  v1s.shape[0]//local_device_count,
  v1s.shape[1]))
v2sp = v2s.reshape(
  (local_device_count,
  v2s.shape[0]//local_device_count,
  v2s.shape[1]))
```

```
if jax.process_index() == 0:
    print('-- v1sp shape: ', v1sp.shape)     # (8, 125000, 3)

dots = jax.pmap(jax.vmap(dot))(v1sp,v2sp)
if jax.process_index() == 0:
    print('-- dots shape: ', dots.shape)     # (8, 125000)

global_sum = jax.pmap(
    lambda x: jax.lax.psum(jnp.sum(x), axis_name='p'),
    axis_name='p'
)(dots)

if jax.process_index() == 0:
    print('-- global_sum shape: ', global_sum.shape)     # (8,)

print(f'== Worker {jax.process_index()} global sum: {global_sum}')

dots = dots.reshape((dots.shape[0]*dots.shape[1]))
if jax.process_index() == 0:
    print('-- result shape: ', dots.shape)     # (1000000,)
local_sum = jnp.sum(dots)
print(f'== Worker {jax.process_index()} local sum: {local_sum}')

print(f'== Worker {jax.process_index()} done')
```

Each host parallelizes dot product calculation across its eight TPU cores.

A separate pmap() runs psum() across all global devices.

Each shard on each TPU core calculates the sum of all elements.

Checks that each process calculated the same global sum

Each process calculates its local sum as well.

Here we first initialize a cluster with `jax.distributed.initialize()`. Then each machine prepares its own array of random vectors. We used different seeds for the random number generator (more on that in the next chapter) to have different values for each worker. The seeds are based on the `jax.process_index()` value, which returns different numbers for different JAX processes in a cluster. You will shard your data and load it separately for each worker.

For diagnostic purposes, we print numbers of global and local devices for the JAX process with index 0.

Then, each host with a TPU board (with eight TPU chips) performs parallelized and vectorized dot product calculation, processing its own data independently. No communication between different hosts happens here.

This is not the case in the next `pmap()` where we calculate the global sum. Each host performs `jax.lax.psum(jnp.sum(x))` on each of its eight TPU cores. On each host, an input to `pmap()` has shape (8, 125000), which is split along the first dimension, and each TPU core gets a vector of 125,000 values (dot products from the previous stage). It calculates the sum of these values using `jnp.sum()` and obtains a single number, and then a collective operation happens. All the TPU cores across all the hosts, now 32 TPU cores, exchange their local sums and calculate an all-reduce sum using `jax.lax.psum()`. As a result, each worker obtains an eight-element array containing the same number, which is the global sum across the whole cluster.

Later, we calculate local sums on each worker and print them so you can manually check that each worker has its own sum, and they sum together into the global sum with the value you obtained in the resulting array.

Now let's create our small TPU Pod slice to run the program.

NOTE TPU Pod slices are expensive. Always check the cost (https://cloud.google .com/tpu/pricing#pod-pricing), and do not forget to delete them when they are no longer needed.

You can see which TPU Pods are available in what zones at https://cloud.google.com/ tpu/docs/regions-zones.

When writing, I found that the v2-32 TPU Pod slice is available in the us-central1-a and europe-west4-a zones. So we can create it:

```
$gcloud compute tpus tpu-vm create tpu-pod
--zone europe-west4-a --accelerator-type v2-32
--version tpu-vm-base
Create request issued for: [tpu-pod]
Waiting for operation [projects/true-poet-371617/
locations/europe-west4-a/operations/
operation-1676557945942-5f4d210d03
274-dd57b5fd-0bfd83f9] to complete...done.
Created tpu [tpu-pod].
```

Congratulations if this is your first TPU supercomputer!

Now the TPU Pod is created, and we need to prepare it for running our JAX program. First, we need to install JAX:

```
$gcloud compute tpus tpu-vm ssh tpu-pod
--zone europe-west4-a --worker=all
--command="pip install 'jax[tpu]>=0.2.16' -f
https://storage.googleapis.com/jax-releases/libtpu_releases.html"
SSH: Attempting to connect to worker 0...
SSH: Attempting to connect to worker 1...
SSH: Attempting to connect to worker 2...
SSH: Attempting to connect to worker 3...
Looking in links: https://storage.googleapis.com/jax-releases/libtpu_
releases.html
Collecting jax[tpu]>=0.2.16
  Downloading jax-0.4.3.tar.gz (1.2 MB)
...
Successfully installed jax-0.4.3 jaxlib-0.4.3 libtpu-nightly-0.1.dev20230207
numpy-1.24.2 opt-einsum-3.3.0 scipy-1.10.0
Successfully installed jax-0.4.3 jaxlib-0.4.3 libtpu-nightly-0.1.dev20230207
numpy-1.24.2 opt-einsum-3.3.0 scipy-1.10.0
```

You may see SSH connection errors if you haven't previously connected to these machines. Check the manual (https://cloud.google.com/tpu/docs/jax-pods) for how to resolve this error.

Now we are ready to distribute our JAX Python program to all the hosts of the TPU Pod slice:

```
$gcloud compute tpus tpu-vm scp worker.py
tpu-pod: --worker=all --zone=europe-west4-a
WARNING: Cannot retrieve keys in ssh-agent. Command may stall.
SCP: Attempting to connect to worker 0...
SCP: Attempting to connect to worker 1...
SCP: Attempting to connect to worker 2...
SCP: Attempting to connect to worker 3...
worker.py                  | 1 kB |   1.8 kB/s | ETA: 00:00:00 | 100%
worker.py                  | 1 kB |   1.8 kB/s | ETA: 00:00:00 | 100%
worker.py                  | 1 kB |   1.8 kB/s | ETA: 00:00:00 | 100%
worker.py                  | 1 kB |   1.8 kB/s | ETA: 00:00:00 | 100%
```

In the final step, we can run our program:

```
gcloud compute tpus tpu-vm ssh tpu-pod
--zone europe-west4-a --worker=all --command "python3 worker.py"
SSH: Attempting to connect to worker 0…
SSH: Attempting to connect to worker 1…
SSH: Attempting to connect to worker 2…
SSH: Attempting to connect to worker 3…
== Running worker:  2
== Worker 2 global sum: [-45.239502 -45.239502 -45.239502 -45.239502
-45.239502 -45.239502 -45.239502 -45.239502]
== Worker 2 local sum: -367.02166748046875
== Worker 2 done
== Running worker:  0
-- global device count: 32
-- local device count: 8
-- JAX version: 0.4.3
-- v1sp shape:  (8, 125000, 3)
-- dots shape:  (8, 125000)
-- global_sum shape:  (8,)
== Worker 0 global sum: [-45.239502 -45.239502 -45.239502
 -45.239502 -45.239502 -45.239502 -45.239502 -45.239502]
-- result shape:  (1000000,)
== Worker 0 local sum: 1397.5830078125
== Worker 0 done
== Running worker:  1
== Worker 1 global sum: [-45.239502 -45.239502 -45.239502
 -45.239502 -45.239502 -45.239502 -45.239502 -45.239502]
== Worker 1 local sum: -992.9242553710938
== Worker 1 done
== Running worker:  3
== Worker 3 global sum: [-45.239502 -45.239502 -45.239502
 -45.239502 -45.239502 -45.239502 -45.239502 -45.239502]
== Worker 3 local sum: -82.87371826171875
== Worker 3 done
```

Here you see the output of all the workers mixed together. Each worker has its own eight-element array with global sum, and each worker also printed its own local sum so you can check everything is correct.

All the communication across 32 TPU cores in the cluster happened successfully.

Now, when everything is done, do not forget to delete the TPU Pod when you no longer need it:

```
$gcloud compute tpus tpu-vm delete tpu-pod --zone europe-west4-a
You are about to delete tpu [tpu-pod]
Do you want to continue (Y/n)?
Delete request issued for: [tpu-pod]
Waiting for operation [projects/true-poet-371617/
 locations/europe-west4-a/operations/operation-
 1676559317550-5f4d262914486-f827e901-ce9ce3f7]
 to complete...done.
Deleted tpu [tpu-pod].
```

The important thing to remember is that on multihost platforms, the input to pmapped functions must have a leading axis size equal to the number of local devices, not global devices. Each host can easily address only its own local devices. Communication between global devices happens using collective ops.

You can read more about multiprocess environments at https://mng.bz/6YgA.

We've finished with explicit parallelization using pmap(). In the next chapter, we will cover another approach to parallelization using tensor sharding.

Summary

- Parallelization can improve the speed of your code by running computations on multiple devices in parallel.
- Parallel map, or pmap(), transformation is a straightforward way to split your computations across different devices. It allows writing SPMD programs and running them on multiple devices.
- pmap() compiles the function with XLA (so you don't need a separate jit() transformation), replicates the function across devices, and executes each replica on its device in parallel.
- The mapped axis size must be less than or equal to the number of local XLA devices available, as returned by jax.local_device_count().
- You need to reshape arrays so that the dimension you parallelize matches the number of devices.
- You can control which axis to map over using the in_axes parameter.
- You can control the output layout with the out_axes parameter.
- The axis_name parameter allows you to use collective operations if your code needs communication between different devices.
- You may use an optional axis_index_groups parameter, which allows performing collective ops for groups that cover the axis, rather than the whole axis at once.
- Thanks to the functional nature of JAX, you can easily combine different transformations—for example, making nested pmap() calls or mixing pmap() and other transformations like vmap() or grad().
- Using the decorator style with pmap() can help you write a bit less code.
- pmap() can be used to implement data parallel neural network training.

- JAX uses the multicontroller programming model where each JAX Python process runs independently, and the same JAX Python program runs in each process.
- In multihost environments, each `pmap()` can see only its local devices, and each JAX process performs computation locally on its own piece of data.
- When collective ops are called inside a function, they run across all global devices, so this looks like `pmap()` is running over an array sharded across different hosts. Each host sees and processes only its own shard, but they communicate using collective ops.

Using tensor sharding

This chapter covers

- Using tensor sharding to achieve parallelization with XLA
- Implementing data and tensor parallelism for training neural networks

The chapter introduces you to an alternative and modern way of parallelizing computations in JAX using tensor sharding. The use case is the same as in the previous chapter: to run some parts of the computation in parallel and perform the whole computation faster. It is especially useful for different ways of parallelizing neural network training, be it data or model parallelism. It can also be applied to inference with large models that do not fit into a single GPU. However, areas other than deep learning can also benefit from this modern technique. If you work with large tensors in bioinformatics, cosmology, weather modeling, or elsewhere, tensor sharding can provide you with an easy way to parallelize your computations.

Parallelization with `pmap()` from the previous chapter gives you the ability to explicitly tell the compiler what you want to do using per-device code and explicit communication collectives. Another school of thought lets the compiler automatically partition functions over devices without specifying too many low-level details. Tensor sharding (or distributed arrays) belongs to the second school. This option to parallelize computations has been available since JAX version 0.4.1, together with the new `jax.Array` type.

Appendix D describes two experimental parallelization techniques that are outdated now, namely `xmap()` and `pjit()`. You might still want to read about these topics either if you are interested in how parallelization was developed in JAX or if you need to understand and support code that uses these techniques. Understanding `xmap()` and `pjit()` will also help you better understand tensor sharding, though it's not strictly required, and this chapter is sufficient in itself.

We are already familiar with `jax.Array`, the topic of chapter 3. Here we will look deeper. Together with `jit()`, `jax.Array` provides automatic compiler-based parallelization. I call it *implicit parallelization*, as you do not use any special language constructs or library functions to parallelize your code explicitly but instead put your tensors on devices in such a way that the computations are performed in parallel on different devices.

The idea is simple. In JAX, computations follow the data placement. So tensor sharding can be viewed as an extension of what we covered in section 3.2.3. There we placed our tensors on different devices (CPUs, GPUs, TPUs), and the computations were performed where the tensors resided. With tensor sharding, it's almost the same, but now you may split a tensor across different devices. During the computation, JAX takes care of how to perform the computation most efficiently without unnecessary data movement.

The `jax.Array` type is a unified array type that subsumes `DeviceArray`, `SharedDeviceArray`, and `GlobalDeviceArray` types from previous versions of JAX. The new `jax.Array` type helps make parallelism a core feature of JAX. It simplifies and unifies JAX internals and allows unifying `jit` and `pjit` (which is why you might be interested in appendix D).

Functions created with `jit()` can operate over distributed arrays (arrays sharded across different devices) without copying data onto a single device. The compiler determines sharding for intermediate variables based on the sharding of input data. You may also influence intermediate variable sharding by setting constraints. The compiler inserts collective ops where necessary. You may have heard the same for `pjit()` if you worked with it, and now this behavior is generalized to `jit()`.

> **NOTE** The features required by `jax.Array` are not supported by the Colab TPU runtime, even if you use an older JAX version that supports Colab TPUs. You need to set up a Cloud TPU as described in appendix C.

Let's first look at the complete example with familiar dot products; then we will discuss all the underlying concepts, and finally, implement parallelized neural network training using this new method.

8.1   *Basics of tensor sharding*

Let's rewrite our good old dot product example to use tensor sharding. In listing 8.1, we shard our arrays before the computations; the relevant code is highlighted in bold in the listing. Then all the computations are performed in a parallel fashion; we do not change any code related to computations.

> **Listing 8.1   Parallelizing dot product calculations using distributed arrays**

```
from jax.experimental import mesh_utils          Imports modules
from jax.sharding import PositionalSharding       for sharding
from jax import random

def dot(v1, v2):                              ◄──   Our familiar function for calculating
  return jnp.vdot(v1, v2)                            a dot product between two vectors

rng_key = random.PRNGKey(42)

vs = random.normal(rng_key, shape=(8_000,10_000))     This time, we generate
v1s = vs[:4_000,:]                                     vectors wider than before.
v2s = vs[4_000:,:]

v1s.shape, v2s.shape

>>> (4000, 10000), (4000, 10000))
                                                    Visualizes sharding; the whole
jax.debug.visualize_array_sharding(v1s)        ◄──  tensor resides on a single device
```

```
>>>  ┌──────────────────────────────────────────┐
>>>  │                                            │
>>>  │                                            │
>>>  │                                            │         Creates 2D
>>>  │                                            │         mesh to
>>>  │                                            │         shard the
>>>  │                   TPU 0                     │         rank-2
>>>  │                                            │         tensor's
>>>  │                                            │         first axis
>>>  │                                            │         across
>>>  │                                            │         eight TPUs
>>>  └──────────────────────────────────────────┘
```

```
sharding = PositionalSharding(mesh_utils.create_device_mesh((8,1)))   ◄──
sharding
```

```
>>> PositionalSharding([[{TPU 0}]
>>>                      [{TPU 1}]
>>>                      [{TPU 2}]
>>>                      [{TPU 3}]          create_device_mesh returns
>>>                      [{TPU 6}]          the most performant ordering
>>>                      [{TPU 7}]          of devices given the shape.
>>>                      [{TPU 4}]
>>>                      [{TPU 5}]])
```

```
v1sp = jax.device_put(v1s, sharding)          Shards tensors
v2sp = jax.device_put(v2s, sharding)          across their first axis
```

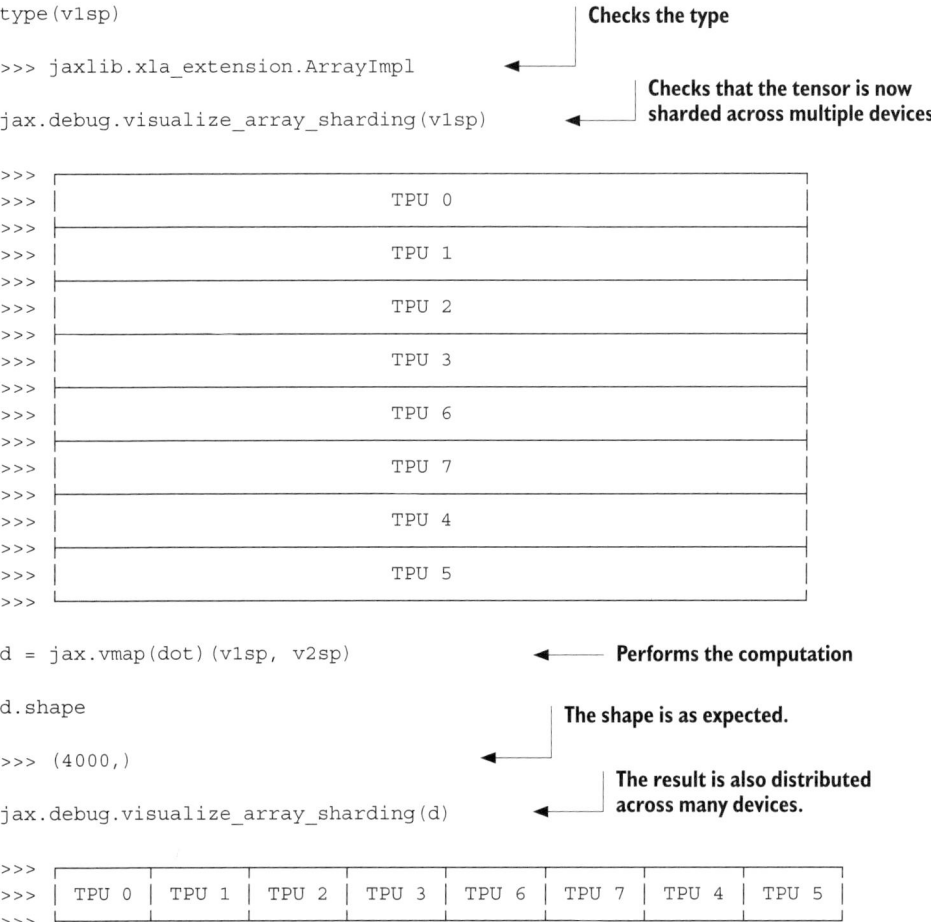

```
type(v1sp)
```
Checks the type

```
>>> jaxlib.xla_extension.ArrayImpl
```

```
jax.debug.visualize_array_sharding(v1sp)
```
Checks that the tensor is now sharded across multiple devices

```
>>>
>>>                          TPU  0
>>>
>>>                          TPU  1
>>>
>>>                          TPU  2
>>>
>>>                          TPU  3
>>>
>>>                          TPU  6
>>>
>>>                          TPU  7
>>>
>>>                          TPU  4
>>>
>>>                          TPU  5
>>>
```

```
d = jax.vmap(dot)(v1sp, v2sp)
```
Performs the computation

```
d.shape
```
The shape is as expected.

```
>>> (4000,)
```

```
jax.debug.visualize_array_sharding(d)
```
The result is also distributed across many devices.

```
>>>
>>> | TPU 0 | TPU 1 | TPU 2 | TPU 3 | TPU 6 | TPU 7 | TPU 4 | TPU 5 |
>>>
```

Many things happen in the example; let's look at the important parts.

First, we created a wider-than-usual version of arrays with vectors. Each vector now contains 10,000 elements. This is for a future example where we will show how easy it is to shard computations across many dimensions. The function itself does not change. We use a `jax.debug.visualize_array_sharding()` function to visualize tensor placement. At the start, the whole tensor resides on a single TPU.

8.1.1   *Device mesh*

We create a *device mesh*, an *n*-dimensional array of devices created by the `mesh_utils` `.create_device_mesh()` function. This function returns the most performant ordering of devices given the shape. This is important, as hardware devices are usually organized in some topology (say, 2D or 3D torus) and are not fully connected. Only the neighbors are connected by some high-speed interconnect.

Here we created a 2D mesh of size (8, 1) to shard the rank-2 tensor's first axis across eight TPUs. You can see that the order of devices is not from one to eight; it is more complicated because of the performance issues.

If you are emulating a multidevice system on a CPU with the XLA flag `--xla_force_host_platform_device_count` according to the recipe in listing 7.2, add the devices parameter to the `create_device_mesh()` function. The call will look like the following:

```
>>> mesh_utils.create_device_mesh((8, 1), devices=jax.devices("cpu"))
```

If we wanted to shard the tensor's second dimension only, we'd use a device mesh with the shape (1, 8) instead of (8, 1).

> **NOTE** The tensor shape you want to shard must be congruent with the sharding's shape. It means that both shapes must have the same length (same number of axes); that's why we used a device mesh of the size (8, 1), not just (8,). Additionally, the number of elements along each tensor's axis must evenly divide the corresponding sharding axis size.

8.1.2 *Positional sharding*

Then we create a `PositionalSharding` object representing a distributed memory layout. It fixes the device order and the initial shape.

We use the familiar `jax.device_put()` function, which we used heavily in chapter 3, to commit data to a device. This function accepts a sharding object instead of a particular device and places the data accordingly. You can check that the tensor placement changes, and the tensor's first axis (with index 0) is sharded across the first axis of the device mesh. The second axis of the sharding object has a size of 1, so the second axis of the tensor is not split.

Then we perform the computation with a function auto-vectorized using `vmap()` as usual and obtain the result, which is also sharded. It happened this way because, on each device, you have a subset of vectors for which it is possible to calculate dot products. These dot products are stored on the same devices where the original vectors reside.

You can check that parallelization really happened by measuring the time consumed by the function.

> **Listing 8.2 Measuring times for sharded and unsharded computations**

```
%timeit jax.vmap(dot)(v1sp, v2sp).block_until_ready()    ◄── Uses sharded tensor

>>> 1.7 ms ± 34.3 µs per loop (mean ± std. dev. of 7 runs, 1,000 loops each)

%timeit jax.vmap(dot)(v1s, v2s).block_until_ready()    ◄── Uses unsharded tensor

>>> 2.22 ms ± 27.2 µs per loop (mean ± std. dev. of 7 runs, 100 loops each)
```

Here we use the same function with sharded and unsharded tensors. The sharded tensors are split across eight devices, and the unsharded reside on a single device. So, in the first run, the calculations are executed on all eight TPU cores, and in the second run, they consume only a single TPU core (with index 0). In the first case, it happens faster. Why not eight times faster? The answer is because we do not use all the available hardware to its full capacity. Performance optimization is a separate interesting topic on its own, and the Roofline model (https://mng.bz/YV8B) highlights many complexities in this field.

8.1.3   *An example with 2D mesh*

Our vectors consist of many components—in our example, 10,000 of them. While such vectors can still fit into each separate device, sharding across the vector dimension might also make sense. The dot product can easily be sharded as it is just a sum of corresponding products of elements of the vectors. Figure 8.1 visualizes this.

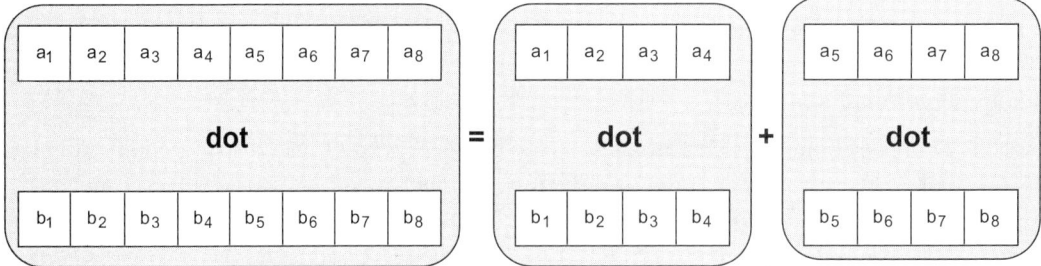

Figure 8.1   Sharding a dot product

To shard across two dimensions (vectors themselves and vector components), we must prepare a 2D mesh. In the following example, we shard two rank-2 input tensors across both dimensions and the output across its only dimension. The process might look pretty complicated, so we start with a diagram visualizing it in figure 8.2.

Let's carefully examine what is happening here. First, we create 4,000 pairs of vectors with 10,000 elements each. These are much wider vectors than we had in previous chapters. So we have two 2D arrays of size (4000, 10000). We will use a 2D hardware mesh of size (2, 4). If we used named sharding (we touch it on this later in the section), we might have named the mesh axes "x" and "y" or "vectors" and "features."

Both input parameters of the dot() function are partitioned across the first and the second dimensions. The first dimension of input arrays (size 4000) is partitioned across the first axis of the mesh (size 2), producing chunks of size 2000, which index subsets of vectors. The second dimension of input arrays (size 10000) is partitioned across the second axis of the mesh (size 4), producing chunks of size 2500, which index subsets of vector components.

The output is partitioned only across a single axis as it is a rank-1 tensor. Here, this axis is equivalent to the first axis of input arrays, which counts vectors.

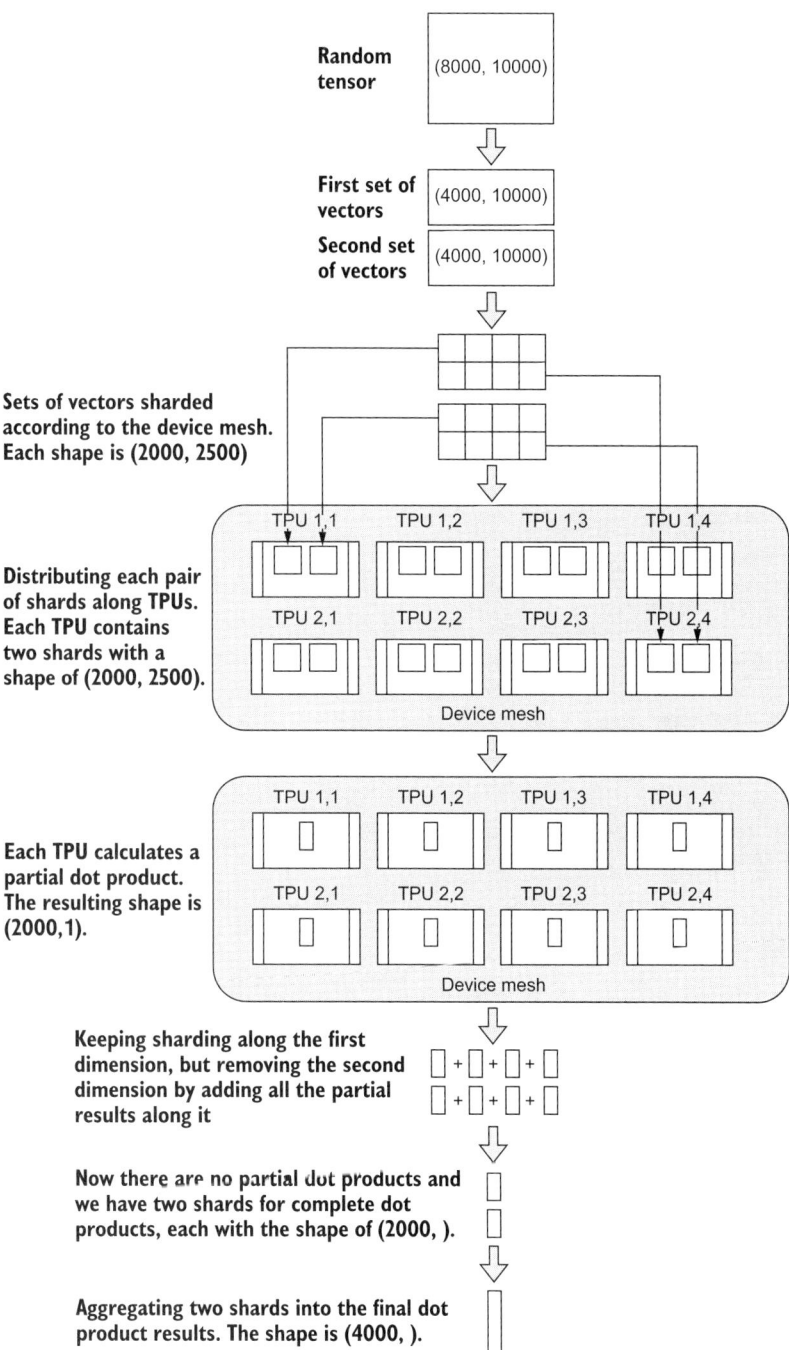

Figure 8.2   A sharding dot product calculation across a 2D mesh

The computation happens this way: each device can calculate the partial dot product based on the shards it has. So, on every device, a 2,500-element chunk of the 10,000-element vector from the first array is multiplied elementwise with a 2,500-element chunk of the 10,000-element vector from the second array, and this is happening for each of the 2,000 pairs of vectors that reside on a particular device. Each partial dot product produces a single number, and then we have to sum all the partial dot products for each vector (there are four such partial dot products) together. This is done with a collective operation hidden from us.

In the end, the first row of the device mesh contains a dot product for the first 2,000 vectors from both arrays. The second row of the device mesh contains a dot product for the second half of vectors from both arrays.

Finally, we just concatenated two remaining shards, producing the final result with 4,000 dot products. It is pretty straightforward to translate this scheme into the code.

Listing 8.3 Sharding across two dimensions

```
from jax.sharding import PartitionSpec as P
from jax.sharding import Mesh
import numpy as np

rng_key = random.PRNGKey(42)

vs = random.normal(rng_key, shape=(8_000,10_000))
v1s = vs[:4_000,:]                                        Distributes the tensors
v2s = vs[4_000:,:]

v1s.shape, v2s.shape

>>> (4000, 10000), (4000, 10000))

sharding = PositionalSharding(
  mesh_utils.create_device_mesh((2,4)))            ◄──── Creates sharding for a 2D mesh

v1sp = jax.device_put(v1s, sharding)                     Distributes the tensors
v2sp = jax.device_put(v2s, sharding)

jax.debug.visualize_array_sharding(v1sp)         ◄──── Visualizes the tensor sharding
```

```
>>>  ┌──────────┬──────────┬──────────┬──────────┐
>>>  │          │          │          │          │
>>>  │  TPU 0   │  TPU 1   │  TPU 2   │  TPU 3   │
>>>  │          │          │          │          │
>>>  │          │          │          │          │
>>>  ├──────────┼──────────┼──────────┼──────────┤
>>>  │          │          │          │          │
>>>  │  TPU 6   │  TPU 7   │  TPU 4   │  TPU 5   │
>>>  │          │          │          │          │
>>>  │          │          │          │          │
>>>  └──────────┴──────────┴──────────┴──────────┘
```

```
d = jax.vmap(dot)(v1sp, v2sp)                    ◄──── Applies the function
```

```
d.shape
```

```
>>> (4000,)
```

```
jax.debug.visualize_array_sharding(d)
```
◄─── **Visualizes the result sharding**

```
>>>  ┌───────────┬───────────┐
>>>  │TPU 0,1,2,3│TPU 4,5,6,7│
>>>  └───────────┴───────────┘
```

Here we created a 2D device mesh and distributed our tensors across it. Tensors are sharded across both their dimensions. They are sharded across the first axis, splitting all the vectors into two groups. They are also sharded across the second axis, which contains vector elements.

The dot product computations happen successfully, though the result now is sharded differently. For example, to calculate a dot product for the first pair of vectors (with index 0), you need to take the corresponding shards from TPU 0 and calculate a partial dot product there, take the shards from TPU 1 and calculate another partial dot product, and repeat the same for TPUs 2 and 3. Then you add four partial dot products (using a collective op) to obtain the final dot product. This way, the same dot product is obtained on TPUs 0, 1, 2, and 3.

Again, you can check that parallelization really happened by measuring the time consumed by the function.

Listing 8.4 Measuring times for 2D-sharded computations

```
%timeit jax.vmap(dot)(v1sp, v2sp).block_until_ready()
```
◄─── **Uses sharded tensor**

```
>>> 1.61 ms ± 39.4 µs per loop (mean ± std. dev. of 7 runs, 1,000 loops each)
```

```
%timeit jax.vmap(dot)(v1s, v2s).block_until_ready()
```
◄─── **Uses unsharded tensor**

```
>>> 2.32 ms ± 15.7 µs per loop (mean ± std. dev. of 7 runs, 100 loops each)
```

Here, we have the same speed improvement as in the 1D sharding case, which is expected as the difference is only in a few summation operations. If you look at the HLO code produced for this function (see the Notebook in the book's repository), you will see the all-reduce operation automatically placed to organize communication between groups.

8.1.4 *Using replication*

Sometimes you may not want to shard a tensor across all the sharding dimensions. In such a case, you can use sharding's `replicate(axis=NUMBER)` method to copy tensor slices to each device along the specified dimension. If no axis is specified, then it replicates along each axis. If we decide not to use the sharding's second dimension for splitting our tensors, we may use the code shown in listing 8.5.

Listing 8.5   Using replication

Still uses a 2D mesh

```
sharding = PositionalSharding(                              Distributes the tensor
  mesh_utils.create_device_mesh((2,4)))          ◄─┐       across the first
                                                   │        dimension but replicates
v1sp = jax.device_put(v1s, sharding.replicate(axis=1))  ◄─┘   along the second one

jax.debug.visualize_array_sharding(v1sp)       ◄─────── Visualizes the tensor sharding
```

```
>>>  ┌────────────────────────────────────────────────┐
>>>  │                                                  │
>>>  │                  TPU 0,1,2,3                     │
>>>  │                                                  │
>>>  │                                                  │
>>>  │                                                  │
>>>  ├──────────────────────────────────────────────────┤
>>>  │                                                  │
>>>  │                  TPU 4,5,6,7                     │
>>>  │                                                  │
>>>  │                                                  │
>>>  │                                                  │
>>>  └────────────────────────────────────────────────┘
```

Here we let JAX know that we do not want to shard our tensor across the second sharding's dimension (with index 1). Devices along this sharding dimension will contain copies of tensors across the tensor's second dimension, so effectively, each device in a group (the groups are {0, 1, 2, 3} and {4, 5, 6, 7}) has a full content of the tensor's second dimension. TPUs 0 to 3 (the same for the second group of TPUs) have the same data in their memory.

Looking at the sharding dimensions, the original sharding has a (2, 4) shape, and after calling `replicate()`, it becomes a (2, 1) shape. Unlike NumPy methods, which will squeeze the dimension with size 1 and the shape will become just (2,), the reduced axis is not squeezed. You can use the optional `keepdims=False` parameter to control this behavior.

This is the natural way to implement distributed matrix multiplication. Suppose we are multiplying two matrices, one on the left and one on the right. For the left matrix, you need to replicate rows so that each device will have a full copy of some row. For the right matrix, you need to replicate columns again to have a full copy of a column on a device. By calculating the `dot()` function on these sharded inputs, you obtain a matrix multiplication result computed in parallel on many devices.

Listing 8.6   Distributed matrix multiplication example

```
sharding = PositionalSharding(mesh_utils.create_device_mesh((2,4)))

A = random.normal(rng_key, shape=(10000,2000))          Generates two
B = random.normal(rng_key, shape=(2000,5000))           random matrices

Ad = jax.device_put(A, sharding.replicate(1))    ◄─┐   Replicates the left
                                                   │    matrix across rows
```

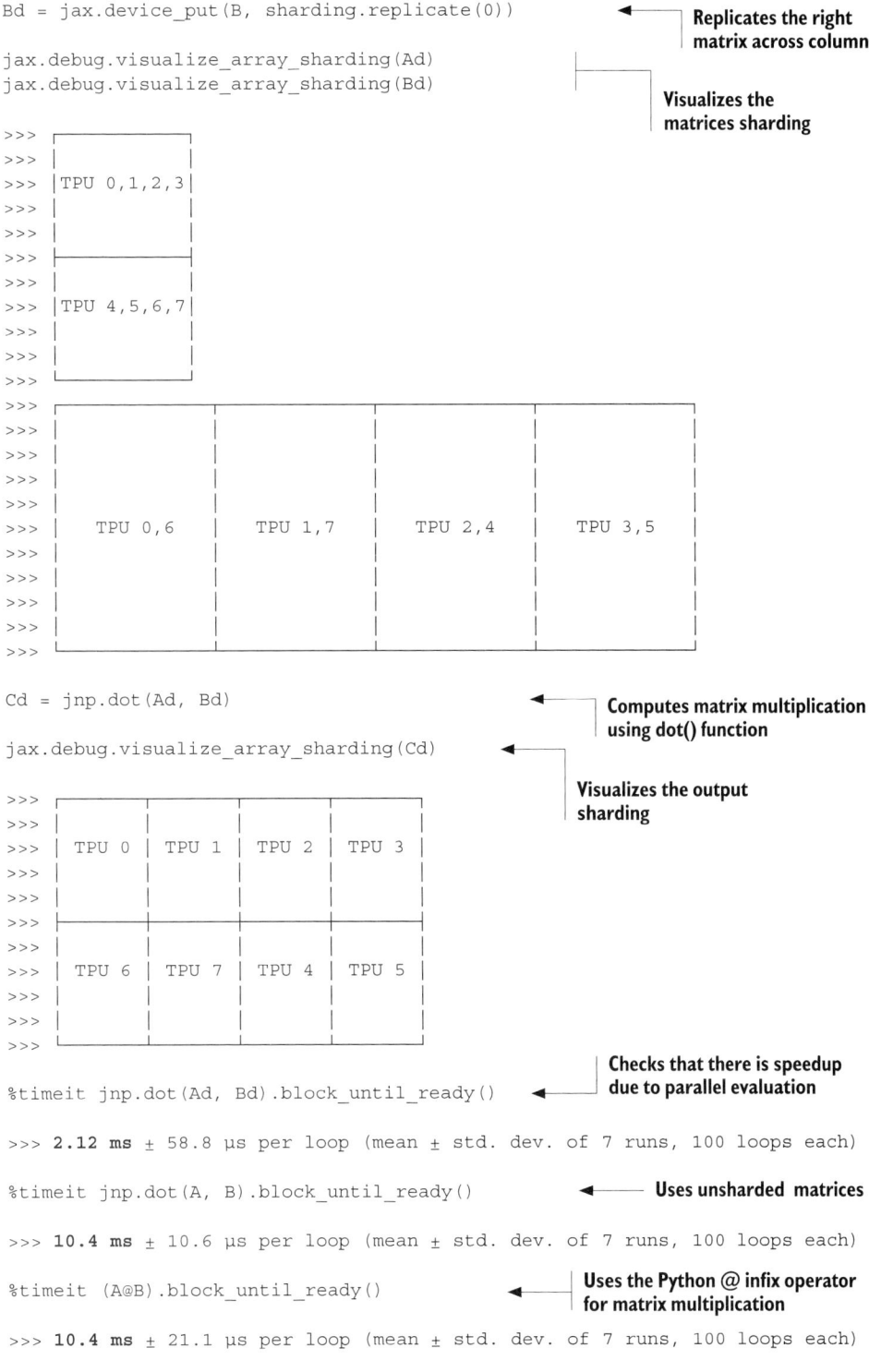

```
Bd = jax.device_put(B, sharding.replicate(0))
```
◄ **Replicates the right matrix across columns**

```
jax.debug.visualize_array_sharding(Ad)
jax.debug.visualize_array_sharding(Bd)
```
Visualizes the matrices sharding

```
>>> ┌───────────┐
>>> │           │
>>> │TPU 0,1,2,3│
>>> │           │
>>> │           │
>>> ├───────────┤
>>> │           │
>>> │TPU 4,5,6,7│
>>> │           │
>>> │           │
>>> └───────────┘
```

```
>>> ┌───────────┬───────────┬───────────┬───────────┐
>>> │           │           │           │           │
>>> │           │           │           │           │
>>> │           │           │           │           │
>>> │           │           │           │           │
>>> │  TPU 0,6  │  TPU 1,7  │  TPU 2,4  │  TPU 3,5  │
>>> │           │           │           │           │
>>> │           │           │           │           │
>>> │           │           │           │           │
>>> │           │           │           │           │
>>> └───────────┴───────────┴───────────┴───────────┘
```

```
Cd = jnp.dot(Ad, Bd)
```
◄ **Computes matrix multiplication using dot() function**

```
jax.debug.visualize_array_sharding(Cd)
```
◄ **Visualizes the output sharding**

```
>>> ┌───────┬───────┬───────┬───────┐
>>> │       │       │       │       │
>>> │ TPU 0 │ TPU 1 │ TPU 2 │ TPU 3 │
>>> │       │       │       │       │
>>> │       │       │       │       │
>>> ├───────┼───────┼───────┼───────┤
>>> │       │       │       │       │
>>> │ TPU 6 │ TPU 7 │ TPU 4 │ TPU 5 │
>>> │       │       │       │       │
>>> │       │       │       │       │
>>> └───────┴───────┴───────┴───────┘
```

```
%timeit jnp.dot(Ad, Bd).block_until_ready()
```
◄ **Checks that there is speedup due to parallel evaluation**

```
>>> 2.12 ms ± 58.8 µs per loop (mean ± std. dev. of 7 runs, 100 loops each)
```

```
%timeit jnp.dot(A, B).block_until_ready()
```
◄ **Uses unsharded matrices**

```
>>> 10.4 ms ± 10.6 µs per loop (mean ± std. dev. of 7 runs, 100 loops each)
```

```
%timeit (A@B).block_until_ready()
```
◄ **Uses the Python @ infix operator for matrix multiplication**

```
>>> 10.4 ms ± 21.1 µs per loop (mean ± std. dev. of 7 runs, 100 loops each)
```

Here we prepared the data in such a way that dot product calculation will be performed efficiently in parallel. We prepared sharded input matrices, performed matrix multiplication using dot product on sharded arrays, and compared the result with an ordinary matrix multiplication for unsharded arrays. We obtained exactly the same result as with ordinary matrix multiplication, though, in our example, it was approximately four times faster.

8.1.5   *Sharding constraints*

In addition to controlling input variables' sharding (which is done using the `jax .device_put()` function), you may give the compiler hints on how to shard intermediate function variables. It might be useful when you do not control input variables, for example. For that, you use the `jax.lax.with_sharding_constraint()` function, which is much like the `jax.device_put()` function but is used inside the `jit`-decorated functions. For example, you may implement a function for matrix multiplication that will force its argument to be sharded in a way that the multiplication becomes parallelized.

Listing 8.7   Using sharding constraints

```
from jax import jit
from functools import partial

@partial(jax.jit, static_argnums=2)
def distributed_mul(a, b, sharding):
  ad = jax.lax.with_sharding_constraint(a, sharding.replicate(1))
  bd = jax.lax.with_sharding_constraint(b, sharding.replicate(0))
  return jnp.dot(ad, bd)

sharding = PositionalSharding(mesh_utils.create_device_mesh((2,4)))

jax.debug.visualize_array_sharding(A)
jax.debug.visualize_array_sharding(B)
```

jit-annotated function with sharding as a static argument

Forces specific way of sharding

Original input arguments are unsharded.

```
>>>   ┌───────┐
>>>   │       │
>>>   │       │
>>>   │       │
>>>   │       │
>>>   │       │
>>>   │ TPU 0 │
>>>   │       │
>>>   │       │
>>>   │       │
>>>   │       │
>>>   └───────┘
>>>   ┌───────────────────────────────────┐
>>>   │                                   │
>>>   │                                   │
>>>   │                                   │
>>>   │                                   │
>>>   │                TPU 0              │
>>>   │                                   │
```

```
>>> |                                          |
>>> |                                          |
>>> |                                          |
>>> └──────────────────────────────────────────┘
```

```
d = distributed_mul(A, B, sharding)
```

```
jax.debug.visualize_array_sharding(d)
```
◀─────── **The result is sharded.**

```
>>> ┌───────┬───────┬───────┬───────┐
>>> |       |       |       |       |
>>> | TPU 0 | TPU 1 | TPU 2 | TPU 3 |
>>> |       |       |       |       |
>>> |       |       |       |       |
>>> ├───────┼───────┼───────┼───────┤
>>> |       |       |       |       |
>>> | TPU 6 | TPU 7 | TPU 4 | TPU 5 |
>>> |       |       |       |       |
>>> |       |       |       |       |
>>> └───────┴───────┴───────┴───────┘
```

Here we annotated computations to let the compiler know how the function's input arguments should be sharded. This is the same sharding pattern we used before for making a distributed multiplication using a dot product. Sharding of the resulting value shows that the constraints were applied.

8.1.6 *Named sharding*

You can also use named sharding to express shardings with names instead of positions in an array as with positional sharding. This is similar to how it is done in `xmap()` and `pjit()`; see appendix D for details.

This is done by defining a hardware mesh context manager, an *n*-dimensional array of devices with named axes. Technically, a hardware mesh is a two-component object:

- *An n-dimensional array of JAX device objects*—These are the same objects you obtain by calling the `jax.devices()` or `jax.local_devices()` functions but are represented as an `np.array` type. Be careful: it is a pure NumPy array (`np.array`), not a JAX NumPy array (`jnp.array`), because a device object is not a valid JAX array type. The `create_device_mesh()` utility function creates a proper performant device mesh with good collective performance.

- *A tuple of resource axes names*—The length of the tuple must match the rank of the device array. So, for example, for a 3D mesh, the tuple contains three resource axes names.

JAX provides a special `Mesh` context manager (https://mng.bz/GN8v). You can create the mesh the following way:

Imports Mesh type

```
from jax.sharding import Mesh
mesh = Mesh(mesh_utils.create_device_mesh((4,2)),

    axis_names=('batch', 'features'))
```

Creates a 2D mesh with two named axes, "batch" and "features"

Here we created a 2D array of available devices and a `Mesh` context manager with two axes along the hardware mesh. We name the first mesh axis the "batch" axis and the second one the "features" axis. Let's rewrite our tensor sharding example using these axes.

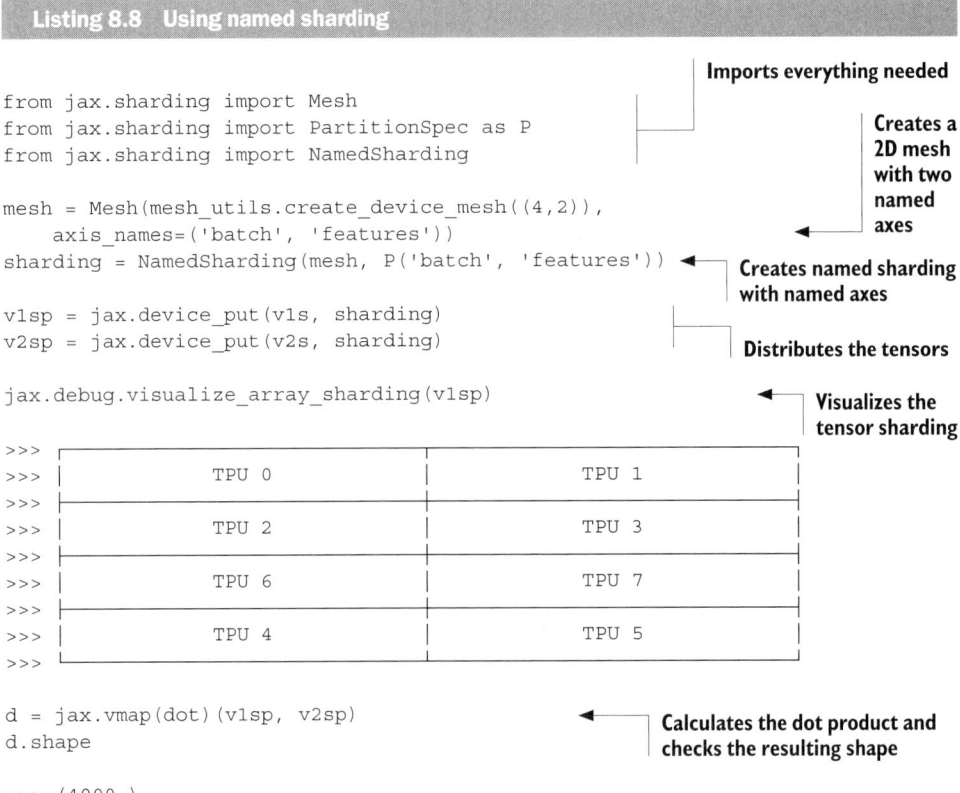

Listing 8.8 Using named sharding

```
from jax.sharding import Mesh
from jax.sharding import PartitionSpec as P        ─── Imports everything needed
from jax.sharding import NamedSharding

mesh = Mesh(mesh_utils.create_device_mesh((4,2)),       ◄─── Creates a 2D mesh with two named axes
    axis_names=('batch', 'features'))
sharding = NamedSharding(mesh, P('batch', 'features'))   ◄─── Creates named sharding with named axes

v1sp = jax.device_put(v1s, sharding)
v2sp = jax.device_put(v2s, sharding)           ─── Distributes the tensors

jax.debug.visualize_array_sharding(v1sp)              ◄─── Visualizes the tensor sharding

>>>
>>> ┌───────────────────────┬───────────────────────┐
>>> │         TPU 0         │         TPU 1         │
>>> ├───────────────────────┼───────────────────────┤
>>> │         TPU 2         │         TPU 3         │
>>> ├───────────────────────┼───────────────────────┤
>>> │         TPU 6         │         TPU 7         │
>>> ├───────────────────────┼───────────────────────┤
>>> │         TPU 4         │         TPU 5         │
>>> └───────────────────────┴───────────────────────┘
>>>

d = jax.vmap(dot)(v1sp, v2sp)          ◄─── Calculates the dot product and
d.shape                                      checks the resulting shape

>>> (4000,)
```

We created a sharding object of the type `NamedSharding` with a partition specification. The `PartitionSpec` is a tuple whose elements can be a `None`, a string name of a mesh axis, or a tuple of mesh axes names. Each element of the tuple describes a mesh dimension across which the input dimension is partitioned.

Our rank-2 tensor will be partitioned across two axes. The first dimension is partitioned across the batch axis of the mesh, and the second is partitioned across the features axis.

You may use `None` values for specifying axes for which you do not need sharding. The data will be replicated across such axes. You may also omit `None` values for trailing axes. So, to replicate the data across the second axis, you may use `NamedSharding(mesh, P('batch', None))` or just `NamedSharding(mesh, P('batch'))`.

8.1.7   *Device placement policy and errors*

The policy for sharded data is a generalization of JAX's policy of following explicit device placement, which we discussed in section 3.2.3. Remember: computations involving committed data are performed on the committed device, and the results will also be committed to the same device. Using `device_put()` with shardings produces tensors committed to a device.

You will get an error when you invoke an operation on arguments committed to different devices (but no error if some arguments are uncommitted). With sharding, if two arguments of computation are placed on different devices or their device orders are incompatible, you will get an error.

Listing 8.9   Different devices

```
sharding_a = PositionalSharding(
  np.array(jax.devices()[:4]).reshape(4,1))          ◄──── Uses first four devices
sharding_b = PositionalSharding(
  np.array(jax.devices()[4:]).reshape(4,1))          ◄──── Uses second four devices

sharding_a

>>> PositionalSharding([[{TPU 0}]
>>>                     [{TPU 1}]
>>>                     [{TPU 2}]
>>>                     [{TPU 3}]])

sharding_b

>>> PositionalSharding([[{TPU 4}]
>>>                     [{TPU 5}]
>>>                     [{TPU 6}]
>>>                     [{TPU 7}]])

v1sp = jax.device_put(v1s, sharding_a)                │ Shards the tensors
v2sp = jax.device_put(v2s, sharding_b)                │

d = jax.vmap(dot)(v1sp, v2sp)          ◄──── Produces an error saying
                                             that inputs are located on
                                             different lists of devices
>>> ...
>>> ValueError: Received incompatible devices for
jitted computation. Got ARG_SHARDING with device ids
 [0, 1, 2, 3] on platform TPU and ARG_SHARDING with
device ids [4, 5, 6, 7] on platform TPU
```

We put the first tensor across the four first devices and the second tensor across the last four devices so they do not intersect. Then the dot product function that worked before produces an error saying that the inputs are located on different lists of devices. The order inside the list of devices is important, and you get the same error even if you use the same devices for both tensors but in a different order.

If you do not explicitly commit a tensor to a device, it is placed uncommitted to the default device (TPU 0 in the case of the Cloud TPU). Uncommitted tensors can be automatically moved and resharded, so it is safe to use uncommitted tensors together with committed ones as arguments of a computation.

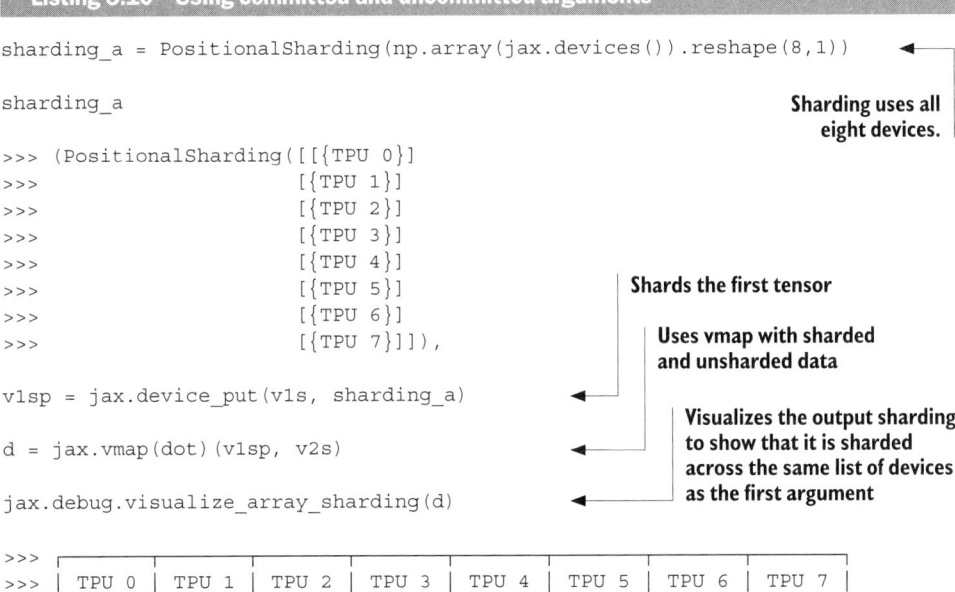

Listing 8.10   Using committed and uncommitted arguments

```
sharding_a = PositionalSharding(np.array(jax.devices()).reshape(8,1))

sharding_a

>>> (PositionalSharding([[{TPU 0}]
>>>                      [{TPU 1}]
>>>                      [{TPU 2}]
>>>                      [{TPU 3}]
>>>                      [{TPU 4}]
>>>                      [{TPU 5}]
>>>                      [{TPU 6}]
>>>                      [{TPU 7}]]),

v1sp = jax.device_put(v1s, sharding_a)

d = jax.vmap(dot)(v1sp, v2s)

jax.debug.visualize_array_sharding(d)

>>>
>>> | TPU 0 | TPU 1 | TPU 2 | TPU 3 | TPU 4 | TPU 5 | TPU 6 | TPU 7 |
>>>
```

Sharding uses all eight devices.

Shards the first tensor

Uses vmap with sharded and unsharded data

Visualizes the output sharding to show that it is sharded across the same list of devices as the first argument

Here, we sharded the first argument and committed its shards to specific devices, but we did nothing with the second argument. The computations happen successfully in this case, and the output is sharded across the same list of devices as the first argument.

With a basic understanding of how tensor sharding works, let's apply it to our guinea pig of MNIST classification using MLP, as we have done many times before.

8.2   MLP with tensor sharding

We start with a simple example of data-parallel training. We aim to parallelize training across multiple devices—here, eight TPU cores. You'll see that the code almost returns to the original version of chapter 2, though having all (or even more) of the benefits of the versions from chapter 7 and experimental parallelization approaches from appendix D.

8.2.1   Eight-way data parallelism

I skip the parts that did not change: the data loading and the MLP structure. The loss and update functions returned to the original state from chapter 2.

Listing 8.11   Loss and update functions

```
INIT_LR = 1.0
DECAY_RATE = 0.95
DECAY_STEPS = 5
NUM_EPOCHS  = 20

def loss(params, images, targets):
    """Categorical cross entropy loss function."""
```

Sets meta-parameters

The same loss function as before

```
  logits = batched_predict(params, images)
  log_preds = logits - logsumexp(logits)
  return -jnp.mean(targets*log_preds)

@jit
def update(params, x, y, epoch_number):
  loss_value, grads = value_and_grad(loss)(params, x, y)
  lr = INIT_LR * DECAY_RATE ** (epoch_number / DECAY_STEPS)
  return [(w - lr * dw, b - lr * db)
          for (w, b), (dw, db) in zip(params, grads)], loss_value
```

jit-annotated update function as before

So this is nothing new; we just returned to the original version of chapter 2. The beautiful thing is that the code at this point has not been modified in any way to accommodate parallelization. All the changes compared to chapter 2 will be in the training loop highlighted in bold in the following listing.

Listing 8.12 The complete training loop

```
@jit
def batch_accuracy(params, images, targets):
  images = jnp.reshape(images, (len(images), NUM_PIXELS))
  predicted_class = jnp.argmax(batched_predict(params, images), axis=1)
  return jnp.mean(predicted_class == targets)

def accuracy(params, data):
  accs = []
  for images, targets in data:
    accs.append(batch_accuracy(params, images, targets))
  return jnp.mean(jnp.array(accs))

sharding = PositionalSharding(jax.devices()).reshape(8, 1)

import time

params = init_params
for epoch in range(NUM_EPOCHS):
  start_time = time.time()
  losses = []
  for x, y in train_data:
    x = jnp.reshape(x, (len(x), NUM_PIXELS))
    y = one_hot(y, NUM_LABELS)
    x = jax.device_put(x, sharding)
    y = jax.device_put(y, sharding)
    params = jax.device_put(params, sharding.replicate())
    params, loss_value = update(params, x, y, epoch)
    losses.append(jnp.sum(loss_value))
  epoch_time = time.time() - start_time

  train_acc = accuracy(params, train_data)
  test_acc = accuracy(params, test_data)
  print("Epoch {} in {:0.2f} sec".format(epoch, epoch_time))
  print("Training set loss {}".format(jnp.mean(jnp.array(losses))))
  print("Training set accuracy {}".format(train_acc))
  print("Test set accuracy {}".format(test_acc))
```

Prepares device mesh

Shards data tensors across eight devices

Replicates model parameters across eight devices

```
>>> Epoch 0 in 1.66 sec
>>> Training set loss 0.803970217704773
>>> Training set accuracy 0.7943314909934998
>>> Test set accuracy 0.8018037676811218
>>> Epoch 1 in 1.04 sec
>>> Training set loss 0.7146415114402771
>>> Training set accuracy 0.8670936822891235
>>> Test set accuracy 0.875896155834198
...
>>> Epoch 19 in 0.88 sec
>>> Training set loss 0.6565680503845215
>>> Training set accuracy 0.9357565641403198
>>> Test set accuracy 0.9364372491836548
```

As you see, the changes are minor and localized. First, you create a sharding configuration. It is an (8,1) grid of TPU cores. Then you assign data tensors to devices according to this sharding. That means both x and y tensors are split along their first dimension (the batch dimension), and these shards are assigned to their own devices. You also replicate the model parameters across all the devices, so each device has its own full copy of the model parameters.

That's it! All of these changes were enough to make code for neural network training, the code that does not know anything about parallelization, fully distributed across eight TPU cores. It's really beautiful and much simpler than SPMD training using pmap() or parallelizing computations with pjit(). You may need to tune the hyperparameters like batch size (we didn't change it compared to the non-parallelized example), to make the training procedure converge faster. It is also very easy to mix data and model parallelism!

8.2.2 *Four-way data parallelism, two-way tensor parallelism*

Here we adjust our code to do both data-parallel and model-parallel training. We use four-way batch data parallelism with two-way model tensor parallelism, which means that our training examples are split across four groups of devices, and the model parameters (some weight matrices) are split across two groups of devices.

Tensor parallelism and pipeline parallelism

There are two kinds of model parallelism: tensor parallelism and pipeline parallelism.

Tensor parallelism (or *sharding*) distributes the computation of some tensor across different devices. For example, a large embedding or a fully connected layer in a neural network may be sharded across different devices so that each device calculates part of this layer output. As a tensor may have more than one dimension, sharding may be applied simultaneously to different (or many) dimensions. For the embedding or fully connected layer example, both weights and activations can be sharded independently.

Pipeline parallelism (or *pipelining*) distributes the computation of a neural network such that different layers are calculated on different devices. For example, in a deep transformer, different transformer blocks may reside on different devices, so device 1 holds layers 1 to 4, and device 2 holds layers 5 to 8.

These types of parallelism are not exclusive; you can mix both when needed (mixing with data parallelism as well).

You can read more about data, tensor, pipeline, and other types of parallelism at https://mng.bz/znJB or https://mng.bz/0MYN.

We modify our sharding and change the function to initialize model parameters, so some layers' weights becomes sharded. We also make our network deeper and wider to be closer to the case when model-parallel training would make sense (though we are still far from it, as the model perfectly fits into a single accelerator).

Listing 8.13 Sharding model weights

```
sharding = PositionalSharding(jax.devices()).reshape(4, 2)          ◀── Creates a 2D sharding

LAYER_SIZES = [28*28, 10000, 10000, 10]          ◀── Makes the network deeper and wider
PARAM_SCALE = 0.01

def init_network_params(sizes, key=random.PRNGKey(0), scale=1e-2):          ◀── No changes in the initialization function
  """Initialize all layers for a fully-connected
neural network with given sizes"""

  def random_layer_params(m, n, key, scale=1e-2):
    """A helper function to randomly initialize
weights and biases of a dense layer"""
    w_key, b_key = random.split(key)
    return (scale * random.normal(w_key, (n, m)),
        scale * random.normal(b_key, (n,)))

  keys = random.split(key, len(sizes))
  return [random_layer_params(m, n, k, scale)
    for m, n, k in zip(sizes[:-1], sizes[1:], keys)]

init_params = init_network_params(
  LAYER_SIZES, random.PRNGKey(0), scale=PARAM_SCALE)

sharded_params = []
for i,(w,b) in enumerate(init_params):
  print(i, w.shape, b.shape)
  if i==0:
    w = jax.device_put(w, sharding.replicate(0))          ┐
    b = jax.device_put(b, sharding.replicate(0))          │ Replicates weights across
  elif i==1:                                              │ axis 0, shards across axis 1
    w = jax.device_put(w, sharding.replicate(0))          │
    b = jax.device_put(b, sharding.replicate(0))          ┘
  elif i==2:
    w = jax.device_put(w, sharding.replicate())          ┐ Replicates weights
    b = jax.device_put(b, sharding.replicate())          ┘ across all axes
  sharded_params.append((w,b))
```

```
>>> 0 (10000, 784) (10000,)
>>> 1 (10000, 10000) (10000,)
>>> 2 (10, 10000) (10,)

for (w,b) in sharded_params:
  jax.debug.visualize_array_sharding(w)
  jax.debug.visualize_array_sharding(b)
```

Visualizes weight sharding

```
>>> ┌──────────┬──────────┐
>>> │          │          │
>>> │          │          │
>>> │          │          │
>>> │          │          │
>>> │          │          │
>>> │TPU 0,2,4,6│TPU 1,3,5,7│
>>> │          │          │
>>> │          │          │
>>> │          │          │
>>> │          │          │
>>> │          │          │
>>> └──────────┴──────────┘
>>> ┌──────────┬──────────┐
>>> │TPU 0,2,4,6│TPU 1,3,5,7│
>>> └──────────┴──────────┘
...
>>>
>>> ┌─────────────────────┐
>>> │                     │
>>> │                     │
>>> │                     │
>>> │                     │
>>> │                     │
>>> │TPU 0,1,2,3,4,5,6,7  │
>>> │                     │
>>> │                     │
>>> │                     │
>>> │                     │
>>> │                     │
>>> └─────────────────────┘
>>> ┌─────────────────────┐
>>> │TPU 0,1,2,3,4,5,6,7  │
>>> └─────────────────────┘
```

Here we created a (4, 2) mesh. Our goal is to shard training items across the mesh's first axis and some model parameters across the second axis.

The function for neural network weights initialization remained the same. We only changed the structure of the network. Now it has more layers, and hidden layers have more neurons.

After generating model weights, we shard specific weight and bias matrices. For the first two layers, we replicate their weights and biases across axis 0 of the grid and shard them across axis 1. This is done by the `sharding.replicate(0)` parameter. The last layer is replicated across the whole mesh completely because it's pretty small.

The sharding visualization shows that the first two layers are split across two groups of devices. Part of the weights is located in a group containing TPU {0, 2, 4, 6}. The other part of the weights is located in a group with TPU {1, 3, 5, 7}. The last layer is replicated across all eight TPUs.

Now that we have model parameters prepared and sharded, we are ready to run the complete training loop.

Listing 8.14 The complete training loop

```
params = sharded_params
for epoch in range(NUM_EPOCHS):
  start_time = time.time()
  losses = []
  for x, y in train_data:
    x = jnp.reshape(x, (len(x), NUM_PIXELS))
    y = one_hot(y, NUM_LABELS)
    x = jax.device_put(x, sharding.replicate(1))
    y = jax.device_put(y, sharding.replicate(1))
    params, loss_value = update(params, x, y, epoch)
    losses.append(jnp.sum(loss_value))
  epoch_time = time.time() - start_time

  train_acc = accuracy(params, train_data)
  test_acc = accuracy(params, test_data)
  print("Epoch {} in {:0.2f} sec".format(epoch, epoch_time))
  print("Training set loss {}".format(jnp.mean(jnp.array(losses))))
  print("Training set accuracy {}".format(train_acc))
  print("Test set accuracy {}".format(test_acc))

>>> Epoch 0 in 14.36 sec
>>> Training set loss 0.7603772282600403
>>> Training set accuracy 0.8505693674087524
>>> Test set accuracy 0.8597139716148376
...
```

> **Replicates training data across the second axis, shards across the first axis**

There are two changes. First, we changed the sharding for training data. They are now replicated across the mesh's second axis (with index 1) but sharded across the first axis (with four groups of devices). Second, the model parameters do not need to be replicated inside the loop as we tuned their sharding before. Gradients will also be calculated locally on the same devices where the model parameters reside, so after the model parameter update, the parameters remain on the device where they were before the update, and their localization does not change. You see how mixing data and tensor parallelism with this new distributed arrays API is easy!

In this particular example, there is not much benefit from model-parallel training because the model is still too small, yet it is a very useful skill in the world of very large models.

Summary

- Tensor sharding and the new distributed arrays API allow easy parallelization with a very modest code change.
- Since version 0.4.1, JAX introduced the `jax.Array`, which is a unified array type that subsumes `DeviceArray`, `ShardedDeviceArray`, and `GlobalDeviceArray` types. The new `jax.Array` type helps make parallelism a core feature of JAX.

- `jax.Array` simplifies and unifies JAX internals and allows unifying `jit()` and `pjit()`: if data is transferred to devices, `jit()` will parallelize it automatically.

- In JAX, computations follow the data placement. Tensor sharding can be viewed as an extension of device placement rules from chapter 3.

- The `mesh_utils.create_device_mesh()` function returns the most performant ordering of devices given the shape.

- `PositionalSharding` acts like an array with sets of devices as elements.

- `NamedSharding` can express shardings with names instead of positions in an array.

- The familiar `jax.device_put()` function can also accept a sharding object instead of a particular device and place the data accordingly.

- You may give the compiler hints on how to shard intermediate function variables. For that, you use the `jax.lax.with_sharding_constraint()` function, which is much like the `jax.device_put()` function but is used inside the `jit`-decorated functions.

- You can use sharding's `replicate(axis=NUMBER)` method to copy tensor slices to each device along the specified dimension. If no axis is specified, then it replicates along each axis.

- With sharding, if two arguments of computation are placed on different devices or their device orders are incompatible, you will get an error.

- It is easy to achieve data and model parallelism with tensor sharding just by changing the data layout and almost without changes in code that performs computations.

Random numbers
in JAX

This chapter covers

- Generating (pseudo) random numbers in JAX
- Differences with NumPy and using keys to represent pseudo-random number generator state
- Working with keys and generating random numbers in real-life applications

Working with randomness is essential, as many machine learning algorithms use stochasticity in some way. Randomness is used to make random splits and samplings from the data, generate random data, and perform random augmentations. It is also required for for specific neural network–related algorithms like Dropout or architectures like variational auto-encoders (VAE) or generative adversarial networks (GANs) and in hyperparameter tuning to search for better hyperparameter values. Randomness is also essential to the process that is at the heart of deep learning: weight initialization. Surely randomness is no less important in other fields outside of machine learning. Random numbers are at the heart of Monte Carlo simulations and statistical sampling and have many applications in computer simulation of real-world processes.

Another important topic in machine learning is reproducibility. It is very common to set a seed so that no matter how often the same process is executed, the same sequence of random numbers is expected to be produced. But by setting a global seed (like NumPy uses), the reproducibility breaks down when concurrency or parallelization is introduced into the code. In addition, XLA might execute code in a different order than it appears but in the most efficient manner. This means that we may not get reproducibility by defining a specific execution order in the code, as we expect.

The random number generation process in JAX is structured very differently than NumPy; the roots of this difference lie in the functional nature of JAX. NumPy uses an internal state inside a random number generator and modifies it on every function call so that the subsequent calls produce different random values. In the functional programming paradigm, having an internal state is bad because it makes your functions not pure, and they should return the same values for the same inputs. So JAX provides an alternative: functionally pure random number generators. These generators consume keys that represent the state of the generator, so you need to manage keys responsibly. Do not use any key twice (or you will have the same "random" numbers), and create a new key each time you need to generate a new set of random values.

In this chapter, you will learn how to work with (pseudo-) random numbers in JAX. First, we will quickly take a glimpse at the example of random number generation for data augmentation. Then, we will dive deeper into the functions for working with random numbers and compare NumPy's approach with JAX's. Finally, we will create a couple of real-life cases that require random numbers: a complete data augmentation pipeline and a random weight initialization for a neural network.

9.1   *Generating random data*

Let's start with a simple example of generating random noise to augment training data. Imagine you have a dataset of images to train your neural network image classifier. To add some robustness to your network (and also to increase the size of the training dataset), you want to perform a set of data augmentations: adding random noise and making random rotations. It is common practice in image classification to augment data by performing such simple transformations to add diversity to the dataset, as this will work as implicit regularization and thus reduce overfitting. In some sense, this is the reverse process for our image filtering example in section 3.1.

Random and pseudo-random numbers

Many computer random number generators (RNGs) are essentially pseudo-random number generators (PRNGs). They use some algorithmic deterministic process to produce sequences of numbers with properties that approximate the properties of true random number sequences from a desired distribution.

The deterministic algorithmic process is initialized and completely determined by some seed value, which creates an internal state of a PRNG. This state is later updated between subsequent calls, either automatically (and hidden from a programmer) or manually, to produce different pseudo-random values. Pseudo-random number generations, which use the same internal state, produce the same numbers.

Since the state space is finite, a PRNG must eventually return to a state it was in previously. The smallest number of steps after which the state returns to some previous value is called a *period* of the generator. The widely used Mersenne Twister PRNG has a period of $2^{19937}-1$ iteration.

A separate class of PRNGs is cryptographic PRNGs with special requirements. In Python, you can use the `os.urandom()` function that uses an OS-specific randomness source, which should be suitable for cryptographic applications—the `random.SystemRandom()` generator uses this function. It does not rely on software state, and sequences are not reproducible.

Hardware RNGs are available on some machines and operating systems. They are typically devises using some physical process to generate truly random numbers. Intel CPUs provide the RDRAND and RDSEED instructions for returning random numbers from an on-chip hardware RNG. Their entropy source uses thermal noise within the chip.

Among more exotic options, there is, for example, a quantum source of randomness by the Australian National University (https://qrng.anu.edu.au/), where random numbers are generated by measuring the quantum fluctuations of the vacuum. The `quantumrandom` module provides a Python API to it.

This chapter is dedicated to PRNGs, and in the text of the chapter, I will not repeat the word "pseudo-random" each time; instead, I'll use the shorter word "random." But be aware that it really means a pseudo-random value in each case.

We will use a new dataset for binary classification between cats and dogs. We will also use it in chapter 11, where we will build a more state-of-the-art neural network for image classification using high-level neural network libraries.

The process for the data augmentation is simple. For each image in the input batch, it will randomly choose one of the two random augmentations: adding a Gaussian noise or flipping an image horizontally. Figure 9.1 demonstrates the process visually.

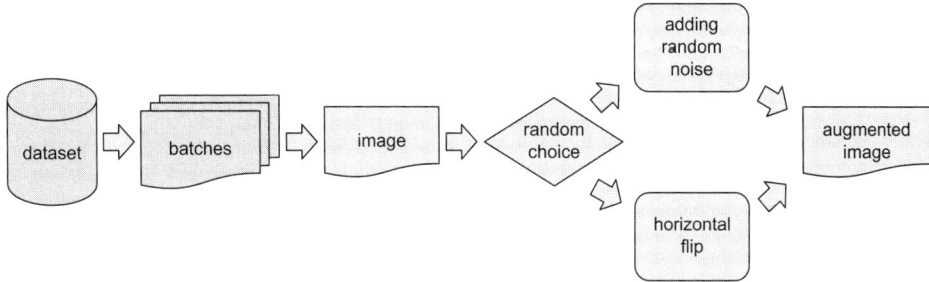

Figure 9.1   Scheme of the data augmentation process

We will implement parts of this process, starting from dataset loading.

9.1.1 Loading the dataset

We will take a well-known Dogs vs. Cats dataset (https://www.kaggle.com/c/dogs-vs
-cats) from Kaggle. Figure 9.2 is a sample from the dataset.

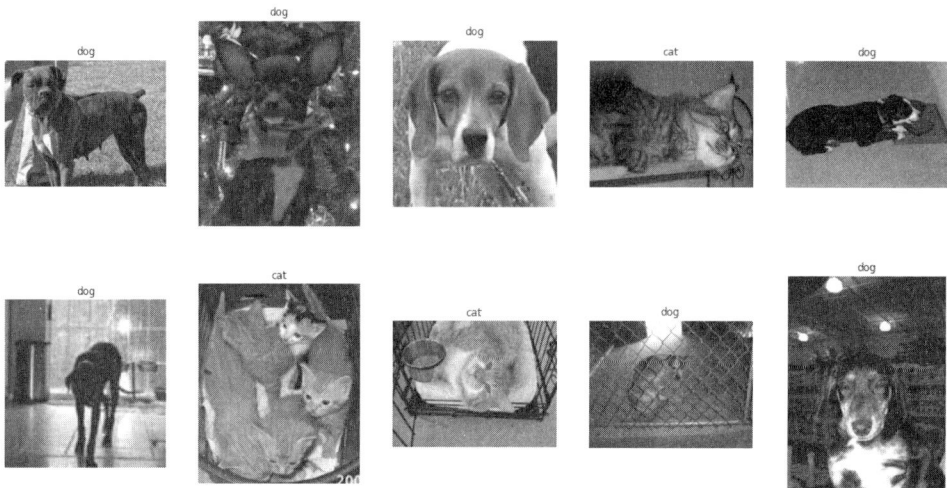

Figure 9.2   Samples from the Dogs vs. Cats dataset

TensorFlow Datasets contain a version of the Dogs vs. Cats dataset under the name
`cats_vs_dogs`; 1,738 corrupted images were dropped from the original dataset, and
the total number of images is 23,262. The dataset contains no train/test split, so we
need to split it on our own.

Listing 9.1   Loading the dataset

```
import tensorflow as tf
# Ensure TF does not see GPU and grab all GPU memory.
tf.config.set_visible_devices([], device_type='GPU')

import tensorflow_datasets as tfds

data_dir = '/tmp/tfds'

# As the dataset does not contain any train/test split
# we make our own split into train and test dataset.
# as_supervised=True gives us the (image, label) as a tuple instead of a dict
data, info = tfds.load(name="cats_vs_dogs",          ◀──── Loads cats_vs_dogs dataset
                       data_dir=data_dir,
                       split=["train[:80%]", "train[80%:]"],   ◀────
                       as_supervised=True,
                       with_info=True)                 Performs 80%/20%
                                                        train/test split using
                                                        TensorFlow Datasets
(cats_dogs_data_train, cats_dogs_data_test) = data     internal functionality
```

We do not implement our own splitting logic, relying instead on the TensorFlow Datasets functionality to split the data into 80%/20% for train and test sets, respectively.

We can look at the samples from the dataset to obtain an image from figure 9.2 with the code in the following listing.

Listing 9.2   Samples from the dataset

```
import matplotlib.pyplot as plt
plt.rcParams['figure.figsize'] = [20, 10]

CLASS_NAMES = ['cat', 'dog']
ROWS = 2
COLS = 5

i = 0
fig, ax = plt.subplots(ROWS, COLS)                    ◄─── Displays a 2 × 5 grid of images
for image, label in cats_dogs_data_train.take(ROWS*COLS):
    ax[int(i/COLS), i%COLS].axis('off')
    ax[int(i/COLS), i%COLS].set_title(CLASS_NAMES[label])
    ax[int(i/COLS), i%COLS].imshow(image)
    i += 1

plt.show()
```

As you can see, the images have different sizes, so to process them similarly and pack multiple images into a batch, we want to add some preprocessing to the dataset.

Preprocessing will resize all the images to the same size, 200 × 200 pixels, also normalizing the pixel RGB values that take values in the range of [0, 255] into the range of [0, 1].

Listing 9.3   Preprocessing the dataset and splitting it into batches

```
HEIGHT = 200
WIDTH  = 200
NUM_LABELS = info.features['label'].num_classes

import jax.numpy as jnp                               ◄─── Simple preprocessing function to apply to each image

def preprocess(img, label):
  """Resize and preprocess images."""
  return tf.image.resize(img, [HEIGHT, WIDTH]) / 255.0, label    ◄─── Resizes and normalizes an image

train_data = tfds.as_numpy(
  cats_dogs_data_train.map(preprocess).batch(32).prefetch(1))
test_data  = tfds.as_numpy(
  cats_dogs_data_test.map(preprocess).batch(32).prefetch(1))
```

We ask the dataloader to apply the preprocess function to each example, pack all the images into a set of batches of the size of 32 items, and prefetch a new batch without waiting for the previous batch to finish processing on the GPU.

Our preprocessing will lose some information, though the images are still recognizable (see figure 9.3).

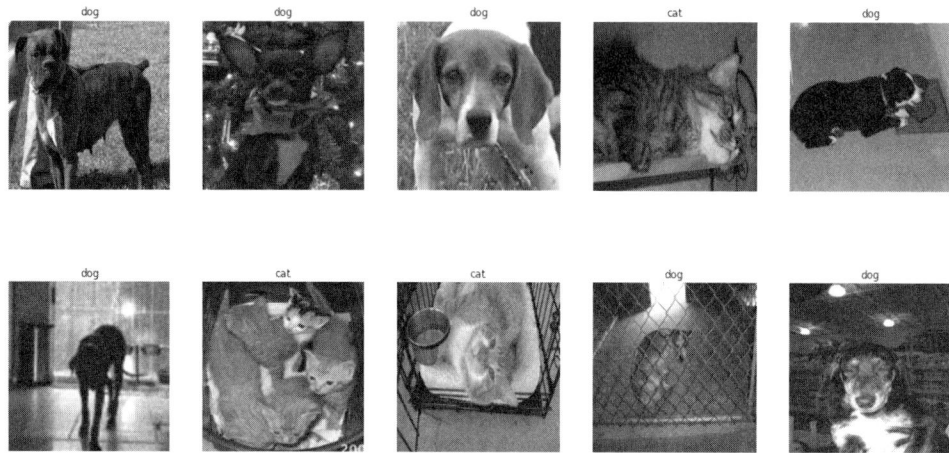

Figure 9.3   Samples from the Dogs vs. Cats dataset after preprocessing

Now let's resume with the dataset augmentation.

9.1.2   *Generating random noise*

The first augmentation will be adding random noise to an image. This way, we can multiply the number of images by creating several noisy images from an original one.

We start with generating random Gaussian noise and adding it to an image. To do that, we need to generate a tensor containing noise with the same shape as the image and then sum the image and the noise tensor, possibly with some weights.

JAX provides a rich set of functions for generating random numbers from different distributions. The full list is available at https://mng.bz/j0rr.

There is a `jax.random.normal()` function for generating random variables from the standard Gaussian distribution with 0 mean and standard deviation of 1. This function resembles the `numpy.random.normal()` function but with different parameters. We will discuss them shortly. First, we load an image.

Listing 9.4   Taking an image

```
import jax

batch_images,batch_labels = next(iter(train_data))     ◀── Takes a batch of images
batch_images[0].shape                                       from the data loader

>>> (200, 200, 3)                    ◀──  This is a color
                                          200 × 200 pixel image.

image = batch_images[0]
image.min(), image.max()             ◀──  Image is described by float
                                          values in the range of [0.0, 1.0]
>>> (0.0, 1.0)

plt.imshow(image)                    ◀──  Draws the image
```

We took the first image from the training dataset (see figure 9.4).

Figure 9.4 The first image from the training dataset

Nothing special happens in this code; we just take the first image of the first batch of the training dataset to use it for augmentations. Now we are ready to prepare a noise tensor with the shape of the image.

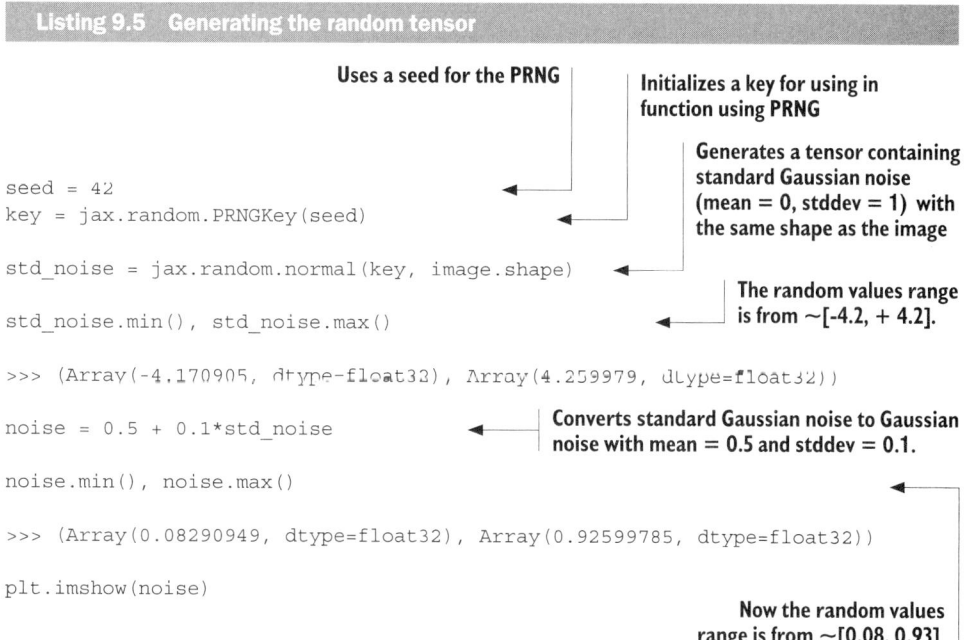

```
Listing 9.5   Generating the random tensor
```

Uses a seed for the PRNG

Initializes a key for using in function using **PRNG**

Generates a tensor containing standard Gaussian noise (mean = 0, stddev = 1) with the same shape as the image

```
seed = 42
key = jax.random.PRNGKey(seed)

std_noise = jax.random.normal(key, image.shape)

std_noise.min(), std_noise.max()
```

The random values range is from ~[-4.2, + 4.2].

```
>>> (Array(-4.170905, dtype=float32), Array(4.259979, dtype=float32))

noise = 0.5 + 0.1*std_noise
```

Converts standard Gaussian noise to Gaussian noise with mean = 0.5 and stddev = 0.1.

```
noise.min(), noise.max()

>>> (Array(0.08290949, dtype=float32), Array(0.92599785, dtype=float32))

plt.imshow(noise)
```

Now the random values range is from ~[0.08, 0.93].

There are several essential things in the code. We use some seed value to initialize a PRNG, which is done using an object called a key. We will dive into the internals of PRNG soon, but what is important now is that any function (here `jax.random.normal()`) that uses a PRNG consumes a key. A key is created by calling the `random.PRNGKey(seed)` function. This function takes in a 64- or 32-bit integer value as a seed to generate a key.

The second parameter of the `jax.random.normal()` function is the shape of the output value. We passed the same shape the image has, so the function essentially generates many random numbers at once.

If you compare this function with the `numpy.random.normal()` function, you will see they differ entirely in their parameters. First, the function from NumPy (https://mng.bz/WVea) consumes the mean and standard deviation as arguments, while the JAX function (https://mng.bz/86yz) assumes the mean is 0 and the standard deviation is 1. Second, the NumPy function does not consume any seed or key, while the JAX function explicitly consumes a key. Finally, both functions allow passing a shape for the output value.

We generated values from the standard Gaussian distribution; then, by multiplying them by 0.1 and adding 0.5, we obtained a Gaussian distribution with a mean of 0.5 and a standard deviation of 0.1.

It's important to say right away that to generate *different* random values, you need to use *different* keys. If you use the same key again, you will get exactly the same pseudorandom values as before. We will explain the different ways of generating keys in the next section. The generated noise is shown in figure 9.5.

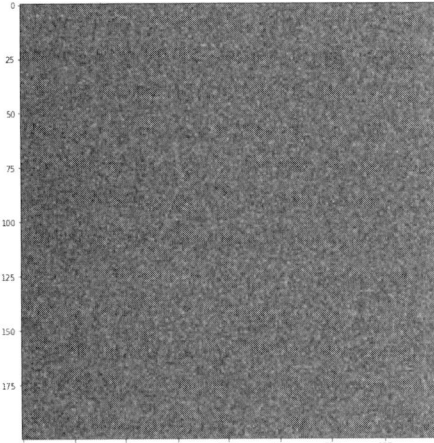

Figure 9.5   Generated random noise

In the end, we are ready to produce a noisy version of the image.

Listing 9.6 Generating a noisy image

```
new_image = image + noise
new_image.min(), new_image.max()
```
◀ **Adds the image and the noise**

```
>>> (Array(0.2063958, dtype=float32),
➥ Array(1.7627949, dtype=float32))
```
◀ **We are out of the [0.0, 1.0] range now.**

```
new_image = (new_image - new_image.min())/(
➥    new_image.max() - new_image.min())
```
◀ **Normalizes the resulting image to have values in the range [0.0, 1.0]**

```
new_image.min(), new_image.max()
```

```
>>> (Array(0., dtype=float32), Array(1., dtype=float32))
```
◀ **Checks that everything is right**

```
plt.imshow(new_image)
```

The final part is straightforward; we add the original image and the generated noise. The only thing to remember is that images contain values in the range of [0.0, 1.0], but we are out of this range after addition. So we have to normalize the result, and finally, we have a noisy version of the image (see figure 9.6).

Figure 9.6 A noisy version of the image

We processed a single image; the next step will be processing batches of images. We will perform this step later in the chapter after we learn more about the keys.

9.1.3 *Performing a random augmentation*

Let's also add another type of random augmentation: a horizontal flip. This operation usually does not change the semantics of an image, and it is safe to generate flipped versions of cat and dog images, while doing a vertical flip may produce unnatural images like upside-down animals. We can make a horizontal flip of a tensor without calling any special function by just reversing each row of an image.

Listing 9.7   Performing a horizontal flip

```
image_flipped = image[:,::-1,:]                    Reverses the second
                                                   axis of the tensor
plt.imshow(image_flipped)
```

We reverse the second axis of the tensor. This axis contains columns of an image. The resulting image is flipped (see figure 9.7.). Alternatively, you may use the `fliplr()` function, which is available in both NumPy and JAX.

Figure 9.7   Horizontally flipped version of the image

Now we are ready to write a function that randomly applies an augmentation, either generating a noisy version of an image or flipping it horizontally. Here, we use a function that chooses only one of the augmentations. In real-life cases, you may want to use a combination of augmentations (unless they do not contradict each other). Treat this possible extension as an exercise.

We already discussed such a function in section 3.4, and using the `jax.lax` control flow primitives is a natural way of doing this. We will use the `jax.lax.switch()` function as it allows adding more augmentations. The important thing here is that we now have two random functions, each requiring a key: one for choosing an augmentation and another (if that branch is chosen) to generate random noise.

Using the same key for both functions would be a mistake, as a key should be used only once. Otherwise, you have very limited randomness, as both function calls will be entangled and produce correlated results.

So we need to generate a new key for the second call, which is done by splitting a key. You can use the `jax.random.split()` function for that. The following listing shows the code for performing a random augmentation.

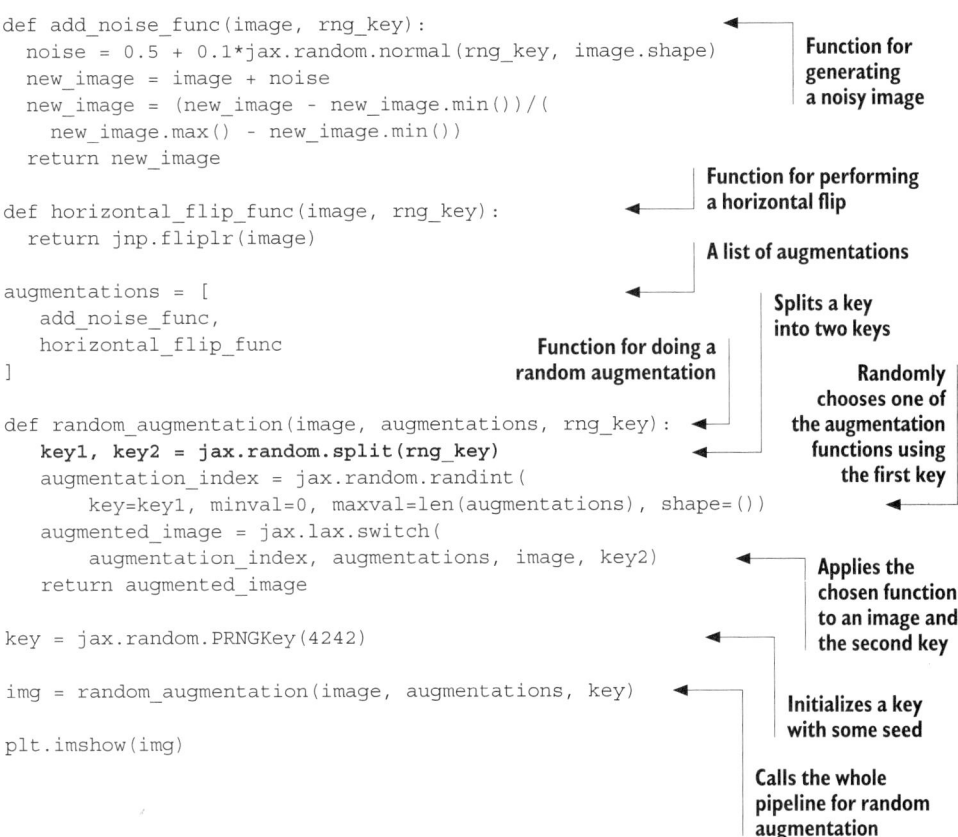

Listing 9.8 Performing a random augmentation

```
def add_noise_func(image, rng_key):                              Function for
  noise = 0.5 + 0.1*jax.random.normal(rng_key, image.shape)      generating
  new_image = image + noise                                      a noisy image
  new_image = (new_image - new_image.min())/(
    new_image.max() - new_image.min())
  return new_image
                                                       Function for performing
def horizontal_flip_func(image, rng_key):              a horizontal flip
  return jnp.fliplr(image)
                                                       A list of augmentations
augmentations = [
  add_noise_func,                                              Splits a key
  horizontal_flip_func                                         into two keys
]                                        Function for doing a
                                         random augmentation     Randomly
def random_augmentation(image, augmentations, rng_key):          chooses one of
  key1, key2 = jax.random.split(rng_key)                         the augmentation
  augmentation_index = jax.random.randint(                       functions using
      key=key1, minval=0, maxval=len(augmentations), shape=())   the first key
  augmented_image = jax.lax.switch(
      augmentation_index, augmentations, image, key2)
  return augmented_image                                       Applies the
                                                               chosen function
key = jax.random.PRNGKey(4242)                                 to an image and
                                                               the second key
img = random_augmentation(image, augmentations, key)
                                                          Initializes a key
plt.imshow(img)                                           with some seed

                                                       Calls the whole
                                                       pipeline for random
                                                       augmentation
```

This code gathers all our previous developments into a pipeline working on a single image. First, we reorganized the code from previous sections into two Python functions and a list of augmentations. Each function must have the same signature (the same list of parameters with the same order); otherwise, we cannot call them in a uniform way from the `jax.lax.switch()` function. Because of that, the function for horizontal flipping also takes in a key for PRNG, though it does not use it.

Then we prepared a function for choosing and applying a random augmentation. This function is almost the same as the function in listing 3.27, with only a single addition of splitting a key.

The function consumes a key for PRNG and splits it into two keys. The first key will be required to generate a random value (an integer index) to choose one of the available augmentations. This key is consumed by the `jax.random.randint()` function. The `randint()` function with parameters `minval=0` and `maxval=2` returns either 0 or 1 but not 2. The second key is required to generate a random noise tensor if the corresponding function was chosen in the previous step. If the horizontal flipping function was chosen instead, we effectively waste the second key, as it is not required for such an operation. But we need to do it this way to be able to call different functions from the `jax.lax.switch()`. You can experiment with different initial key values to see how the function works. You may also extend this function by adding other augmentations.

Now we have seen enough to dive deeper into the PRNG internals and to understand why JAX organizes work with random numbers this way.

9.2 Differences with NumPy

Before discussing JAX, let's look at NumPy; this should help us better understand the differences between the NumPy way of doing things and the JAX way of doing things.

9.2.1 How NumPy works

To generate random numbers in NumPy, you just call functions to provide random values sampled from different distributions and choose the output shape you want. What's important is that the subsequent calls return different values. The process of generating a random number in NumPy is shown schematically in figure 9.8.

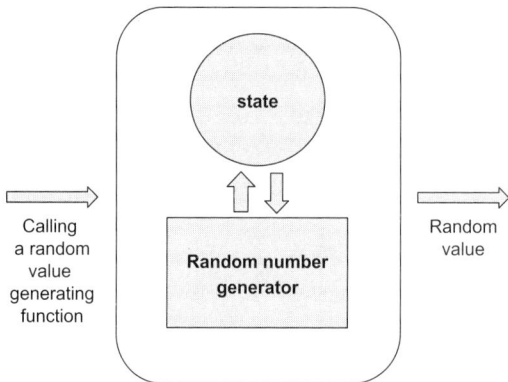

Figure 9.8   Random number generation in NumPy; the state is internally updated by the RNG.

In older versions of NumPy, you call methods from the `numpy.random` module; in the newer versions since 1.17, you call methods of an RNG object. In the following listing, we generate random values from the normal distribution using the new and the legacy NumPy API.

Listing 9.9   Generating random values in NumPy

```
from numpy import random
vals = random.normal(loc=0.5, scale=0.1, size=(3,5))
more_vals = random.normal(loc=0.5, scale=0.1, size=(3,5))
```

Uses legacy random generation

Generates random normal values

Generates more random normal values

```
vals
>>> array([[0.41442475, 0.66198785, 0.42058724, 0.54404004, 0.43972029],
>>>        [0.41518162, 0.36498766, 0.54380958, 0.63188696, 0.40681366],
>>>        [0.49568808, 0.45086299, 0.49072887, 0.40336257, 0.41021533]])

more_vals
>>> array([[0.37960004, 0.48809215, 0.59210434, 0.53701619, 0.60282681],
>>>        [0.60296999, 0.42870291, 0.61688912, 0.43114899, 0.41913782],
>>>        [0.45572322, 0.48780771, 0.482078  , 0.59348996, 0.41206967]])

from numpy.random import default_rng
rng = default_rng()
vals = rng.normal(loc=0.5, scale=0.1, size=(3,5))
more_vals = rng.normal(loc=0.5, scale=0.1, size=(3,5))

vals
>>> array([[0.49732516, 0.41752651, 0.54104826, 0.60639913, 0.49745545],
>>>        [0.39052283, 0.57229021, 0.54367553, 0.70409461, 0.44481841],
>>>        [0.4184092 , 0.48017174, 0.32490981, 0.30408382, 0.45733146]])

more_vals
>>> array([[0.39426541, 0.6461455 , 0.38793849, 0.50340449, 0.62198861],
>>>        [0.4760281 , 0.43383763, 0.41066168, 0.57226022, 0.36438518],
>>>        [0.71569246, 0.52847295, 0.61811126, 0.45912844, 0.59835265]])
```

Subsequent calls produce different values.

Uses new approach for random generation

Generates random normal values

Generates more random normal values

Subsequent calls produce different values.

We used the legacy approach for random number generation using the `random.normal()` function and the new approach using a separate RNG and the `normal()` generator method.

I want to highlight that the subsequent calls of the same function with the same parameters produce different numbers. It may look handy for a programmer, who generates more numbers when needed, but it is against the functional approach, as such a function is not functionally pure. Functionally pure functions should return the same values given the same parameters. That's precisely the reason JAX needs to use a different approach, and we will cover it shortly.

Now let's dive deeper into NumPy random number generation to understand better how it works and what needs to be changed to adapt it to JAX.

9.2.2 Seed and state in NumPy

First, there is a notion of a *seed* to initialize a PRNG. We used it occasionally in our code examples where we needed some randomness. Using the same seed number for a PRNG helps maintain reproducibility. Repeating a sequence of random number generations will obtain the exact same numbers if you reinitialize the PRNG it with the same seed. We demonstrate this behavior in listing 9.10.

Listing 9.10   Using seed to reproduce random values

Uses the same
seed for both calls

```
random.seed(42)
vals = random.normal(loc=0.5, scale=0.1, size=(3,5))
random.seed(42)
more_vals = random.normal(loc=0.5, scale=0.1, size=(3,5))
```

Calls are exactly
the same.

```
vals
```

Produces
the same
numbers

```
>>> array([[0.54967142, 0.48617357, 0.56476885, 0.65230299, 0.47658466],
>>>        [0.4765863 , 0.65792128, 0.57674347, 0.45305256, 0.554256  ],
>>>        [0.45365823, 0.45342702, 0.52419623, 0.30867198, 0.32750822]])
```

```
more_vals
```

```
>>> array([[0.54967142, 0.48617357, 0.56476885, 0.65230299, 0.47658466],
>>>        [0.4765863 , 0.65792128, 0.57674347, 0.45305256, 0.554256  ],
>>>        [0.45365823, 0.45342702, 0.52419623, 0.30867198, 0.32750822]])
```

As you can see, identical calls with the same seed value produce the same numbers.

Another interesting guarantee is the *sequential equivalent guarantee* that NumPy provides. This means that no matter whether you sample *N* individual numbers or an array of *N* numbers, the resulting random sequence will be the same, as you can see in the following listing.

Listing 9.11   Demonstrating sequential equivalent guarantee

Uses the same
seed as before

Generates the
same number
of random
numbers
sequentially

```
random.seed(42)
even_more_vals = np.array(
    [random.normal(loc=0.5, scale=0.1) for i in range(3*5)]
).reshape((3,5))
```

Produces the
same numbers

```
even_more_vals
```

```
>>> array([[0.54967142, 0.48617357, 0.56476885, 0.65230299, 0.47658466],
>>>        [0.4765863 , 0.65792128, 0.57674347, 0.45305256, 0.554256  ],
>>>        [0.45365823, 0.45342702, 0.52419623, 0.30867198, 0.32750822]])
```

Here we generated a list of random normal values sequentially, value by value. We created a NumPy array and reshaped it to the (3, 5) shape we had before. The resulting matrix is precisely the same as we had in listing 9.10.

Second, NumPy PRNGs are *stateful*, meaning the generator has an internal *state*. This state is deterministically initialized using the seed provided (or some default value). Then the state is updated after each generator call, so subsequent calls of the same function with the same parameters use a different state value and return different values. You can look at the state using the `random.get_state()` function.

Listing 9.12 Looking at the PRNG state for the legacy approach

```
random.seed(42)
```
◄——— **Uses the same seed as before**

```
random.get_state()
```
◄——— **Gets the state**

```
>>> ('MT19937', array([        42, 3107752595, 1895908407, 3900362577,
>>> ...
>>>         2783561793, 1329389532,  836540831,   26719530], dtype=uint32),
>>>         624, 0, 0.0)
```

```
vals = random.normal(loc=0.5, scale=0.1, size=(3,5))
```
◄——┐ **Generates some**
      random values

```
random.get_state()
```
◄——— **Gets the updated state**

```
>>> ('MT19937', array([ 723970371, 1229153189, 4170412009, 2042542564,
>>> ...
>>>         3446775024, 1857191784, 1432291794, 4088152671], dtype=uint32),
>>>         40, 1, -0.5622875292409727)
```

You can see that the state is a tuple of five elements. The first element of the tuple contains information about the algorithm behind the PRNG; it is MT19937 here. Then there is an array of 624 integers with three more numbers. We will not dive into the internals of the MT19937 and its state here.

The state after initialization and the state after calling the `random.normal()` function are different states. If you set the seed to the same value of 42, you will return to the same state you had at the beginning of the example. The new NumPy approach for RNG uses a combination of a `BitGenerator` to create sequences of random numbers (typically unsigned integer words filled with sequences of either 32 or 64 random bits) and a `Generator` that transforms sequences of random bits from a `BitGenerator` into sequences of numbers that follow a specific probability distribution.

`BitGenerator` manages the state, and seeds are passed to `BitGenerators`. By default, they use a PCG64 generator (which may change in future versions) with better statistical properties than the legacy MT19937 generator. You can use the older MT19937 bit generator if you want, though it is not recommended.

MT19937, PCG64, Threefly, and other PRNGs

Internals of random number generation aren't essential for using JAX, but they may be interesting for some readers.

Mersenne Twister is a widely known general-purpose (not cryptographic) PRNG and is the default PRNG in many software programs. It was developed by Makoto Matsumoto (松本 眞) and Takuji Nishimura (西村 拓士) in 1997. Its period length is chosen to be a Mersenne prime, so that's the name. Its period is $2^{19937}-1$, so that's the number in the name *MT19937* of a standard 32-bit implementation. The state consists of 624 32-bit unsigned integers plus a single integer value that indexes the current position within this array. It has poor throughput and a large state and is not Crush-resistant, as it passes many, but not all, tests for statistical randomness from the TestU01 library.

(continued)

A PRNG is called Crush-resistant if it passes all the tests from Crush batteries (Small Crush, Crush, and Big Crush) from the TestU01 library (https://mng.bz/EOnd).

Permuted congruential generator (PCG) is a PRNG developed by Dr. M.E. O'Neill in 2014. It has a small state size, it's fast, and it demonstrates excellent statistical performance. See the author's page for more details about this algorithm: https://www.pcg-random .org/. *PCG-64* is the default implementation in NumPy. There is also its upgraded variant for heavily parallel use cases called *PCG64DXSM*.

There are other PRNGs as well; see the following page for the details and recommendations: https://mng.bz/NBdn.

JAX uses the *Threefry* counter-based PRNG described in the paper "Parallel Random Numbers: As Easy as 1, 2, 3" (https://mng.bz/Dp8R) with a functional array-oriented splitting model described in another paper, "Splittable Pseudorandom Number Generators Using Cryptographic Hashing" (https://dl.acm.org/doi/10.1145/2578854.2503784). It is a fast PRNG with reduced cryptographic strength. Threefry is the fastest Crush-resistant PRNG on CPUs without AES hardware support and is among the fastest PRNGs on GPUs.

You can read more about JAX PRNG design at https://mng.bz/lrE2.

You can access the state stored inside the `BitGenerator` using the `state` attribute.

Listing 9.13   Looking at the PRNG state using a new approach

```
from numpy.random import default_rng          ◀──────  Imports default RNG
rng = default_rng(42)                          ◀──
rng.bit_generator.state                              Uses the same
                                                     seed as before

>>> {'bit_generator': 'PCG64',
>>>  'state': {'state': 274674114334540486603088602300644985544,
>>>   'inc': 332724090758049132448979897138935081983},    Gets the state
>>>  'has_uint32': 0,
>>>  'uinteger': 0}

vals = rng.normal(loc=0.5, scale=0.1, size=(3,5))  ◀──  Generates some
                                                        random values
rng.bit_generator.state

>>> {'bit_generator': 'PCG64',
>>>  'state': {'state': 45342206775459714514805635519735197061,
>>>   'inc': 332724090758049132448979897138935081983},    Gets the state,
>>>  'has_uint32': 0,                                      it is changed.
>>>  'uinteger': 0}
```

Here again, we see there is some internal RNG state that is changed between subsequent calls, and this leads to different results for function calls with the same explicit arguments. The state here is an implicit argument that is not visible from the outside, as you do not work with the state explicitly.

9.2.3 *JAX PRNG*

Figure 9.9 visualizes the process of random number generation in JAX. As you can see, NumPy PRNGs use some global state. This goes against the functional approach used in JAX and may lead to problems with reproducing results and parallelization. If we are using any multithread, multiprocess, or multihost logic with NumPy (e.g., implementing data-parallel computation), we cannot get away with just a single seed, and likely we can't even control the concurrency of internal state mutation. Hence, the randomness becomes a race condition. But in JAX, such a problem is ruled out in principle. Also, as you remember from chapter 5, JIT may work incorrectly with impure functions.

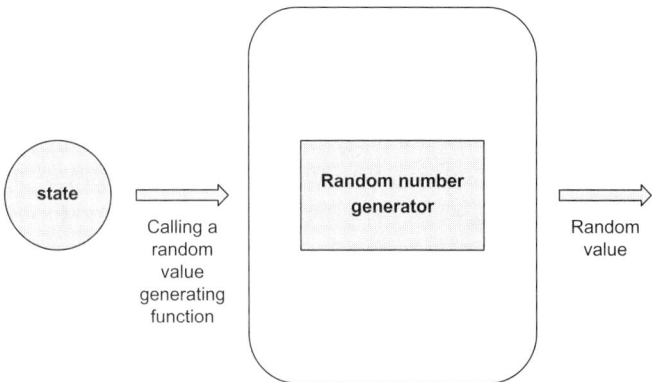

Figure 9.9 Random number generation in JAX; the state is explicitly consumed and not updated by the random number generator.

JAX does not use the global state; instead, JAX random functions explicitly consume the state. JAX introduces the concept of a *key* that explicitly represents the PRNG state. A key is created by calling the `random.PRNGKey(seed)` function. This function takes in a 64- or 32-bit integer value as a seed to generate a key.

Random functions consume the key, but their behavior differs from NumPy. They do not update a key in any way; they just use it as an external state. So if you pass the same key to a function multiple times, you will get the same result each time.

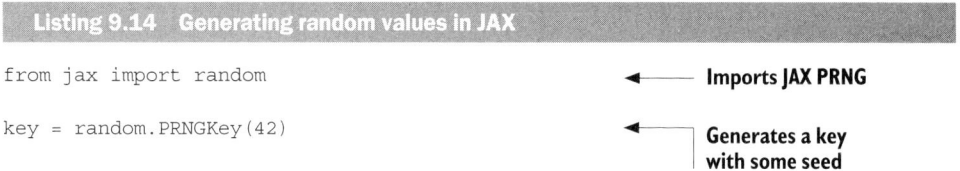

Listing 9.14 Generating random values in JAX

```
from jax import random          ◄——— Imports JAX PRNG

key = random.PRNGKey(42)        ◄——┐ Generates a key
                                    └ with some seed
```

Generates random normal values

Generates some more random normal values

```
vals = random.normal(key, shape=(3,5))
more_vals = random.normal(key, shape=(3,5))

vals

>>> Array([[-0.716899  , -0.20865498, -2.5713923 ,  1.0337092 , -1.4035789 ],
>>>        [ 1.3873734 , -0.8396519 ,  0.3010434 ,  0.1421263 , -1.7631724 ],
>>>        [-1.6755073 ,  0.31390068,  0.5912831 ,  0.5325395 , -0.9133108 ]],
>>>        dtype=float32)
```

Produces the same numbers

```
more_vals

>>> Array([[-0.716899  , -0.20865498, -2.5713923 ,  1.0337092 , -1.4035789 ],
>>>        [ 1.3873734 , -0.8396519 ,  0.3010434 ,  0.1421263 , -1.7631724 ],
>>>        [-1.6755073 ,  0.31390068,  0.5912831 ,  0.5325395 , -0.9133108 ]],
>>>        dtype=float32)
```

We made two subsequent calls with the same key. The result was similar to listing 9.10, where we deliberately set the seed before each call. Using the same key in JAX is equivalent to setting the seed before each call in NumPy. It is completely different from the results in listing 9.9, where between calls, NumPy functions modify the hidden PRNG state. If we look at the state, we see it is just an array of two 32-bit unsigned integer values.

Listing 9.15   Looking at the key

```
key = random.PRNGKey(42)
```

Generates a key with some seed

```
type(key)

>>> jaxlib.xla_extension.Array
```

The type is an Array.

```
key

>>> Array([ 0, 42], dtype=uint32)
```

The key contains two uint32 values.

As you can see, the state represented by the key is simpler than the state we saw in NumPy. This is because JAX uses a different PRNG.

If you want multiple random values, you basically have two options:

- You may request more than one random number with a single key by providing a shape parameter. This is precisely how we generated random tensors earlier in this chapter. Here, we could ask to generate a twice larger matrix (say, 6×5) and then split it into two matrices (two 3×5).
- You may split a key into two or more keys to use the different keys in subsequent random value–generating function calls.

The first method is useful when you know in advance how many random values you will need and have memory to store them. Sometimes, you either need too many numbers, so it's impractical to generate and store them in advance, or you do not know in advance how many of them you will need. In such a case, splitting a key is a better option.

Splitting a key is easy; you do it using the `random.split()` function. The function consumes a key and an integer indicating how many new keys to produce (with the default value of 2). It returns an array-like object with the requested number of new PRNG keys.

The `split()` function deterministically converts one key into many keys that can generate independent values. You can further split any newly obtained keys if you need more.

NOTE A key shouldn't be used more than once. If you provided a key as an argument for the `split()` function, you should throw the old key away after splitting.

Sometimes, the `split()` results are called a *key* and *subkey* (or subkeys). By convention, the keys used to generate other keys are called just keys, and the keys used to generate random values are called subkeys. But it doesn't represent any hierarchy between the keys; they all have equal status. It doesn't matter which of them you will later use for splitting and which for random value generation.

In the following listing, we generate two subsequent random normal matrices equivalently to the NumPy example in listing 9.9.

Listing 9.16 Generating different random values in JAX

```
from jax import random

key = random.PRNGKey(42)          ◄─── Generates a key with some seed

key

>>> Array([ 0, 42], dtype=uint32)

key1, key2 = random.split(key, num=2)   ◄─── Splits a key into two keys

key1                                      ◄──┐ The two keys are different.

>>> Array([2465931498, 3679230171], dtype=uint32)
                                             │ Generates random normal
                                             │ values with the first key
key2                                      ◄──┘

>>> Array([255383827, 267815257], dtype=uint32)
                                                 Generates some
                                                 more random
vals = random.normal(key1, shape=(3,5))   ◄──   normal values with
more_vals = random.normal(key2, shape=(3,5))  ◄─ the second key
```

```
vals
```
◀——— **Produces different numbers**

```
>>> Array([[-0.95032114,  0.89362663, -1.9382219 , -0.9676806 , -0.3920417 ],
>>>        [ 0.6062024 ,  0.37990445,  0.30284515,  1.3282853 ,  1.1882905 ],
>>>        [-0.95166105,  1.2611355 ,  0.41334143, -0.7831721 ,  0.09786294]],
>>>        dtype=float32)
```

```
more_vals
```
◀——— **Produces different numbers**

```
>>> Array([[ 0.7679137 ,  0.46966743, -1.4884446 , -1.155719 , -1.2574353 ],
>>>        [-0.66447204, -1.3314192 ,  1.5208852 , -0.55124223, -0.3213504 ],
>>>        [ 1.1168208 , -0.4216216 ,  0.32398054,  1.3500887 , -0.22909231]],
>>>        dtype=float32)
```

We split the key into two different keys and use the `random.normal()` function twice with different keys. This way, the function produces different results.

NOTE   Never reuse keys unless you want identical outputs!

It is easy to generate as many new keys as you want. In the following example, we generate 100 keys; the first one will be further used for key splitting, and all the rest will be used for random number generation.

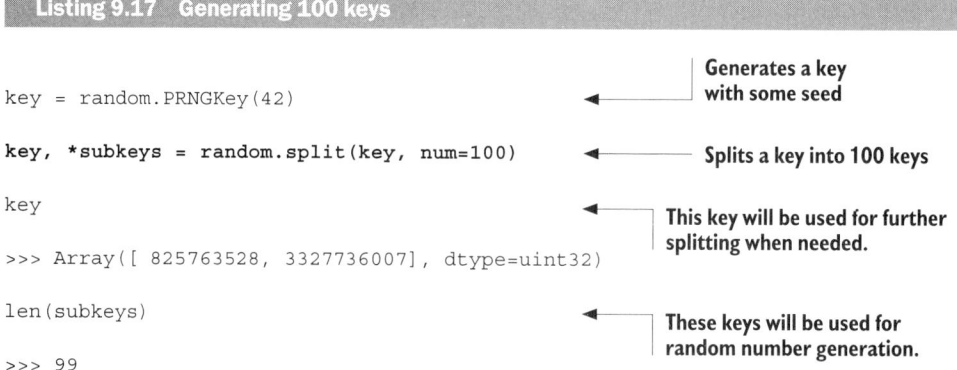

Listing 9.17   Generating 100 keys

```
key = random.PRNGKey(42)
```
◀——— **Generates a key with some seed**

```
key, *subkeys = random.split(key, num=100)
```
◀——— **Splits a key into 100 keys**

```
key
```
◀——— **This key will be used for further splitting when needed.**

```
>>> Array([ 825763528, 3327736007], dtype=uint32)
```

```
len(subkeys)
```
◀——— **These keys will be used for random number generation.**

```
>>> 99
```

We decided to use the first key after splitting as a key for further splitting and all the other keys for random number generation. However, all the keys are equal, and you may use any of them however you want.

Another way to create new keys based on an existing key and some data is to use the `fold_in()` function. This function takes in an existing key and an integer and folds the data into the key, returning a new key that is statistically safe for producing a stream of new pseudo-random values. A real-life use case is when you have a loop at each iteration for which you want to have a separate key. One option is to prepare a list of keys in advance and index it in the loop. However, it may be memory consuming for large loops, or you might not know the number of iterations in advance.

Listing 9.18   Using `fold_in()` to generate new keys

```
key = random.PRNGKey(42)                          ◄───   Generates a key
                                                          with some seed
for i in range(5):
  new_key = random.fold_in(key, i)          ◄────────   Generates a
  print(new_key)                                         new key
  vals = random.normal(new_key, shape=(3,5))   ◄──       based on the
  # do something with values       Generates data        existing key
                                   with a new key         and iteration
>>> [1832780943   270669613]                              number
>>> [  64467757 2916123636]
>>> [2465931498   255383827]
>>> [3134548294   894150801]
>>> [2954079971 3276725750]
```

We generate a new key on each loop iteration. We do not have to prepare a list of keys in advance. You can see that each key is a new key.

The `fold_in()` function takes in only an integer as additional data. If you want to fold other data types, you need to convert them to integers. For example, you may have some strings—say, neural network layer names. In this case, you may use some deterministic hash function for transforming string data into an integer. The Python `hashlib` library provides different options. In the following listing, we use the SHA-1 hash from this library to generate an integer.

Listing 9.19   Using `fold_in()` with strings

```
import hashlib                              A function for generating
                                            integers from strings
def my_hash(s):
  return int(hashlib.sha1(s.encode()).hexdigest()[:8], base=16)  ◄───

some_string = 'layer7_2'
some_int = my_hash(some_string)      ◄───   Generates a 32-bit
                                            integer from a string
some_int

>>> 2649017889

key = random.PRNGKey(42)
new_key = random.fold_in(key, some_int)   ◄───   Generates a new key
                                                 from the existing key
new_key                                          and an integer

>>> Array([3110527424, 3716265121], dtype=uint32)
```

We take a string, calculate the SHA-1 digest from it, convert the digest into a string with hexadecimal digits, and cut the first 8 digits. Since each hex code encodes 4 bits, 8 hex codes encode 32 bits, making it easy to convert into a 32-bit integer. With this integer, it is easy to generate a new key by calling the `fold_in()` function.

NOTE   Using Python's built-in `hash()` function for getting integers from strings might lead to irreproducible results as the `hash()` function is randomized by default. See more on this topic at https://mng.bz/Bg51.

An important distinction between NumPy and JAX is that JAX does not provide a *sequential equivalent guarantee*. This is because it would interfere with vectorization on SIMD hardware (and also because there are no known users or examples for which this property is important).

In the following listing, we demonstrate this by generating a 3×5 random array using a single function call with a single key and comparing it with an array generated sequentially using keys produced from the original key.

Listing 9.20   No sequential equivalent guarantee in JAX

```
import jax.numpy as jnp

key = random.PRNGKey(42)                      ← Generates a key with some seed
subkeys = random.split(key, num=3*5)          ← Splits a key into 15 new keys

vals = random.normal(key, shape=(3,5))        ← Generates a 3 × 5 matrix using a single function call

more_vals = jnp.array(
    [random.normal(key) for key in subkeys]   ← Generates a 3 × 5 matrix sequentially
).reshape((3,5))

vals

>>> Array([[-0.716899  , -0.20865498, -2.5713923 ,  1.0337092 , -1.4035789 ],
>>>        [ 1.3873734 , -0.8396519 ,  0.3010434 ,  0.1421263 , -1.7631724 ],
>>>        [-1.6755073 ,  0.31390068,  0.5912831 ,  0.5325395 , -0.9133108 ]],
>>>       dtype=float32)

more_vals

>>> Array([[-0.46220607, -0.33953536, -1.1038666 ,  0.34873134, -0.577846  ],
>>>        [ 1.9925295 ,  0.02132202,  0.7312121 , -0.40033886, -0.9915146 ],
>>>        [-0.03269025,  1.1624117 ,  0.15050009, -1.3577023 , -1.7751262 ]],
>>>       dtype=float32)
```

The results are different.

We generate two matrices in different ways and see that they are different. Moreover, there is no normal way to generate many values sequentially from a single key. If we used the same key for each generation, all the values would be identical.

9.2.4   *Advanced JAX PRNG configuration*

NumPy provides several PRNG implementations, and JAX does the same, though with a different set of PRNGs. As we mentioned, by default, JAX uses the Threefry counter-based PRNG. There is also an experimental PRNG that uses the XLA `RngBitGenerator` (https://mng.bz/dZNo).

The benefits of the original Threefry PRNG are that it is identical across shardings, CPUs/GPUs/TPUs, and different JAX and XLA versions. However, you might not want to use the default PRNG if it is slow to compile or execute on TPU or if you want efficient sharding.

> **NOTE** These experimental implementations haven't been thoroughly empirically tested (say, using Big Crush), and they do not provide any guarantee that they do not change between JAX versions.

In addition to the default Threefry PRNG, internally called `threefry2x32`, there are two experimental PRNGs called `rbg` and `unsafe_rbg`.

The `rbg` PRNG uses the same Threefry PRNG as the standard PRNG for splitting but XLA RBG for data generation. The `unsafe_rbg` PRNG is for demonstration purposes only. It uses RBG for both splitting and generation. Both `rbg` and `unsafe_rbg` PRNGs are faster on TPUs and also identical across shardings. XLA RBG is not guaranteed to be deterministic between backends and different compiler versions. You can turn these experimental PRNGs on by setting the `jax_default_prng_impl` flag when initializing JAX, as in the following listing.

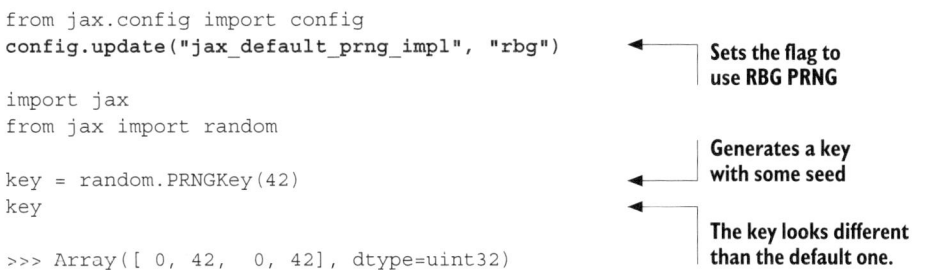

Listing 9.21 Using experimental PRNGs

```
from jax.config import config
config.update("jax_default_prng_impl", "rbg")      ◄── Sets the flag to
                                                       use RBG PRNG
import jax
from jax import random
                                                   ◄── Generates a key
                                                       with some seed
key = random.PRNGKey(42)
key                                                ◄──
                                                       The key looks different
>>> Array([ 0, 42,  0, 42], dtype=uint32)             than the default one.
```

Here we set the `jax_default_prng_impl` flag to use the `rbg` PRNG and generated a key to demonstrate that it differs from a key generated by the default PRNG.

There is ongoing work toward pluggable PRNG implementations (https://mng.bz/V21W), but it is not finished yet.

There is another flag called `jax_threefry_partitionable`. This flag turns on the new Threefry PRNG implementation, which is more efficiently shardable. The problem with the original Threefry PRNG is that, because of historical reasons, its implementation is not automatically partitionable. So it involves some cross-device communication to produce partitioned output.

Setting the `jax_threefry_partitionable` flag to `True` (the default value is `False`) switches to the new implementation (which is still under development). The new implementation removes communication overhead, though the random values generated may be different than without the flag set. They are still deterministic and will be the same at a given JAX version but may vary across releases.

We are done with JAX PRNGs, and the most important thing to remember is that JAX PRNG requires you to pass a PRNG state represented by a key. This is very different from NumPy, which hides a PRNG state in its internals. We know everything we need to implement a complete data augmentation pipeline and do other practical things.

9.3   *Generating random numbers in real-life applications*

We will discuss two cases:

- Building a complete pipeline for data augmentation, which can work on batches of images
- Implementing a neural network initialization

Let's start with the case from section 9.1 and finalize our data augmentation pipeline so it will work not on a single example but continuously on each arriving batch.

9.3.1   *Building a complete data augmentation pipeline*

The only big missing thing for our image augmentation pipeline is key management. We have to organize our loop over the data loader so that we generate enough keys to process all the images when working with each batch. We can complete this task with all the knowledge we obtained in previous sections.

I skip most redundant code for loading, preprocessing, and visualizing the data. You can find it in the book's repository. I only show the main loop to highlight working with keys.

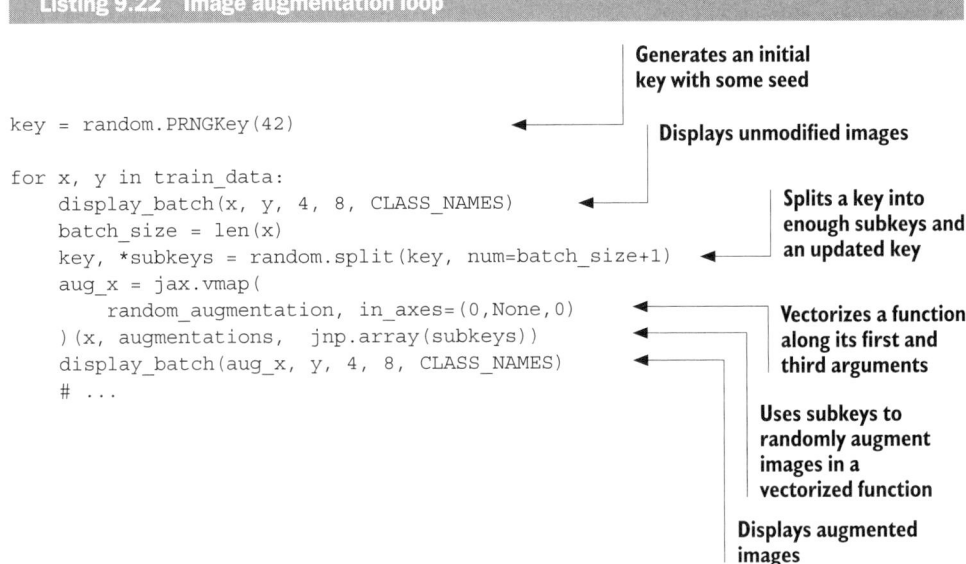

Listing 9.22   Image augmentation loop

```
key = random.PRNGKey(42)                          ◄── Generates an initial key with some seed

for x, y in train_data:
    display_batch(x, y, 4, 8, CLASS_NAMES)        ◄── Displays unmodified images
    batch_size = len(x)
    key, *subkeys = random.split(key, num=batch_size+1)   ◄── Splits a key into enough subkeys and an updated key
    aug_x = jax.vmap(
        random_augmentation, in_axes=(0,None,0)           ◄── Vectorizes a function along its first and third arguments
    )(x, augmentations,  jnp.array(subkeys))              ◄── Uses subkeys to randomly augment images in a vectorized function
    display_batch(aug_x, y, 4, 8, CLASS_NAMES)            ◄── Displays augmented images
    # ...
```

```
# do some other processing and neural network training
# ...
```

The main thing is to generate enough subkeys to process every image in a batch. Also, remember to update the key so that we can repeat the process during the subsequent batch processing.

Instead of processing images in a batch one by one, we use our knowledge of vectorization from chapter 6 to vectorize a single-image function `random_augmentation()` and apply it to the whole batch of images. We need to provide an array of subkeys, so we converted a Python `list` into a JAX `Array`.

I intentionally skipped the part related to neural network training. You may adapt the code to use it with a neural network similar to the one we used in MNIST image classification. Chapter 11 will use a high-level neural network library to implement a modern convolutional neural network. An augmented batch looks like figure 9.10.

Figure 9.10   An augmented batch of images

You can check yourself that some images are horizontally flipped while others are noisy versions of corresponding originals.

9.3.2   *Generating random initializations for a neural network*

Another real-life use case is neural network initialization. To train a neural network from scratch, you need to start with some random initialization. Proper initialization is an important topic in deep learning, and many papers propose methods that lead to better results. We will not dive into the topic of which initialization is better, but we will implement a general approach that you can adapt and change by yourself.

Actually, we have already used this code in previous chapters without focusing on how it works. Here we highlight the parts responsible for random number generation and key splitting. We use a simple multilayer perceptron with the same structure as in previous image classification examples.

Say there is an input layer that consumes 200×200–pixel color images. This fully connected layer has 2,048 neurons. The following fully connected layer consists of 1,024 neurons, and the final layer is a fully connected layer for two-class classification.

For each fully connected layer, there is a weight matrix with the size of (number of inputs) × (number of neurons). There is also a bias term of the size (number of neurons). These variables, usually called w (from weights) and b (from biases), must be randomly initialized. We will use a standard normal distribution with a 0 mean and a standard deviation of 0.01.

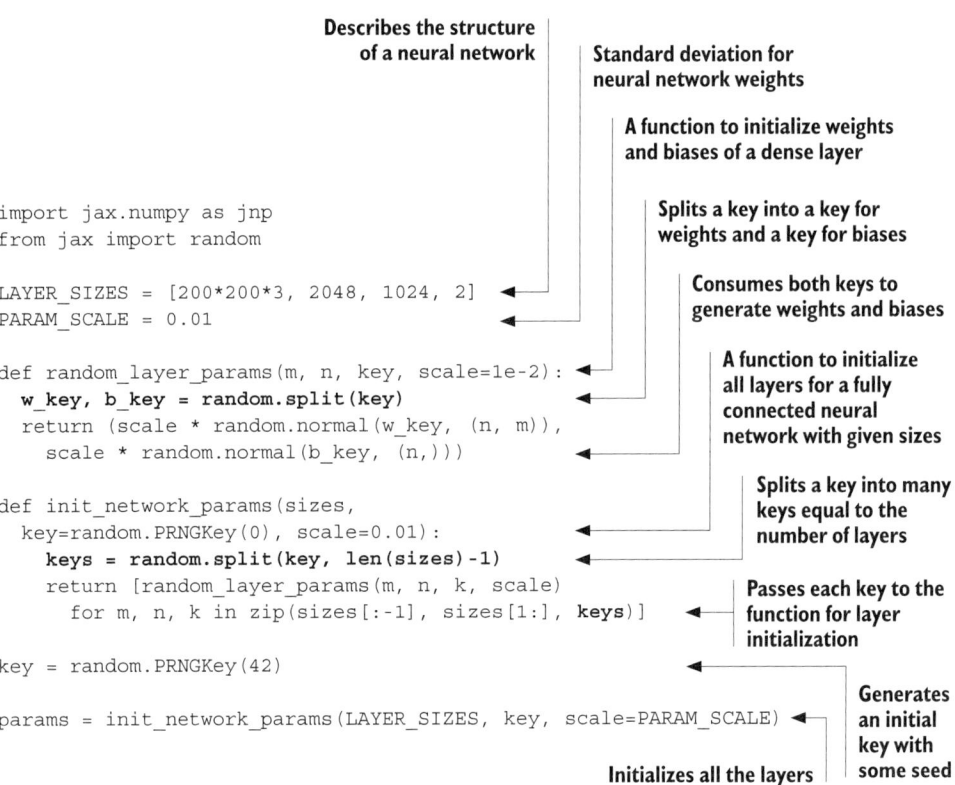

Listing 9.23   Neural network random initialization

We start from a single key; then we split this key into many keys equal to the number of layers and pass each key to a separate call of the function for layer initialization.

Inside the function for layer initialization, we again split the key into two: one for weights and one for biases. Then, finally, we consume both keys by generating random values.

Summary

- PRNGs use some algorithmic deterministic process to produce sequences of numbers with properties that approximate the properties of true random number sequences from a desired distribution.

- `jax.random` provides a rich set of functions for generating random numbers from different distributions.

- A seed is used to initialize a PRNG.

- A NumPy PRNG is stateful, meaning the generator has an internal state.

- In NumPy, the state is deterministically initialized using the seed provided. Then the state is updated after each generator call, so subsequent calls of the same function with the same parameters use a different state value and return different values.

- NumPy provides a *sequential equivalent guarantee*, meaning that the resulting random sequence will be the same whether you sample *N* individual numbers or an array of *N* numbers.

- Using a global state goes against the functional approach used in JAX and may lead to problems with reproducing results and parallelization. As you remember from chapter 5, JIT may work incorrectly with impure functions.

- JAX does not use global state; instead, JAX random functions explicitly consume the state.

- JAX introduces the concept of a key that explicitly represents the PRNG state. A key is created by calling the `random.PRNGKey(seed)` function.

- In JAX, random functions consume the key, but unlike NumPy, they do not update a key in any way; they just use it as an external state. So if you pass the same key to a function multiple times, you will get the same result each time.

- If you want multiple random values, you basically have two options:
  - You may request more than one random number with a single key by providing a shape parameter.
  - You may split a key into two or more keys to use the different keys in subsequent random value–generating function calls.

- The `split()` function deterministically converts one key into many keys that can generate independent values.

- Another way to create new keys based on an existing key and some data is to use the `fold_in()` function. This function takes in an existing key and an integer and folds the data into the key, returning a new key that is statistically safe for producing a stream of new pseudo-random values.

- A key shouldn't be used more than once. You should throw the old key away after splitting if you provided a key as an argument for the `split()`, `fold_in()`, or any random number–generating function.

- An important distinction between NumPy and JAX is that JAX does not provide a *sequential equivalent guarantee*. This is done because it would interfere with vectorization on SIMD hardware.
- There is also an experimental PRNG that uses the XLA RBG algorithm.
- The `jax_threefry_partitionable` flag turns on the new Threefry PRNG implementation, which is more efficiently shardable.

Working with pytrees

10

This chapter covers

- Representing complex data structures as pytrees
- Using functions for working with pytrees
- Creating custom pytree nodes

In previous chapters, we mostly used tensors to represent data and model parameters. That's enough for simple cases, but it is not very convenient when your models and datasets become more complex.

Working with machine learning tasks frequently requires working with objects represented as lists of `dicts`, lists of arrays, `dicts` of arrays, and so on. For example, dataset elements can be represented this way, and neural network weights are typically organized in some hierarchy with weights and biases stored for each layer. If you continue to work with this complexity using low-level tools like tensors and basic tensor operations, your code quickly becomes larger and less clear. Finally, you have to invent your own higher-level abstractions and more complex data structures. Other domains like astrophysics, bioinformatics, weather modeling, and so on may have their own convenient data structures.

Fortunately, JAX has some batteries included; some of these tools are provided in core JAX. JAX refers to such tree-like data structures built out of container-like Python objects as *pytrees* and supports them in many library functions.

For example, to store all the weights and biases for a multilayer neural network, having a single hierarchical data structure is very convenient. This structure has a list representing layers of the neural network, and each element of the list stores another list or dictionary with layer weights and biases represented as a matrix and a vector, respectively. Such a nested list is an example of a pytree.

It is very convenient to pass this structure to all the functions that require model parameters and not to pass them separately. It is also handy to be able to work with such a structure when doing JAX transformations like calculating gradients or auto-vectorizing a function. Fortunately, we can do just this: JAX functions work natively with pytrees. JAX also provides a toolset for working with pytrees, a set of functions to transform these structures with a map-like operation, functions to flatten and unflatten the structure, functions to perform a reduce-like operation popular in functional programming, and so on.

You can also define your own container classes to use in pytrees. It is helpful when you build your own higher-level abstractions for neural network layers and want a pytree to understand its internal structure. Hence, all the pytree-processing functions work correctly with your classes.

This chapter will cover all these essentials of working with pytrees. In the book's last chapters, we will learn even more powerful batteries from the JAX ecosystem that equip you with higher-level abstractions for neural network layers, optimizers, and so on.

We start with the case of storing neural network parameters for a multilayer perceptron to demonstrate the idea of pytrees and the basic ways to work with them. In the next section, we will see more advanced operations on pytrees, and in section 10.3, we will learn how to customize pytrees.

10.1   *Representing complex data structures as pytrees*

In a multilayer feedforward neural network or multilayer perceptron, each layer consists of a weight matrix and a bias vector. In previous chapters, we used pretty complex Python structures to store model parameters. The structure containing these weights and biases is a list of tuples containing two elements: a weight matrix as the first element of the tuple and a bias vector as the second element. Figure 10.1 shows the structure visually for the case of an input and an output layer and a hidden layer between them, from the example in listing 9.23. In essence, it is a nested tree-like structure. This is called a *pytree* in JAX.

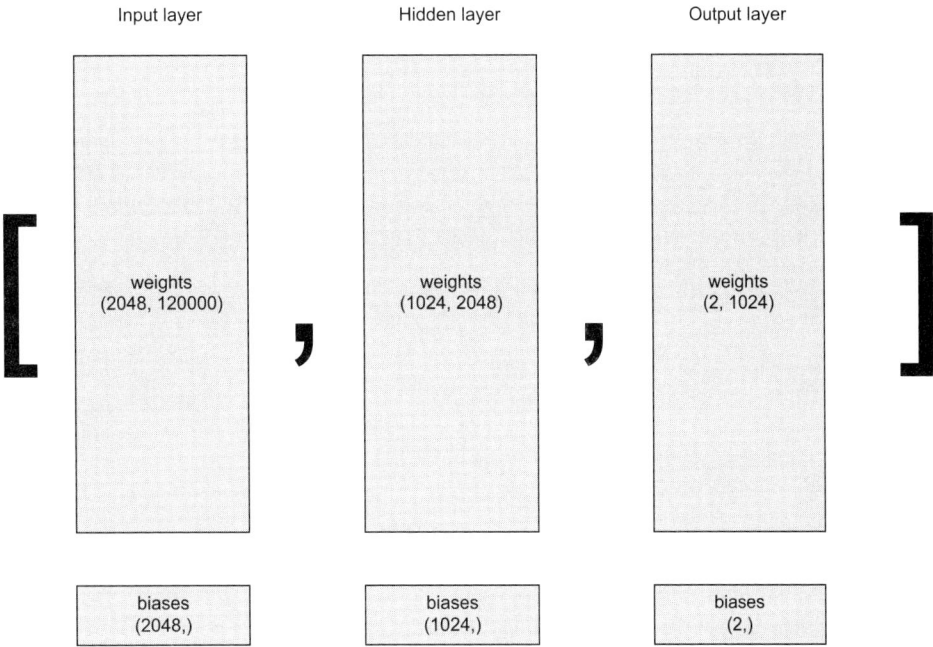

Figure 10.1 A pytree with model weights and biases

A pytree refers to a tree-like structure built out of container-like `lists`, `tuples`, `dicts`, and a few more. This set can be extended by registering your container class. We will do this in section 10.3. In the following listing, we reproduce the code from listing 9.23 to initialize these weights and biases.

Listing 10.1 Neural network random initialization (from listing 9.23)

```
import jax.numpy as jnp
from jax import random

LAYER_SIZES = [200*200*3, 2048, 1024, 2]          ◄─── Describes the structure
PARAM_SCALE = 0.01                                      of a neural network
                                                    ◄─── Standard deviation for
                                                         neural network weights
def random_layer_params(m, n, key, scale=1e-2):   ◄─── A function to initialize weights
  w_key, b_key = random.split(key)                       and biases of a dense layer
  return (scale * random.normal(w_key, (n, m)),
    scale * random.normal(b_key, (n,)))

def init_network_params(sizes, key=random.PRNGKey(0), scale=0.01):   ◄───┐
  keys = random.split(key, len(sizes)-1)
  return [random_layer_params(m, n, k, scale)      A function to initialize all layers
    for m, n, k in zip(sizes[:-1], sizes[1:], keys)]   for a fully connected neural
                                                         network with given sizes
```

```
key = random.PRNGKey(42)
```
                                                              ◀──┐ **Generates an initial**
                                                                 key with some seed

```
params = init_network_params(LAYER_SIZES, key, scale=PARAM_SCALE)
```
                                                                          ◀──┐
                                                              Initializes all the layers

We can walk over such a tree structure and print its properties. In the following listing, we print shapes for weights and biases from each layer.

Listing 10.2   Walking over the data structure

```
for i,layer in enumerate(params):          ◀─── Iterates over layers
  w,b = layer
  print(i, w.shape, b.shape)               ◀──┐ Prints shapes for
                                               weights and biases
>>> 0 (2048, 120000) (2048,)
>>> 1 (1024, 2048) (1024,)
>>> 2 (2, 1024) (2,)
```

The problem with this function is that it needs to know the structure in advance to parse it meaningfully. We can write more sophisticated code to work with different structures, but we don't need to do that: there is a `jax.tree_util` package with many useful functions. We will look closer into these functions in section 10.2; here, we will use the `jax.tree_util.tree_map()` function.

`jax.tree_util.tree_map()` maps a function over pytree arguments and produces a new pytree. It's like Python `map()` but for pytrees. We can easily map our structure into another structure containing shapes to produce almost the same result as in listing 10.2.

Listing 10.3   Walking over the data structure using `tree_map()`

```
shapes = jax.tree_util.tree_map(lambda p: p.shape, params)   ◀──┐ Maps a pytree
                                                                 into a pytree
for i,shape in enumerate(shapes):          ◀──┐                  of shapes
  print(i, shape)                          ◀──┘
                                               Iterates over layers
>>> 0 ((2048, 120000), (2048,))
>>> 1 ((1024, 2048), (1024,))            Prints shapes for
>>> 2 ((2, 1024), (2,))                  weights and biases
```

A pytree consists of *leaves* and *nodes*. A node is a pytree itself (recursive definition) and can be represented by a container-like Python object. These container types are registered in the pytree container registry, including `list`, `tuple`, `dict`, `namedtuple`, `OrderedDict`, and `None` by default. Note that `None` is treated as a node without children, not as a leaf. Other types are leaves by default, which include numeric values, `dataclasses`, `Array`, and `ndarray` types. The `jax.tree_util.tree_leaves()` function returns the leaves of a pytree.

We use a toy example with different types instead of a pytree with large arrays to demonstrate this behavior.

Listing 10.4 Extracting leaves from a pytree

```
import jax
import numpy as np
import jax.numpy as jnp                              Does necessary
import collections                                   preparations
Point = collections.namedtuple('Point', ['x', 'y'])

example_pytree = [                    ◄─── Creates a pytree containing different types
    {
        'a': [1, 2, 3],              ◄─── Leaves from the list inside the dict
        'b': jnp.array([1, 2, 3]),   ◄─┐
        'c': np.array([1, 2, 3])     ◄─┤ The JAX array is a leaf.
    },                                 │ The NumPy array is a leaf.
    [42, [44, 46], None],    ◄─┐ Leaves from a nested
    31337,                     │ list; None is not a leaf.
    (50, (60, 70)),      ◄─┐ Number is a leaf.
    Point(640, 480),              ◄─── Leaves from a tuple
    collections.OrderedDict([('a', 100), ('b', 200)]),  ◄─┐
    'some string'                                          │ Leaves from a
]                             ◄─────────────────────        namedtuple

                                              Leaves from an
jax.tree_util.tree_leaves(example_pytree)     OrderedDict

>>> [1,                                        String is a leaf.
>>>  2,              Leaves from the list
>>>  3,              inside the dict
>>>  Array([1, 2, 3], dtype=int32),   ◄─── The JAX array is a leaf.
>>>  array([1, 2, 3]),                ◄─┐
>>>  42,                                │ The NumPy array is a leaf.
>>>  44,              Leaves from the nested
>>>  46,             list; None is not a leaf.
>>>  31337,                            ◄─── Number is a leaf.
>>>  50,
>>>  60,             Leaves from the tuple
>>>  70,
>>>  640,
>>>  480,            Leaves from the namedtuple
>>>  100,
>>>  200,            Leaves from the OrderedDict
>>>  'some string']                    ◄─── String is a leaf.
```

Here we see that list, tuple, dict, namedtuple, OrderedDict, and None work as containers, and strings, numeric values, Array, and ndarray types are leaves.

Many JAX functions, like jax.lax.scan() or jax.lax.map(), operate over pytrees. JAX function transformations can also be applied to functions that accept as input and produce as output pytrees of arrays (not arrays of pytrees—that's important).

Our previous examples with neural networks for the MNIST or Cats vs. Dogs image classification used a similar structure for storing model parameters. Now we know those were pytrees. These pytrees are passed to the function for calculating gradients, and the returning value is also a pytree with the same structure.

To highlight many cases when we used pytrees, here we replicate some code from listings 2.5 to 2.13 that works with a pytree with model parameters. This is not a complete example; please use the corresponding notebook if you want to run the code yourself.

Listing 10.5   Replicating model training code from listings 2.5 to 2.13

```
init_params = init_network_params(
  LAYER_SIZES, random.PRNGKey(0), scale=PARAM_SCALE)
```
◄— **Generates initial parameter values**

```
def predict(params, image):
  """Function for per-example predictions."""
  activations = image
  for w, b in params[:-1]:
    outputs = jnp.dot(w, activations) + b
    activations = swish(outputs)
  final_w, final_b = params[-1]
  logits = jnp.dot(final_w, activations) + final_b
  return logits
```
◄— **Function for per-example prediction using model parameters**

```
batched_predict = vmap(predict, in_axes=(None, 0))
```
◄— **Function for batched prediction**

```
def loss(params, images, targets):
  """Categorical cross entropy loss function."""
  logits = batched_predict(params, images)
  log_preds = logits - logsumexp(logits)
  return -jnp.mean(targets*log_preds)
```
◄— **Loss function that uses batched prediction**

```
@jax.jit
def update(params, x, y, epoch_number):
  shapes = jax.tree_util.tree_map(lambda p: p.shape, params)
  print(f"Params shapes: {shapes}")
  loss_value, grads = value_and_grad(loss)(params, x, y)
  grad_shapes = jax.tree_util.tree_map(lambda p: p.shape, grads)
  print(f"Grads shapes: {grad_shapes}")
  lr = INIT_LR * DECAY_RATE ** (epoch_number / DECAY_STEPS)
  return [(w - lr * dw, b - lr * db)
          for (w, b), (dw, db) in zip(params, grads)], loss_value
```
◄— **Function for making a single gradient update step**

```
params, loss_value = update(init_params, x, y, 0)
```
◄— **Parameter pytree before the update**

```
>>> Params shapes: [((512, 784), (512,)), ((10, 512), (10,))]
>>> Grads shapes: [((512, 784), (512,)), ((10, 512), (10,))]
```
◄— **Pytree with gradients**

Our pytree with model parameters passed through functions after three function transformations. First, there was the `vmap()` for creating the batched version of the `predict()` function. Then, there was the `value_and_grad()` transformation for obtaining the gradients. Finally, there was also the `jit()` transformation. None of the transformations had problems working with a pytree as a function parameter.

Remember the `in_axes` parameter for `vmap()` and `pmap()`. In listing 6.12, we mentioned that it can work with nested Python containers. Now you know that we meant pytrees. The parameter can accept a pytree if the corresponding parameter of the mapped function is also a pytree. In the preceding example, we used just `None`, as we didn't want to map over the model parameters. Still, potentially, it allows you to do some complicated things—for example, having a separate set of weights for each item in the batch or having separate biases for each batch item while using the same weights. We will not dive into such exotic cases here, but remember, you can have very fine-grained control.

In addition to supporting pytrees in JAX transformations and standard library calls, there is also a special useful package for working with pytrees, which we will discuss in the next section.

10.2 Functions for working with pytrees

The `jax.tree_util` package provides many helpful functions for working with pytrees that can make your life easier. For example, you might frequently want to iterate over your pytree, performing the same operation with each element—say, reshaping it. There is a map-like transformation for that. Or you could flatten your pytree to serialize the model parameters and then deserialize and restore the pytree structure. There are functions for doing each of these things and more. Here we will describe the most important and useful functions to help you work with pytrees.

> **NOTE** Previously, many `jax.tree_util` routines could be accessed from the top-level JAX package—say `jax.tree_leaves()` instead of `jax.tree_util.tree_leaves()`. These imports are deprecated and will be removed in a future release.

10.2.1 Using tree_map()

We are already familiar with the `jax.tree_util.tree_leaves()` that returns the leaves of a pytree. We are also familiar with the `jax.tree_util.tree_map()`, which maps a function over pytree arguments and produces a new pytree. We used it to traverse a tree and log the shapes of all the arrays along the tree, but in the same way, you can create modified pytrees. For example, it is easy to scale each array—say, multiplying each tensor by 10. Remember: you cannot make changes in place; you produce a new modified version of the existing structure.

Listing 10.6 Modifying a data structure

```
params = init_network_params(LAYER_SIZES, key, scale=PARAM_SCALE)   ◄── Generates
                                                                        some
scaled_params = jax.tree_util.tree_map(lambda p: 10*p, params)   ◄──    neural
                                                                        network
                             Scales model weights by                    weights
                        multiplying each weight by 10
```

It's also easy to use `tree_map()` to replicate model parameters across many devices in case of data-parallel training. We can slightly change the MNIST data-parallel training example from section 7.3. Originally, on each training step, we broadcasted model parameters to every device, and then each device calculated global gradients using collective ops, so we had two potentially large between-device communications regarding the model weights (see figure 10.2).

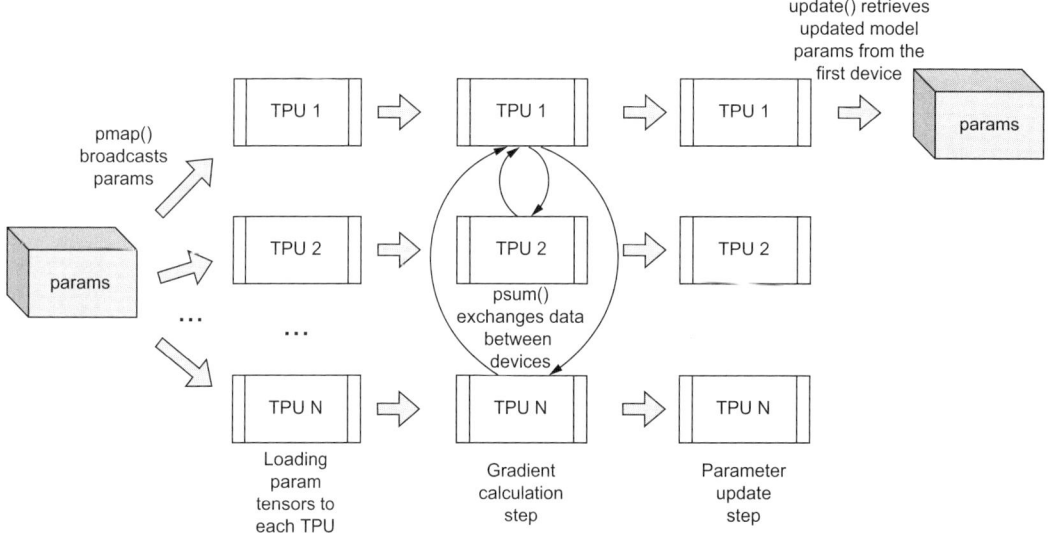

Figure 10.2   Data-parallel training scheme from chapter 7. On each step, the model parameters are broadcasted to each TPU.

As mentioned in chapter 7, constantly storing a separate copy of model parameters on each device and updating them locally using aggregated gradients would be more efficient. To do so, simply prepare a pytree of model parameters; then in the `pmap()` call, specify that the model parameters are also mapped over. This approach uses the `in_axes` parameter (see figure 10.3).

To modify model parameters accordingly, we need to add an additional leading axis to each matrix with weights and each vector with biases and replicate (copy) the weights and bias values into the new dimension (this only happens once, at the beginning of training). The `pmap()` will map over this new axis so that each device will have its own complete copy of the model parameters.

To replicate values across a newly created axis, we will use the `jnp.broadcast_to()` function (https://mng.bz/BgD1). In listing 10.7, we provide incomplete code with only relevant parts that differ from listings 7.26 to 7.29.

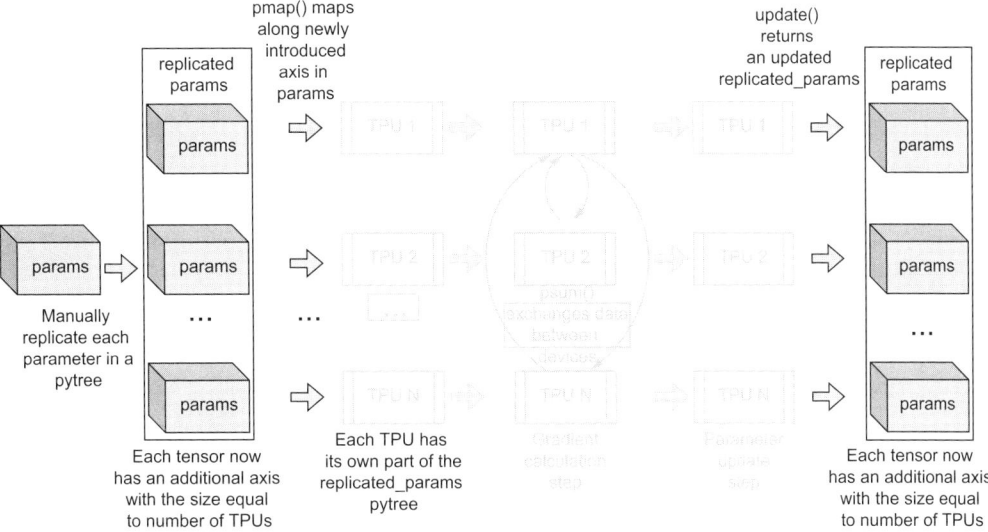

Figure 10.3 Optimized data-parallel training scheme. Model parameters are manually replicated before the training, so broadcasting them on each step is unnecessary.

Listing 10.7 Modified data-parallel training from chapter 7

```
from jax.tree_util import tree_map                    ◄──── Imports tree_map()

init_params = init_network_params(                    ┐ Generates initial
  LAYER_SIZES, random.PRNGKey(0), scale=PARAM_SCALE) ◄┘ model parameters
replicate_array = lambda x: jnp.broadcast_to(
  x, (NUM_DEVICES,) + x.shape)
replicated_params = tree_map(replicate_array, init_params)  ◄──

@partial(jax.pmap, axis_name='devices', in_axes=(0, 0, 0, None)) ◄─┐  Replicates
def update(params, x, y, epoch_number):                              the neural
  loss_value, grads = value_and_grad(loss)(params, x, y)            network
  grads = [(jax.lax.psum(dw, 'devices'), jax.lax.psum(db, 'devices')) parameters
    for dw, db in grads]                                            multiple
  lr = INIT_LR * DECAY_RATE ** (epoch_number / DECAY_STEPS)         times so
  return [(w - lr * dw, b - lr * db)                                that each
          for (w, b), (dw, db) in zip(params, grads)], loss_value   device will
                                                                    have its
for epoch in range(NUM_EPOCHS):                                     own copy
  start_time = time.time()              Uses pmap to parallelize    with the
  losses = []                           function and map over its   same
  for x, y in train_data:               first three parameters      structure
    num_elements = len(y)
    x = jnp.reshape(x, (NUM_DEVICES, num_elements//NUM_DEVICES, NUM_PIXELS))
    y = jnp.reshape(
      one_hot(y, NUM_LABELS),
      (NUM_DEVICES, num_elements//NUM_DEVICES, NUM_LABELS))
```

```
    replicated_params, loss_value = update(
      replicated_params, x, y, epoch)
    losses.append(jnp.sum(loss_value))
  epoch_time = time.time() - start_time

  params = tree_map(lambda x: x[0], replicated_params)
  train_acc = accuracy(params, train_data)
  test_acc = accuracy(params, test_data)
  print("Epoch {} in {:0.2f} sec".format(epoch, epoch_time))
  print("Training set loss {}".format(jnp.mean(jnp.array(losses))))
  print("Training set accuracy {}".format(train_acc))
  print("Test set accuracy {}".format(test_acc))
```

◄── **Uses manually
replicated parameters**

**Extracts parameters for the
first device only to calculate
accuracy on a single device**

Notice how we replicate the model parameters here. We introduce a new leading axis
with a size equal to the number of devices and copy (or broadcast) the model parameters into the new dimension. We do this for every leaf in the pytree, storing the model
parameters, using the `tree_map()` function.

A significant yet hard-to-notice change is that we use `in_axes=(0, 0, 0, None)`
instead of `in_axes=(None, 0, 0, None)` from listing 7.27. It means we do not rely on
automatic replication, as we manually replicated the model parameters and now want
to map over them. We also got rid of the `out_axes=(None,0)` because we don't need to
return the updated model parameters from the first device only. Now we don't need to
return model parameters at all; they are stored on each device separately (thanks to the
array sharding). The only place where we extract the model parameters from the first
device is when we calculate accuracy. We do this using only a single device, but you can
rewrite this part to use multiple devices as well.

10.2.2 *Flatten/unflatten a pytree*

In real life, you need to communicate with external libraries. Many libraries allow only
simple lists or 1D arrays on their inputs. You may also want to have highly performant
functions optimized to work with 1D arrays or lists. Or you may wish to store model
parameters somewhere in external storage or to file. In all these cases, it may be impossible to work with pytrees, and you need a way to convert a pytree into a simpler structure and then restore it back to its original form.

There is a useful set of functions to flatten and unflatten a pytree—namely, the `jax`
`.tree_util.tree_flatten()`, `jax.tree_util.tree_unflatten()`, `jax.flatten_`
`util.ravel_pytree()`, and the companion `jax.tree_util.tree_structure()`
functions.

The `jax.tree_util.tree_structure()` function returns the structure for a
pytree represented with a `PyTreeDef` type. The `jax.tree_util.tree_flatten()`
returns the flattened version of a pytree using a deterministic procedure corresponding to a left-to-right depth-first tree traversal. It also returns a `PyTreeDef` representing
the structure of the flattened tree, the same thing produced by the `tree_structure()`
function.

Both functions allow an optional `is_leaf` parameter that specifies a function with a Boolean return value that will be called at each flattening step. If it returns `True`, then the traversal stops, and the whole subtree is treated as a leaf. Otherwise, with the `False` value, the flattening procedure traverses the current object.

The `jax.tree_util.tree_unflatten()` performs the reverse function. With a tree structure in a `PyTreeDef` and an iterable of leaves (produced by `tree_flatten()`), it reconstructs the original pytree.

You can simulate the `tree_map()` by first flattening a tree, then performing an ordinary Python map over the iterable of leaves, and then restoring the tree with the `tree_unflatten()` function.

Listing 10.8 Flattening/unflattening a pytree

```
some_pytree = [                                          ◄──── Creates a pytree
    [1,1,1],
    [
        [10,10,10], [20, 20]
    ]
]

jax.tree_util.tree_map(lambda p: p+1, some_pytree)       ◄──── Processes the pytree
                                                               using tree_map()
>>> [[2, 2, 2], [[11, 11, 11], [21, 21]]]

leaves, struct = jax.tree_util.tree_flatten(some_pytree) ◄──── Flattens the pytree

leaves

>>> [1, 1, 1, 10, 10, 10, 20, 20]                        ◄──── Contains the values

struct
                                                               Contains the
>>> PyTrecDef([[*, *, *], [[*, *, *], [*, *]]])          ◄──── pytree structure

updated_leaves = map(lambda x: x+1, leaves)              ◄──── Maps the values

jax.tree_util.tree_unflatten(struct, updated_leaves)     ◄──── Restores the pytree with
                                                               the given structure
>>> [[2, 2, 2], [[11, 11, 11], [21, 21]]]
```

You typically don't have to use `flatten/unflatten` to process a tree, as the `tree_map()` function does this job perfectly. However, you might want to use `tree_flatten()/tree_unflatten()` when serializing/deserializing complex structures to store them in some external storage or to communicate between different processes.

As you can see, the `tree_flatten()` produces an ordinary Python list. If you are working with arrays instead of lists, you might also prefer a 1D array after flattening. This is a typical case for different machine learning libraries, as they mostly use tensors and arrays, not lists. In that case, there is a separate `jax.flatten_util.ravel_pytree()` function. It returns a 1D array representing the flattened and concatenated leaf values; plus, instead of a `PyTreeDef` structure, it returns a function for unflattening a 1D vector of the same length back to a pytree of the same structure as the input one.

Listing 10.9   Flattening/unflattening a pytree using a 1D array

```
from jax.flatten_util import ravel_pytree          ◄————  Necessary import

leaves, unflatten_func = ravel_pytree(some_pytree)  ◄————┐ Flattens the pytree
                                                         │ into a 1D array
leaves

>>> Array([ 1,   1,   1, 10, 10, 10, 20, 20], dtype=int32)  ◄———┐ Contains the values
                                                                │ in a 1D array
unflatten_func

>>> <function jax._src.flatten_util.ravel_pytree.
  <locals>.<lambda>(flat)>                            ◄———┐ Function to restore
                                                           │ a pytree
unflatten_func(leaves)

>>> [[Array(1, dtype=int32), Array(1, dtype=int32), Array(1, dtype=int32)],
>>>  [[Array(10, dtype=int32), Array(10, dtype=int32), Array(10, dtype=int32)],
>>>   [Array(20, dtype=int32), Array(20, dtype=int32)]]]
```

Here we started with a list-based structure, the same structure we used in the flatten/unflatten example. Because the `ravel_pytree()` function targets 1D arrays, it promotes the types of input elements to a suitable 1D array (see the following page for the details of type promotion: https://mng.bz/dZPo). In other words, `unravel(ravel(x))` is not idempotent, unlike `unflatten(flatten(x))`. So be careful if you have a really complex structure with different types mixed inside. They will all be promoted to a single type. But that's typically not the case for machine learning applications.

10.2.3   Using tree_reduce()

Sometimes you want to apply a function to all of the leaves of a pytree and return a single value, like calculating a sum of the pytree. One possible use case is to calculate some aggregate of the weights of the network and to add this as a penalty term to the loss function.

A function you may find useful is the `jax.tree_util.tree_reduce()` function. It basically resembles a traditional `reduce` function popular in functional programming. Internally, it uses the standard Python `functools.reduce()` function (https://mng.bz/r1BJ) over pytree leaves.

This function applies a two-argument function cumulatively to the iterable over the list of leaves left to right, starting with an optional initial value (or the first element of the iterable). In the end, it reduces the leaves to a single value. For example, it is easy to calculate the sum of all values over a pytree.

```
Listing 10.10   Reducing a pytree
```

```
some_pytree = [                                          ◄──── Creates a pytree
    [1,1,1],
    [
        [10,10,10], [20, 20]
    ]
]
```

```
jax.tree_util.tree_reduce(lambda acc,value: acc+value, some_pytree,
initializer=0)                              ◄──┐
                                               │ Reduces the pytree using a
>>> 73                                           function to accumulate values
```

Here we pass a function that accumulates a value over all iterables starting with some initial value—in this case, 0. The function traverses over all leaves, and for each leaf, it is called with the current accumulator value (initially, zero) and the leaf value. It sums both values, and then the result becomes the accumulator value for the next function call.

10.2.4 Transposing a pytree

Sometimes you need to transpose a pytree, meaning to transform a pytree with some hierarchical structure of the type (outer, inner) into a pytree with a transposed structure of the type (inner, outer). For example, a list of pytrees can be turned into a pytree of lists. Let's look at a specific example.

Imagine you have a structure representing a point in a 2D space; let it be a namedtuple with the fields named x and y. You have an array of such points, and you want to apply a function for rotation around the origin for every point in this array.

```
Listing 10.11   Working with 2D points
```

```
import math
from collections import namedtuple

Point = namedtuple('Point', ['x', 'y'])           ◄──── Creates namedtuple type

points = [                                          ◄──── Creates a list of points
    Point(0.0, 0.0),
    Point(3.0, 0.0),
    Point(0.0, 4.0)
]

def rotate_point(p, theta):                         ◄──── A function for rotating a point
  x = p.x * math.cos(theta) - p.y * math.sin(theta)
  y = p.x * math.sin(theta) + p.y * math.cos(theta)
  return Point(x,y)

rotate_point(points[1], math.pi)                    ◄──── Rotates one point

>>> Point(x=-3.0, y=3.6739403974420594e-16)
```

The most naive approach would be to process each point manually, but remember, there is automatic vectorization in JAX, and we'd like to use its powers.

The straightforward approach with vmap() will not work, as vmap() supports pytrees in the form of a "struct of arrays" rather than an "array of structs." This is because the "array of struct" form can't be operated on efficiently, which is in turn because XLA supports numeric array dtypes only. So you can't apply vmap to vectorize along an array of structures; you instead need to reorganize the points to be a structure of arrays. This means there should be a single structure containing arrays of coordinates for all the points.

Listing 10.12   Applying vmap to a list of 2D points

We assume we want to map over the array, but it doesn't work.

```
jax.vmap(rotate_point, in_axes=(0, None))(points, math.pi)    ◄

>>> ...
>>> ValueError: vmap was requested to map its argument along axis 0, which
implies that its rank should be at least 1, but is only 0 (its shape is ())
```

We need to transform our list of structs into a struct of arrays. The solution is to use the jax.tree_util.tree_transpose() function. The outer structure here is a list, and the inner structure here is the structure containing a single point.

Listing 10.13   Looking at the inner and outer structures

```
jax.tree_util.tree_structure(points)        ◄─┐ Returns the outer
                                               │ tree structure
>>> PyTreeDef([CustomNode(namedtuple[Point], [*, *]),
CustomNode(namedtuple[Point], [*, *]), CustomNode(namedtuple[Point], [*, *])]])

jax.tree_util.tree_structure(points[0])     ◄─┐ Returns the inner
                                               │ tree structure
>>> PyTreeDef(CustomNode(namedtuple[Point], [*, *]))
```

To be precise, when we say we return the outer structure, in this example, we actually return both the outer and the inner structures, as there are both the outer list and the inner namedtuple details there.

To extract the outer structure only, we have to replicate the list without the details of the list elements.

Listing 10.14   Looking at the outer structure only

```
jax.tree_util.tree_structure([0 for p in points])    ◄─┐ Returns the outer
                                                        │ tree structure
>>> PyTreeDef([*, *, *])
```

Providing the tree_transpose() function with all the necessary parameters, we can "transpose" our structure into the required form.

Listing 10.15 Transposing the pytree

```
points_t = jax.tree_util.tree_transpose(
  outer_treedef = jax.tree_util.tree_structure(
    [0 for p in points]),
  inner_treedef = jax.tree_util.tree_structure(points[0]),
  pytree_to_transpose=points
)

points_t

>>> Point(x=[0.0, 3.0, 0.0], y=[0.0, 0.0, 4.0])
```

Passes the outer
tree structure

Passes the
inner tree
structure

Gets the transposed
structure

Notice again how we passed the tree structure for the outer level. We passed a simplified list without any internal structure of elements. If we passed the original list itself, then it would contain both the outer and inner levels, and the function call would fail.

There is only one single step missing. We transformed the "list of structs" into a "struct of lists," but vmap() does not work on lists—it works on arrays. So the last step is to convert lists to arrays, which is simple.

Listing 10.16 Converting lists into arrays

Converts two lists
into two arrays

```
points_t_array = Point(jnp.array(points_t.x),jnp.array(points_t.y))

points_t_array
```

Shows the structure now contains arrays

```
>>> Point(x=Array([0., 3., 0.], dtype=float32), y=Array([0., 0., 4.],
dtype=float32))
```

Finally, we can apply vmap() to the converted structure (more correctly, we apply vmap() to a function processing a single element and then the transformed function to the converted structure).

Listing 10.17 Successfully applying a vectorized function

Vectorizes and applies the function
to the converted structure

```
jax.vmap(rotate_point, in_axes=(0, None))(points_t_array, math.pi)

>>> Point(x=Array([-0.0000000e+00, -3.0000000e+00,
   -4.8985874e-16], dtype=float32),
   y=Array([ 0.0000000e+00,  3.6739406e-16,
   -4.0000000e+00], dtype=float32))
```

Shows the successfully
applied function

We have finally succeeded, and you can see that the points are rotated by 180 degrees, and their coordinates changed signs. So transposing can be very useful.

We've worked with a lot of handy functions from the `jax.tree_util` package. The only important set of functions we didn't cover is the set related to creating custom containers. That's the topic of the next section.

10.3 Creating custom pytree nodes

You may have your own classes containing data that you'd like to work with as containers, not leaves, and the classes representing neural network layers are a perfect example of this situation.

Please note this is a pedagogical example. In real-life cases, good libraries have already solved this problem. So, just in case you are using `dataclasses` (which are leaves by default) and want to make them pytree nodes, there is a nice Chex library (https://mng.bz/V2qy) to help you (with just a single annotation). If you use Flax (the topic of chapter 11) to create neural networks, there is a `flax.struct.dataclass` annotation (https://mng.bz/x6Jd) there. As an alternative, you may also use `equinox .Module` (https://mng.bz/Aa2o) from the small, beautiful, and extremely useful Equinox library. However, here I will show you how to make it yourself.

Imagine you have a class representing a neural network linear layer, storing the layer's name together with a matrix of weights and a vector of biases.

Listing 10.18   A custom class for a neural network linear layer

```
class Layer:
  def __init__(self, name, w, b):
    self.w = w                          ◄———  Matrix with weights
    self.b = b                          ◄———  Vector with biases
    self.name = 'name'                  ◄———  Name of the layer
```

This is nothing special—just a simple structure holding together some related data.

You can create a pytree that includes a newly created layer and another leaf containing some data.

Listing 10.19   A pytree with the custom class

```
h1 = Layer('hidden1', jnp.zeros((100,20)), jnp.zeros((20,)))   ◄———  Creates a layer

pt = [                                          ◄———  Creates a pytree
    jnp.ones(50),
    h1
]

jax.tree_util.tree_leaves(pt)                   ◄———  Dumps leaves of the pytree

>>> [Array([1., 1., 1., 1., 1., 1., 1., 1., 1., 1., 1., 1., 1., 1., 1., 1.,
>>>         1., 1., 1., 1., 1., 1., 1., 1., 1., 1., 1., 1., 1., 1., 1., 1.,
>>>         1., 1., 1., 1., 1., 1., 1., 1., 1., 1., 1., 1., 1., 1., 1., 1.],
>>>        dtype=float32),
>>>  <__main__.Layer at 0x7fc87db04490>]
```

As you can see, the layer object is treated as a separate leaf. That might be okay, but we know that it really is a container for some other data, and we potentially want to apply some functions to this data using `tree_map()`. If we try to, say, increment or multiply all the values in this pytree, we'll fail as our class does not support a suitable operation.

Listing 10.20 Applying `tree_map` to a pytree with the custom class

```
jax.tree_map(lambda x: x*10, pt)                    ◄─── Multiplies all values by 10

                                                         Returns an error
>>> ...
>>> TypeError: unsupported operand type(s) for *: 'Layer' and 'int'    ◄──
```

We can solve the problem by implementing all the required operators for the class. But we have another option. We can register our class as a container and let JAX know what is inside the container and how to work with this data.

To do this, you must tell JAX how to flatten and unflatten the container by providing two corresponding functions.

The flattening function returns (1) an iterable for the children to be flattened and (2) an optional auxiliary data to be stored in the tree definition but which does not appear as a child (basically, some metadata). In our case, we'd like to see both weights and biases as leaves, but we don't want to see the layer name as a leaf, so it's a perfect candidate for auxiliary data.

The unflattening function takes two arguments—the auxiliary data and the flattened children—and restores the original object. Let's write both these functions for the `Layer` class.

Listing 10.21 Flattening and unflattening functions for the custom class

```
def flatten_layer(container):                       Packs data items
  flat_contents = [container.w, container.b]   ◄─── into a flat list
  aux_data = container.name                     ◄──
  return flat_contents, aux_data                    Returns layer name
                                                    as auxiliary data
def unflatten_layer(aux_data, flat_contents):
  return Layer(aux_data, *flat_contents)        ◄── Restores the
                                                    original object
```

Here we take both weights and biases and pack them in a flat list. The layer name is not packed in the same list as we don't want to see it as a leaf in a pytree, so we return it as auxiliary data. The unflattening function does the reverse; it takes the auxiliary data and the flat list of children and restores the original object.

The last thing to do is to register our container in the pytree container registry. This is done using the `jax.tree_util.register_pytree_node()` function. The function takes in a Python type to treat as an internal pytree node and two functions for flattening and unflattening (listing 10.22).

Listing 10.22   Registering our container in the pytree container registry

```
jax.tree_util.register_pytree_node(                          Registers the container
    Layer, flatten_layer, unflatten_layer)
                                                             Now we see new
jax.tree_util.tree_leaves(pt)                                leaves in the pytree.

>>> [Array([1., 1., 1., 1., 1., 1., 1., 1., 1., 1., 1., 1., 1., 1., 1., 1.,
>>>         1., 1., 1., 1., 1., 1., 1., 1., 1., 1., 1., 1., 1., 1., 1., 1.,
>>>         1., 1., 1., 1., 1., 1., 1., 1., 1., 1., 1., 1., 1., 1., 1.],
>>>       dtype=float32),
>>>  Array([[0., 0., 0., ..., 0., 0., 0.],
>>>         [0., 0., 0., ..., 0., 0., 0.],
>>>         [0., 0., 0., ..., 0., 0., 0.],
>>>         ...,
>>>         [0., 0., 0., ..., 0., 0., 0.],
>>>         [0., 0., 0., ..., 0., 0., 0.],
>>>         [0., 0., 0., ..., 0., 0., 0.]], dtype=float32),
>>>  Array([0., 0., 0., 0., 0., 0., 0., 0., 0., 0., 0., 0., 0., 0., 0.,
>>>         0., 0., 0.], dtype=float32)]
                                                  Calling tree_map successfully changes
pt2 = jax.tree_map(lambda x: x+1, pt)             the data inside the container.

>>> [Array([2., 2., 2., 2., 2., 2., 2., 2., 2., 2., 2., 2., 2., 2., 2., 2.,
>>>         2., 2., 2., 2., 2., 2., 2., 2., 2., 2., 2., 2., 2., 2., 2., 2.,
>>>         2., 2., 2., 2., 2., 2., 2., 2., 2., 2., 2., 2., 2., 2., 2.],
>>>       dtype=float32),
>>>  Array([[1., 1., 1., ..., 1., 1., 1.],
>>>         [1., 1., 1., ..., 1., 1., 1.],
>>>         [1., 1., 1., ..., 1., 1., 1.],
>>>         ...,
>>>         [1., 1., 1., ..., 1., 1., 1.],
>>>         [1., 1., 1., ..., 1., 1., 1.],
>>>         [1., 1., 1., ..., 1., 1., 1.]], dtype=float32),
>>>  Array([1., 1., 1., 1., 1., 1., 1., 1., 1., 1., 1., 1., 1., 1., 1., 1.,
>>>         1., 1., 1.], dtype=float32)]
```

Here it is! After registering our container, we can apply `tree_map()` to the data inside this container, and the leaves of the pytree now contain the data items from the container internals rather than just the class object.

We are done with pytrees. You will frequently use them as many real-world tasks require complex hierarchical data storage structures. In the field of deep learning, almost all model parameters are stored this way.

Summary

- Pytree is a nested tree-like structure built from container-like Python objects.
- A pytree consists of *leaves* and *nodes*.
- A node is a pytree itself and can be represented by a container-like Python object. These container types are registered in the pytree container registry and include `list`, `tuple`, `dict`, `namedtuple`, `OrderedDict`, and `None` by default.

- Other types are leaves by default, which include numeric values, `Array`, and `ndarray` types.

- Many library JAX functions and function transformations can work with pytrees.

- The `jax.tree_util` package provides many useful functions for working with pytrees.

- The `jax.tree_util.tree_map()` maps a function over pytree arguments and produces a new pytree.

- The `jax.tree_util.tree_leaves()` function returns the leaves of a pytree.

- The `jax.tree_util.tree_structure()` function returns the structure for a pytree represented with a `PyTreeDef` type.

- The `jax.tree_util.tree_flatten()` returns the flattened version of a pytree in a list, and a `PyTreeDef` represents the structure of the flattened tree.

- The `jax.tree_util.tree_unflatten()` does the reverse; with a tree structure in a `PyTreeDef` and an iterable of leaves (produced by `tree_flatten()`), it reconstructs the original pytree.

- The `jax.flatten_util.ravel_pytree()` function returns a 1D array representing the flattened and concatenated leaf values; plus, instead of a `PyTreeDef` structure, it returns a function for unflattening a 1D vector.

- The `jax.tree_util.tree_reduce()` function resembles a traditional reduce function popular in functional programming. It applies a two-argument function cumulatively to the iterable over the list of leaves from left to right, reducing the leaves to a single value.

- The `jax.tree_util.tree_transpose()` function transforms a pytree with some hierarchical structure of the type (outer, inner) into a pytree with a transposed structure of the type (inner, outer).

- You can register a custom container class in the JAX container registry to let JAX know what is inside the container and how to work with this data.

- To register a custom pytree container, you must tell JAX how to flatten and unflatten the container by providing two corresponding functions and using the `jax.tree_util.register_pytree_node()` function.

Part 3

Ecosystem

Part 3 introduces you to the vibrant ecosystem surrounding JAX, showcasing the libraries and tools that extend its functionality into various domains of deep learning and beyond. This section highlights how JAX fits into a broader context, enabling you to leverage its power in conjunction with other specialized libraries. Through two comprehensive chapters, you'll discover the high-level neural network libraries that simplify model building and training, as well as other members of the JAX ecosystem that cater to a wide array of scientific and computational needs.

Chapter 11 discusses higher-level neural network libraries, focusing on Flax and its Linen API, along with Optax for gradient transformations. You'll learn how to construct models more intuitively, manage training states, and interact with the Hugging Face ecosystem to access state-of-the-art models. This chapter bridges the gap between JAX's core capabilities and the practical needs of deep learning projects, providing you with the tools to build, train, and deploy complex models efficiently.

Chapter 12 takes a broader look at the JAX ecosystem, showcasing libraries for various machine learning tasks, including reinforcement learning and evolutionary computations. We'll also explore JAX modules for other scientific fields like physics, chemistry, and more.

By the end of part 3, you'll have a comprehensive understanding of the JAX ecosystem and be ready to apply JAX to a wide range of exciting and challenging problems.

Higher-level neural network libraries

11

This chapter covers

- Building an MLP for MNIST digit classification using Flax and its Linen API
- Using the Optax gradient transformation library for model training
- Using the `TrainState` `dataclass` for representing a training state and storing metrics
- Building a residual neural network for image classification and working with model state variables
- Using Hugging Face libraries with JAX/Flax transformers and diffusers

Core JAX is a powerful but pretty low-level library. Just as you will rarely ever build a complex neural network in pure NumPy or with basic TensorFlow primitives, in most cases, you will also not do so with pure JAX. And just as there are higher-level neural network libraries for TensorFlow (Keras, Sonnet) and PyTorch (torch.nn, Pytorch Lightning, fast.ai), there are also such libraries for JAX.

One of the most well-known high-level neural network libraries is Flax by Google. There was also Haiku by DeepMind, but now Haiku is in maintenance mode and Google DeepMind recommends that new projects adopt Flax instead of Haiku. There is also a brand-new Keras 3.0 with multibackend support, and Equinox. In this chapter, we will use Flax, but other libraries have much in common, so it shouldn't be a problem to master another library once you are familiar with Flax. These libraries provide high-level primitives that help you build neural networks from existing blocks, like dense, convolutional, or LSTM layers, multihead self-attention, activation functions, etc.

Unless you need something very special and custom, most of your basic needs are covered by these standard blocks. You can save a lot of time reusing these well-tested and optimized solutions, reducing the risk of introducing bugs into your own implementations.

Why even bother with higher-level JAX neural network libraries when you already have TensorFlow and PyTorch? Because the composable function transformation approach in JAX helps you make your code more maintainable, scalable, and high performance.

The philosophy of Flax is to offer an API familiar to those who have experience with Keras, PyTorch, or Sonnet. The API in Flax is called Linen. It is fundamentally a functional system for defining neural nets in JAX, which is different from the mostly object-oriented approaches of the TensorFlow and PyTorch ecosystems.

Flax supports the ecosystem philosophy of JAX with decoupled well-maintained libraries. It is designed to be easily integrated with other parts of the ecosystem. For example, it uses Optax, a separate library for optimizers and, more broadly, for composable gradient transformations.

In this chapter, we will start with a familiar example of MNIST digits classification and iteratively rewrite it using Flax to understand its basics. Then, in the next section, we will build a more modern and complicated example with a residual network and learn more advanced features of Flax.

Flax is also the third most popular library (after PyTorch and TensorFlow) among the models published on Hugging Face (https://mng.bz/ZVZR). Hugging Face provides a hub with state-of-the-art models for different NLP and image processing tasks, so with Flax, you can quickly start working with the best available open LLMs and diffusion models, using pretrained models, fine-tuning them, and training your own models from scratch. In the last section, we will use Hugging Face models for image diffusion and text generation.

11.1 *MNIST image classification using an MLP*

So let's start with the MNIST digits classification using a multilayer perceptron (MLP). We have already spent a lot of time developing different versions of this solution, starting from the basic example in chapter 2 to the parallelized versions in chapters 7 and 8. Now it's time to look at how the same network would look if you used Flax instead of core JAX.

We start with the simplest way of switching to Flax—by replacing the network definition and the `predict()` function that applies a neural network to some input data. Then, in the next step, we will do it more Flax-like by using a `dataclass` that represents the entire training state and an external optimizer from the Optax library.

11.1.1 MLP in Flax

The simplest way to start is to replace the network definition with layers provided by the Flax library, more precisely, by its Linen API.

Linen API

Linen, or `flax.linen`, is a second-generation neural network API. The older API was `flax.nn`.

Linen provides a `Module` abstraction that behaves much more like vanilla Python objects. The Linen `Module` API is stable and currently recommended for new projects. The authors strive to offer an API familiar to those experienced with Keras/Sonnet/PyTorch. At the same time, Linen is fundamentally a functional system for defining neural nets in JAX.

The Flax philosophy is described at https://mng.bz/RNGZ. You can find the introduction to the Linen design goals at https://mng.bz/2gAg.

First, let's reproduce the pure JAX code from chapter 2, where we manually initialized all the weight and bias tensors (listing 2.4) and wrote a `predict()` function (listing 2.5) that performed all the necessary matrix multiplications, activation functions, and so on.

Listing 11.1 Initializing and applying MLP in pure JAX (reproducing listings 2.4 and 2.5)

```
from jax import random
import jax.numpy as jnp
from jax.nn import swish                          The list with layer sizes

LAYER_SIZES = [28*28, 512, 10]                    Parameter for scaling
PARAM_SCALE = 0.01                                random values

def init_network_params(sizes, key=random.PRNGKey(0), scale=1e-2):
  """Initialize all layers for a fully-connected neural network with given
sizes"""

  def random_layer_params(m, n, key, scale=1e-2):
    """A helper function to randomly initialize
weights and biases of a dense layer"""
    w_key, b_key = random.split(key)
    return (scale * random.normal(w_key, (n, m)),
       scale * random.normal(b_key, (n,)))        Generates random values for
                                                  the layer parameters w and b
  keys = random.split(key, len(sizes))
  return [random_layer_params(m, n, k, scale)
```

```
      for m, n, k in zip(sizes[:-1], sizes[1:], keys)]

params = init_network_params(
  LAYER_SIZES, random.PRNGKey(0), scale=PARAM_SCALE)

def predict(params, image):
  """Function for per-example predictions."""
  activations = image
  for w, b in params[:-1]:
    outputs = jnp.dot(w, activations) + b
    activations = swish(outputs)

  final_w, final_b = params[-1]
  logits = jnp.dot(final_w, activations) + final_b
  return logits
```

Generates random values for all the layers

Initializes activations with input image pixels

Loops from the first to the penultimate layer

Successively updates activations with the output of each layer

For the last layer, we do not apply the activation function.

The code for parameter initialization and neural network forward pass is pretty straightforward but low-level and thus a bit wordy. There is no single place where the network structure is described. Some network descriptions are contained in Python lists with layer sizes; other parts are incorporated in the predict() function, and you have to manually parse this code to infer the network structure unless you documented it in the comments. Even if you documented the network structure (which is a good practice), you still have to maintain it separately from the code and remember to update it when you change the code. There are still risks that the description and the code might misalign at some point in time.

Flax provides you with a Module abstraction familiar to many developers using PyTorch or TensorFlow. It is stateful inside, and you write your networks in a stateful object-oriented way. But to use JAX transformations, Module needs to provide pure functions. Flax creates pure functions from Modules, so it is functional outside. These functions do not maintain a state: they return and consume it. This is the same pattern we saw with the JAX random number generators (chapter 9) that differ from their NumPy analogs by having no internal state.

Flax provides an easy way to describe the neural network structure in a self-documenting way. Figure 11.1 visually describes this process.

To write a neural network in Flax, first you describe the network as a sequence of layers in a way very similar to Keras or torch.nn. This step has no corresponding procedure in the pure JAX example. To do this, subclass the flax.linen.Module class and, using the @nn.compact annotation, define your forward calculation within the __call__ method, which we'll use shortly.

The @nn.compact annotation is a simple and compact way of defining a neural network. It allows writing your network's logic directly within a single "forward-pass" method. A more capable way of defining a neural network is using the separate setup() method. It may be required for more complex configurations with multiple forward-pass methods (for example, if you have one such function for the encoder part of the network and another one for the decoder), but we don't need it in our case. You can read more about the setup() method at https://mng.bz/1a7X. You then instantiate the object of the newly defined class.

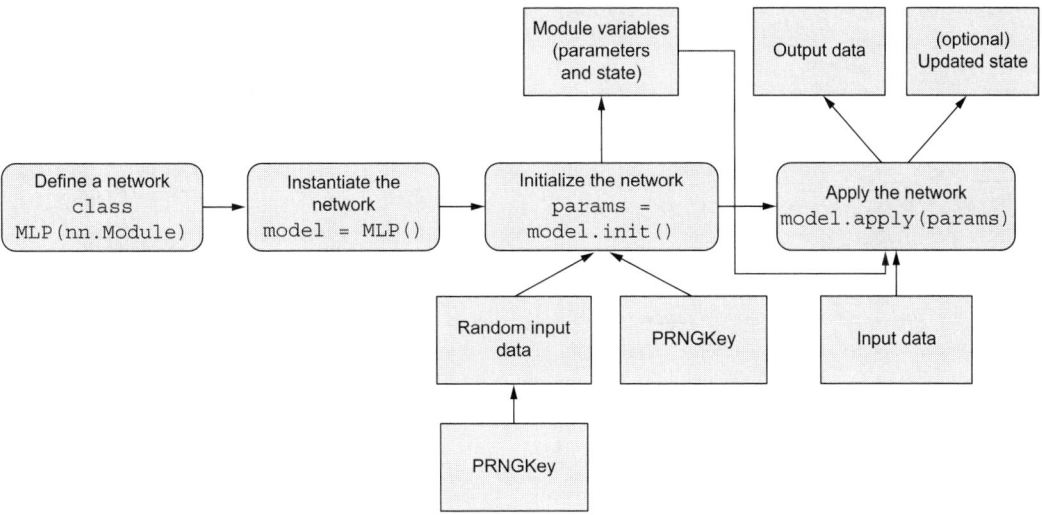

Figure 11.1   The process of initializing and applying a neural network in Flax

Then, you generate dummy input data to initialize the `Module` variables. These variables include the parameters of the `Module` (weights and biases) and any other state variables (say, statistics for batch normalization layers). Model variables (or parameters) are initialized by the `init()` method on the instantiated `Module`. The `model .init()` call needs a PRNGKey and dummy input data. This is equivalent to the `init_ network_params()` call in the pure JAX example, except that there, you didn't have to pass dummy data to infer tensor shapes because you explicitly determined the shapes by yourself. Flax does shape inference, so you only have to declare the number of neurons, not the input sizes, and then Flax automatically determines the shapes of weight matrices. If, for some reason, in addition to the initialized parameters, you need the output of the forward pass on the dummy data, you can use the `init_with_output()` function instead of `init()`. It has the same input parameters and returns a tuple of the output and initialized parameters.

Finally, to conduct a forward pass of the model using a given set of parameters, call the `apply()` method on the instantiated `Module`. `apply()` takes the initialized variables as well as the input data. This step completely replaces the `predict()` function we used before, and you can just replace all the `predict()` invocations with `model .apply()` calls. If a model has some internal state, it will also be updated during this call. Our MNIST example contains no state, but we will implement a more complicated example with a state later in section 11.2.

NOTE   Parameters are never stored within the model. The `init()` and `apply()` functions return state rather than maintain state.

The resulting code for defining and initializing a model looks like listing 11.2.

Listing 11.2 Defining and applying MLP in Flax

```
from jax import random
from flax import linen as nn

class MLP(nn.Module):
  """A simple MLP model."""

  @nn.compact
  def __call__(self, x):
    x = nn.Dense(features=512)(x)
    x = nn.activation.swish(x)
    x = nn.Dense(features=10)(x)
    return x

model = MLP()

key1, key2 = random.split(random.PRNGKey(0))
random_flattened_image = random.normal(key1, (28*28*1,))
params = model.init(key2, random_flattened_image)
jax.tree_util.tree_map(lambda x: x.shape, params)

>>> dict({
>>>     params: {
>>>         Dense_0: {
>>>             bias: (512,),
>>>             kernel: (784, 512),
>>>         },
>>>         Dense_1: {
>>>             bias: (10,),
>>>             kernel: (512, 10),
>>>         },
>>>     },
>>> })

model.apply(params, random_flattened_image)

>>> Array([ 0.43500084,  0.20896661, -0.9779186 ,  0.3447541 ,  0.05475511,
>>>         0.29811084, -0.24472891, -0.30921277,  0.2945502 , -0.34386003],
>>>       dtype=float32)
```

- Necessary imports
- Class for our MLP, subclass of flax.linen.Module
- Uses nn.compact declaration mode
- Defines a net directly within a single forward-pass method
- Instantiates an object for the MLP
- Prepares a dummy input (you may also use an array of zeros as well)
- Initializes the model parameters
- Checks output shapes for the model parameters
- Applies the model to input data

In the MLP training code, there are just two places where predict() calls need to be updated with model.apply(): in the loss function and in the accuracy function.

In our case we don't need to change gradient calculations. The grad() function just works with the updated loss function as before. You only need to slightly change the update() function to apply the gradients to model parameters. Because the model parameters are now structured differently, using a dict, it's easier to modify them with the help of the jax.tree_util.tree_map() function you are familiar with from the previous chapter.

And that's it. The training code with the loss() and update() functions looks the following listing.

Listing 11.3 Doing a gradient update step for the MLP in Flax

```
def loss(params, images, targets):
  """Categorical cross entropy loss function."""
  logits = model.apply(params, images)                    Calls model.apply()
  log_preds = logits - jax.nn.logsumexp(logits)           instead of predict()
  return -jnp.mean(targets*log_preds)

@jax.jit
def update(params, x, y, epoch_number):
  loss_value, grads = jax.value_and_grad(loss)(params, x, y)    Uses the tree_map,
  lr = INIT_LR * DECAY_RATE ** (epoch_number / DECAY_STEPS)     which is better
  return jax.tree_util.tree_map(                                suited for pytrees
      lambda p, g: p - lr * g, params, grads), loss_value
```

This is an incomplete example that highlights only the changed parts. For the complete working example, see the Chapter_11.1_MNIST_MLP_Flax_Simple example in the book's repo on GitHub.

Flax follows the JAX functional conventions of storing data in pytrees. Researchers frequently need to manually interact with this data, so Flax uses nested dictionaries with meaningful default keys and offers several utilities (like traversals) for handling them directly.

> **NOTE** If you use a Flax version earlier than 0.7.1, you may see that Flax uses FrozenDict data structure for storing model parameters (https://mng.bz/PN8w). It is an immutable variant of the Python `dict`, which helps deal with the functional nature of JAX by preventing any mutation of the underlying `dict` and making the user aware of it. An additional benefit of the `FrozenDict` data structure is that this is an accelerated version of a Python frozen dictionary that caches its JAX-flattened form to speed up jitted function call overheads. However, after lengthy discussions (https://github.com/google/flax/issues/1223), the team switched to using regular Python `dicts` when calling the `init()`, `init_with_output()`, and `apply()` Module methods. Internally, Flax still uses `Frozen-Dicts` to ensure variable `dicts` aren't accidentally mutated.

The beauty of this code lies in two aspects. First, the neural network definition is clear, and it's harder to make a mistake doing all the tensor operations. The data structure containing the model parameters is also self-descriptive. You just see which parts of the `dict` are responsible for which layers. A `tabulate()` function returns the model description in the string form. It has the same signature and internally calls the `Module.init()` method, but instead of returning the variables, it returns the string summarizing the `Module` in a table. You can easily print it for debugging purposes:

```
print(model.tabulate(key2, random_flattened_image))
```
◄――― **Generates a string with model description**

MLP Summary

path	module	inputs	outputs	params
	MLP	float32[784]	float32[10]	
Dense_0	Dense	float32[784]	float32[512]	bias: float32[512] kernel: float32[784,512] 401,920 (1.6 MB)
Dense_1	Dense	float32[512]	float32[10]	bias: float32[10] kernel: float32[512,10] 5,130 (20.5 KB)
			Total	407,050 (1.6 MB)

Total Parameters: 407,050 (1.6 MB)

With this data structure, it is also much easier to introspect, do network surgery if you need to change anything in the pretrained network, or write a conversion procedure if you need to import or export your neural network. For example, Flax users have utilized this to map TensorFlow and PyTorch checkpoints to Flax.

Second, all the JAX function transformations work perfectly well, and you don't have to change your code significantly when doing the same things in Flax. Moreover, you don't even need to use `jax.vmap()`. In Flax, you write models as "single-example" code, and the framework introduces batching automatically.

What we did was not the most Flax-like way of doing things. There is a common pattern in Flax for how you structure the entire training state, including model parameters, optimizer state, iteration number, and so on. But before doing this, let's get acquainted with the Optax gradient transformation library.

11.1.2 *Optax gradient transformations library*

Originally, Flax had its own `flax.optim` API for optimization. It contained some optimizers and `dataclasses` helpful in the process of model training. However, the list of optimizers was far from exhaustive, and the pattern used for training was relatively complex and quite verbose. The maintainers proposed making a switch (https://mng.bz/JN8o) to a dedicated library—*Optax*—that was already developed by DeepMind.

Optax (https://github.com/google-deepmind/optax) implements a wide range of optimizers and provides a framework to compose new optimizers from reusable gradient transformations.

At first sight, Optax provides an extensive list of predefined state-of-the-art optimizers that you can use off the shelf. But it is more than just a collection of optimizers. In the same way as JAX itself is more than just a multidimensional array library but the library for *composable function transformations*, Optax is rather a library of *gradient transformations*. Optax is designed to facilitate research by providing building blocks that can be easily recombined in custom ways.

An initial Optax prototype was made available in JAX's experimental folder as `jax.experimental.optix`, but later, it was eventually moved out of experimental as a standalone open source library, renamed `optax`. Here we will only use Optax for well-tested and efficient implementations of optimizers, but keep in mind that Optax is much more than that.

USING OPTAX OPTIMIZERS

A high-level diagram of using an Optax optimizer is shown in figure 11.2.

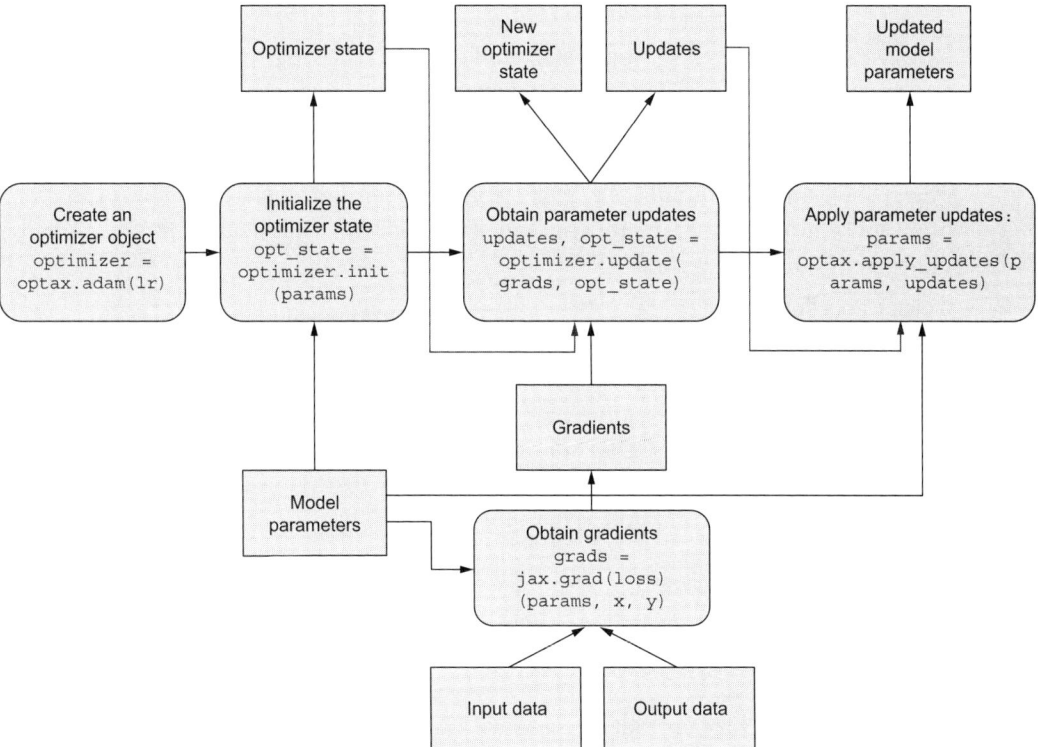

Figure 11.2 The process of using an optimizer in Optax (only a single gradient update step is shown)

The scheme may look complicated, but when described as a sequence of steps, the process is straightforward:

1 Create an optimizer object, for example, Adam optimizer: `optimizer = optax` `.adam(learning_rate)`.

2 Initialize the optimizer state (e.g., a momentum vector) using the `init()` function called with parameters of the model: `opt_state = optimizer` `.init(params)`.

3 In the model update loop, you have a loss function that can be differentiated by JAX to obtain the gradients, like `grads = jax.grad(loss_function)(params,` `x, y)`.

4 The gradients are then converted via an `optimizer.update()` call to obtain the parameter updates. This function also consumes and updates the optimizer state: `updates, opt_state = optimizer.update(grads, opt_state)`.

5 The parameter updates should be applied to the current `params` to obtain the new ones. You can use the handy `optax.apply_updates()` function for this: `params = optax.apply_updates(params, updates)`.

As you can see, Optax uses a pattern similar to Flax, having one function for initialization (in both cases `init()`) and another one for application (`apply()` in Flax, `update()` in Optax).

Technically, every optimizer implements the `GradientTransformation` interface. The `init()` function initializes a set of statistics (or optimizer state), and the `update()` function transforms a candidate gradient given some statistics (state) and (optionally) the current value of the parameters.

OTHER OPTAX COMPONENTS

A gradient transformation does not return updated model parameters but rather processed gradients. This allows the ability to combine arbitrary transformations into a custom optimizer and to combine transformations for different gradients that operate on a shared set of variables. One common application is to create a chain of gradient transformations that involves calculating gradients by some optimizer, scaling them according to some learning rate schedule, and then clipping them to fit in a specified range.

Optax provides classes and wrappers for composing gradient transformations: `chain()` for applying a list of chainable update transformations and `multi_transform()` for partitioning model parameters and applying a different transformation to each subset.

There are also wrappers that take a `GradientTransformation` as input and return a new `GradientTransformation` that modifies the behavior of the inner transformation in a specific way. For example, one wrapper flattens gradients into a single vector before applying a gradient transformation and then unflattens the result. This can be used to reduce the overhead of performing many calculations on many small variables at the cost of slightly increased memory usage. Another wrapper makes an optimizer robust to NaNs or Infs. Another helps mask some parameters from an update, such as skipping weight decay for the BatchNorm scale and all bias parameters.

Schedules can be used to create time-dependent components in an optimizer. A common example of this is annealing the learning rate or some other hyperparameter. There are also a number of standard losses used in deep learning, such as l2_loss, softmax_cross_entropy, cosine_distance, kl_divergence, and ctc_loss.

We have covered the most important elements of Optax, though Optax has additional useful features discussed in the documentation (https://optax.readthedocs.io/en/latest/index.html). In the next section, I will show you how to use Optax with Flax.

11.1.3 Training a neural network the Flax way

Here we will incorporate an Optax optimizer into the training procedure, add metrics calculation, and use a special data structure for storing a training state.

There is a flax.training.train_state.TrainState class (https://mng.bz/r1PD) for representing a simple training state for the common case with a single Optax optimizer. If you want to add anything to the training state—say, quality metrics—you would create a subclass of it. Let's start with a basic case with only an Optax optimizer added.

ADDING TRAINSTATE

You use the TrainState.create() function by passing

- apply_fn—A function to apply the neural network, usually set to model.apply
- params—The model parameters used by apply_fn and to be updated by an optimizer (the next item, tx)
- tx—An optimizer that implements the Optax GradientTransformation interface

There are also parameters for a training step number and an optimizer state, but for our purposes, the three mentioned parameters are enough. TrainState simplifies the process of using an Optax optimizer. Of the five steps listed in the previous section, you will only see steps 1, 3, and combined steps 4 and 5.

Here we create a training state with a simple optimizer: stochastic gradient descent (SGD) with momentum. This way, we implement step 1 from the procedure of using an Optax optimizer (create an optimizer object) and step 2 (initializing the optimizer state), though the latter step is hidden inside the TrainState.create() method call.

Listing 11.4 Creating a training state

```
from flax.training import train_state        ◄—— Imports TrainState
import optax                                   ◄—┐
                                                  │ Imports Optax
                                                  │ optimization library
```

```
state = train_state.TrainState.create(          ◀──── Creates a training state
    apply_fn=model.apply,
    params=params,
    tx=optax.sgd(learning_rate=1.0, momentum=0.9))   ◀──┐ Uses an SGD optimizer
                                                         └ from the optax library
```

Now we have a training state and can arrange a training loop.

Inside the training loop, you use almost the same loss function, with the only change being that instead of calling `model.apply()` directly, you call the apply function from the `TrainState` object, `train_state.apply_fn()`.

In the `update()` function, you obtain gradients the same way as before (step 3 of the procedure of using an Optax optimizer), but then applying gradients to the model weights is simpler and is done by the `train_state.apply_gradients(grads)` call. Internally, it calls a couple of functions to update an optimizer state, produces updates for the model parameters (step 4), and applies these updates (step 5). The resulting training loop looks like the following listing. (For the full listing, see the book's GitHub repo.)

Listing 11.5   Updated training loop

```
@jax.jit
def update(train_state, x, y):
    """A single training step"""
    def loss(params, images, targets):
        """Categorical cross entropy loss function."""        ──┐ Applies the model
        logits = train_state.apply_fn(params, images)   ◀──────┘ to input images
        log_preds = logits - jax.nn.logsumexp(logits)
        return -jnp.mean(targets*log_preds)                     ┐ The gradient
    loss_value, grads = jax.value_and_grad(loss)(              │ calculation remained
        train_state.params, x, y)                       ◀──────┘ the same.
    train_state = train_state.apply_gradients(grads=grads)   ◀──┐
    return train_state, loss_value                              │
                                                                │ Updates the model
...                                                             │ parameters and the
                                                                └ optimizer state
for epoch in range(num_epochs):
    start_time = time.time()
    losses = []
    for x, y in train_data:
        x = jnp.reshape(x, (len(x), NUM_PIXELS))
        y = jax.nn.one_hot(y, NUM_LABELS)                       ┐ Updates the
        state, loss_value = update(state, x, y)   ◀────────────┘ training state
        losses.append(loss_value)
    epoch_time = time.time() - start_time
```

The code has become even more high-level, hiding some low-level details about parameter updating.

ADDING METRICS CALCULATION WITH THE CLU LIBRARY

Another thing that can be done in a more Flax-like way is metrics calculation. There is a common pattern for adding metrics to the training state.

For calculating metrics, we will use another library in the JAX ecosystem from Google called *Common Loop Utils* (CLU) (https://github.com/google/CommonLoopUtils). It contains common functionality for writing machine learning training loops with the goal of making them short and readable without removing the flexibility required for research. CLU is designed to work perfectly with JAX and Flax.

Among other things, the CLU library defines a functional metric computation interface `Metric` that relies on metrics accumulating intermediate values and then uses these intermediate values to compute the final metric value. It works for averageable metrics. In a few words, this is done the following way:

1 For each batch, you compute local batch metrics from the model outputs. The "model output" is a dictionary of values with unique keys that all have a specific meaning (such as "loss," "logits," and "labels"). Every metric depends on at least one such model output by name. The `Metric` interface provides the function `from_output()` to specify the name of the model output that will be used for the metric calculation.

2 Local or intermediate metrics from different batches are aggregated using the `merge()` function.

3 The final metrics are computed from aggregated intermediate values using the `compute()` function.

CLU also provides an interface called `metrics.Collection` to compute a collection of metrics from model outputs all at once. It uses the function `single_from_model_output()` for the non-distributed setting and `gather_from_model_output()` for the distributed setting.

To add metrics to the training state, we first declare a `dataclass` for storing the metrics, loss, and accuracy. Then we create a subclass for the `TrainState` to include metrics. Finally, we instantiate the newly defined `TrainState` class and initialize all the relevant fields, including metrics. The code for this looks like the following listing.

Listing 11.6 Adding metrics to the training state

```
from flax.training import train_state
from clu import metrics
import flax
import optax

@flax.struct.dataclass
class Metrics(metrics.Collection):        Defines our own class for metrics
  accuracy: metrics.Accuracy            ◄── Adds an accuracy metric
  loss: metrics.Average.from_output('loss')  ◄──
                                             Adds a loss metric
```

```
class TrainState(train_state.TrainState):
  metrics: Metrics
```
◄── Adds metrics to the TrainState

```
state = TrainState.create(
    apply_fn=model.apply,
    params=params,
    tx=optax.sgd(learning_rate=0.01, momentum=0.9),
    metrics=Metrics.empty())
```
◄── Initializes metrics with an empty collection

Next, we must change the training loop to include the metrics calculation. We will use a function to calculate all the metrics and call this function on each training batch. Inside this function, we use a function from Optax to calculate cross-entropy loss (which will save us several lines of code). We use an existing metric from CLU for the accuracy metric, and the library knows how to aggregate the state and calculate the final metric from intermediate values. If you need another metric, like precision or recall, you might need to implement it independently, which isn't difficult.

To calculate test set metrics, we clone a `TrainState` with empty metrics and compute all the metrics in the same way as we do during training.

Listing 11.7   Calculating the metrics inside the training loop

The function does all the metric calculations and updates the TrainState with new metrics.

Gets the output of the model

```
@jax.jit
def compute_metrics(state, x, y):
  logits = state.apply_fn(state.params, x)
  loss = optax.softmax_cross_entropy_with_integer_labels(
        logits=logits, labels=y).mean()
  metric_updates = state.metrics.single_from_model_output(
    logits=logits, labels=y, loss=loss)
  metrics = state.metrics.merge(metric_updates)
  state = state.replace(metrics=metrics)
  return state

for epoch in range(num_epochs):
  start_time = time.time()
  for x, y in train_data:
    x = jnp.reshape(x, (len(x), NUM_PIXELS))
    y = y.astype(jnp.int32)     # by default it is int64 and clu expects int32
    state, loss_value = update(state, x, y)
    state = compute_metrics(state, x, y)
  epoch_time = time.time() - start_time
  print("Epoch {} in {:0.2f} sec".format(epoch, epoch_time))

  for metric,value in state.metrics.compute().items():
    print(f"Training set {metric} {value}")
  state = state.replace(metrics=state.metrics.empty())

  test_state = state
  for x, y in test_data:
```

Uses the softmax loss function from Optax library

Provides the model output dictionary to calculate all the intermediate metrics in a collection

Aggregates intermediate metrics

Updates the TrainState with aggregated metrics

Updates metrics during the training loop

Computes final metrics

Resets metrics after each epoch

Clones the state with empty metrics for evaluation

```
x = jnp.reshape(x, (len(x), NUM_PIXELS))
y = y.astype(jnp.int32)
test_state = compute_metrics(test_state, x, y)

for metric,value in test_state.metrics.compute().items():
  print(f"Test set {metric} {value}")
```

Computes metrics on the test set after each training epoch

We've trained a neural network using Flax, but the model was still a very simple MLP, which is far from the state of the art. The next section will implement the more advanced residual network for image classification.

11.2 *Image classification using a ResNet*

You likely know that using MLPs for image processing tasks is typically not optimal, as more specialized and efficient solutions like convolutional neural networks (CNNs) exist. CNNs have evolved over many years, and usually, people use residual networks (ResNets).

Here we will take the Dogs vs. Cats dataset from chapter 9 and implement a rather simple ResNet, which might be the right choice for such a task.

Modern computer vision

A typical real-world solution to the image classification problem likely involves a CNN. A CNN is a type of neural network well suited to work with images. It has remarkable properties, like translation equivariance and the ability to learn local features.

CNNs were long considered the best neural network type for working with images, and many improvements pushed the frontier further. ResNets (https://arxiv.org/abs/1512.03385) were one of them. So CNNs were a natural choice for computer vision tasks. Yet, in the last few years, the situation has changed.

Transformers (https://arxiv.org/abs/1706.03762) emerged in 2017 and were first applied to NLP tasks such as machine translation. In 2018, a model called BERT (https://arxiv.org/abs/1810.04805) was developed that could be applied to almost any NLP task.

In 2020, a network called Vision Transformer (ViT) (https://arxiv.org/abs/2010.11929) demonstrated exceptional performance on images. This work started a vast wave of transformer applications for images and videos.

In 2021, a model called MLP-Mixer (https://arxiv.org/abs/2105.01601) emerged along with several other similar works. These works finally found a way to use good old MLPs in computer vision tasks and showed results comparable to transformers.

CNN architectures didn't stand still all that time, and many other improvements appeared. ConvNeXt (https://arxiv.org/abs/2201.03545) and EfficientNetV2 (https://arxiv.org/abs/2104.00298) were among the top performers on image classification tasks in 2022.

Interestingly enough, both ViT and MLP-Mixer were created with JAX.

You can find the complete code for the dataset loading and preprocessing in the book's GitHub repo. This code is not crucial here, so we will now jump to ResNet creation.

11.2.1 *Managing state in Flax*

Previously, we used simple neural network layers without any internal state. However, some widely used layer types use an internal state; the most popular example is the batch normalization layer (`BatchNorm`).

A `BatchNorm` normalizes layer activations. This helps train models faster and obtain better performance. There are many other types of normalization, such as layer normalization, group normalization, instance normalization, etc.

> **BatchNorm**
>
> The `BatchNorm` technique was introduced in 2015 by Sergey Ioffe and Christian Szegedy in a paper titled "Batch Normalization: Accelerating Deep Network Training by Reducing Internal Covariate Shift" (https://arxiv.org/abs/1502.03167).
>
> A visual explanation of how `BatchNorm` works can be found at https://mng.bz/GNyR.
>
> `BatchNorm` is a layer with different behavior during training and inference. It works the following way.
>
> During training, `BatchNorm` calculates batch statistics, namely mean and variance, across a batch for each activation. Then it normalizes each activation by subtracting the mean and dividing it by the standard deviation (the square root of the variance). Then it applies a learned linear transformation that does scaling (by a different standard deviation) and shifting (by a different mean). As with many other neural network layer weights, these two coefficients for scaling and shifting are learned by backpropagation. It is essential to have this learned transformation in addition to the normalization part so the `BatchNorm` can learn an identity transformation if needed.
>
> `BatchNorm` also keeps an exponential moving average of the mean and variance as it is a good proxy for the mean and variance of the whole data, and it is much easier to calculate. These moving average values are stored inside a layer state but separately from learned model parameters.
>
> During inference, a neural network might work using a single-input data point without any batch, so no batch statistics are available. `BatchNorm` uses stored values of moving average mean and variance for normalization and fixed learned weights for scale and shift transformations.
>
> Flax has its own guide on how to apply `BatchNorm` provided by the library: https://mng.bz/znXX.

The problem with `BatchNorm` and other layers with an internal state is that with Flax's functional approach, there should be no side effects or internal state, and changing the program state is one kind of side effect. The state should be passed as an external

parameter to resolve this, so the classes and functions become stateless (https://mng
.bz/0MKl). Again, this is precisely the same pattern as JAX random number generators
(chapter 9), which use an external state as a PRNGKey.

BatchNorm is an essential part of a ResNet; it follows convolutional layers. Flax provides implementations for many popular neural network layers in the flax.linen
module (https://mng.bz/KDeZ). This includes convolutional layers (https://mng
.bz/PNPY) and BatchNorm (https://mng.bz/JNDK).

The dictionary with initialized variables for BatchNorm will contain, in addition to
a params collection, a separate batch_stats collection containing all the running
statistics.

The Flax BatchNorm module contains a use_running_average parameter, which
is set to True when the statistics stored in batch_stats should be used (during
inference) or False when we need to compute the batch statistics on the input and
update the batch_stats collection (during training). In our code, we will use a
Boolean flag to distinguish training mode from inference, and this flag will determine
the use_running_average parameter of BatchNorm layers.

The code in listing 11.8 defines a small ResNet model with 18 layers (ResNet18). In
the notebook for the chapter, you will find code for other larger ResNets as well, with
34, 50, 101, 152, or 200 layers. For the complete working example, see the Colab notebook. Here we will only highlight important parts worth our attention right now. This
code is based on the ImageNet example from the Flax repository. Flax examples provide a great way to start experimenting with real-life models while learning Flax.

> ### Listing 11.8 Defining a 18-layer ResNet

```
from flax import linen as nn
from functools import partial                          ◄── Import for partial
from typing import Any, Callable, Sequence, Tuple      ◄──   function application

ModuleDef = Any                                         Import for type
                                                        annotations

class ResNetBlock(nn.Module):                          ◄── Class for a ResNet
  """ResNet block."""                                       building block
  filters: int
  conv: ModuleDef
  norm: ModuleDef
  act: Callable
  strides: Tuple[int, int] = (1, 1)

  @nn.compact
  def __call__(self, x,):
    residual = x                                                 Convolutional layer
    y = self.conv(self.filters, (3, 3), self.strides)(x)   ◄──
    y = self.norm()(y)                                     ◄── Normalization layer
    y = self.act(y)
    y = self.conv(self.filters, (3, 3))(y)                       Activation
    y = self.norm(scale_init=nn.initializers.zeros_init())(y)
```

```
      if residual.shape != y.shape:
        residual = self.conv(self.filters, (1, 1),
                             self.strides, name='conv_proj')(residual)
        residual = self.norm(name='norm_proj')(residual)

      return self.act(residual + y)

class ResNet(nn.Module):                          ◄─────  Class for a
  """ResNetV1."""                                         complete ResNet
  stage_sizes: Sequence[int]
  block_cls: ModuleDef
  num_classes: int
  num_filters: int = 64                           ◄─────  Uses linen.relu
  dtype: Any = jnp.float32                                activation
  act: Callable = nn.relu                          ◄─────
  conv: ModuleDef = nn.Conv                        ◄─────  Uses linen.Conv layer

  @nn.compact
  def __call__(self, x, train: bool = True):       ◄─────  Uses a
    conv = partial(self.conv, use_bias=False, dtype=self.dtype)    parameter to
    norm = partial(nn.BatchNorm,                   ◄─────          distinguish
                   use_running_average=not train,  ◄─────          training and
                   momentum=0.9,                                   inference
                   epsilon=1e-5,                                   modes
                   dtype=self.dtype)
                                                          Uses linen.BatchNorm
    x = conv(self.num_filters, (7, 7), (2, 2),            layer
             padding=[(3, 3), (3, 3)],
             name='conv_init')(x)                   Defines how to use
    x = norm(name='bn_init')(x)                     running averages
    x = nn.relu(x)                                  depending on the mode
    x = nn.max_pool(x, (3, 3), strides=(2, 2), padding='SAME')
    for i, block_size in enumerate(self.stage_sizes):
      for j in range(block_size):
        strides = (2, 2) if i > 0 and j == 0 else (1, 1)
        x = self.block_cls(self.num_filters * 2 ** i,   ◄─────  Uses ResNetBlocks
                           strides=strides,                     as building blocks
                           conv=conv,
                           norm=norm,
                           act=self.act)(x)
    x = jnp.mean(x, axis=(1, 2))
    x = nn.Dense(self.num_classes, dtype=self.dtype)(x)
    x = jnp.asarray(x, self.dtype)
    return x

ResNet18 = partial(ResNet, stage_sizes=[2, 2, 2, 2],    ◄─────  Sets parameters for
                   block_cls=ResNetBlock)                       an 18-layer ResNet

model = ResNet18(num_classes=NUM_LABELS)
```

You can see a much more advanced neural network here than in our previous examples. The code here is similar to the model definition in TensorFlow or PyTorch. You may use something like this or a deeper ResNet from the notebook to solve your own real-life image classification tasks.

There is nothing special here except for new layers we previously didn't use and a separate parameter to distinguish training and inference modes. The model state is hidden inside `BatchNorm` layers, and the only place that links to the internal state is the `use_running_average` parameter, whose value depends on the mode we are in: training or inference.

The `model.init()` function is pretty much the same as before; it still returns all the model variables. Now, variables include not only the model parameters but also the model state (`BatchNorm` statistics). The resulting `dict` after initialization contains the `params` key for trainable model parameters as before, as well as the `batch_stats` key with `mean` and `var` variables for storing each layer's running averages. You can visualize it using the `model.tabulate()` method.

Listing 11.9 Initializing the ResNet

```
key1, key2 = random.split(random.PRNGKey(0))          Initializes the model
variables = model.init(key2, images)

model_state, params = flax.core.pop(variables, 'params')    Separates the model
                                                            state and parameters

print(model.tabulate(key2, images))               Displays all the model variables
                                                  (state and parameters) visually
>>>
>>>                           ResNet Summary
>>>
>>> ┌──────────┬──────────┬───────────┬───────────┬─────────────┬───────────┐
>>> │path      │ module   │ inputs    │ outputs   │ batch_stats │ params    │
>>> ├──────────┼──────────┼───────────┼───────────┼─────────────┼───────────┤
>>> │          │ ResNet   │ float32[3…│ float32[3…│             │           │
>>> ├──────────┼──────────┼───────────┼───────────┼─────────────┼───────────┤
>>> │conv_init │ Conv     │ float32[3…│ float32[3…│             │ kernel:   │
>>> │          │          │           │           │             │ float32[7…│
>>> │          │          │           │           │             │           │
>>> │          │          │           │           │             │ 9,408     │
>>> │          │          │           │           │             │ (37.6 KB) │
>>> ├──────────┼──────────┼───────────┼───────────┼─────────────┼───────────┤
>>> │bn_init   │ BatchNorm│ float32[3…│ float32[3…│ mean:       │ bias:     │
>>> │          │          │           │           │ float32[64] │ float32[6…│
>>> │          │          │           │           │ var:        │ scale:    │
>>> │          │          │           │           │ float32[64] │ float32[6…│
>>> │          │          │           │           │             │           │
>>> │          │          │           │           │ 128 (512 B) │ 128 (512  │
>>> │          │          │           │           │             │ B)        │
>>> └──────────┴──────────┴───────────┴───────────┴─────────────┴───────────┘
>>> …
```

Here you see that both model state and parameters become explicit after initialization. Later, they will be used in training and inference. We incorporate both variables into the `TrainState` we used before. Other parts of the code related to the `model.apply()` function, optimizer, and metrics remain the same.

The `model.apply()` function (now called using `train_state.apply_fn`) is changed compared to our MLP example without state. It still consumes a dictionary with model variables as before, yet now model variables include the state as well. The second argument (`x`) is an input to be processed as before. And there are two more new arguments. One named argument passes the Boolean `train` parameter to distinguish training from inference. Another argument named `mutable` specifies which collections inside `dict` model variables should be treated as mutable. Now we have a mutable state that needs to be updated inside the training loop, so we must pass keys from the model state part of variables.

Previously, in the MLP example, the `model.apply()` function returned just the model output or the logits. Now, with the mutable part, we also need to return an updated model state, so when the `mutable` parameter is set to `True`, it returns a tuple of `(output, vars)`, where `vars` is a `dict` of the modified collections, here running averages for data mean and variances. Also, when calculating gradients, we need to remember this auxiliary data with the model state, so the `grad()` (or `value_and_grad()`) transformation needs to know about these additional return values. We will use the `has_aux=True` parameter we discussed in chapter 4.

All of these changes will be incorporated into the `update()`, `evaluate()` functions and the `TrainState`. The training loop will be the same. Long story short: it's easier to look at the code than read all these lengthy explanations.

Listing 11.10 Updated training loop with model state

```
class TrainState(train_state.TrainState):
  metrics: Metrics
  model_state: Any                              Adds model state (non-trainable
                                                parameters) to the TrainState

state = TrainState.create(
    apply_fn=model.apply,
    params=params,
    model_state=model_state,                    Stores model state and
    tx=optax.sgd(learning_rate=0.01, momentum=0.9),    model parameters separately
    metrics=Metrics.empty())

@jax.jit
def update(train_state, x, y):
  """A single training step"""
  def loss(params):
    """Categorical cross entropy loss function."""
    logits, new_model_state = train_state.apply_fn(
        {'params': params, **train_state.model_state},
        x,
        mutable=list(model_state.keys()),
        train=True)
    loss_ce = optax.softmax_cross_entropy_with_integer_labels(
        logits=logits, labels=y).mean()
    return loss_ce, (logits, new_model_state)
```

The model apply function returns both the output and updated state

Reassembles full model variables that include model parameters and model state

Marks model state variables as mutable

Lets the apply function know that we are in the training mode

```
  grad_fn = jax.value_and_grad(loss, has_aux=True)
  (loss_value, (logits, new_model_state)), grads = \
    grad_fn(train_state.params)
```

Returns auxiliary parameters (model state) after the gradient transformation

```
  train_state = train_state.apply_gradients(grads=grads,
model_state=new_model_state)
  train_state = compute_metrics(train_state, loss=loss_value,
logits=logits, labels=y)
  return train_state, loss_value
```

Updates the model state inside the TrainState

```
@jax.jit
def evaluate(train_state, x, y):
  """A single eval step"""
  logits = train_state.apply_fn(
    {'params': train_state.params, **train_state.model_state},
    x,
    mutable=False,
    train=False)
  loss_ce = optax.softmax_cross_entropy_with_integer_labels(
    logits=logits, labels=y).mean()
  train_state = compute_metrics(
    train_state, loss=loss_ce, logits=logits, labels=y)
  return train_state
```

During evaluation, we do not update the model state.

Lets the apply function know that we are **NOT** in the training mode

```
for epoch in range(num_epochs):
...
  for x, y in train_data:
    state, loss_value = update(state, x, y)
...

  for x, y in test_data:
    state = evaluate(state, x, y)
...
```

The training loop is as usual with separate training and evaluation parts.

As you can see, since we started using `TrainState`, it has become much simpler to make changes without constantly modifying function signatures after adding each new feature to a model. Now, everything related to the training state is incorporated into this data structure, which is available inside the training and evaluation functions of the training loop.

We've now implemented and trained a ResNet. The final step is to save the trained model so it can be used later.

11.2.2 Saving and loading a model using Orbax

To save and load Flax checkpoints, using another library from the JAX ecosystem, Orbax (https://github.com/google/orbax) is recommended. Flax has its legacy `flax.training.checkpoints` API, but now the recommended way of saving a model is Orbax.

With Orbax, you can save and load any given JAX pytree, even customized classes extended from `flax.struct.dataclass`. So you can store not only your model parameters but almost any data generated, including arrays, dictionaries, metadata, configs, and so on.

Orbax includes a checkpointing library oriented toward JAX users, supporting various features required by different frameworks, including asynchronous checkpointing, various types, and various storage formats. To install Orbax, run the following command:

```
pip install orbax-checkpoint
```

Orbax also includes a serialization library for JAX users, enabling the exporting of JAX models to the TensorFlow `SavedModel` format. To install this functionality, run the following command:

```
pip install orbax-export
```

To save and restore model parameters, create a checkpointer (a special class in Orbax; we will use a checkpointer for `PyTree`, `PyTreeCheckpointer`). For saving a model, call its `save()` method, passing a path and a pytree to save. For restoring a model, call its `restore()` method with a path in a filesystem. By default, the checkpointer stores each parameter in a pytree as a separate directory. There is an optional parameter `save_args`. It is recommended for performance speedups, as it bundles smaller arrays in your pytree into a single large file instead of multiple smaller files.

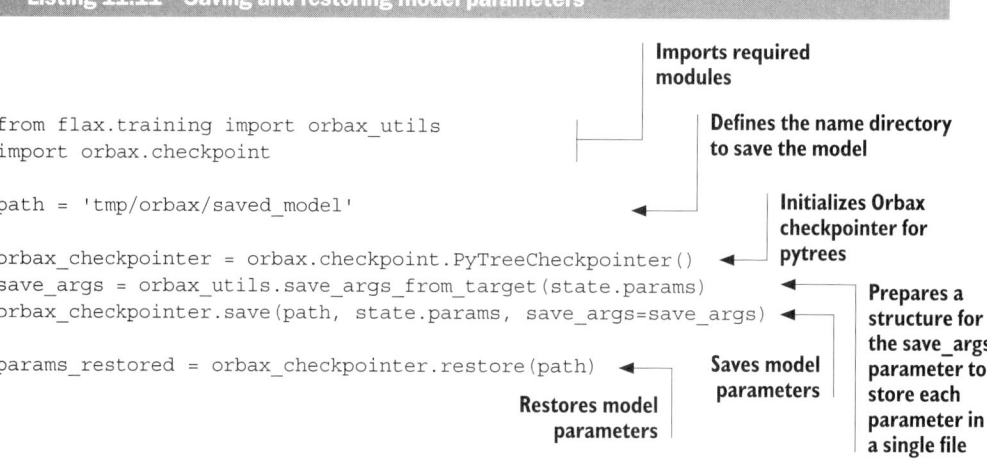

Listing 11.11 Saving and restoring model parameters

```
from flax.training import orbax_utils
import orbax.checkpoint

path = 'tmp/orbax/saved_model'

orbax_checkpointer = orbax.checkpoint.PyTreeCheckpointer()
save_args = orbax_utils.save_args_from_target(state.params)
orbax_checkpointer.save(path, state.params, save_args=save_args)

params_restored = orbax_checkpointer.restore(path)
```

Imports required modules

Defines the name directory to save the model

Initializes Orbax checkpointer for pytrees

Prepares a structure for the save_args parameter to store each parameter in a single file

Saves model parameters

Restores model parameters

So saving and restoring is easy. You can also use versioning and automatic bookkeeping features—for example, saving a model checkpoint after each epoch. To do this, you need to wrap `orbax.checkpoint.CheckpointManager` over the checkpointer. The `CheckpointManager` has parameters that control the interval at which checkpoints should be saved, the maximum number of checkpoints to keep, a prefix for directories, and so on. With a checkpoint manager, the training loop may look like the following listing.

Listing 11.12 Using a checkpoint manager to regularly make checkpoints

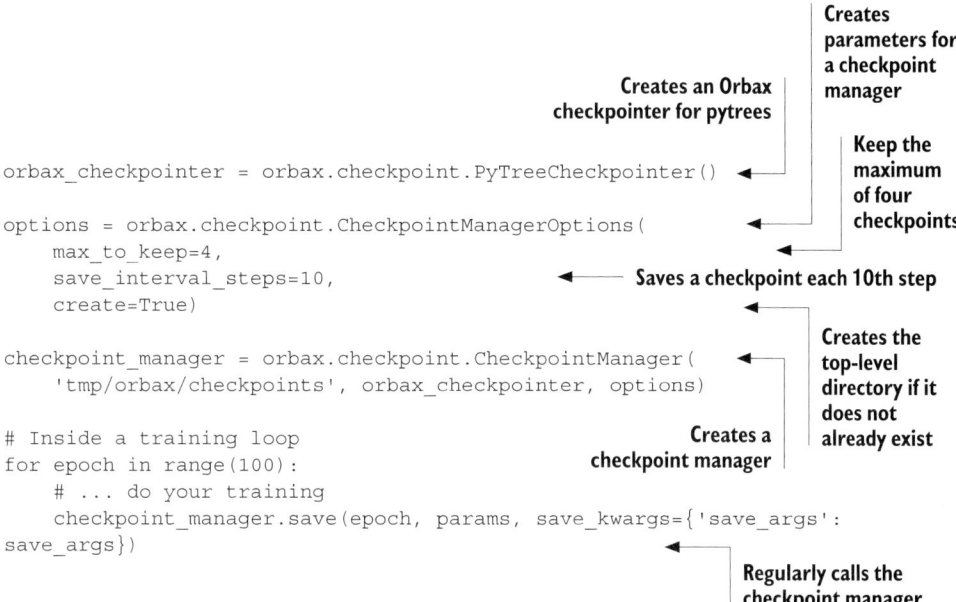

```
orbax_checkpointer = orbax.checkpoint.PyTreeCheckpointer()

options = orbax.checkpoint.CheckpointManagerOptions(
    max_to_keep=4,
    save_interval_steps=10,
    create=True)

checkpoint_manager = orbax.checkpoint.CheckpointManager(
    'tmp/orbax/checkpoints', orbax_checkpointer, options)

# Inside a training loop
for epoch in range(100):
    # ... do your training
    checkpoint_manager.save(epoch, params, save_kwargs={'save_args':
save_args})
```

Creates an Orbax
checkpointer for pytrees

Creates
parameters for
a checkpoint
manager

Keep the
maximum
of four
checkpoints

Saves a checkpoint each 10th step

Creates the
top-level
directory if it
does not
already exist

Creates a
checkpoint manager

Regularly calls the
checkpoint manager

This way, it is easy to save all the intermediate results without adding much additional logic into your training loop. Other checkpointers are available, including an asynchronous one, where save operations take place in a background thread so that you can perform computation alongside the saves.

Orbax also supports saving and loading pytrees with multiprocess arrays in the same fashion as single-process pytrees. Saving checkpoints in a multiprocess context uses the same API as in a single-process context. However, using an asynchronous checkpointer is recommended for saving large multiprocess arrays.

That is it with Flax for now. We have just scratched the surface of what you can do with Flax. Nonetheless, we demonstrated the basics with which you can easily go further. Flax provides excellent documentation and a set of examples so that you can clone it and start experimenting on your own. There are recipes for parallel training, model inspection and surgery, PyTorch model conversion, and so on.

In previous sections, we got a good grasp of the JAX ecosystem. We used Flax for high-level neural network modeling, Optax for model optimization, CLU for structuring a training loop, and Orbax for saving and loading models. This highlights the modular approach adopted by members of the ecosystem. Now we will switch to a larger ecosystem of ML models—namely, Hugging Face transformers.

11.3   *Using the Hugging Face ecosystem*

In this section, we will touch on the Hugging Face ecosystem and learn how to use pretrained models from the Hugging Face Model Hub for natural language processing and image generation tasks. Hugging Face provides beautiful transformers and diffusers libraries and a huge model hub with thousands of open source models. The most popular framework there is PyTorch, though there are also more than 9,500 JAX models (https://huggingface.co/models?library=jax) at the moment of writing this chapter.

Among interesting open source models, there are many GPT-like LLMs (large language models), including the latest Llama and Gemma families:

- *Meta's Llama* family of models (https://huggingface.co/meta-llama).
- *Google's Gemma 2* (https://huggingface.co/collections/google/gemma-2-release -667d6600fd5220e7b967f315) family of open LLMs.

There are also older families like

- *EleutherAI's GPT-J-6B* (https://huggingface.co/EleutherAI/gpt-j-6b) and its predecessor GPT-Neo with model sizes of 125M (https://huggingface.co/EleutherAI/ gpt-neo-125m), 1.3B (https://huggingface.co/EleutherAI/gpt-neo-1.3B), and 2.7B (https://huggingface.co/EleutherAI/gpt-neo-2.7B).
- *BigScience* Large Open-science Open-access Multilingual Language Model BLOOM LM with up to 176B parameters (https://huggingface.co/models?other= bloom&search=bigscience).
- *OpenAI's GPT-2* (https://huggingface.co/gpt2-xl). The company stopped publishing its models after GPT-2, but it still might be a good start to train your own LLM.

Other (not GPT-like) transformer models include

- Half a thousand models from *Google*, including the latest from the T5 family *UMT5* (https://huggingface.co/google/umt5-xxl) supporting 102 languages, and instruction fine-tuned *FLAN-T5* with sizes up to 11.3B (https://huggingface .co/google/flan-t5-xxl), and many other interesting models like summarization *PEGASUS* (https://huggingface.co/google/pegasus-large).
- Tons of *BERT-like* general and specialized models, like *FinBERT* for analyzing the sentiment of financial texts (https://huggingface.co/ProsusAI/finbert) or *BioBERT* for biomedical text mining (https://huggingface.co/dmis-lab/ biobert-v1.1), to name a few.
- Image generation *DALL·E Mini* (https://huggingface.co/dalle-mini/dalle -mini) and *Mega* models (https://huggingface.co/dalle-mini/dalle-mega).

- *OpenAI's* speech recognition *Whisper* (https://huggingface.co/openai/whisper -large-v2), and joint image and text embedding *CLIP* models (https://mng .bz/5ONB).

You can find a table with models implemented in the Hugging Face Transformers library, showing support of different frameworks, namely PyTorch, TensorFlow, and JAX at https://mng.bz/gANE.

Let's start with a simple example of using a pretrained GPT-like model from the Hugging Face Model Hub.

For this chapter, you might need to install the transformers library:

```
pip install -q git+https://github.com/huggingface/transformers.git
```

11.3.1 *Using a pretrained model from the Hugging Face Model Hub*

There are many different GPT-like models of different sizes available. We start with GPT-J-6B (https://huggingface.co/EleutherAI/gpt-j-6b), which is a 6B parameter open source English autoregressive language model trained by EleutherAI on the Pile.

At time of printing, there are many newer and more capable models available (I recommend trying Llama 3 or Gemma 2 families), and likely many more are to come, so keep an eye on this highly dynamic field. For demonstration purposes, we stick to GPT-J-6B, but the basics are the same for newer models. If GPT-J-6B is too large for your machine, you may try something smaller, say, Gemma 2B (https://huggingface .co/google/gemma-2b).

The Pile is an 825 Gb diverse, open source language modeling dataset that consists of 22 smaller, high-quality datasets combined (https://pile.eleuther.ai/). It was also collected by EleutherAI. You can use it if you decide to train your own LLM.

There are a series of LLMs trained on the Pile. Initially, EleutherAI trained GPT-3-like language models called GPT-Neo. These came in 125M, 1.3B, and 2.7B parameter variants. Then GPT-J-6B was created. At the time of its release, GPT-J-6B was the largest publicly available GPT-3-style language model in the world.

> **WARNING** GPT-J-6B is not intended for deployment without fine-tuning, supervision, and/or moderation. It is not in itself a product and cannot be used for human-facing interactions. For example, the model may generate harmful or offensive text. Please evaluate the risks associated with your particular use case.

GPT-J-6B used the Mesh Transformer JAX library (https://mng.bz/6Yjo) built upon Haiku. It relied on using the `xmap/pjit` operators in JAX for model parallelism of transformers. This library is designed for scalability up to approximately 40B parameters on TPUv3s, beyond which different parallelism strategies should be used. Since 2023, this project is not actively developed, so if you consider training your own LLMs from scratch, look at more recent and actively developed libraries. We will touch on this topic in chapter 12.

GPU memory requirements

You need a GPU or TPU with sufficient memory to run these models. To estimate the required memory size, you can multiply the model parameter number (say, 1.3B for GPT-Neo-1.3B or 6B for GPT-J-6B) by the size of a 32-bit floating-point number (FP32), which is a typical format for distributing models. With a single parameter taking 4 bytes, the whole GPT-Neo-1.3B model will require 1.3B × 4 = 7.2 billion bytes or approximately 7.2 Gb of memory just to store the model. The GPT-J-6B will require 6B × 4 = 24 Gb just for storing, which does not fit into many low-end GPU cards. You really need more to store intermediate activations. For training and fine-tuning, you need even more memory to store gradients.

For larger models like GPT-J-6B, you might need a more capable and expensive GPU, like A100, with 40 or 80 Gb memory or multi-GPU/TPU configuration. If you have something with 16 Gb memory, like NVIDIA T4 or RTX 4080, or even a 24 Gb RTX 3090/4090 card, try a smaller model like GPT-Neo. You can also run these models for inference on a CPU with enough memory available, but doing so will be very slow.

There are ways to reduce the memory footprint—for example, by converting a model to a 16-bit floating-point number (`float16` or `bfloat16`, as described in section 3.3.2). In the upcoming example, we use a variant of GPT-J-6B converted to FP16 to save some space. There are even more aggressive options, like quantization and converting a model to INT4, but we do not focus on these things in the book.

Loading a model from the Model Hub and using it for text generation is easy.

The Hugging Face transformers library provides an easy way to load different models called *auto classes* (https://mng.bz/o0Nd). The exact architecture you want to use can be guessed from the name of the pretrained model you are supplying to the `from_pretrained()` method. Auto classes retrieve the relevant model automatically.

There are different auto classes for different tasks and for each backend, such as PyTorch, TensorFlow, or Flax. You can find more about auto classes at https://mng.bz/n0Qa.

There is a general class for Flax GPT-like models designed to generate text called `FlaxAutoModelForCausalLM` (https://mng.bz/vJN7). When provided a model name (here, `"EleutherAI/gpt-j-6B"`) it instantiates a model of the `FlaxGPTJForCausalLM` type. In the case of the `"EleutherAI/gpt-neo-1.3B"` model, it would be `FlaxGPT-NeoForCausalLM` type.

Each model requires the input text to be preprocessed in a specified way, and it is handled by a tokenizer. A tokenizer splits a text into tokens (usually subword units), which in turn are processed by the model generating the input text continuation, token by token. Different models may use different tokenization strategies and different token vocabularies. The `AutoTokenizer` class automatically handles the task of choosing the right tokenizer.

Now we are ready to load a model from the Model Hub.

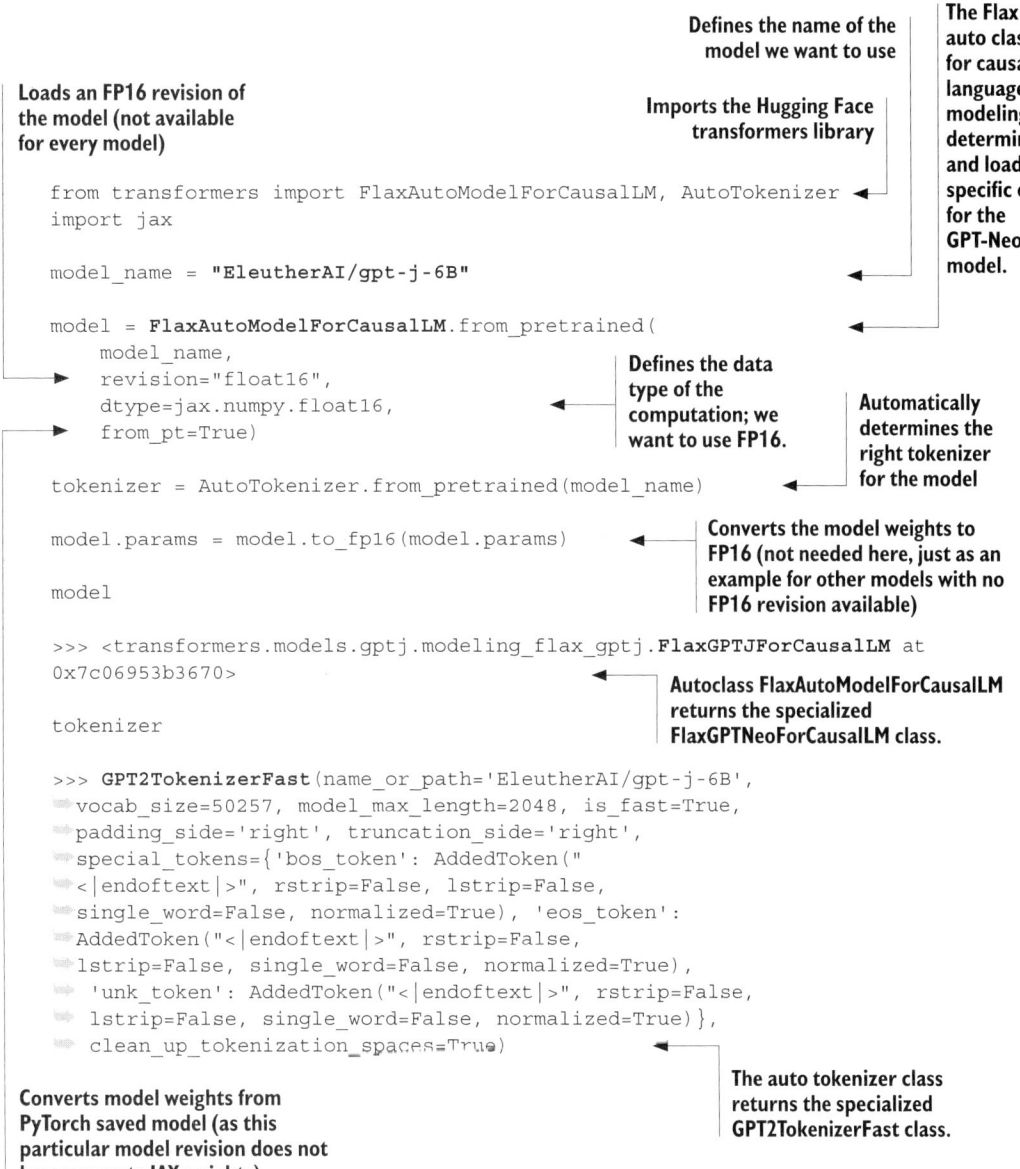

Listing 11.13 Loading the GPT-J-6B model from the Hugging Face Model Hub

Loads an FP16 revision of the model (not available for every model)

Defines the name of the model we want to use

Imports the Hugging Face transformers library

The Flax auto class for causal language modeling determines and loads a specific class for the GPT-Neo model.

```
from transformers import FlaxAutoModelForCausalLM, AutoTokenizer
import jax

model_name = "EleutherAI/gpt-j-6B"

model = FlaxAutoModelForCausalLM.from_pretrained(
    model_name,
    revision="float16",
    dtype=jax.numpy.float16,
    from_pt=True)

tokenizer = AutoTokenizer.from_pretrained(model_name)

model.params = model.to_fp16(model.params)

model
```

Defines the data type of the computation; we want to use FP16.

Automatically determines the right tokenizer for the model

Converts the model weights to FP16 (not needed here, just as an example for other models with no FP16 revision available)

```
>>> <transformers.models.gptj.modeling_flax_gptj.FlaxGPTJForCausalLM at
0x7c06953b3670>

tokenizer
```

Autoclass FlaxAutoModelForCausalLM returns the specialized FlaxGPTNeoForCausalLM class.

```
>>> GPT2TokenizerFast(name_or_path='EleutherAI/gpt-j-6B',
vocab_size=50257, model_max_length=2048, is_fast=True,
padding_side='right', truncation_side='right',
special_tokens={'bos_token': AddedToken("
<|endoftext|>", rstrip=False, lstrip=False,
single_word=False, normalized=True), 'eos_token':
AddedToken("<|endoftext|>", rstrip=False,
lstrip=False, single_word=False, normalized=True),
'unk_token': AddedToken("<|endoftext|>", rstrip=False,
lstrip=False, single_word=False, normalized=True)},
clean_up_tokenization_spaces=True)
```

The auto tokenizer class returns the specialized GPT2TokenizerFast class.

Converts model weights from PyTorch saved model (as this particular model revision does not have separate JAX weights)

Here we deliberately loaded a version of the model in FP16 weights (the `revision` parameter). Such lower-precision versions are not available for every model, so for other models, you may want to explicitly convert a model from FP32 to FP16. Notice there are two relevant places. First, the dtype parameter of FlaxAutoModelForCausalLM defines the data type of the computation. It does not affect the type of the model weights themselves. So, if there were no FP16 versions available, we would need a separate explicit conversion using the to_fp16() method. There is also a to_bf16() method for conversion to BF16 type.

Also notice that a general FlaxAutoModelForCausalLM class returns a specialized FlaxGPTJForCausalLM class, and a general AutoTokenizer returns a specific GPT2-TokenizerFast class. This is not an error, as the EleutherAI GPT-Neo and GPT-J models use the same tokenizer as the OpenAI GPT-2 model. The tokenizer class also contains important properties like vocabulary size, a list of special tokens to mark the beginning and end of the sentence, and so on.

> ### Large language models and causal language models
>
> The term *large language models* (LLMs) is a very broad term covering many different models that work with natural language. At the moment, the term LLM is the most frequently used for an OpenAI GPT-like family of models that use the *transformer decoder* architecture. There are other models using different transformer architectures, like BERT, which is a *transformer encoder*, or T5, which is a full *transformer encoder-decoder*. There is a great series of posts about different transformer architectures by Jay Alammar:
>
> - Full transformer encoder-decoder (http://jalammar.github.io/illustrated -transformer/)
> - Transformer encoder (https://mng.bz/4pOw)
> - Transformer decoder (http://jalammar.github.io/illustrated-gpt2/)
>
> Non-transformer models built using other architectures also exist—for example, recurrent neural networks like RWKV (https://github.com/BlinkDL/RWKV-LM), or state space models like Mamba (https://mng.bz/QVQG).
>
> In short, GPT-like LLMs perform the task of completing an input text. You pass an input text, usually called the *prompt*, and the model generates the completion for the prompt. Such LLMs are sometimes called *causal language models* (CLMs).
>
> Technically, at the lower level, the model performs the task of predicting the next token in the following manner. First, the input text is tokenized or split by tokens according to the tokenizer vocabulary. Tokens are usually subword units that frequently appear in the training dataset. Then, a sequence of text tokens is passed to the model input, and the model internally produces a sequence of token embeddings on each of its layers. At the last layer, the CLM returns the probability distribution for the next token. The next token is selected according to this distribution; then the token is added to the prompt, and the process repeats.
>
> There are many strategies for selecting the next token (or decoding strategies). You may use *greedy decoding,* which takes the token with the maximum probability; *multinomial sampling,* which randomly samples a token from the distribution; or the so-called *beam search*, which keeps several hypotheses at each time step and at the end chooses the

hypothesis with the highest overall probability for the entire sequence. There are other types of decoding as well (https://mng.bz/XVgv).

A parameter called *temperature* is frequently used in sampling methods. It controls the sharpness of the probability distribution. When the temperature is 0, then the distribution is the sharpest. When you raise the temperature (the typical value may be 0.7 or 1.0), then the distribution gets flatter, and you have higher chances for sampling rare (with lower probabilities) tokens. In some sense, with higher temperatures, a model becomes less deterministic and more "creative." An excellent visual explanation of the temperature can be found at https://mng.bz/yozB.

For more details, feel free to follow the Hugging Face tutorial on LLMs (https://mng .bz/M1OW) and look at the open source LLM ecosystem (https://huggingface.co/blog/ os-llms).

Now we are ready to use the model for text generation. We will use a prompt that asks to generate an SQL query from a text explaining what we want to do. We will tokenize the prompt and use a multinomial sampling generation strategy, but feel free to try other methods as well.

Listing 11.14 Using the GPT-J-6B model for text generation

```
prompt = """Generate SQL query from the text inside triple backticks
```select all the users from table 'users' older than 20 years```
"""

inputs = tokenizer(prompt, return_tensors="jax")

inputs

>>> {'input_ids': Array([[ 8645,   378, 16363, 12405,   422,   262,  2420,
...
>>>          812, 15506,    63,   198]], dtype=int32),
>>> 'attention_mask': Array([[1, 1, 1, … 1, 1, 1]], dtype=int32)}

generated_ids = model.generate(
    **inputs,
    do_sample=True,
    num_beams=1,
    max_new_tokens=300,
    temperature=0.7,
    pad_token_id = model.config.eos_token_id,
    prng_key=jax.random.PRNGKey(4232),
    no_repeat_ngram_size=2)

generated_text = tokenizer.decode(
  generated_ids['sequences'].squeeze(0))
print(generated_text)
```

Defines a prompt

Tokenizes the prompt

Generates prompt continuation

Uses a multinomial sampling generation strategy

Sets the maximum length of the generated text

Sets model temperature (a parameter that defines model "creativity")

Provides a PRNGKey for random sampling

Decodes a sequence of token IDs into text tokens
```

```
>>> Generate SQL query from the text inside triple backticks
>>> ```select all the users from table 'users' older than 20 years```
>>>
>>> ```
>>> SELECT * FROM `users` WHERE age > 20
>>> ```
>>>
>>> ```
>>> SELECT * FROM `users` WHERE age > `20 years`
>>> ```
>>>
>>> ```
>>> SELECT * FROM `users` WHERE `age` > 20`
>>> ```
>>>
>>> <!--end-query-->
>>> …
```

The model output contains a prompt following the generated text.

Here we tokenized the prompt using the corresponding tokenizer. The main output of this step is just a sequence of numbers contained in the `input_ids` field. Another field called `attention_mask` marks token positions that a transformer decoder should attend to; here, it is every position of the prompt. Be careful, and do not use tokenizers from different models as they will produce a different text split with different token IDs, so the model will interpret it incorrectly.

Then we set several parameters for generation, with the temperature and the parameters related to the decoding strategy being the most important—notice also that we provide the PRNGKey here for reproducibility. The model then generates a sequence of token IDs, which we decode back into text tokens using the same tokenizer. Notice that the input prompt is also included in the output. Also, the model keeps generating the same output after the `<!--end-query-->` mark, so I skipped it.

The particular output for our example prompt contains something relevant, though it may not be exactly what we want, and usually, it cannot be used as is. Here, we could not use the generated SQL commands directly as (1) there is a formatting text around them, so they are not directly executable; (2) there are multiple answers in the model output (plus the model keeps generating the text repeatedly); and (3) some SQLs contain errors—for example, an unmatched single quote in the third example. Tuning prompts and getting what you want from a model is a separate topic, usually called *prompt engineering*, and is outside the book's scope.

Prompt engineering

Prompt engineering is a set of techniques for structuring prompts (input texts) to obtain the results you want. There are many different techniques, with "chain of thought" (https://mng.bz/aVd7) being among the most well known. The field is constantly evolving, so keep an eye on it.

For a simple start, I'd recommend a short introductory course on prompt engineering for developers: https://mng.bz/75je.

Prompt engineering is not always enough; there is a growing tendency to incorporate LLMs into software programs—for example, see "Large Language Model Programs" (https://arxiv.org/abs/2305.05364). The program then splits the solution into steps, manages the state across the steps, prepares prompts, and does other orchestration.

That's it on the basic use of LLMs. But using pretrained models is only a part of the story. In many cases, that's not enough to achieve the required quality, and you need to create custom solutions.

11.3.2 *Going further with fine-tuning and pretraining*

When you solve tasks with LLMs, you typically start with pretrained models and prompt engineering. In some cases, when the resulting quality is not good enough, you need to go beyond using pretrained models. You need to customize the models, and there are two main ways of doing this:

- *Training a new large model from scratch.* In the context of LLMs, this is also called pretraining. This process usually requires huge amounts of training data and training for a long time using multi-GPU/TPU configurations. Depending on the resources required, this may cost you from tens of thousands to tens of millions of dollars for computing. Many people cannot afford this.

- *Fine-tuning an existing pretrained model.* This way, you rely on someone else's pretrained model and fine-tune (or adapt) a model for your own task. Sometimes it makes sense even if you pretrain the model yourself, as pretraining usually uses broadly available vast general data, and fine-tuning uses more scarce specialized data. There are different approaches to fine-tuning, from classical transfer learning with updates to all or some network layers to low-rank adaptation (like LoRa), which produces small adjustments (called a *delta file*) to the original weights. This approach is usually much cheaper and affordable; sometimes you can obtain a useful fine-tuned model with just a few hundred dollars spent on cloud GPUs. You may also use reinforcement learning from human feedback (RLHF) to fine-tune models.

Retrieval augmented generation (RAG) is complementary to fine-tuning and might be an easy way to make a pretrained model more up to date. We will not discuss RAG in the book. You can read about it, for example, at https://mng.bz/gAVV.

If you go these roads, there are some examples and manuals provided on how to use Hugging Face Transformers. Here are a few:

- A tutorial on pretraining a GPT-like causal language model (https://mng.bz/eVDQ) describes training an autoregressive causal language model, a distilled version of GPT-2, on one of the languages of the huge multilingual OSCAR corpus, obtained by language classification and filtering of the Common Crawl corpus. The tutorial includes defining the model architecture, training a tokenizer, preprocessing a dataset, and finally, pretraining a model on a TPUv3-8.

- Though not strictly about Hugging Face Transformers, Google has great tutorials on how to use their recent open LLM Gemma (https://huggingface.co/blog/gemma) for inference (https://ai.google.dev/gemma/docs/jax_inference) and fine-tuning (https://ai.google.dev/gemma/docs/jax_finetune) using JAX and Flax.

- Also, chapter 12 of this book contains a section on JAX modules to train your own LLMs.

- A tutorial on pretraining a BERT-like masked language model (https://mng.bz/pxyz) describes training a RoBERTa-base model on the same OSCAR dataset.

- A tutorial on fine-tuning a pretrained BERT model for a text-classification task on the GLUE Benchmark (https://mng.bz/Om9E) uses the `FlaxAutoModel-ForSequenceClassification` class with a freshly initialized new classification head.

- Additional Flax language modeling examples (https://mng.bz/YVeA) include training another `roberta-base` and a small version of GPT-2 for Norwegian, span-masked language modeling with T5-base, and denoising language modeling with `bart-base`.

- There are more examples for image captioning (https://mng.bz/GN4O), question answering (https://mng.bz/znlQ), summarization (https://mng.bz/0M76), text (https://mng.bz/KDE0) or token (https://mng.bz/9ow1) classification, and image classification (https://mng.bz/j05P) using Vision Transformer.

There are numerous examples, and it does not make sense to replicate all of them in this book. This is a good place to start your own small experiments and expand them if you have a budget.

Another big topic is the widely popular text-to-image diffusion models like DALL·E 2, Stable Diffusion, or Midjourney, which generate images based on textual descriptions. They are worth a separate section as there is a special diffusers library for them in the Hugging Face ecosystem.

11.3.3 *Using the diffusers library*

Diffusers is a library for state-of-the-art pretrained diffusion models for generating images, audio, and even 3D structures of molecules. Diffusers is both a simple inference solution and a means of training your own diffusion models.

Diffusion models

Diffusion models are a modern physics-inspired approach to image generation. You may read a beautiful article on them in *Quanta Magazine* (https://mng.bz/WVO1).

There are many popular models and products like DALL·E 3, Stable Diffusion, Midjourney, etc., and the field is quickly developing.

These models typically encode a textual description using some textual encoder, an optional image by some image encoder, and then run the image generation multistep diffusion process.

An early history of image generation models is presented in my blog post at https://mng .bz/86zw. Jay Alammar also has a great visual explanation of how diffusion models work internally: https://mng.bz/mRy4.

Diffusion models are also used for video generation, sound synthesis, and so on.

Diffusers offers three core components:

- *State-of-the-art diffusion pipelines* that can be run in inference with just a few lines of code. There are pipelines for image generation using text prompts, image variation, inpainting, upscaling, 3D object generation, text-to-audio, and even text-to-video generation, and more.
- *Interchangeable noise schedulers* for different diffusion speeds and output quality.
- *Pretrained models* that can be used as building blocks and, combined with schedulers, to create your own end-to-end diffusion systems. The Model Hub contains thousands (more than 30,300 at the moment of writing) of pretrained diffusion models (https://mng.bz/EO1O).

To install the diffusers library with Flax support (it supports Flax since version 0.5.1), run the following command:

```
pip install --upgrade diffusers[flax]
```

Do you want to develop something like Midjourney? It is easy to start using existing models to generate your own images and build your own image generation pipeline. But remember to check a model license. We will use the well-known Stable Diffusion model created by researchers and engineers from CompVis, Stability AI, and LAION. There are several versions of the model; we will use `runwayml/stable-diffusion-v1-5` (https://mng.bz/NBe1), which can generate images with a resolution of 512×512. We run our generation on eight TPUs in parallel, but you can easily change your code to work on a GPU or CPU.

We will use the BF16 floating-point type that is supported by TPU. For the following example, we run a Cloud TPU VM (as described in appendix C) and connect Colab notebook to a local kernel. To adapt the code for a GPU, you may need to switch to FP16 or FP32, depending on the GPU type and supported formats. You can also run this code on a CPU; just remove the sharding and replication parts.

The field evolves very fast, and it's likely that at the moment you read this, there are new, much better image generation models; the diffusers library has most likely changed. Please read the library documentation.

The diffusers library provides the `FlaxStableDiffusionPipeline` class (https://mng.bz/DpNw) for using Stable Diffusion models. As usual with functional frameworks, models are stateless, and parameters are stored outside them, so the pipeline initialization method returns both the pipeline and the model parameters. `Flax-StableDiffusionPipeline` requires the transformers library, so install that first if it is missing from your environment.

The general approach is to load model weights and initialize the model, preprocess text, replicate model weights and preprocessed text prompts on each device, and finally, generate several images in parallel.

We can use the `prepare_inputs()` function for tokenizing prompts, the `flax.jax_utils.replicate()` function to replicate model parameters to each device, and the `flax.training.common_utils.shard()` to shard a pytree of arrays by local devices (determined by the `local_device_count()` function).

The code in the following listing implements this approach.

Listing 11.15   Generating images using the diffusers library

```
from jax.lib import xla_bridge                          Checks that we use TPU
print(xla_bridge.get_backend().platform)

>>> tpu

import jax
import jax.numpy as jnp
from flax.jax_utils import replicate
from flax.training.common_utils import shard            Imports everything
from PIL import Image
from diffusers import FlaxStableDiffusionPipeline        Loads the Stable
                                                         Diffusion 1.5 model
pipeline, params = FlaxStableDiffusionPipeline.from_pretrained(
    "runwayml/stable-diffusion-v1-5",
    revision="bf16",                      Uses the BF16 floating-point format (you
    dtype=jnp.bfloat16,                   may need to switch to FP16 for GPU)
)
                                                    Prepares eight prompts
prompts = [
    "Three leopards holding a scarlet rose and in the centre a green rat.",
    "A large glass bottle full of tiny elephants of different colors",
    "HAL-9000 in the style of Picasso",
    "Pink panther drinking a coffee. ",
    "Golden tiger fighting vikings in a modern city, Van Gogh style",
    "A blue Axolotl sitting on an emerald throne.",
    "A pumpkin-shape spaceship spinning around the Moon",
```

```
    "Black panther doing his homework",
]

p_params = replicate(params)
```
Replicates model parameters to each TPU core

```
prompt_ids = pipeline.prepare_inputs(prompts)
prompt_ids = shard(prompt_ids)
```
Preprocesses prompts and shards them across eight TPUs

```
seed = 42
rng = jax.random.PRNGKey(seed)
rng = jax.random.split(rng, jax.device_count())
```
Prepares eight PRNGKeys

```
images = pipeline(prompt_ids, p_params, rng, jit=True).images
```
Runs the pipeline and returns generated images

```
def image_grid(imgs, rows, cols):
    w,h = imgs[0].size
    grid = Image.new('RGB', size=(cols*w, rows*h))
    for i, img in enumerate(imgs): grid.paste(img, box=(i%cols*w, i//cols*h))
    return grid
```
Function for drawing a grid of images

```
images = images.reshape((images.shape[0], ) + images.shape[-3:])
images = pipeline.numpy_to_pil(images)
image_grid(images, 2, 4)
```
Draws the images

Gets rid of unneeded batch dimension

You can see that the code is pretty compact, and the model loading and image generation part fits on a single screen. Generating new images is easy.

The first run of the pipeline may take some time as the JIT compilation happens at this moment (thus the `jit=True` flag). This parameter is also responsible for running `pmap()` versions of the generation and safety scoring functions. The output of the model generation is shown in the figure 11.3.

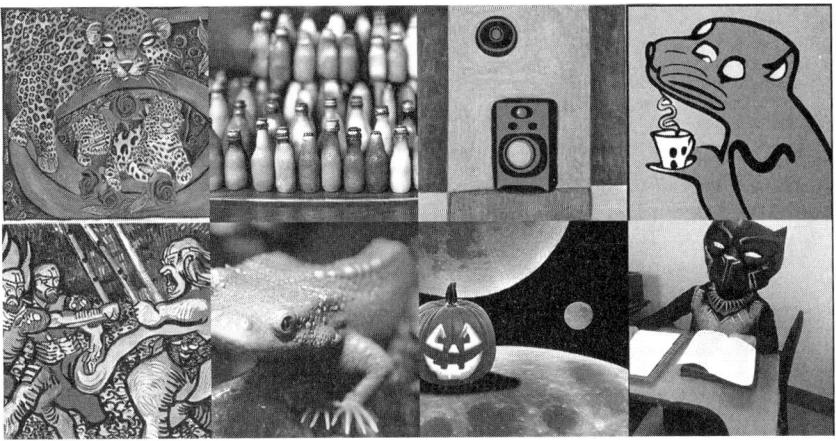

Figure 11.3   Eight images generated by the Stable Diffusion model

The pipeline also has other parameters influencing the image generation process, so please consult the `FlaxStableDiffusionPipeline` documentation. The internals of the Stable Diffusion model and the meaning of the parameters that influence the image generation process are well described in the blog article at https://huggingface .co/blog/stable_diffusion.

You can explore plenty of available pipelines from the diffusers library at https:// mng.bz/lro8.

The diffusers library is much more than just a collection of pretrained models. You can train new diffusion models from scratch or fine-tune existing models on your data-sets. The official documentation provides extensive guides on this process, so if you are interested in it, please start from the basic training manual (https://mng.bz/BgY8) and follow the main part (https://mng.bz/dZxO).

There are many interesting examples, and the library supports data types other than images as well. One single topic I'd like to highlight is the Low-Rank Adaptation of LLM (LoRA). It is a training method that accelerates the fine-tuning of large models while consuming less memory. It is a very popular approach for fine-tuning Stable Diffusion models. A great blog post by Pedro Cuenca and Sayak Paul on this topic can be found at https://huggingface.co/blog/lora.

The greater memory efficiency of LoRA allows you to run fine-tuning on consumer GPUs like the Tesla T4, RTX 3080, or even the RTX 2080 Ti! GPUs like the T4 are free and readily accessible in Kaggle or Google Colab notebooks. LoRA is still an experi-mental feature in the diffusers library, and its API may change in the future.

That's it for the Hugging Face ecosystem, and we are done with high-level neural network libraries for now. You now have the background and tools to dive into Flax, any other high-level library above JAX, or the diverse Hugging Face ecosystem. The next chapter will provide you with a wider overview of the JAX ecosystem, including the tools to train your own LLM.

Summary

- High-level libraries provide high-level primitives that help you build neural net-works from existing blocks, like dense, convolutional, or LSTM layers; multihead self-attention; activation functions; etc.
- One of the most well-known high-level neural network libraries is Flax by Google. Other options are Keras and Equinox.
- The philosophy of Flax is to offer an API familiar to those who have experience with Keras, PyTorch, or Sonnet.
- The Flax API is called Linen. It is fundamentally a functional system for defining neural nets in JAX, which is different from the mostly object-oriented approaches of the TensorFlow and PyTorch ecosystems.
- The Flax `Module` abstraction is stateful inside and stateless outside. You write your networks in a stateful, object-oriented way. But to use JAX transformations,

Flax creates pure functions from `Modules`. These functions do not maintain a state; they return and consume it.

- Model variables (or parameters) are initialized by the `init()` method on the instantiated `Module`.

- To conduct a forward pass with the model with a given set of parameters, you call the `apply()` method on the instantiated `Module`, passing the initialized variables and the input data.

- There is a `flax.training.train_state.TrainState` class for representing a simple training state.

- Optax is a library for composable gradient transformations. It provides an extensive list of predefined state-of-the-art optimizers, loss functions, schedulers, classes, and wrappers for composing gradient transformations and more.

- The CLU library contains common functionality for writing machine learning training loops, including a functional metric computation interface.

- Flax supports models with internal state like `BatchNorm` layers. Like model parameters, the state should be passed externally to make the classes and functions stateless.

- Hugging Face provides beautiful transformers and diffusers libraries and a huge Model Hub with thousands of open source models. JAX is the third framework here by the number of supported models.

- The Hugging Face transformers library provides an easy way to load different models called auto classes.

- There is a general class for Flax GPT-like models designed to generate text: `FlaxAutoModelForCausalLM`.

- With Hugging Face transformers, you can train a new large model from scratch or fine-tune an existing pretrained model.

- Hugging Face diffusers is a library for state-of-the-art pretrained diffusion models for generating images, audio, and even 3D structures of molecules. Diffusers is both a simple inference solution and a means for training your own diffusion models.

- LoRA is a training method that accelerates the fine-tuning of large models while consuming less memory.

Other members of the
JAX ecosystem

12

This chapter covers

- Utility libraries, libraries for LLMs, and other high-level neural network libraries for JAX
- Libraries for other machine learning fields, including reinforcement learning and evolutionary computations
- Other JAX modules for computer science, physics, chemistry, and more

By *the JAX ecosystem*, I mean a broad set of libraries, modules, and packages built on top of JAX or created to be interoperable with JAX or other ecosystem members. The JAX ecosystem is vibrant and dynamic, with hundreds of modules dedicated to solving problems in diverse fields. As you know, JAX is great not only for deep learning but for the broader areas of machine learning, optimization, and other computer science fields.

There is growing adoption of JAX in other compute-intensive fields, like protein folding, chemical modeling, and especially physics, including molecular dynamics, fluid dynamics, rigid body simulation, quantum computing, astrophysics, ocean modeling, etc. New applications are emerging constantly.

In this final chapter of the book, we look at the broader JAX ecosystem. We start with deep learning, then go to the wider fields of machine learning and computer science in general, and finish with physics and related fields.

This chapter is more a catalog than a comprehensive description of how to use each module. It would be impossible to describe everything, and just providing examples of using each module would take enough space to fill a separate book. Searching GitHub for JAX across Python repositories (https://mng.bz/RNP0) already produces more than 2,000 results at the time of writing. Things are also quickly changing, so the chapter will likely be quickly outdated. Use this chapter as a starting point and refer to the original module documentation.

12.1 Deep learning ecosystem

In the previous chapter, we mentioned many different modules for deep learning. Here I provide a wider summary of modules in the ecosystem, also mentioning some deprecated modules you may find in different examples.

12.1.1 High-level neural network libraries

Let's start with high-level neural network libraries. We have already gotten used to the Flax library, but here I will provide you with a broader picture:

- *Flax* (https://github.com/google/flax), the high-level neural network library by Google, is the first choice if you need higher-level neural network abstractions than pure JAX provides. We already discussed and used this library in chapter 11.

- *Equinox* (https://github.com/patrick-kidger/equinox) is a one-stop JAX library for everything you need that isn't already in core JAX, including neural networks with easy-to-use PyTorch-like syntax, filtered APIs for transformations, useful pytree manipulation routines, and advanced features like support for raising runtime errors. You may find it very useful.

- *Keras 3.0* (https://keras.io/keras_3/) is the new generation of the well-known Keras library that makes it possible to run Keras workflows on top of TensorFlow, JAX, and PyTorch. It also enables you to seamlessly integrate Keras components (like layers, models, or metrics) into low-level TensorFlow, JAX, and PyTorch workflows.

- *Ivy* (https://github.com/unifyai/ivy) is an ML transpiler and a framework currently supporting JAX, TensorFlow, PyTorch, and NumPy. Ivy unifies all ML frameworks, enabling you to not only write code that can be used with any of these frameworks as the backend but also convert (or transpile) any function, model, or library written in any of them to your preferred framework.

- *AXLearn* (https://github.com/apple/axlearn) by Apple is a library built on top of JAX and XLA to support the development of large-scale deep learning models. It takes an object-oriented approach to software engineering.

There are other libraries, some of which are not actively developed, though you may see them:

- *Haiku* (https://github.com/google-deepmind/dm-haiku) is a JAX-based neural network library by Google DeepMind. Since July 2023, Google DeepMind recommends that new projects adopt Flax instead of Haiku. Haiku will remain best-effort supported; however, the project will enter maintenance mode, meaning that development efforts will be focused on bug fixes and compatibility with new releases of JAX. You can still find many examples of people using it in the wild.

- *Trax* (https://github.com/google/trax) by Google is an end-to-end library for deep learning that focuses on clear code and speed. Trax includes basic models (like ResNet, LSTM, Transformer) and RL algorithms (like REINFORCE, A2C, PPO).

- *Objax* (https://github.com/google/objax), also by Google, is a minimalist object-oriented framework with a PyTorch-like interface. Its name comes from the contraction of Object and JAX. Objax is designed by researchers for researchers with a focus on simplicity and understandability. Its users should be able to easily read, understand, extend, and modify it to fit their needs.

- *Stax* (https://mng.bz/2gJd), originally an experimental part of JAX, is now more of an example library. It might still be useful if you want to understand how to build a small but flexible neural net specification library from scratch.

- *Elegy* (https://github.com/poets-ai/elegy) is a high-level API for deep learning in JAX by poets-ai. It doesn't seem to be actively developed anymore.

- *Mesh Transformer JAX* (https://github.com/kingoflolz/mesh-transformer-jax) is the framework that was used to build the GPT-J-6B language model. It provides model parallel transformers in JAX and Haiku and is designed for scalability up to approximately 20B parameters on TPUv3s. Since 2023, this project is not actively developed.

A separate subset of high-level neural network libraries is the libraries for large language models (LLMs).

12.1.2 *LLMs in JAX*

With the enormous progress in LLMs in the last few years, this topic has become extremely hot. There are already many commercial models like OpenAI's GPT-4, Google's PaLM 2 and Gemini, Anthropic Claude family, and Cohere models, Amazon Titan, etc. Open source is also blooming now with all the releases of Llama 3, Gemma 2, Mistral, and others with all their community fine-tuned versions, and that's just the beginning.

If you work in a large company or received a grant for using Cloud GPUs/TPUs, you may have the resources to train your LLMs from scratch. Here I've gathered some modern libraries that may be useful for this:

- *EasyLM* (https://github.com/young-geng/EasyLM) is developed by the Berkeley AI Research team as a one-stop solution for pretraining, fine-tuning, evaluating, and serving LLMs in JAX/Flax. EasyLM is designed to be easy to use by hiding the complexities of distributed model/data parallelism but exposing the core training and inference details of LLMs, making it easy to customize. EasyLM can scale up LLM training to hundreds of TPU/GPU accelerators without the need to write complicated distributed training code by leveraging JAX's `pjit` functionality. EasyLM authors created a truly open source version of LLaMa 1 (which had a license not suitable for commercial use cases) called OpenLLaMa (https://github.com/openlm-research/open_llama). The framework contains an example script to pretrain a 7B LLaMa model on a TPU v4-512 pod and a script to serve a pretrained LLaMa on a GPU machine or a single TPU v3-8 VM.

- *Paxml (or Pax)* (https://github.com/google/paxml, current version 1.4.0) by Google is a JAX-based machine learning framework for training large-scale models—models so large that they span multiple TPU accelerator chip slices or pods. Pax has been focusing on scaling efficiently. It allows for advanced and fully configurable experimentation and parallelization and has demonstrated industry-leading model flop utilization rates. A set of tutorials to start using Pax can be found at https://mng.bz/1awV.

- *MaxText* (https://github.com/google/maxtext) also by Google, is a simple, performant, and scalable JAX LLM written in pure Python/JAX and targeting Google Cloud TPUs. It achieves high model flop utilization (MFU)—here, 50% to 70%, compared to 21.3% for GPT-3 and 46.2% for PaLM—and scales from a single host to very large clusters while staying simple and "optimization-free" thanks to the power of JAX and the XLA compiler. There are three recommended patterns for running MaxText: running locally, running on a cluster experimentally, or spawning a production style managed by Google Compute Engine (GCE). So it's easy to start with Local Development, then move to Cluster Experimentation for some ad hoc development, and finally run long-running jobs on GCE. Like Pax, MaxText provides high-performance and scalable implementations of LLMs in JAX. Pax focuses on enabling powerful configuration parameters, allowing developers to change the model by editing config parameters. By contrast, MaxText is a simple, concrete implementation of an LLM that encourages users to extend by forking and directly editing the source code.

- *T5X* (https://github.com/google-research/t5x), also by Google, is an older library, and is a successor of its T5 transformer code base. It is a modular, composable, research-friendly framework for high-performance, configurable, self-service training, evaluation, and inference of language sequence models at many scales. It has examples of how to run it on Google's Vertex AI cloud service (https://

cloud.google.com/vertex-ai). Examples include training and fine-tuning machine translation models.

- *Levanter* (https://github.com/stanford-crfm/levanter) by the Stanford Center for Research on Foundation Models is a framework for training LLMs and other foundation models that strives for legibility, scalability, and reproducibility. It uses its companion named tensor library *Haliax* (https://github.com/stanford -crfm/haliax), which is in some sense an alternative to JAX's own `xmap()` mechanism. Levanter scales to large models and can train on various hardware, including GPUs and TPUs, with scale proven up to 20B parameters and up to a TPU v3-256 pod slice. It also achieves high MFU (https://mng.bz/PNO9).

- *Jaxformer* (https://github.com/salesforce/jaxformer) by Salesforce is a minimal library to train LLMs on TPU in JAX with data and model parallelism using `pjit()`.

- *JaxSeq* (https://github.com/Sea-Snell/JAXSeq) is built on top of Hugging Face's Transformers library and enables training LLMs in JAX. Currently, it supports GPT2, GPT-J, T5, and OPT models.

- *Alpa* (https://github.com/alpa-projects/alpa) is a system for training and serving large-scale neural networks. Alpa automatically parallelizes users' single-device codes on distributed clusters with data, operator, and pipeline parallelism. Examples include training/fine-tuning vision transformer (ViT) for image classification, fine-tuning OPT language models on AWS p3.16xlarge instances with $8 \times 16GB$ V100 GPUs, and a GPT-2-like example similar to the Hugging Face one.

The landscape is highly dynamic and changes frequently, so keep an eye on it, as after the book is published, new interesting projects may emerge.

12.1.3 Utility libraries

The JAX ecosystem contains many utility libraries that will simplify and improve your life with JAX:

- Optimization:
  - The *Optax* library (https://github.com/google-deepmind/optax) was developed by DeepMind, which we discussed in chapter 11. It's a framework to compose new optimizers from reusable gradient transformations, and it's almost impossible not to use it for training your neural networks.
  - *JAXopt* (https://github.com/google/jaxopt) is another library for hardware-accelerated, batchable, and differentiable optimizers in JAX.
  - *Optimistix* (https://github.com/patrick-kidger/optimistix) is a library for nonlinear solvers in JAX and Equinox.
  - *Lineax* (https://github.com/patrick-kidger/lineax) is a library for linear solvers and linear least squares.

- There are also more special optimization libraries, like *KFAC-JAX* (https://github.com/google-deepmind/kfac-jax), built for second-order optimization of neural networks and for computing scalable curvature approximations.

- Writing better code:
  - *Common Loop Utils* (CLU) (https://github.com/google/CommonLoopUtils) by Google was also used in chapter 11. It contains common functionality for writing machine learning training loops with the goal of making them short and readable without removing the flexibility required for research.
  - *Chex* (https://github.com/google-deepmind/chex) by DeepMind is a library of utilities for helping to write reliable JAX code. Chex provides various utilities, including JAX-aware unit testing, `dataclasses`, assertions of properties of JAX datatypes, mocks and fakes, and multidevice test environments.
  - *Jax-verify* (https://github.com/google-deepmind/jax_verify) is another library from DeepMind that contains JAX implementations of many widely used neural network verification techniques.
  - *jaxtyping* (https://github.com/patrick-kidger/jaxtyping) provides type annotations and runtime checking for `shape` and `dtype` of JAX/NumPy/PyTorch/etc. arrays.

- Deployment-related tools:
  - *Orbax* (https://github.com/google/orbax), another library by Google used in chapter 11, includes checkpointing and serialization libraries oriented toward JAX users. It supports a variety of different features required by different frameworks, including asynchronous checkpointing, various types and various storage formats, and exporting of JAX models to the TensorFlow Saved-Model format.
  - The *JAX2TF* tool (https://www.tensorflow.org/guide/jax2tf), by Google, also provides an easy way to convert a JAX model into a TensorFlow SavedModel and deploy your models with the help of a well-developed TensorFlow ecosystem. Using this tool, you can run inference on a server using TF Serving, on a device using TFLite, or on the web using TensorFlow.js. You can also perform fine-tuning by continuing to train a JAX-trained model in TensorFlow with your existing training data and setup. You can even do fusion by combining parts of models trained using JAX with those trained using TensorFlow.
  - *Saxml* or *Sax* (https://github.com/google/saxml) is another project by Google. It is an experimental system that serves JAX, Paxml (see the previous section on LLMs), and PyTorch models for inference. A Sax cell (aka Sax cluster) consists of an admin server and a group of model servers. The admin server keeps track of model servers, assigns published models to model servers to serve, and helps clients locate model servers serving specific published models. This project just reached its 1.2.0 release.

- *TF2JAX* (https://github.com/google-deepmind/tf2jax) is an experimental library by DeepMind for converting TensorFlow functions/graphs to JAX functions, allowing existing TF models to be reused and fine-tuned in JAX codebases.

- *JAX ONNX Runtime* (https://github.com/google/jaxonnxruntime) is a toolchain that enables the seamless execution of ONNX models using JAX as the backend.

- Some other useful libraries:

  - *JMP* (https://github.com/google-deepmind/jmp) is a mixed precision library for JAX. It allows the use of a mix of full and half-precision floating-point numbers during training to reduce the memory bandwidth requirements and improve the computational efficiency of a given model.

  - *Transformer Engine* (https://github.com/NVIDIA/TransformerEngine) is an NVIDIA library for accelerating transformer models on NVIDIA GPUs, including using 8-bit floating-point (FP8) precision on Hopper GPUs to provide better performance with lower memory utilization in both training and inference.

  - *JAXline* (https://github.com/google-deepmind/jaxline) is a distributed JAX training and evaluation framework designed to be forked, covering only the most general aspects of the experiment boilerplate.

  - *Tree-math* (https://github.com/google/tree-math) makes it easy to implement numerical algorithms that work on JAX pytrees, such as iterative optimization and equation-solving methods.

  - *Haliax* (https://github.com/stanford-crfm/haliax) is a library for building neural networks with named tensors, an alternative to the `xmap()` mechanism.

  - *einops* (https://github.com/arogozhnikov/einops) is a flexible and powerful tensor operations library for readable and reliable code.

  - *Penzai* (https://github.com/google-deepmind/penzai) is a research toolkit for building, editing, and visualizing neural networks. It focuses on making it easy to do things with models after they have been trained, so it is a great choice for research involving reverse engineering, model surgery, debugging, inspecting and probing internal activations, and more.

12.2 *Machine learning modules*

There is good coverage of other machine learning subfields in the JAX ecosystem.

12.2.1 *Reinforcement learning*

Reinforcement learning (RL) has been a very popular field in the last decade, and not surprisingly, there is a set of libraries focused on it:

- *RLax* (https://github.com/google-deepmind/rlax) by DeepMind provides useful building blocks for implementing reinforcement learning agents. The components in RLax cover a broad spectrum of algorithms and ideas: TD-learning, policy gradients, actor critics, MAP, proximal policy optimization, nonlinear value transformation, general value functions, and a number of exploration methods.

- *Coax* (https://github.com/coax-dev/coax) is a modular RL Python package by Microsoft for solving OpenAI Gym environments (now Gymnasium) with JAX.

- *Dopamine* (https://github.com/google/dopamine) by Google is a research framework for fast prototyping of reinforcement learning algorithms. It aims to fill the need for a small, easily grokked codebase in which users can freely experiment with their ideas.

- *Acme* (https://github.com/google-deepmind/acme) by DeepMind is a library of RL building blocks that strives to expose simple, efficient, and readable agents.

- `gymnax` (https://github.com/RobertTLange/gymnax) provides JAX-accelerated RL environments.

- *Mctx* (https://github.com/google-deepmind/mctx) by DeepMind is a library with a JAX-native (fully supporting JIT-compilation) implementation of Monte Carlo tree search (MCTS) algorithms such as AlphaZero, MuZero, and Gumbel MuZero.

- *Jumanji* (https://github.com/instadeepai/jumanji) is a diverse suite of scalable reinforcement learning environments written in JAX.

12.2.2 *Other machine learning libraries*

If you want to use graph neural networks, there is a library for that:

- *Jraph* (https://github.com/google-deepmind/jraph) is a library for graph neural networks by DeepMind. It provides a data structure for graphs, a set of utilities for working with graphs, and a "zoo" of forkable graph neural network models.

There are also libraries in the JAX ecosystem if you are working with evolutionary computations:

- *EvoJAX* (https://github.com/google/evojax) is a scalable, general-purpose, hardware-accelerated neuroevolution toolkit. It enables neuroevolution algorithms to work with neural networks running in parallel across multiple TPU/GPUs.

- *Evosax* (https://github.com/RobertTLange/evosax) is a vast library of evolution strategies in JAX.

Some libraries are dedicated to probabilistic programming and Bayesian optimization:

- *Oryx* (https://github.com/jax-ml/oryx) is a library for probabilistic programming and deep learning built on top of JAX.
- *NumPyro* (https://github.com/pyro-ppl/numpyro) is a lightweight probabilistic programming library that provides a NumPy backend for Pyro, a deep probabilistic programming library. NumPyro relies on JAX for automatic differentiation and JIT compilation.
- *Bayex* (https://github.com/alonfnt/bayex) is a high-performance Bayesian global optimization library using Gaussian processes. It is written completely in JAX.
- *BlackJAX* (https://github.com/blackjax-devs/blackjax) is a Bayesian inference library designed for ease of use, speed, and modularity. It is a library of samplers for JAX, not a probabilistic programming library.

There are also means for federated learning:

- *FedJAX* (https://github.com/google/fedjax) is a JAX-based open source library for federated learning simulations emphasizing ease of use in research.
- *Flower* (https://flower.ai/) is a friendly federated learning framework with JAX support.

There is a set of tools for graphics and computer vision as well:

- *PIX* (https://github.com/google-deepmind/dm_pix) is an image processing library in JAX. Its goal is to provide image processing functions and tools to JAX so that they can be optimized and parallelized through `jit()`, `vmap()`, and `pmap()`.
- *Scenic* (https://github.com/google-research/scenic) is a codebase focusing on research around attention-based models for computer vision. It is a set of shared lightweight libraries solving tasks commonly encountered when training large-scale vision models and several projects containing fully fleshed-out problem-specific training and evaluation loops using these libraries.
- You can also do differentiable rendering with JAX. A beautiful example can be found at https://mng.bz/JNz0.
- *visu3d* (https://github.com/google-research/visu3d) is an abstraction layer between Torch/TF/Jax/NumPy and your program that provides standard primitives for 3D geometry.
- *Big Vision* (https://github.com/google-research/big_vision) is the official codebase used to develop Vision Transformer, SigLIP, MLP-Mixer, and more.

Other interesting special libraries include

- *JaxPruner* (https://github.com/google-research/jaxpruner) is an open source JAX-based pruning and sparse training library for machine learning research.

- *Rax* (https://github.com/google/rax) is a learning-to-rank library that provides off-the-shelf implementations of ranking losses and metrics to be used with JAX.
- *OTT-JAX* (https://github.com/ott-jax/ott) is a library to compute optimal transport at scale and on accelerators.
- *CoDeX* (https://github.com/google/codex) contains learned data compression tools for JAX.
- *Foolbox* (https://github.com/bethgelab/foolbox) is a Python library that lets you easily run adversarial attacks against machine learning models like deep neural networks.
- `metax` (https://github.com/smonsays/metax) is a meta-learning library in JAX for research. It bundles various meta-learning algorithms and architectures that can be flexibly combined and is simple to extend.

Last but not least are libraries for privacy-preserving machine learning:

- *JAX-Privacy* (https://github.com/google-deepmind/jax_privacy) by DeepMind contains the JAX implementation of algorithms for privacy-preserving machine learning.

12.3 JAX modules for other fields

This section does not pretend to be an exhaustive overview of JAX modules. The goal is to demonstrate a very wide JAX applicability and to highlight that JAX is not limited to deep learning or machine learning.

There are modules dedicated to differentiable physics:

- *JAX, M.D.* (https://github.com/jax-md/jax-md) by Google is a framework for accelerated, differentiable molecular dynamics. It provides differentiable, hardware-accelerated molecular dynamics built on top of JAX.
- *Brax* (https://github.com/google/brax) is a fast and fully differentiable physics engine used for research and development of robotics, human perception, materials science, reinforcement learning, and other simulation-heavy applications.

There are also more specialized modules dedicated to specific areas of physics:

- `jax-cosmo` (https://mng.bz/w5lq) is a differentiable cosmology library.
- *j-Wave* (https://github.com/ucl-bug/jwave) is a library of simulators for acoustic applications.
- *JAX-Fluids* (https://github.com/tumaer/JAXFLUIDS) is a differentiable fluid dynamics package.
- *Veros* (https://github.com/team-ocean/veros) is a versatile ocean simulator. It aims to be the Swiss army knife of ocean modeling. It is a full-fledged primitive equation ocean model that supports anything between idealized toy models and realistic, high-resolution, global ocean simulations.

- *JAXChem* (https://github.com/deepchem/jaxchem) is a JAX-based deep learning library for complex and versatile chemical modeling.
- *OptimiSM* (https://github.com/sandialabs/optimism) is a library for posing and solving problems in solid mechanics using the finite element method.
- *qujax* (https://github.com/CQCL/qujax) is a JAX-based Python library for the classical simulation of quantum circuits. It is designed to be simple, fast, and flexible.
- *PennyLane* (https://github.com/PennyLaneAI/pennylane) is a cross-platform Python library for the differentiable programming of quantum computers.
- *NetKet* (https://github.com/netket/netket) is an open source project delivering cutting-edge methods for studying many-body quantum systems with artificial neural networks and machine learning techniques.
- *DeepXDE* (https://github.com/lululxvi/deepxde) is a library for scientific machine learning and physics-informed learning, such as with physics-informed neural networks (PINNs).
- *Diffrax* (https://github.com/patrick-kidger/diffrax) is a JAX-based library providing numerical differential equation solvers.

I'd like to stop here. Any such list in a book will not be exhaustive and will become outdated soon. Just keep an eye on the JAX ecosystem, look at GitHub, and follow the lists of modules like the one at https://github.com/n2cholas/awesome-jax.

Summary

- JAX has many high-level neural network libraries, including Flax, Equinox, Keras 3.0, and other exciting options.
- The JAX ecosystem has a vast collection of libraries focused on LLM training and inference.
- Many libraries help in different aspects of deep learning: organizing training loops, performing gradient transformations and optimization, making code and neural networks reliable, etc.
- A separate set of modules helps with deployment and inference using a well-developed TensorFlow ecosystem.
- Many JAX libraries are built for specific areas of machine learning, like reinforcement learning, computer vision, federated learning, probabilistic programming, evolutionary computation, etc.
- JAX is not limited to deep learning, and you may find many tools for using JAX for physics, chemistry, cosmology, quantum computing, and other fields.
- The JAX ecosystem is actively developing, so before writing something from scratch, look at the vast and vibrant JAX ecosystem. You will likely find something that helps you.

appendix A
Installing JAX

JAX is published as two separate Python packages:

- `jax`—A pure Python package
- `jaxlib`—A mostly C++ package that contains libraries such as XLA, pieces of LLVM used by XLA, MLIR infrastructure with MHLO Python bindings, and JAX-specific C++ libraries for fast JIT and pytree manipulation

JAX installation process will differ depending on whether your target architecture is a CPU, GPU, or TPU.

A.1 Installing JAX on CPUs

JAX is designed for high-performance computing and especially shines on a TPU or GPU, although, thanks to the XLA compiler, you still get a boost even on a CPU. You may also want to use CPU installation for local development. The easiest way to install JAX on the CPU is to use `pip`, the package installer for Python.

To install the CPU-only version of JAX, you can run

```
pip install --upgrade pip
pip install --upgrade "jax[cpu]"
```

The current release of `jaxlib` supports the following platforms and architectures:

- Linux x86_64
- Mac x86_64

- Mac ARM
- Windows x86_64, native or using WSL2, Windows Subsystem for Linux

On Windows, you may also need to install the Microsoft Visual Studio 2019 Redistributable if it is not already installed on your machine. Please consult the official documentation for more details: https://mng.bz/6Ywo.

Other architectures, like Linux aarch64, require building JAX from source. Running `pip install` may successfully install `jax`, but `jaxlib` will not be installed, and JAX will fail at run time.

A.2   Installing JAX on GPUs

There are several ways to install and run JAX on GPUs (here, we assume NVIDIA GPUs):

- Using CUDA and CuDNN installed from `pip` wheels (this is the easiest way, but wheels are only available for Linux x86_64)
- Using a self-installed CUDA/CuDNN
- Using a Docker container

The pip installations might not work with Windows. Experimental support exists only for Windows WSL2 x86_64 at the time of this writing

For AMD GPUs, there is experimental support for Linux x86_64 that requires building JAX from source. More details on it can be found at https://mng.bz/o0md. There is also experimental support for Apple GPUs. More details on this topic can be found at https://mng.bz/n0va. Please consult the official documentation for any updates: https://mng.bz/vJl7.

A.2.1   pip installation with CUDA

JAX supports NVIDIA GPUs with Maxwell architecture or newer (with compute capability 5.2 or higher). Note that JAX no longer supports Kepler-series GPUs since NVIDIA has dropped support for Kepler GPUs in its software.

You can check the compute capability for your GPU at https://mng.bz/4pew. If you want to learn more about the compute capabilities, read https://mng.bz/QV0G.

First, you must install the NVIDIA driver. Installing the newest driver available from NVIDIA is recommended, but the driver must be version ≥525.60.13 for CUDA 12 on Linux.

Then use the following commands to install CUDA and JAX:

```
pip install --upgrade pip

# CUDA 12 installation
# Note: wheels only available on linux.
pip install -- upgrade "jax[cuda12]"
```

That's it: it's the easiest way!

A.2.2   *pip installation with self-installed CUDA/CuDNN*

You may already have some CUDA/CuDNN versions installed. Check your CUDA version with the command:

```
nvcc --version
```

If there is no CUDA/CuDNN installed, follow these steps: first, install the NVIDIA driver. Installing the newest driver available from NVIDIA is recommended, but the driver must be version ≥525.60.13 for CUDA 12 on Linux. Then install CUDA (https://developer.nvidia.com/cuda-downloads) and CuDNN (https://developer.nvidia.com/CUDNN).

> **NOTE**   Your CUDA installation and the NVIDIA driver must be new enough to support your GPU.

Then it's time to install JAX. JAX currently supports one CUDA wheel variant:

- Built with CUDA 12.3, CUDNN 9.0, NCCL 2.19
- Compatible with CUDA >= 12.1, CUDNN >= 9.0, <10.0, NCCL >= 2.18

You may use a JAX wheel with your local CUDA/CuDNN installation if the major version of your CUDA and CuDNN matches and the minor version is at least as new as the version JAX expects.

To install JAX wheels, run the following commands:

```
pip install --upgrade pip

# Installs the wheel compatible with CUDA 12 and cuDNN 8.9 or newer.
# Note: wheels only available on linux.
pip install --upgrade "jax[cuda12_local]"
```

If there are any errors or issues with the installation, please check the JAX installation documentation.

A.2.3   *Using Docker containers*

NVIDIA provides the JAX Toolbox (https://github.com/NVIDIA/JAX-Toolbox) with Docker containers that include JAX and some JAX libraries like T5x, Paxml, and Transformer Engine.

A.3   *Installing JAX on TPUs*

JAX provides prebuilt wheels for Google Cloud TPU. To install JAX along with appropriate versions of `jaxlib` and `libtpu`, run the following in your cloud TPU VM:

```
pip install jax[tpu] -f \
https://storage.googleapis.com/jax-releases/libtpu_releases.html
```

Appendix C explains how to set up a Google Cloud TPU, run a Cloud TPU instance, and connect it to Google Colab.

NOTE   The Colab TPU runtime in Google Colab differs from the Google Cloud TPU. It provides less control and is no longer supported by JAX since version 0.4.

With previous versions of JAX and Colab TPUs, you must run the following cell before importing JAX:

```
import jax.tools.colab_tpu
jax.tools.colab_tpu.setup_tpu()
```

appendix B
Using Google Colab

Google Colaboratory (https://colab.google/), or Colab for short, is a hosted Jupyter notebook service that requires no setup and provides free access to computing resources, including GPUs and TPUs. Colab is especially well suited to machine learning, data science, and education. Colab is free, though there are paid plans with an increased amount of compute units, faster GPUs, more memory, and other features. A huge collection of curated notebooks is available at https://colab.google/notebooks/.

A notebook is a list of cells. Cells contain either explanatory text or executable code and its output. You can interactively run cells and observe their outputs (see figure B.1). The Colab basic features are explained in the following notebook: https://mng.bz/XVpv.

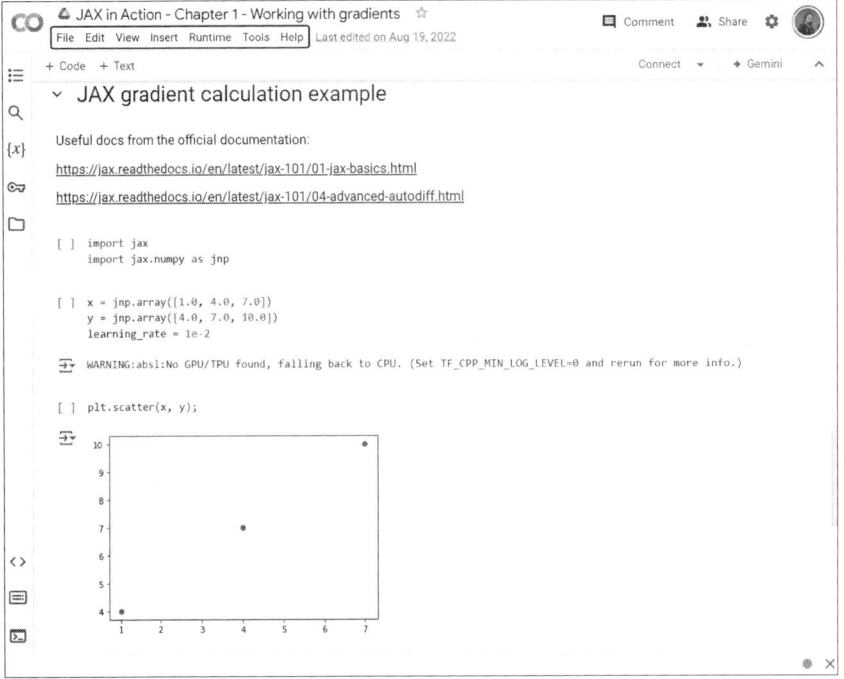

Figure B.1   A Colab notebook is a collection of cells with code and text.

Among factors especially relevant for our book is the ability to change the runtime between CPUs, GPUs, and TPUs. You can do this in the Runtime menu (see figure B.2).

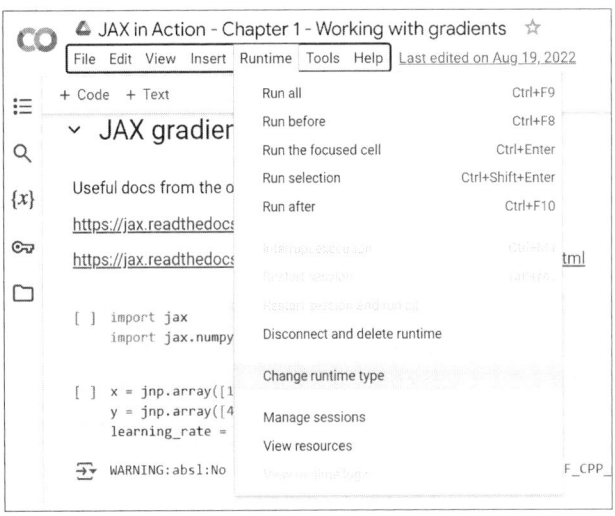

Figure B.2   The Runtime menu allows changing runtime type.

Depending on your subscription—free or paid—specific options available may differ. In my Colab free subscription at the moment of writing, the options listed in figure B.3. are available.

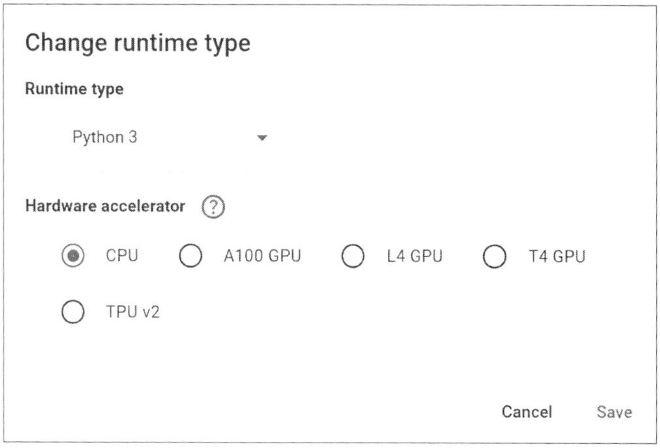

Change runtime type

Runtime type

Python 3   ▾

Hardware accelerator   ⑦

◉ CPU   ○ A100 GPU   ○ L4 GPU   ○ T4 GPU

○ TPU v2

Cancel   Save

Figure B.3   Runtime types available. Depending on your subscription (free or paid), specific options may vary.

Colab is very useful for learning JAX and prototyping your solutions. The TPU available among the runtimes is a Colab TPU, which is different from the Google Cloud TPU. It provides less control and is no longer supported by JAX since version 0.4. Appendix C explains how to set up a Cloud TPU and attach it to a Colab notebook.

Another option to use JAX in cloud interactive notebooks with TPU support is the Kaggle notebooks (https://www.kaggle.com/docs/notebooks). You can use up to 20 hours per week of TPUs and up to 9 hours at a time in a single session. More details on TPU in Kaggle are available at https://www.kaggle.com/docs/tpu.

appendix C
Using Google
Cloud TPUs

C.1 Setting up a Cloud TPU project

You must set up a Google Cloud account and prepare a toolset for working with Cloud TPUs.

> **WARNING** Using Cloud TPUs brings you some expenses, as the Google Cloud Free Tier credits do not cover GPU and TPU costs. The current TPU costs range from approximately \$1.20 to \$4.20 per chip hour, depending on the region. You may find the actual pricing at https://cloud.google.com/tpu/pricing. You may also obtain credits for using Google Cloud through various initiatives for startups (https://cloud.google.com/startup), education (https://mng .bz/yoyB), and research (https://cloud.google.com/edu/researchers and https://sites.research.google/trc/about/).

Follow these steps:

1 Set up a Google Cloud account and create a new project there. This process is described at https://mng.bz/M1dW.
2 Install the `gcloud` CLI (command-line interface) utility. You can do many things manually in the Google Cloud console, though using `gcloud` makes life easier. You can find the instructions at https://cloud.google.com/sdk/docs/ install.

3 Enable the Cloud TPU API using `gcloud` or the Google Cloud console. To enable the Cloud TPU API, run the following command in your command prompt:

```
gcloud services enable tpu.googleapis.com
```

4 Then run the following command to create a service identity:

```
gcloud beta services identity create --service tpu.googleapis.com
```

Now you are ready to create cloud machines with a TPU.

C.2 *Running a Cloud TPU instance and connecting it to Google Colab*

Now you have the `gcloud` CLI installed and set up; you are ready to run and connect to a TPU machine.

C.2.1 *Running and deleting a Cloud TPU node*

To run a machine, you need to choose a zone (here, us-central1-b), an accelerator type (here, TPU v2-8), and choose a name for the newly created node (here, node-jax):

```
$gcloud compute tpus tpu-vm create node-jax --zone \
us-central1-b --accelerator-type v2-8 --version tpu-vm-base
```

TPU availability may change depending on the zones, so you may have to try different zones and accelerator types.

You can always look at the list of running TPUs in a specified zone using the following command:

```
$gcloud compute tpus tpu-vm list --zone us-central1-b
```

To delete a node (do not forget to do it; you may have unexpected expenses), use the following command:

```
$gcloud compute tpus tpu-vm delete node-jax --zone us-central1-b
```

C.2.2 *Preparing a Cloud TPU node*

After successfully creating a node, you can log into it using SSH. To use the node as a local runtime for your Google Colab or Jupyter notebook, you must create an SSH tunnel to forward requests to a specified local port (here, 8888) to the remote machine. This is done using the following command:

```
$gcloud compute tpus tpu-vm ssh --zone us-central1-b \
 node-jax -- -L 8888:localhost:8888
```

If you are using Windows PowerShell, be careful—the double dash should be quoted:

```
$gcloud compute tpus tpu-vm ssh --zone us-central1-b \
node-jax '--' -L 8888:localhost:8888
```

Now you are on an empty machine, and you have to install everything you need. To install JAX and start experimenting with it in a console right away, run the following command:

```
$pip install jax[tpu] -f \
https://storage.googleapis.com/jax-releases/libtpu_releases.html
```

If you want to use Google Colab or Jupyter notebooks, you need to do more. First, install the necessary modules:

```
$pip install -U jinja2
$pip install notebook
```

By default, Jupyter installs locally and does not change the PATH variable. You may need to update it to include the directory where Jupyter is installed (it will display warning messages during the installation). Change the following path to the path you have; it will have a different home directory:

```
$export PATH=$PATH:/home/grigo/.local/bin
```

Install the jupyter extension:

```
$pip install jupyter_http_over_ws
```

Start the jupyter server and allow connections from Google Colab:

```
$jupyter notebook \
  --NotebookApp.allow_origin='https://colab.research.google.com' \
  --port=8888 \
  --NotebookApp.port_retries=0
```

After running the jupyter server, it displays the link to access the notebook. In my case, it was the following: http://localhost:8888/?token=5dd75b993902ba1e9710471a5b0a6 c2b887bc0c35841b1c7. The token value in the URL will change between different runs, and you need to copy this URL.

This process is also described at https://mng.bz/o0pp.

C.2.3   *Connecting to a Cloud TPU node from a Colab notebook*

Now you can connect Colab to this newly established runtime. To do that, in Google Colab, go to "Reconnect -> Connect to a Local Runtime" (see figure C.1).

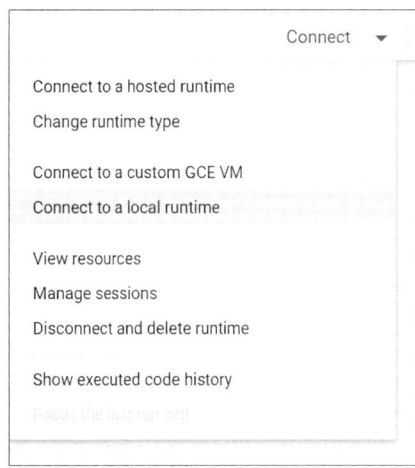

Figure C.1
Connecting a
Colab notebook
to a local runtime

Paste the link into the Backend URL field and click Connect (figure C.2). If a notebook didn't connect because of a timeout, click Reconnect.

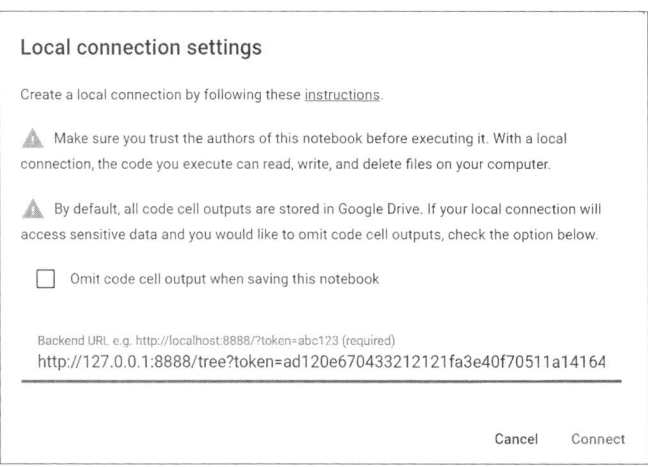

Figure C.2 Entering the backend URL for a local runtime

C.3 Resources

- More about managing TPUs
  https://mng.bz/n0M2
- Quickstart on how to run a calculation on a Cloud TPU VM
  https://mng.bz/vJz4
- Cloud TPU VM architectures
  https://mng.bz/4pZj
- Using TPU Pod slices
  https://cloud.google.com/tpu/docs/jax-pods
- Check TPU availability in different zones
  https://cloud.google.com/tpu/docs/regions-zones
- Create a deep learning VM instance by using the `gcloud` CLI
  https://mng.bz/QVmv
- Create a deep learning VM instance by using the Google Cloud console
  https://mng.bz/XVda
- Deep learning VM image
  https://cloud.google.com/deep-learning-vm
- Cloud TPU pricing
  https://cloud.google.com/tpu/pricing

appendix D
Experimental parallelization

In this appendix, we gather two (and a half) experimental parallelization techniques, namely, xmap() (plus the half, shmap()) and pjit(). xmap() is an older technique that was deleted in the JAX version 0.4.31 (July 29, 2024). However, it still might be interesting for those who need to understand legacy code or who want to understand the evolution of parallelization in JAX better.

The xmap() transformation helps parallelize functions easier than pmap(), with less code, replacing nested pmap() and vmap() calls, and without manual tensor reshaping. It also introduces the named-axis programming model that helps you write more error-proof code.

At some point in time, xmap() stopped being actively developed in favor of pjit() (the next topic of our story). Despite its deprecated status, it is very logical to describe it here, as xmap() provides a very natural way of generalizing pmap() and vmap(). If you don't need this feature and there is no legacy code you need to support, you can safely skip this part.

One of the possible xmap() replacements comes from the JAX ecosystem—the Haliax library for building neural networks with named tensors. Another alternative comes from the core JAX—the shmap(), which now has the status of JAX Enhancement Proposals (JEPs) and is a replacement for xmap().

Sometimes your functions (or neural networks) may be so large that they do not fit into a single GPU/TPU, and running computations on a cluster is required. This is common with large language models (LLMs) training and inference. Modern LLMs, like GPT-3 and 4, the largest versions of LLaMa 2, Falcon, and many others, require multi-GPU systems. JAX allows you not only to distribute (or split, or shard) data processing across different machines (data parallelism) but also to split large computations into parts performed across different machines (so-called model parallelism).

One way to shard large computations is `pjit()`, which became more popular than `xmap()` at some point. Older LLMs like GPT-J-6B used `xmap()` (see the case at https://mng.bz/KDMX), and newer LLMs tend to use `pjit()` more (see the case of Cohere: https://mng.bz/9oMj).

`pjit()` and `jit()` (the topic of chapter 5) have been merged into a single unified interface, so please use `jit()` instead. Also, tensor sharding with distributed arrays (the topic of chapter 8) provides a modern way for compiling and executing JAX functions in multihost or multicore environments.

You can safely skip this part if you don't need to support older code with `pjit()` and do not have plans to directly use `jit()` with sharding specifications.

D.1 Using xmap() and named-axis programming

`xmap()` is an interesting experimental feature that can simplify your programs in several ways (see figure D.1). First, it introduces the named-axis programming model, switching from tensor axis indices to axis names. It makes your code more error proof and easier to understand and change.

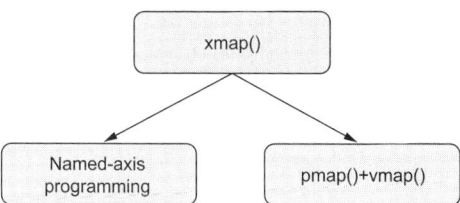

Figure D.1 `xmap()` **capabilities**

Second, it allows replacing both `pmap()` and `vmap()` with a single function capable of doing both things and of getting rid of some technical things that related to *how* things should be done, not *what* should be done: namely, eliminating nested `pmap()`/`vmap()` calls and reshaping your data before calling `pmap()`. With `xmap()`, you don't care about the number of available devices and do not need to reshape your data, adding a special dimension to map over and then removing it after the computation. All this happens behind the curtain in just a single `xmap()` call.

We start with the named-axis programming paradigm. Then we add the parallelization part.

Previously, we built neural network examples using operations on tensors where a particular tensor layout was important, and the functions were typically written the way they relied upon that specific tensor dimension containing the thing they expected.

See, for example, the `predict()` and `loss()` calls in listings 7.25 and 7.26, which worked if the input tensors were of specific shapes like (`batch_size`, etc.) for the tensor-containing images. The code relied on the specific positions of different tensor axes. But if you change a tensor layout, your computations will fail due to dimension mismatch or (in the worst case) continue without errors but semantically calculate the wrong thing.

Such problems with tensor dimensions are usually hard to debug, and different solutions emerge in deep learning. One helpful way to prevent these sorts of errors is the named tensor model proposed by Alexander Rush from the Harvard NLP group in the post "Tensor Considered Harmful" (https://nlp.seas.harvard.edu/NamedTensor) and described in detail in the paper "Named Tensor Notation" (https://arxiv.org/abs/2102.13196).

The idea is to give explicit names to tensor dimensions, say, a batch, features, height, width, or channel dimension. When most tensor operations that take dimension parameters accept dimension names, you can avoid the need to track dimensions by position.

In addition, it can provide extra safety by automatically checking that APIs are being used correctly at run time. Rearranging dimensions by names instead of positions can be easier to write and understand; consequently, it is harder to make errors.

There is a PyTorch implementation of named tensors (https://mng.bz/WVdg). Mesh TensorFlow (https://github.com/tensorflow/mesh) used named tensor and mesh dimensions. JAX has a slightly different experimental implementation of this idea described in the tutorial on `xmap()` (https://mng.bz/ZVq5).

NOTE   `xmap()` was an experimental API and was deleted in JAX version 0.4.31 (July 29, 2024).

D.1.1   *Working with named axes*

The idea is to introduce named axes in addition to tensor positional axes so that a tensor will have both `.dtype` and `.shape` attributes describing its positional axes as a usual NumPy array and an additional `.named_shape` attribute describing its named axes.

Named axes cannot be added to a standalone tensor. Currently, the only way to introduce named axes is to use the `xmap()` call. You will see it shortly.

The `.dtype` attribute stores the element type (e.g., `np.float32`); the `.shape` attribute stores a tuple of integers defining the shape of the array (e.g., (`3, 5`) for a 3×5 array); and the `.named_shape` attribute is a `dict` mapping axis names to integer sizes (e.g., {`'batch': 32, 'channel': 10`} for two additional array axes of size 32 and 10, respectively).

The axis names are arbitrary hashable objects, with strings being a common choice, but you may also use other types. The order of the named axes has no meaning, and they are unordered, resulting in named shapes {`'batch': 32, 'channel': 10`} and {`'channel': 10, 'batch': 32`} being equal.

For backward-compatibility reasons, the meanings of .ndim and .size are not modified, and they are always equal to len(shape) and the product of .shape elements, respectively. However, the true rank of an array with non-empty named axes is len(shape)+len(named_shape), as the actual number of elements stored in such an array is equal to the product of sizes of all dimensions, both positional and named. For example, a tensor containing images with the shape (200, 200) and the named shape {'batch': 32, 'channel': 3} has a true rank of 4.

ADDING AND REMOVING NAMED AXES

Currently, the only way to introduce named axes is to use xmap() because all top-level JAX operations work in the NumPy model with purely positional axes. It may change at some point.

> ### Named-axis programming and axis_name in vmap()/pmap()
>
> Remember, the vmap() and pmap() functions have a separate parameter called axis_name. In some sense, you can treat the axis_name parameter as a very limited form of named-axis programming, which applies only to an axis you map over, and the only place where you can use it is inside collective ops.

You can think of xmap() as a wrapper or an adapter that takes in standard arrays (tensors) with positional axes, making some of the axes named (as specified by the in_axes parameter), calling the function that it wraps, and converting named axes back to positional (using the out_axes parameter).

You can specify axis mappings in two ways:

- Using dictionaries that map positional axes to axis names. For example, {0: 'batch', 3: 'channel'} maps the axis with position 0 to the name "batch" and the axis with position 3 to the name "channel" (beware, this is different with the .named_shape attribute described previously, as numbers meant axes sizes there, but here they mean axes positions).
- Using lists of axes names terminated by the Ellipsis Python object (... or Ellipsis, https://mng.bz/NBYE) to map a prefix of the positional dimensions to given names; for example, ['device', 'batch', ...] for the case when you map the first two positional dimensions of a tensor to the named "device" and "batch" dimensions, keeping other dimensions positional. The order here is important.

The in_axes structure should match the signature of the wrapped function arguments, and the same is true for the out_axes parameter responsible for the function return value.

All the positional axes mentioned in the in_axes parameter are converted to named axes. All the named axes mentioned in the out_axes parameter are inserted in the positions specified in this parameter.

These named axes are essentially removed from input tensors before calling the wrapped function; the function is mapped over them, and then these mapped axes are reinserted into specified positions. The result is the same as if we applied `vmap()` over each named axis (however, it's much more than just `vmap()`; it's more like a way to interpolate between `vmap()`- and `pmap()`-style execution seamlessly, as you will see shortly).

Let's return to our example from listing 7.17, where we calculated dot products between two large arrays organized so that the batch dimension was not the first. Here we reproduce the scheme from chapter 7 to represent what is happening during the processing (see figure D.2).

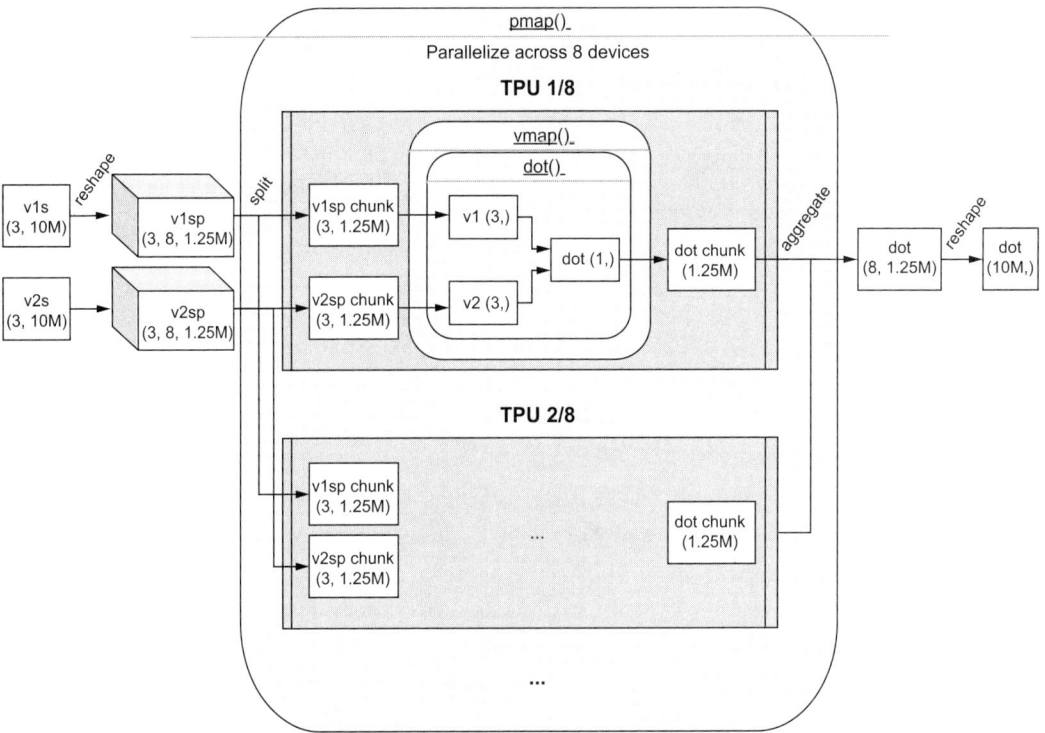

Figure D.2   Scheme of data processing for the large transposed array example (reproducing figure 7.1)

Remember, we reshape our tensors to have a separate dimension with a size equal to the number of available devices, call `pmap()` to distribute computations over this new technical dimension, use `vmap()` internally to process a batch of elements on each device, and then get rid of this extra dimension after calculations are done.

This code is complicated: first, there is a composition of two functions, `pmap()` and `vmap()`. Second, and most importantly, in both `pmap()` and `vmap()` calls, we must keep track of array axis indices using the `in_axes` parameter. It is pretty complicated as you cannot easily adapt your function to a new tensor layout; you must carefully recalculate what indices each function should work with, keeping in mind that each function sees its own shapes. With more nested calls, it would be even harder, and such code that heavily relies on tensor indices is very error prone. And that is precisely what the authors of "Tensor Considered Harmful" stand against.

The following code requires eight devices to parallelize your computations, so either create Cloud TPU and use it as a local runtime in Colab (see appendix C or the example in section 3.2.5 if you need help here) or create eight virtual CPU devices as we described in chapter 7. Alternatively, if you have access to a multi-GPU system, you can adapt this code for your system.

Listing D.1 Reproducing the code from listing 7.17

```
from jax import random
rng_key = random.PRNGKey(42)

def dot(v1, v2):
  return jnp.vdot(v1, v2)

vs = random.normal(rng_key, shape=(20_000_000,3))
v1s = vs[:10_000_000,:].T                    Now arrays are transposed
v2s = vs[10_000_000:,:].T                    versions of the original arrays.

v1s.shape, v2s.shape                         The first dimension contains
                                             components of a vector, and the
>>> ((3, 10000000), (3, 10000000))           second dimension contains vectors.

v1sp = v1s.reshape((v1s.shape[0], 8, v1s.shape[1]//8))
v2sp = v2s.reshape((v2s.shape[0], 8, v2s.shape[1]//8))     We split the second
v1sp.shape, v2sp.shape                                     dimension, which
                                                           contains vectors,
>>> ((3, 8, 1250000), (3, 8, 1250000))    Now we have eight  into two dimensions:
                                          groups of vectors. groups and vectors.
dot_parallel = jax.pmap(
    jax.vmap(dot, in_axes=(1,1)),         We ask vmap to use the second
    in_axes=(1,1)                         dimension to map over (vmap does not
)                                         see the group dimension, so its second
                                          dimension is the vector dimension).
x_pmap = dot_parallel(v1sp,v2sp)
                                          We ask pmap to use the second (group)
x_pmap.shape                              dimension, which will not be visible to vmap.

>>> (8, 1250000)                          We obtain eight groups of dot products.

x_pmap = x_pmap.reshape((x_pmap.shape[0]*x_pmap.shape[1]))
x_pmap.shape
                                          We eliminate the
>>> (10000000,)                           group dimension.
```

Let's rewrite this code using named tensors and xmap(). Let's ignore how exactly the parallelization part performs (we will look at it later in this section) and concentrate on the programmer's experience of writing such processing with named axes.

We will use a single `xmap()` call instead of a nested `pmap()`/`vmap()` call. By default, `xmap()` vectorizes the computation like `vmap()` does, and it doesn't perform any parallelization; the code executes on a single device. So, right now, our example is not equivalent to the code with a nested `pmap()`/`vmap()` call. We will add the parallelization part in the next section.

Figure D.3 depicts adding and removing named axes when using `xmap()`. Please ignore the increased visual size of the tensors after adding named axes; this is done only to fit more text inside the box. The tensor sizes in terms of number of elements remain the same.

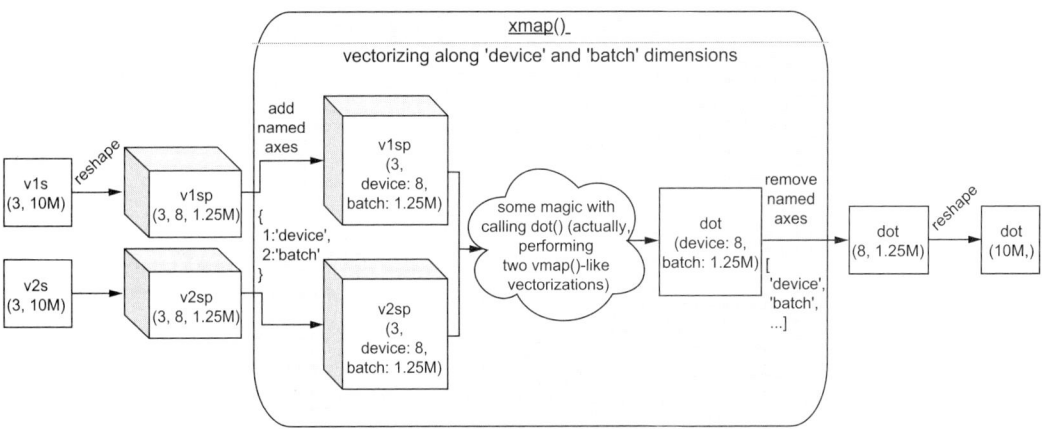

Figure D.3   **Scheme of data processing for the large transposed array example with** `xmap()` **and named axes**

In the code, we have to say that we want to map the `dot()` function over the dimensions with index 1 (we named it the "device" dimension) and 2 (the "batch" dimension), and to do this we use the `{1:'device', 2:'batch'}` notation for both function parameters inside the `in_axes` parameter. For the output, we want to insert these dimensions into positions 0 and 1, respectively, by setting `out_axes=['device', 'batch', ...]`. The order in the list determines the numerical position starting from 0.

Listing D.2   Rewriting using `xmap()`

```
from jax.experimental.maps import xmap          ◄──── Importing xmap

vs = random.normal(rng_key, shape=(20_000_000,3))
v1s = vs[:10_000_000,:].T
v2s = vs[10_000_000:,:].T

v1s.shape, v2s.shape

>>> ((3, 10000000), (3, 10000000))

v1sp = v1s.reshape((v1s.shape[0], 8, v1s.shape[1]//8))
v2sp = v2s.reshape((v2s.shape[0], 8, v2s.shape[1]//8))
```

```
v1sp.shape, v2sp.shape

>>> ((3, 8, 1250000), (3, 8, 1250000))

f = xmap(dot,
         in_axes=(
             {1:'device', 2:'batch'},
             {1:'device', 2:'batch'}
         ),
         out_axes=['device', 'batch', ...]
)

x_xmap=f(v1sp,v2sp)

x_xmap.shape

>>> (8, 1250000)

x_xmap = x_xmap.reshape((x_xmap.shape[0]*x_xmap.shape[1]))
x_xmap.shape

>>> (10000000,)

jax.numpy.all(x_xmap == x_pmap)

>>> Array(True, dtype=bool)
```

Using xmap() as a
function transformation

Signature for the
first dot() argument

Signature for the
second dot() argument

Signature for the
dot() return value

Calling the
transformed function

Checks that the result is
the same as for the
pmap-calculated result

What is better with this code? First, there is just one function transformation, xmap(), instead of two, vmap() and pmap(). Second, you don't have to track indices of different tensor dimensions. You just provide them in the in_axes parameter to convert these axes into named axes, let the wrapped function work with the rest of the positional axes, and for the returning tensor, convert axes specified in the out_axes parameter back to positional axes in the positions indicated by its respective out_axes value.

In the preceding example, we have used mapping specified by dictionaries for input arguments, as the dimensions we want to map over were not the leading dimensions (the leading dimension with index 0 is the dimension that stores individual vector components). We have used mapping specified by lists for the output data; in this case, they are the first dimensions that form the prefix of the positional dimensions.

Here a single xmap() call is equivalent to two nested vmap() calls. This code does not use parallelization, so I want to highlight it and talk about two vmap() calls instead of pmap()+vmap().

Einsum

Einstein summation (or einsum) is a useful function for expressing dot products, outer products, matrix-vector, and matrix-matrix multiplications. It is a generalization of products to multiple dimensions.

For example, a matrix multiplication can be expressed using einsum() in the following way:

(continued)

```
import numpy as np

A = np.array([
    [1, 1, 1],
    [2, 2, 2],
    [3, 3, 3]
])

B = np.array([
    [1, 0, 0],
    [0, 1, 0],
    [0, 0, 1]
])

np.einsum("ij,jk->ik", A, B)

>>> array([[1, 1, 1],
>>>        [2, 2, 2],
>>>        [3, 3, 3]])
```

At the heart of einsum lies Einstein's summation notation. It is a very elegant way to express many operations on tensors. It uses a simple domain-specific language (DSL), resembling the named-axes approach. This DSL can sometimes be compiled into high-performing code (that was the case with the manually vectorized function in section 6.1.2).

Einsum takes in a list of input tensors and a special format string, like `"ij,jk->ik"`. The part at the left of the `->` symbol relates to the input parameters, and the part at the right relates to the output. The format string labels tensor dimensions for all input tensors and the output, with each letter corresponding to a dimension.

For the names that appear both in input and output (so-called free indices, `i` and `k` in the example here), einsum essentially makes an outer loop for these indices. For other indices (called summation indices, `j` in the example here), it makes an inner loop with a summation for dimensions with the same index.

The example string `"ij,jk->ik"` expresses two outer loops: one along the first dimension (`i`) of the first tensor and another along the second dimension (`k`) of the second tensor. For the second dimension of the first tensor and the first dimension of the second tensor (both named `j`), it performs an elementwise product with a summation. So the einsum on two matrices with the chosen format string performs matrix multiplication.

Other useful examples are `"a,a->"` for two-vector inner product, `"ii->i"` for a matrix diagonal, `"ab->ba"` for matrix transpose, and `"Yab,Ybc->Yac"` for batch matrix multiply. For the vectorized dot product we use as an example, the format string will be `"ib,ib->b"`.

Einsum is implemented in NumPy and almost any deep learning framework, including TensorFlow, PyTorch, and JAX. `xmap()` can be seen as a generalized einsum, as it treats named axes as first-class objects, and you can implement a function to manipulate them. Einsum never lets you interact with named axes directly. You can read more about einsum at https://rockt.github.io/2018/04/30/einsum.

RULES FOR NAMED-AXIS PROPAGATION

Let's look at how named axes propagate throughout the program. Named axes never implicitly interact with any positional axes, so you can invoke (using xmap()) a function that knows nothing about named axes with inputs that have positional axes. The result will be the same as if you called vmap() for each separately named axis. We did exactly this in the preceding example.

If a binary operation is applied to arguments with different named axes, these axes are broadcast by their names. So, for example, if one operand has a named axis a, and another operand has a named axis b, then a binary operation (say, addition) for these operands will produce a result with both axes a and b.

All axes with equal names are expected to have equal (or broadcastable) shapes for all arguments in a broadcasting operation. So, if one operand has a named axis a, and another has an axis with the same name, both these axes must have equal sizes or one of them is 1. The named shape of the result becomes a union of the named shapes of its inputs.

In the following example, we use a function that processes two arguments with different named shapes. Each one has a unique named axis. You will see that the result has both named axes as each was broadcast, and the resulting shape became a union of input named shapes.

Listing D.3 Broadcasting in xmap()

```
image = random.normal(rng_key, shape=(480,640,3))
filters = random.normal(rng_key, shape=(5,3,3))

from jax.scipy.signal import convolve2d

def apply_filter(channel, kernel):
  return convolve2d(channel, kernel, mode="same")

apply_filters_to_image = xmap(apply_filter,
      in_axes=(
          {2:'channel'},
          {0:'filter'}
      ),
      out_axes={0:'filter', 3: 'channel'}
)

res = apply_filters_to_image(image, filters)

res.shape

>>> (5, 480, 640, 3)
```

- Generates a random RGB image 640 × 480px
- Generates five matrix filters of size 3 × 3
- A function for applying one filter to a single image channel
- Generates a function to apply many filters to many image channels
- Maps over channel dimension for image
- Maps over filter dimension for a set of filters
- Puts filter dimension at the first position of the output and the channel dimension at the last
- The result has both named dimensions (filters, h, w, channels).

We applied a 2D convolution function to arguments with different named axes. The 2D convolution function works on a single image with a single kernel. We add a named dimension for image channels to the function's first argument and another for separate filter kernels to the second argument. As expected, the result has both dimensions; each was broadcast to the other tensor. For the output value, we have chosen specific positions for these dimensions: the filter dimension became the first dimension, and the color channel dimension became the last one. So the resulting tensor can be treated as five color images stacked together. Each image comprises three color channels and results from applying a separate matrix filter to the original image. As named axes should be equivalent to positional axes, you can use reductions over named axes.

> **NOTE**   Only a few functions from the JAX NumPy interface support named axes. Now only `jnp.sum()`, `jnp.max()`, `jnp.min()` are supported.

In the following example, we have a 2D matrix with named axes called "row" and "col." We run a function that performs a reduction of the "row" axis, calculating a sum (using `jnp.sum()`) of corresponding elements from this axis. Another axis is preserved, and as a result, we obtain a sum of each column (as rows are reduced).

Listing D.4   Reducing axis using `jnp.sum()`

```
f = xmap(
    lambda x: jnp.sum(x, axis=['row']),      Calculates sum along
    in_axes=['row', 'col'],                  the row axis
    out_axes=['col']                         Declares two named
)                                            axes at the input
                                             Declares a single named
C = jnp.array([                              axis at the output
    [1,2,3],
    [4,5,6],
    [7,8,9]
])

f(C)
                                             The result contains
>>> Array([12, 15, 18], dtype=int32)         the sum along rows.
```

You can also use collective ops. All the collectives working inside the `pmapped` function also work with named axes. We can rewrite our global array normalization function from listing 7.23.

Listing D.5   Nested `pmap()` example, reproducing listing 7.23

```
arr = jnp.array(range(8)).reshape(2,4)       Generating a
arr                                          small matrix

>>> Array([[0, 1, 2, 3],
>>>        [4, 5, 6, 7]], dtype=int32)
```

```
n_pmap = jax.pmap(
    jax.pmap(
        lambda x: x/jax.lax.psum(
            x, axis_name=('rows','cols')),
        axis_name='cols'
    ),
    axis_name='rows')
```
◀─── **Doing nested pmap over rows and columns**

```
jnp.sum(n_pmap(arr))

>>> Array(1., dtype=float32)
```
◀─── **Checking normalization result**

With `xmap()`, it is easy to rewrite the same processing in a simpler way using the same function for processing a single element and using the same collective call.

Listing D.6　Rewriting nested `pmap()` example using `xmap()`

```
arr = jnp.array(range(8)).reshape(2,4)
arr
```
◀─── **Generates a small matrix**

```
>>> Array([[0, 1, 2, 3],
>>>        [4, 5, 6, 7]], dtype=int32)

n_xmap = xmap(
    lambda x: x/jax.lax.psum(x, axis_name=('rows','cols')),
    in_axes=['rows', 'cols', ...],
    out_axes=['rows', 'cols', ...]
)
```
Uses the same function for normalization

Introduces named axes in a single xmap() call

```
jnp.sum(n_xmap(arr))

>>> Array(1., dtype=float32)
```
◀─── **Checks normalization result**

The code becomes more straightforward while producing the same result. However, right now, it doesn't use parallel devices. It is analogous to two `vmap()` calls running on a single device. Here it is natural to look at the `xmap()`'s real killer feature—its ability to parallelize code over supercomputer-scale hardware meshes!

D.1.2　Parallelism and hardware meshes

By default, `xmap()` vectorizes the computation in the same way `vmap()` does, and it doesn't perform any parallelization; the code executes on a single device.

To parallelize your computations, you must use *resource axes*. A resource axis is a way to control how `xmap()` evaluates the computation.

Each axis introduced by `xmap()` is assigned to one or more resource axes. Resource axes come from a *hardware mesh*, an *n*-dimensional array of devices with named axes.

Technically, a hardware mesh is a two-component object:

- *An n-dimensional array of JAX device objects*—These are the same objects you obtain by calling `jax.devices()` or `jax.local_devices()` functions but are represented as `np.array` type. Be careful: it is a pure NumPy array (`np.array`), not a JAX NumPy array (`jnp.array`), because a device object is not a valid JAX array type.

- *A tuple of resource axes names*—The length of the tuple must match the rank of the device array. So, for a 3D-mesh, the tuple contains three resource axes names.

A typical TPU (at least of the currently available generations 2, 3, and 4) has four chips (each with two cores) on a card (https://mng.bz/DpRy). TPU v2 and v3 use 2D torus topology, and TPU v4 uses 3D torus topology. So we can represent a default Cloud TPU as a 2 × 2 grid of chips or a 4 × 2 grid of cores (the device visible to JAX is a core).

While physical devices are connected to a physical mesh, you can create a logical mesh above. It abstracts the physical device mesh and may be reshaped depending on your computation needs.

JAX provides a special `Mesh` context manager (https://mng.bz/lr1j). You can create the mesh as shown in the following listing.

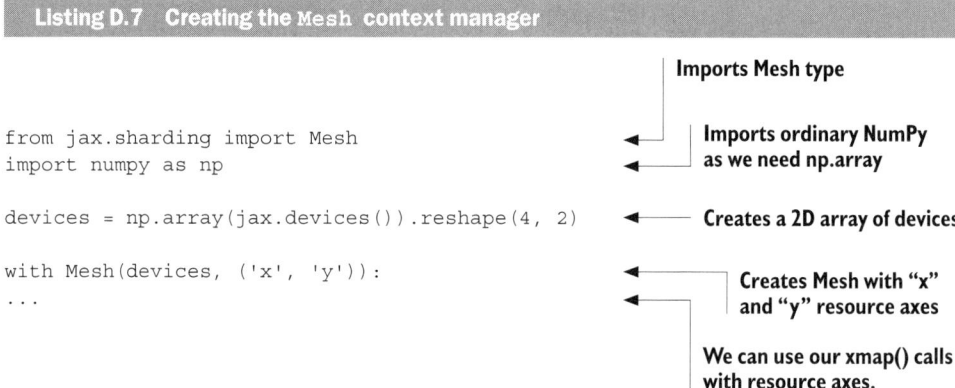

Listing D.7 Creating the `Mesh` context manager

```
from jax.sharding import Mesh
import numpy as np

devices = np.array(jax.devices()).reshape(4, 2)

with Mesh(devices, ('x', 'y')):
    ...
```

Imports Mesh type

Imports ordinary NumPy as we need np.array

Creates a 2D array of devices

Creates Mesh with "x" and "y" resource axes

We can use our xmap() calls with resource axes.

Here we created a 2D array of available devices and a `Mesh` context manager with two axes along the hardware mesh, the "x" and the "y." You can now split your computations along these axes.

Now you can map your logical axes introduced by `xmap()` to resource axes introduced by `Mesh`. Say we want to partition "rows" and "columns" named axes across the "x" and "y" resource axes. There is the `axis_resources` argument to perform this mapping.

The `axis_resources` is a `dict` that maps the axes introduced in this `xmap()` to one or more resource axes. Each value with a named axis will be partitioned over all mesh axes assigned to the named axis using the `axis_resources` parameter. The size of a logical axis must be a multiple of the corresponding mesh dimension size. We parallelize our computation across the device mesh.

Listing D.8   Parallelizing `xmap()` computation

```
arr = jnp.array(range(10000)).reshape(100,100)

with Mesh(devices, ('x', 'y')):
  n_xmap = xmap(
    lambda x: x/jax.lax.psum(x, axis_name=('rows','cols')),
    in_axes=['rows', 'cols', ...],
    out_axes=['rows', 'cols', ...],
    axis_resources={'rows': 'x', 'cols': 'y'}          ◄─── Assigns logical axes
  )                                                          to resource axes

  res = n_xmap(arr)

type(res), res.shape                                   
                                                       ┌── The result is a
>>> (jaxlib.xla_extension.ArrayImpl, (100, 100))  ◄───┘    large array.
```

We assigned the logical axes introduced by `xmap()` to the resource axes provided by our hardware mesh with the `axis_resources` dictionary.

The beauty of this example is that we didn't care about the number of available devices and the corresponding reshaping of our data. Remember, with `pmap()`, we cannot send more data than available devices, so we had to reshape our data to have the mapped dimension size not greater than the number of devices (as we did in listing 7.22). All this happened behind the curtain in just a single `xmap()` call. That's great!

This way, the `xmap()`'s default `vmap()`-like behavior becomes closer to the `pmap()`-like behavior. And you can see `xmap()` as a seamless way to interpolate between `vmap()` and `pmap()`-style execution. We can use `xmap()` as a drop-in replacement for `pmap()`, which makes programming for multidimensional hardware meshes much easier, automatically partitioning the computation over multiple devices.

The `xmap()` transformation performs two actions: *split* (or *partitioning*) and *replication*:

- A logical axis A with size x mapped over a resource axis B with size y is *partitioned* across it, meaning it is split into chunks (of size x/y; x should be divisible by y without remainder), and each chunk is distributed to its own device.
- A logical axis not mapped to any resource axis, is *replicated* across all the devices, meaning each device gets a full copy of this particular axis.

For example, suppose we have a 2D tensor with the shape (1000, 20) with the first axis named "rows" and the second "columns" and a hardware mesh for a single Cloud TPU card with eight cores shaped with two axes, x and y, of sizes 4 and 2, respectively.

If we perform some computation and do not map axes "rows" and "columns" to any resource axes, then this tensor is fully replicated across all the Cloud TPU cores.

If we use `axis_resources={'rows': 'x', 'columns': 'y'}`, then the first (`'rows'`) dimension of the tensor (of size 1000) is split into four chunks of size $1,000/4 = 250$, and the second (`'columns'`) dimension (of size 20) is split into two chunks of size $20/2 = 10$.

If only one dimension is mapped to a resource axis, then this particular dimension is split into chunks, and another unmapped dimension is replicated across all the devices.

Finally, we can simplify our example from listing D.2, a direct adaptation of an older `pmap()`-based example. In that adaptation, we removed tensor dimension indices and switched to using named axes. Also, we used a single `xmap()` call instead of two `vmap()` and `pmap()` calls.

After getting to know hardware meshes, we can finally use them to parallelize our computations over the devices. However, we still relied on manual tensor reshaping to match the number of available devices, but we do not need to do it this way. With `xmap()`, you can use automatic partitioning across a chosen axis, so manual reshaping is no longer needed! The following listing demonstrates this approach.

Listing D.9   Getting rid of reshaping for listing D.2

```
from jax.experimental.maps import xmap            ◀──── Imports xmap

rng_key = random.PRNGKey(42)

vs = random.normal(rng_key, shape=(20_000_000,3))
v1s = vs[:10_000_000,:].T
v2s = vs[10_000_000:,:].T

v1s.shape, v2s.shape
                                                         No reshaping to match
>>> ((3, 10000000), (3, 10000000))               ◀──── device number

with Mesh(np.array(jax.devices()), ('device')):   ◀──── Uses ID mesh of devices
  f = xmap(dot,
        in_axes=(
            {1:'batch'},                           ◀──── Maps over the
            {1:'batch'}                            ◀──── batch dimension
        ),
        out_axes=['batch', ...],                   ◀──── Shards batch dimension
        axis_resources={'batch': 'device'}         ◀──── over device mesh
  )
  x_xmap=f(v1s,v2s)                                ◀──── Calls the transformed function

x_xmap.shape
                                                         We've got 10M
>>> (10000000,)                                   ◀──── dot products.
```

We dropped tensor reshaping to match available devices. We also created a 1D logical mesh of devices. Finally, we partition the "batch" dimension over the "device" hardware mesh dimension. This way, we automatically shard our computation for available devices without needing manual tensor reshaping.

An additional benefit is that our code becomes more universal. It does not depend on a particular number of devices and can be efficiently run on almost any hardware configuration with devices grouped into a 1D grid.

The important thing is that any assignment of `axis_resources` doesn't ever change the results of the computation (at least up to floating-point inaccuracy problems because of a different order of computations). It never changes program semantics; it changes only how the computation is carried out and which devices are used.

This way, it is easy to try different ways of partitioning a single program in many distributed scenarios and choose the most performant one. You can easily transfer your code between small-scale (your laptop) and large-scale (a TPU Pod) systems.

We skip a larger neural network example with `xmap()` as the work on this experimental feature has essentially been stopped in an incomplete state. It is not straightforward to translate our SPMD MNIST example, as some features are still missing (differentiation rule for `lax.pmax()`), and others (like `lax.pdot()` function) are undocumented. The `in_axes/out_axes` arguments become too complicated for a tree-like structure (see the book repository for a prospective example). The named-axis parallelism will probably be revised soon, and the JAX authors may change it.

However, `xmap()` can already help you make your code simpler and more clear, without manual reshaping, as we did it replacing nested `pmap()` and `vmap()` calls.

There are some other interesting things worth mentioning. First, I point to the `shmap` (or `shard_map()`; jokingly, it is also called `shpecialized_xmap`) as a modern replacement for `xmap()`. At the time of writing, `shmap` has a status of JAX Enhancement Proposals (JEPs) (https://mng.bz/BgRv).

Second, other approaches to named tensors exist in the JAX ecosystem. We mention a few relevant modern libraries in chapter 12. At the time of writing, the Haliax library (https://github.com/stanford-crfm/haliax) looks like an interesting option.

D.2 *Using pjit() for tensor parallelism*

The parallelism provided by `pmap()`, or `xmap()` with resource axes, was designed for the case when you need to split data across different accelerators and run a single function across these different chunks of data. This is called *data parallelism*.

There is a different case when you need to split the function instead of the data. It might be required, for example, for large neural networks that do not fit into a single accelerator. Modern large neural networks like GPT-3 with 175B parameters or the 530B-parameter Megatron-Turing NLG are typical examples of neural networks that do not fit into any single GPU. Or you might want to speed up computations by performing them in parallel if they do not depend on each other.

In such a case, you may split a model into different parts (for example, by layers, or even a single layer may be split). This is called *model parallelism*, and JAX supports it with the help of the `pjit()` transformation.

As you remember, `pmap()` allows you to run the same program on multiple devices. Each device gets its own shard of input data. You also must write a program to process data so that if you need communication between different devices, you can manually organize it with the help of collective ops.

With `pjit()`, you can shard both data and function (weights for the neural network case) over an existing hardware mesh. It is the same mesh we used in the `xmap()` section.

Specify how you want to partition input and output data. Then the partitioning of the function over devices happens automatically by the propagation of the input and output partitioning. For all the intermediate tensors, `pjit()` automatically determines the sharding pattern. However, you may also use sharding constraints for selected tensors inside your program, as it may help you improve function performance. You don't need to insert any collective ops in your program; `pjit()` does it when needed.

It essentially compiles your program into XLA representation as if only one large virtual device exists. You tell the compiler to shard the arrays according to a sharding policy, and then it uses the XLA SPMD partitioner to generate an identical program for *N* devices that performs communications between devices through collective ops. It is still the single-program, multiple-data (SPMD) code as it was with `pmap()`. However, you program it on a higher level of abstraction.

The function returned by the `pjit()` transformation preserves the semantics of the original function but is compiled into an XLA computation that runs across multiple devices. In this sense, it is similar to `xmap()`, which never changes program semantics but changes only how the computation is carried out and which devices are used.

The appeal of `pjit()` is that it requires very few changes to your code, and you can get things done faster, compared to `pmap()`, which requires more effort but provides more control. `pjit()` has an interface similar to `jit()` and may work as a decorator on a function that needs to be compiled. `pjit()` is very popular now and is used much more frequently than `xmap()`, especially if you work with large-scale model parallel transformers.

The internals of the XLA SPMD partitioner are described in the paper "GSPMD: General and Scalable Parallelization for ML Computation Graphs" (https://arxiv.org/abs/2105.04663), and `pjit()` is the API exposed for the XLA SPMD partitioner in JAX. The topic of how the XLA SPMD partitioner works is out of the book's scope, and I recommend you start with this paper if you are interested in these details.

For the examples in this section, I create an eight-core Cloud TPU and connect it as a local runtime to Colab. Now let's dive into `pjit()`!

D.2.1 Basics of pjit()

You need three things to use `pjit()`:

- *A mesh specification.* This is the same mesh specification we used in the `xmap()` section. It is a logical multidimensional mesh over a physical hardware mesh and is defined by the `jax.sharding.Mesh()` context manager (https://mng.bz/lr1j). The function will use the `Mesh` definition provided when you call the function, not the `Mesh` definition at the time of calling `pjit()`.

- *The sharding specification.* Here you define input and output data partitioning using the `in_shardings` and `out_shardings` parameters (`in_axis_resources` and `out_axis_resources` in older versions) of the `pjit()` function (https://mng.bz/dZ4D).

- *Sharding constraints (optional).* To specify such constraints for selected intermediate tensors inside a function, you can provide hints using the `jax.lax.with_sharding_constraint()` (originally `jax.experimental.pjit.with_sharding_constraint()`). It can lead to improved performance. We touch on the sharding constraints in section 8.3.1.

Let's look at some examples.

A SIMPLE EXAMPLE WITH 1D MESH

First, we return to our regular example of calculating dot products between two large lists of vectors. In the following example, we use two large lists of random vectors for which we want to calculate pairwise dot products in a parallel fashion. We did that with `pmap()` in listings 7.6 to 7.9 and 7.17 and `xmap()` in listings D.2 and D.9. Here we will create a mesh and try to parallelize the calculation using `pjit()`. Figure D.4 depicts the steps of the process.

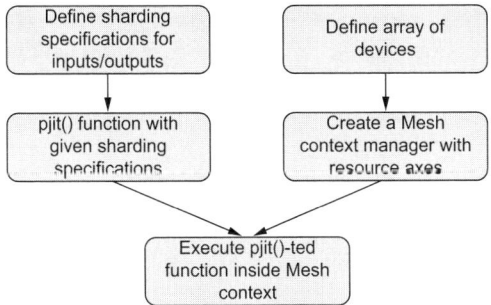

Figure D.4 **The process of using** `pjit()` **for a function and a device mesh**

There are several important parts here. First, for the `Mesh`-related part of the scheme, we need two things to organize a mesh:

- A plain NumPy array, as the `Mesh` context manager accepts an `np.array` of devices
- Resource axes names, which are provided as a tuple

We use a plain 1D mesh with a single axis. To do so, we use a 1D array of `devices=np.array(jax.devices())`, and in the `Mesh()` constructor, we use a one-element tuple to name the "devices" axis using the call `Mesh(devices, ('devices',)).`

Second, for the `pjit()`-related part of the scheme, we provide input and output sharding annotation. This is controlled by the `in_shardings` and `out_shardings` parameters.

The sharding annotation value must either be a `None`, a `PartitionSpec`, or a tuple of length equal to the number of positional arguments of the function we parallelize. The `PartitionSpec` is a tuple whose elements can be a `None`, a string name of a mesh axis, or a tuple of mesh axes names. Each element of the tuple describes a mesh dimension across which the input dimension is partitioned.

For example, for a rank-3 tensor (tensor with three dimensions), the `Partition-Spec('x', 'y', None)` means that the first dimension of data is sharded across the "x" axis of the mesh, the second dimension is sharded across the "y" axis of the mesh, and the third dimension is not sharded (so it is replicated).

In our example, we do not use input sharding, so we pass the `in_shardings=None` value. This means that input values are replicated across all the devices, and each device will have a copy of the input. For sharding the output, we use `out_shardings=PartitionSpec('devices')`, which means the function output tensor should be sharded across the "devices" axis.

Listing D.10 Applying `pjit()` to parallelize dot product calculations

```
from jax import random

def dot(v1, v2):                          ◀── Our familiar function for
  return jnp.vdot(v1, v2)                      calculating a dot product
                                               between two vectors

rng_key = random.PRNGKey(42)

vs = random.normal(rng_key, shape=(20_000_000,3))    Generates some
v1s = vs[:10_000_000,:]                               random vectors
v2s = vs[10_000_000:,:]

v1s.shape, v2s.shape

>>> ((10000000, 3), (10000000, 3))

from jax.sharding import Mesh                  Imports for using
from jax.sharding import PartitionSpec         pjit() and Mesh
import numpy as np                        ◀──
                                               We need plain NumPy
devices = np.array(jax.devices())    ◀──        for creating a Mesh.
devices
                                               We will use a 1D mesh.
```

```
>>> array([TpuDevice(id=0, process_index=0, coords=(0,0,0), core_on_chip=0),
>>>        TpuDevice(id=1, process_index=0, coords=(0,0,0), core_on_chip=1),
>>>        TpuDevice(id=2, process_index=0, coords=(1,0,0), core_on_chip=0),
>>>        TpuDevice(id=3, process_index=0, coords=(1,0,0), core_on_chip=1),
>>>        TpuDevice(id=4, process_index=0, coords=(0,1,0), core_on_chip=0),
>>>        TpuDevice(id=5, process_index=0, coords=(0,1,0), core_on_chip=1),
>>>        TpuDevice(id=6, process_index=0, coords=(1,1,0), core_on_chip=0),
>>>        TpuDevice(id=7, process_index=0, coords=(1,1,0), core_on_chip=1)],
>>>        dtype=object)
```

```
f = pjit(dot,                                        ◄─── Calling pjit() on the dot() function
         in_shardings=None,                          ◄─── Do not partition the
         out_shardings=PartitionSpec('devices')           input (replicate it).
         )                                           ◄─── Partition output across the
                                                          "devices" axis of the mesh

with Mesh(devices, ('devices',)):                    ◄─── Creates Mesh
  x_pjit=f(v1s,v2s)                                       context manager

>>> ...                                              ◄─── Calls our pjit-ted
>>> ValueError: One of pjit outputs is incompatible with its   function
sharding annotation NamedSharding(mesh={'devices': 8},
 spec=PartitionSpec('devices',)): Sharding NamedSharding(
mesh={'devices': 8}, spec=PartitionSpec('devices',))
is only valid for values of rank at least 1, but was
applied to a value of rank 0. For scalars the
PartitionSpec should be P()
```

We are almost right here; however, we get an error describing that this partitioning is only valid for tensors with rank 1 or higher. Our dot() function returns a scalar (rank-0 tensor), so we have this error. The problem is that our function works on a pair of vectors producing a single number and is not vectorized (it cannot work on batches of vector pairs). We know it is easy to fix: just create a vectorized function that will work on arrays of vectors. In the following listing, we fix it and obtain the expected result.

Listing D.11 Applying `pjit()` to parallelize dot product calculations (fixed)

```
f = pjit(jax.vmap(dot),                              ◄─── Auto-vectorizes the
         in_shardings=None,                               dot() function with
         out_shardings=PartitionSpec('devices')          vmap() transformation
         )

with Mesh(devices, ('devices',)):                    ◄─── Calculates parallelized
  x_pjit=f(v1s,v2s)                                        function

x_pjit.shape

>>> (10000000,)                                      ◄─── Gets the expected result
```

The only change here is that we passed an auto-vectorized function inside pjit(). Now the transformed function produces correct results (see figure D.5).

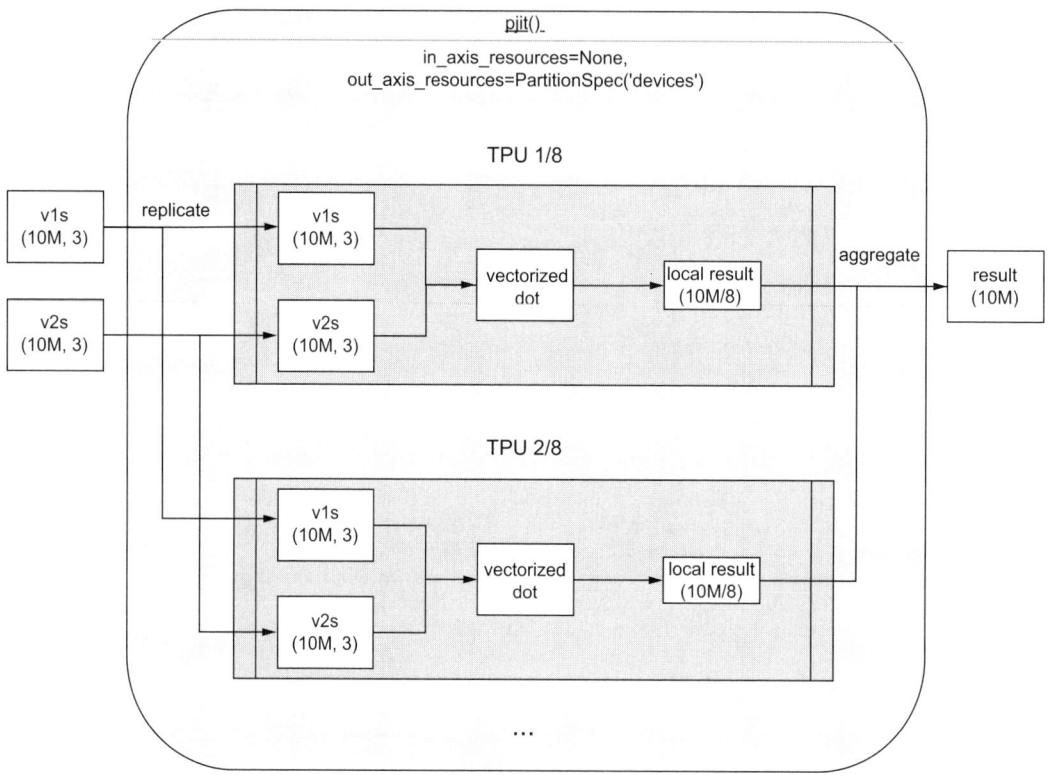

Figure D.5   Visualizing data processing from listing D.11

A deeper understanding of what is happening in this example is worthwhile. First, we have prepared a function capable of processing arrays of vectors and producing arrays of dot products. This is a familiar part from chapter 6, as we used the `vmap()` transformation to create such a function automatically.

Then we marked the input as non-partitioned. This input is replicated across all the devices so that each device will have a full copy of the input array. In our case, it is suboptimal, as we do not need the full input array to calculate a part of the output. For that part of the output, we only need a corresponding part of the input. We will fix that soon.

Then, for the output, we marked that it should be sharded across the "devices" axis. Our mesh is a 1D mesh with eight devices. The output is also a 1D array of pairwise dot products, and here it is split into eight parts and sharded across all eight devices.

Essentially, this means each device is given two full arrays of shape (10M, 3) each, but computes an array of shape (10M/8) consuming only 1/8 of the input arrays.

Let's make this code more efficient and partition our input data as well. In the following listing, we change the value of in_shardings to allow input partitioning.

Listing D.12 Adding input partitioning

```
f = pjit(jax.vmap(dot),
         in_shardings=PartitionSpec('devices'),          ◄──── Adds input partitioning
         out_shardings=PartitionSpec('devices')
         )

with Mesh(devices, ('devices',)):
  x_pjit=f(v1s,v2s)

x_pjit.shape

>>> (10000000,)                                          ◄──── Gets the same result
```

We added input partitioning across the same "devices" axis. But there is a small caveat here. Our function is a two-argument function, but the in_shardings value does not look like it refers to two values. So what does it really mean?

As we already said, the in_shardings value must either be a None, a Partition-Spec, or a tuple of length equal to the number of positional arguments of the function we parallelize. We already used the None value in the previous example, and now we use the PartitionSpec value.

However, in_shardings=PartitionSpec('devices') does not look like it refers to two function arguments. In effect, this specification makes the first array sharded into eight parts across its first dimension, and the second array replicated fully across all eight devices.

The complete specification would be in_shardings=(PartitionSpec('devices', None), PartitionSpec('devices', None)) to shard both function input arguments across the first dimension (with index 0).

In our example with the in_shardings=PartitionSpec('devices') specification and two rank-2 tensors (first and second inputs of the dot() function, which are both arrays of vectors), the resulting sharding will be equivalent to in_shardings=(PartitionSpec('devices', None), None).

In our case, it is also equivalent to both in_shardings=PartitionSpec('devices', None) or in_shardings=(PartitionSpec('devices'), None), as all of them shard only the first function argument across the first dimension; however, strictly speaking, they describe different things. The None in in_shardings=PartitionSpec('devices', None) explicitly refers to the second dimension of the first input parameter, and the None in in_shardings=(PartitionSpec('devices'), None) explicitly refers to the second parameter (see figure D.6).

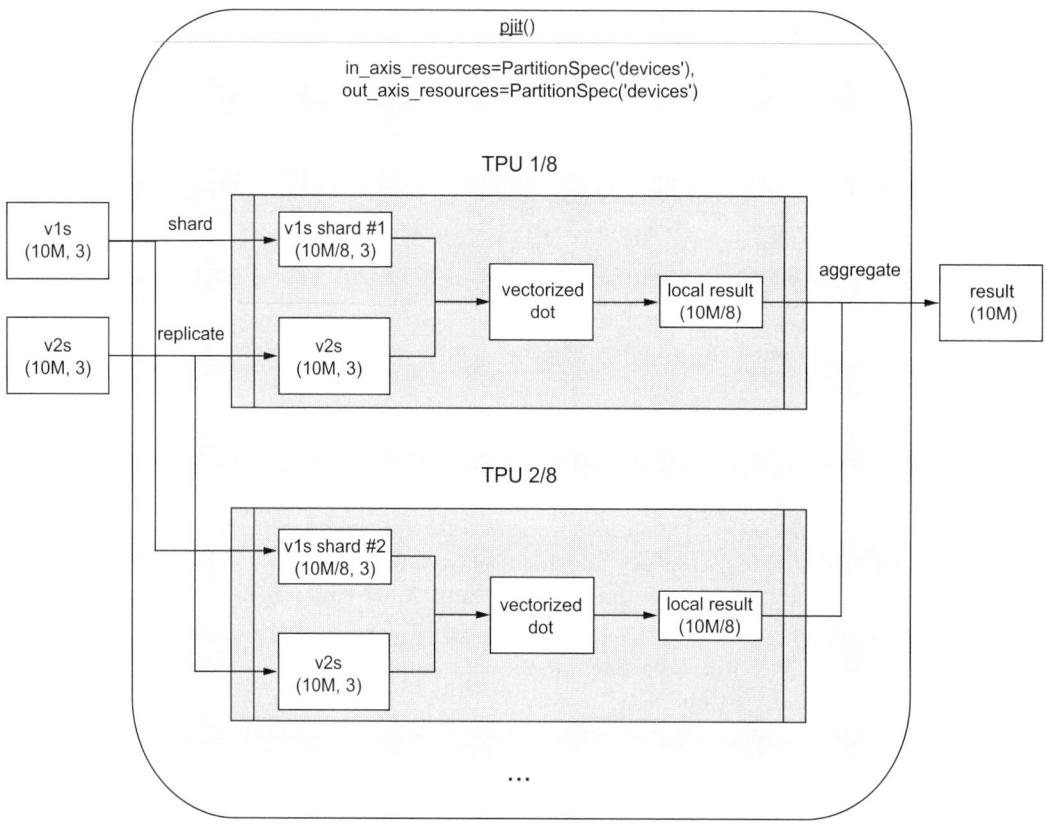

Figure D.6   Visualizing data processing from listing D.12

To shard both arrays, we need to change the `in_shardings` value to refer to both function arguments.

Listing D.13   Adding input partitioning for both arguments

```
f = pjit(jax.vmap(dot),
        in_shardings=(PartitionSpec('devices'), PartitionSpec('devices')), ◄─┐
        out_shardings=PartitionSpec('devices')
        )                                            Adds input partitioning for
                                                     both input parameters
with Mesh(devices, ('devices',)):
  x_pjit=f(v1s,v2s)

x_pjit.shape

>>> (10000000,)                              ◄──── Checks the shape
```

We have finally partitioned both input arguments, so now each device works on its own part of both inputs only; thus, we have used our resources efficiently (see figure D.7).

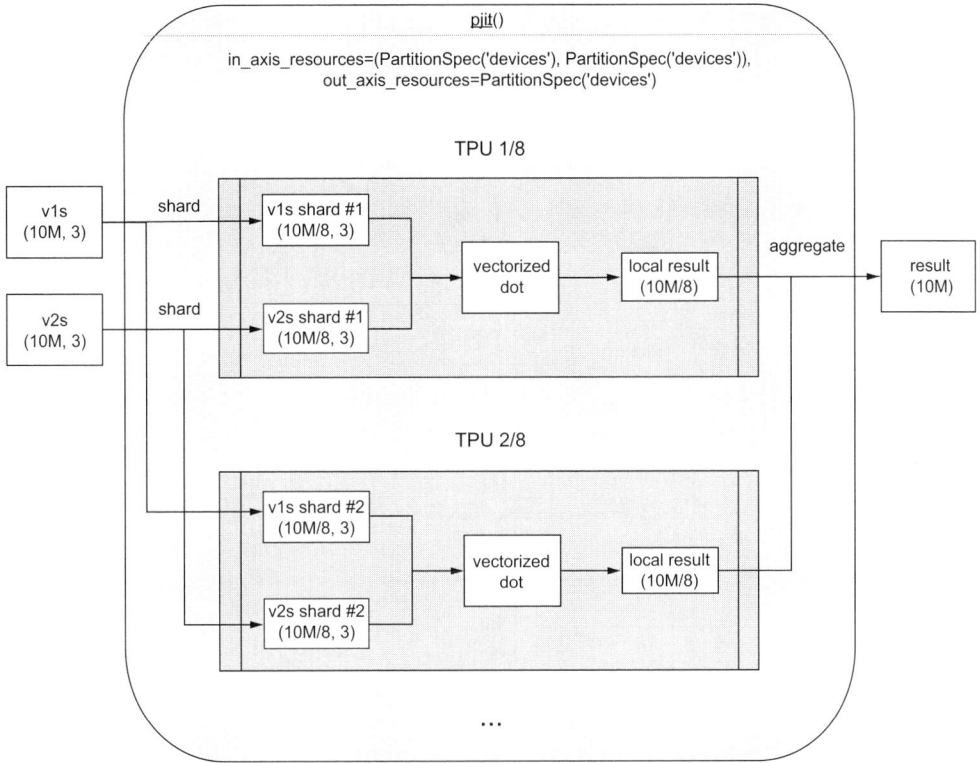

Figure D.7   Visualizing data processing from listing D.13

Now we are ready to move to a more complicated example with a 2D mesh.

AN EXAMPLE WITH 2D MESH

Imagine we have very large vectors, consisting not of just three components as before but of, say, 10,000 components. While such vectors can still fit into each separate device, it might also make sense to distribute the vectors across multiple devices. The dot product can easily be sharded as it is just a sum of corresponding products of elements of this vector (see figure D.8).

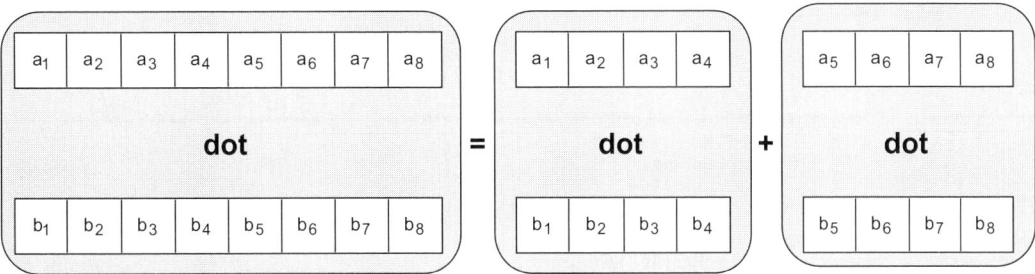

Figure D.8   How to shard a dot product

To shard across two dimensions (vectors themselves and vector components), we must prepare a 2D mesh. In the following example, we shard two rank-2 input tensors across both dimensions and the output across its only dimension. The process might look pretty complicated, so we start with a diagram visualizing it in figure D.9.

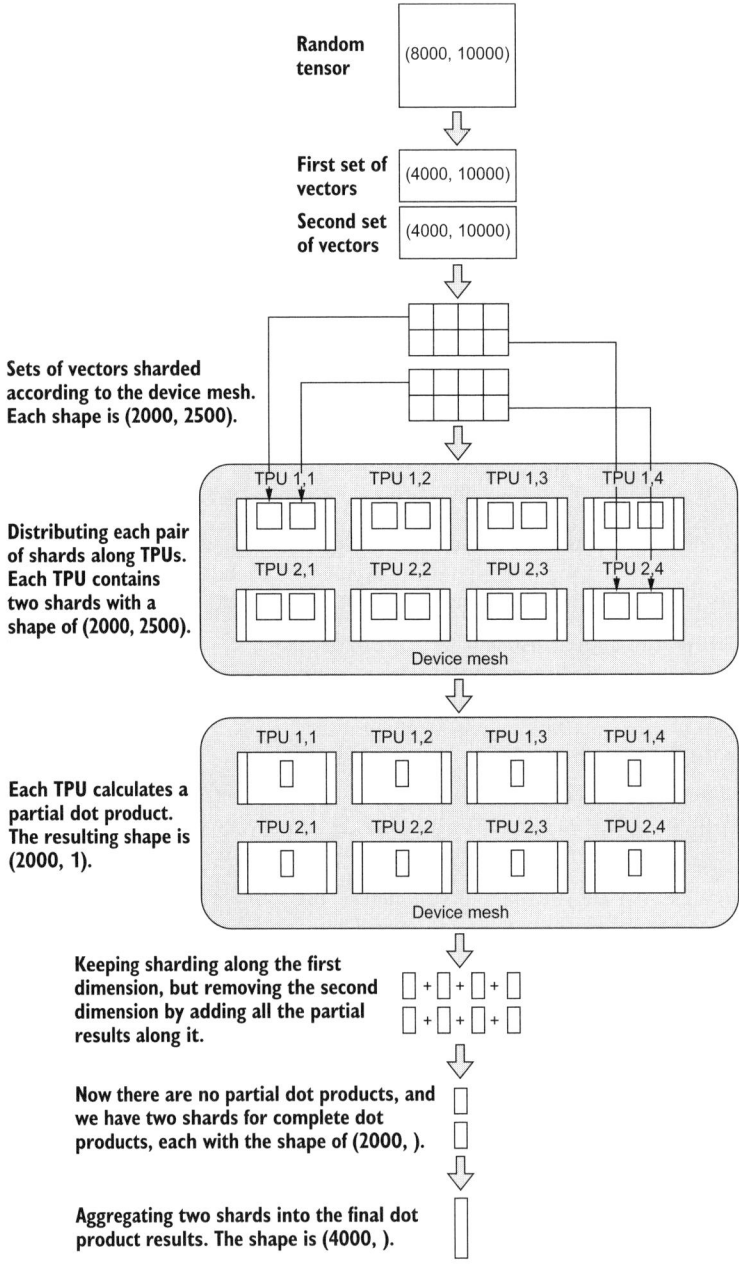

Figure D.9   Sharding dot product calculation across a 2D mesh

Here we did much more sharding than before. Let's carefully examine what is happening here. First, we created 4,000 pairs of vectors with 10,000 elements each. These are much wider vectors than we had before. Then, we created a 2 × 4 array of devices to use in a mesh. Later, we named the mesh axes "x" and "y."

Both input parameters of the dot() function are partitioned across the first and the second dimensions. The first dimension (of size 4000) is partitioned across the "x" axis (of size 2), producing chunks of size 2000, which index subsets of vectors. The second dimension (of size 10000) is partitioned across the "y" axis (of size 4), producing chunks of size 2500, which index subsets of vector components. The output is partitioned only across a single axis (here, "x") as it is a rank-1 tensor.

The computation happens this way: each device can calculate a partial dot product based on the shards it has. So, on every device, a 2,500-element chunk of the 10,000-element vector from the first array is multiplied elementwise with a 2,500-element chunk of the 10,000-element vector from the second array, and this is happening for each of the 2,000 pairs of vectors that reside on a particular device. Each partial dot product produces a single number, and then we have to sum all the partial dot products for each vector (there are four such partial dot products) together. This is done with a collective operation hidden from us.

In the end, the first row of the device mesh contains a dot product for the first 2,000 vectors from both arrays. The second row of the device mesh contains a dot product for the second half of vectors from both arrays. Finally, we just concatenate two remaining shards, producing the final result with 4,000 dot products.

Now it is pretty straightforward to translate this scheme into the code.

Listing D.14 Sharding across a 2D mesh

```
from jax.sharding import PartitionSpec as P          ◄─── Such import helps
from jax.sharding import Mesh                              reduce typing.
import numpy as np

rng_key = random.PRNGKey(42)

vs = random.normal(rng_key, shape=(8_000,10_000))        Generates 8,000
v1s = vs[:4_000,:]                                       "wide" vectors of
v2s = vs[4_000:,:]                                       10,000 components

v1s.shape, v2s.shape

>>> (4000, 10000), (4000, 10000))
                                                         Prepares a 2D array of
devices = np.array(jax.devices()).reshape(2, 4)    ◄─── devices for the mesh
devices

>>> array([[TpuDevice(id=0, process_index=0, coords=(0,0,0),
    core_on_chip=0),
>>>         TpuDevice(id=1, process_index=0, coords=(0,0,0),
    core_on_chip=1),
>>>         TpuDevice(id=2, process_index=0, coords=(1,0,0),
```

```
core_on_chip=0),
>>>           TpuDevice(id=3, process_index=0, coords=(1,0,0),
core_on_chip=1)],
>>>          [TpuDevice(id=4, process_index=0, coords=(0,1,0),
core_on_chip=0),
>>>           TpuDevice(id=5, process_index=0, coords=(0,1,0),
core_on_chip=1),
>>>           TpuDevice(id=6, process_index=0, coords=(1,1,0),
core_on_chip=0),
>>>           TpuDevice(id=7, process_index=0, coords=(1,1,0),
core_on_chip=1)]],
>>>         dtype=object)

def dot(v1, v2):
  return jnp.vdot(v1, v2)

f = pjit(jax.vmap(dot),
         in_shardings=(P('x', 'y'), P('x', 'y')),
         out_shardings=P('x')
         )

with Mesh(devices, ('x','y')):
  x_pjit=f(v1s,v2s)

x_pjit.shape

>>>  (4000,)
```

Both input dot() parameters (v1 and v2) are sharded across both tensor dimensions.

Output parameter is sharded across the first dimension only (it is the only dimension it has).

Creates and uses Mesh resource manager

Checks the shape of the output

The most interesting part is inside the pjit() call where we provide sharding specifi-cations. Everything else happens automatically.

If you want to look at the generated code to see the automatically added collective ops, you need to go deeper than the level of Jaxpr. It can only be seen after the compi-lation in the resulting HLO. In the accompanying notebook, you can find the code to produce HLO representation after compilation, and you can see all-reduce operations there.

You can find more examples of partitioning in a great blog post at https://irhum .github.io/blog/pjit.

In the last example, we used pjit() for both data and tensor parallelism. Our lists of vectors were split into chunks (data parallelism), and each vector was split into parts (tensor parallelism).

Finally, let's look at the MLP example for MNIST classification.

D.2.2   *MLP example with pjit()*

As we said, pjit() can be very helpful for sharding large neural network models. We will use our example with a small network for MNIST image classification to let you compare the code with other approaches we tried. We start loading the dataset, which is the same as before, and we reproduce it here for convenience.

```
import tensorflow as tf
import tensorflow_datasets as tfds

data_dir = '/tmp/tfds'

data, info = tfds.load(name="mnist",
                       data_dir=data_dir,
                       as_supervised=True,
                       with_info=True)

data_train = data['train']
data_test  = data['test']

HEIGHT = 28
WIDTH  = 28
CHANNELS = 1
NUM_PIXELS = HEIGHT * WIDTH * CHANNELS
NUM_LABELS = info.features['label'].num_classes
NUM_DEVICES = jax.device_count()
BATCH_SIZE  = 32

def preprocess(img, label):
  """Resize and preprocess images."""
  return (tf.cast(img, tf.float32)/255.0), label

train_data = tfds.as_numpy(
    data_train.map(preprocess).batch(
        NUM_DEVICES*BATCH_SIZE).prefetch(1)
)
test_data  = tfds.as_numpy(
    data_test.map(preprocess).batch(
        NUM_DEVICES*BATCH_SIZE).prefetch(1)
)

len(train_data)

>>> 235
```

A new constant for the number of computing devices

Asking for larger batches with the size of 32 × number of devices

There are 235 large batches in this dataset.

Then we use the same MLP structure without any changes. We also reproduce the code here for convenience.

```
import jax
import jax.numpy as jnp
from jax import grad, jit, vmap, value_and_grad
from jax import random
from jax.nn import swish, logsumexp, one_hot

LAYER_SIZES = [28*28, 512, 10]
PARAM_SCALE = 0.01
```

Specifies number of neurons in each fully connected layer

```
def init_network_params(sizes, key=random.PRNGKey(0), scale=1e-2):
  """Initialize all layers for a fully-connected
neural network with given sizes"""

  def random_layer_params(m, n, key, scale=1e-2):
    """A helper function to randomly initialize
weights and biases of a dense layer"""
    w_key, b_key = random.split(key)
    return scale * random.normal(w_key, (n, m)),
        scale * random.normal(b_key, (n,))

  keys = random.split(key, len(sizes))
  return [random_layer_params(m, n, k, scale)
      for m, n, k in zip(sizes[:-1], sizes[1:], keys)]

init_params = init_network_params(
    LAYER_SIZES, random.PRNGKey(0), scale=PARAM_SCALE)

def predict(params, image):
  """Function for per-example predictions."""
  activations = image
  for w, b in params[:-1]:
    outputs = jnp.dot(w, activations) + b
    activations = swish(outputs)

  final_w, final_b = params[-1]
  logits = jnp.dot(final_w, activations) + final_b
  return logits

batched_predict = vmap(predict, in_axes=(None, 0))
```

The function for random parameter initialization

Prepares the initial parameters

The forward-pass function

Generates a batched forward-pass function

Finally, we need to adjust our code for loss and update functions. We return to the original functions we had in chapter 2, as we do not need to organize communication manually using collective ops. The new part will be the `pjit()` call.

Listing D.17   Loss and update functions

```
from jax.experimental.pjit import pjit
from jax.sharding import PartitionSpec as P
from jax.sharding import Mesh
import numpy as np

INIT_LR = 1.0
DECAY_RATE = 0.95
DECAY_STEPS = 5
NUM_EPOCHS  = 20

def loss(params, images, targets):
  """Categorical cross entropy loss function."""
  logits = batched_predict(params, images)
  log_preds = logits - logsumexp(logits)
  return -jnp.mean(targets*log_preds)

def update(params, x, y, epoch_number):
```

Organizes required imports

The same loss function as before

The same update function as in chapter 2

```
        loss_value, grads = value_and_grad(loss)(params, x, y)
        lr = INIT_LR * DECAY_RATE ** (epoch_number / DECAY_STEPS)
        return [(w - lr * dw, b - lr * db)
                for (w, b), (dw, db) in zip(params, grads)], loss_value

f_update = pjit(update,
        in_shardings=(None, P('x'), P('x'), None),
        out_shardings=None
        )
```

← Calls pjit on our update function

← Shards both x and y parameters across the "x" mesh axis (this will be the batch axis)

Output is not sharded.

The interesting part here is highlighted in bold. All the other parts are the same as we had in chapter 2.

First, we have new imports. This is straightforward and does not require any comments. Second, our `update()` function becomes simple again. We do not need to call collective ops and organize communication between devices manually. We also do not need to replicate neural network parameters manually across all the devices. Our code becomes simpler, which is great. Compare it to listing 7.26.

Third is the `pjit()` call. We specify that the first input of the `update()` function, the `params`, should be replicated. The second and the third parameters (the x and y) are sharded across the first dimension of the corresponding tensors. This is essentially the batch dimension. The fourth parameter is just a scalar, so it is replicated. Output is not sharded here as the `update()` function returns an updated set of neural network weights, and we do not shard weights in this example.

Then, finally, we organize the training loop.

Listing D.18 The complete training loop

```
devices = np.array(jax.devices())                          ← Prepares device mesh
devices

>>> array([CpuDevice(id=0), CpuDevice(id=1), CpuDevice(id=2), CpuDevice(id=3),
>>>        CpuDevice(id=4), CpuDevice(id=5), CpuDevice(id=6), CpuDevice(id=7)],
>>>       dtype=object)

def batch_accuracy(params, images, targets):
    images = jnp.reshape(images, (len(images), NUM_PIXELS))
    predicted_class = jnp.argmax(batched_predict(params, images), axis=1)
    return jnp.mean(predicted_class == targets)

f_batch_accuracy = pjit(batch_accuracy,
        in_shardings=(None, P('x'), P('x')),
        out_shardings=None
        )

def accuracy(params, data):
    accs = []
```

← Creates JIT-compiled sharded function for calculating accuracy on batch

We shard the function across images and targets parameters.

```
    for images, targets in data:
      accs.append(f_batch_accuracy(params, images, targets))
    return jnp.mean(jnp.array(accs))

import time

params = init_params
with Mesh(devices, ('x',)):
  for epoch in range(NUM_EPOCHS):
    start_time = time.time()
    losses = []
    for x, y in train_data:
      x = jnp.reshape(x, (len(x), NUM_PIXELS))
      y = one_hot(y, NUM_LABELS)
      params, loss_value = f_update(params, x, y, epoch)
      losses.append(jnp.sum(loss_value))
    epoch_time = time.time() - start_time

    train_acc = accuracy(params, train_data)
    test_acc = accuracy(params, test_data)
    print("Epoch {} in {:0.2f} sec".format(epoch, epoch_time))
    print("Training set loss {}".format(jnp.mean(jnp.array(losses))))
    print("Training set accuracy {}".format(train_acc))
    print("Test set accuracy {}".format(test_acc))

>>> Epoch 0 in 39.10 sec
>>> Training set loss 0.41040703654289246
>>> Training set accuracy 0.9299499988555908
>>> Test set accuracy 0.931010365486145
>>> Epoch 1 in 37.77 sec
>>> Training set loss 0.37730318307876587
>>> Training set accuracy 0.9500166773796082
>>> Test set accuracy 0.9497803449630737
...
```

Annotations:
- Using a JIT-compiled sharded function (points to `f_batch_accuracy`)
- Sets the Mesh context manager (points to `with Mesh(devices, ('x',)):`)
- Calls a JIT-compiled sharded function for updating parameters (points to `f_update`)

Here it is! If we organized our pjit() calls as function annotations, our code would be almost similar to the code we had in chapter 2. The only significant difference would be using pjit() instead of jit() and introducing the device mesh.

This code is much simpler than the SPMD code from section 7.1 using pmap(). However, it achieves almost the same result as the manually parallelized code.

There could still be some differences, as the SPMD partitioner is heuristic-based and might not get everything right. It may sometimes lead to worse performance than manually partitioning using pmap().

So the tradeoff is the following: either you write simpler code faster and use pjit(), or you have explicit guarantees and better performance with more complicated code using pmap() that might also require specialized skill sets for achieving desired hardware utilization.

Summary

- `xmap()` transformation helps parallelize functions easier than with `pmap()`, with less code, replacing nested `pmap()` and `vmap()` calls, and without manual tensor reshaping.
- `xmap()` is an experimental feature that introduces the named-axis programming model by introducing named axes in addition to tensor positional axes.
- Named axes never implicitly interact with any positional axes.
- Resource axes come from a hardware mesh; it is an *n*-dimensional array of devices with named axes represented by the `Mesh` context manager.
- Each axis introduced by `xmap()` is assigned to one or more resource axes.
- `xmap()` is a seamless way to interpolate between `vmap()`- and `pmap()`-style execution.
- You can use `xmap()` as a drop-in replacement for `pmap()`, which makes programming for multidimensional hardware meshes much easier, automatically partitioning the computation over multiple devices.
- `xmap()` is now deprecated in favor of `shard_map()`, and it is deleted in JAX version 0.4.31 (July 29, 2024).
- `pjit()` is another experimental feature that helps you shard both data and a function (weights for the neural network case) over an existing hardware mesh.
- With `pjit()`, you specify how you want to partition input and output data. Then the partitioning of the function over devices happens automatically by propagating the input and output partitioning.
- You may give the compiler hints on how to shard intermediate function variables using the `jax.lax.with_sharding_constraint()` function, which is much like the `jax.device_put()` function but is used inside the `jit`-decorated functions.
- `pjit()` essentially compiles your program into XLA representation as if only one large virtual device exists. It uses the XLA SPMD partitioner to generate an identical program for *N* devices that performs communications between devices through collective ops.
- `pjit()` uses the same mesh specification as `xmap()`.
- Now `pjit()` and `jit()` (the topic of chapter 5) have been merged into a single unified interface, so please use `jit()` instead.
- Tensor sharding with distributed arrays (the topic of chapter 8) provides a modern way for compiling and executing JAX functions in multihost or multicore environments.

index

Symbols

@jit annotation   38, 121, 122, 149, 150

A

abs() function   12
Acme library   331
activation functions   28
adjoint   114
all_gather() function   168
All-gather pattern   194
All-reduce pattern   194
All-to-all pattern   194
Alpa library   328
AOT (ahead-of-time) compilation   120, 121, 143
argnums parameter   106, 107
array axes, controlling   160–163
array() function   63
arrays   47
  asynchronous dispatch   69
  device-related operations   65
  NumPy
    differences with   74–80
  overview   63
  running computations on TPUs   71–72
  switching to JAX NumPy-like API   61
Array type   47, 64

ASIC (Application-specific Integrated Circuit)   66
asynchronous dispatch   69
autodiff (automatic differentiation)   13, 33–38
  calculating gradients, reverse mode   114
  evaluation trace   109
  forward and reverse mode   108
Autodiff Cookbook   117
Autograd   12
AutoTokenizer class   312, 314
auto-vectorization   9
axis_index_groups parameter   196
axis_name argument   167, 193, 195
AXLearn library   325

B

backend   139
backend parameter   123
BatchNorm   302
batch_stats collection   303
Bayex library   331
beam search   314
BERT-like models   310
Big Vision library   332
BioBERT   310
BitGenerator   251
BlackJAX library   331

block_until_ready() method   69, 70

BLOOM LM   310

Brax   333

Broadcast function   194

broadcast_to() function   166

BYOL (Bootstrap your own latent)   4

C

calculating, metrics with CLU library   299

chain() function   296

Chex library   329

CLIP   311

clip() function   59

CLMs (Causal Language Models)   314

Cloud TPU   71

CLU (Common Loop Utils) library , metrics
    calculation with   299, 329

CNNs (convolutional neural networks)   56, 301

Coax library   331

code vectorization, real-life use cases for
    vmap()   168–175

CoDeX library   333

Colab TPU runtime   71

collective operations   166–168, 193
   communicating between processes   192

committed data   67

compiling code   119
   AOT compilation   143
   Jaxpr   130–131
   JIT (just-in-time) compilation   38, 121
     and pure functions   128
     compiling and running on specific
       hardware   123
     optimization-related arguments   127
     using jax.jit as transformation or
       annotation   121
     using static arguments   125
   XLA (Accelerated Linear Algebra)   138

complex data structures, representing as
    pytrees   266–271

composable function transformations   13

compute() function   299

cond() primitive   137

consts attribute   131

controlling vmap() behavior   160–168
   controlling array axes to map over   160–163
   controlling output array axes   163

using collective operations   166–168
   using decorator style   166
   using named arguments   164–166

conv() function   12

conv_general_dilated function   81

ConvNeXt   301

convolution   56

convolutional neural networks (CNNs)   56, 301

convolve2d() function   62

core_on_chip attribute   73

cosine_distance   297

cost_analysis() function   146

cotangent   114

CPU (central processing unit)   65

create_device_mesh() function   219, 227

ctc_loss   297

D

DALL·E Mini   311

data, generating random   238–248

data augmentation, building complete
    pipeline   260

data parallel neural network training
    example   199–208

data structures, representing complex data
    structures as pytrees   266–271

decorator style   166

DeepXDE   334

detach() method   103

DeviceArray   63

device() method   67

device parameter   123

device_put() function   70

device-related operations   65
   committed and uncommitted data   67
   local and global devices   66

Diffrax   334

diffusers library   310, 318

diffusion models   319

directional derivative   111

donate_argnums function   127

Dopamine library   331

dot_general() function   159

DSP (Digital Signal Processing)   55

E

EasyLM library 327
EfficientNetV2 301
eight-way data parallelism 230–232
Einops library 330
Elegy library 326
Equinox library 325
equinox.Module 280
evaluation trace 109
EvoJAX library 331
Evosax library 331
exp() function 12

F

FedJAX library 332
filter kernels 55
    applying to image 58
FinBERT 310
fine-tuning 41, 317
FIR (finite impulse response) 55, 56
FLAN-T5 310
Flax
    managing state in 302
    training neural networks 297
FlaxAutoModelForCausalLM class 312, 314
FlaxAutoModelForSequenceClassification
        class 318
FlaxGPTJForCausalLM class 312, 314
FlaxGPTNeoForCausalLM class 312
flax.jax_utils.replicate() function 320
Flax library 325
flax.linen module 303
FlaxStableDiffusionPipeline class 320
flax.struct.dataclass annotation 280
flax.training.checkpoints API 308
flax.training.common_utils.shard() function 320
flax.training.train_state.TrainState class 297
flip() function 54
fliplr() function 246
float16/bfloat16 support 79
float64 support 78–79
Flower library 332
fold_in() function 257, 258
Foolbox library 333
fori loop 131
for loops 10

forward mode 110
    autodiff 108
    calculations 110
    directional derivative and jvp() 111
four-way data parallelism 232–235
from_output() function 299
from_pretrained() method 312
frontend 139
functions
    for working with pytrees 271–280
    vectorizing 158–159
functools.partial function 127
functools.reduce() function 276
functorch library 15
fusion 41

G

GANs (generative adversarial networks) 237
gather_from_model_output() function 299
Gather pattern 194
Gaussian blur filter 57
GELUs (Gaussian error linear units) 28
Generator 251
GlobalDeviceArray type 216
global devices 66, 208
GPT2TokenizerFast class 314
GPT-J-6B (EleutherAI's GPT-like model) 5
GPT-Neo 310
GPUs (graphics processing units) 5, 65
grad() function 10, 13, 14, 104, 306
gradient descent procedure 33
gradients
    calculating, reverse mode 114
    evaluation trace 109
    forward mode and jvp() 110–111
    higher-order derivatives 104
    multivariable case 106–107
    reverse mode 114–115
GradientTransformation interface 296, 297
grad() transformation 35, 119, 171
greedy decoding 314
Gymnax library 331

H

Haiku library 326
Haliax library 328, 330

has_aux=True parameter 306
hash() function 258
hashlib library 257
hessian() function 107
Hessian matrix 107
higher-order derivatives 104
high-level and low-level interfaces 80–83
Hugging Face Transformers library 311
hyperbolic tangent function 28

I

if statements 10
image filtering 55
    applying filter kernel to image 58
    creating filter kernel 55
image processing, with NumPy arrays 48
images
    adding noise to 54
    loading into NumPy arrays 49
    saving tensors as 61
img_as_float() function 54
immutability 74–77
    index update functionality 75
    out-of-bounds indexing 76
impure functions 147
in_axes argument 169, 195
index update functionality 75
inference 41
init() function 296
inline=True parameter 128
input and output mapping axes, controlling 187
    large array example 190
    using in_axes parameter 187
    using out_axes parameter 189
input_ids field 316
IR (intermediate representation) 130
is_leaf parameter 275
Ivy library 325

J

jacfwd() function 106, 111
Jacobian matrix 106
jacrev() function 106
JAX2TF tool 329
jax.Array type 63, 216
JAXChem 334

jax.core.ClosedJaxpr type 131
jax.core.Jaxpr type 131
jax.core.Tracer class 131
Jax-cosmo 333
jax.custom_jvp() function 117
jax.custom_vjp() function 117
jax.debug.visualize_array_sharding() function 218
jax.default_device() context manager 67
jax_default_prng_impl flag 259
jax.device_count() function 66, 201
jax.device_get() function 68
jax.device_put() function 8, 67, 68, 219, 226
jax.devices() function 66, 67, 123, 227
jax.distributed.initialize() function 208
jax_enable_x64 configuration variable 79
jax.flatten_util.ravel_pytree() function 274, 276
JAX-Fluids 333
Jaxformer library 328
jax.jit() function 121, 122, 127, 132
JAX (Just After eXecution) 5
jax.lax 159
jax.lax.cond() primitive 137
jax.lax.fori_loop() primitive 136, 137
jax.lax.map() function 269
jax.lax module 131
jax.lax.scan() function 148, 269
jax.lax.stop_gradient() function 103
jax.lax.switch() function 246, 247
jax.lax.with_sharding_constraint() function 226
jaxlib package 147
jaxlib.xla_extension.ArrayImpl type 62, 184
JAXline library 330
jax.local_device_count() function 66, 182
jax.local_devices() function 66, 227
jax.make_jaxpr() function 130
JAX, M.D. (differentiable molecular dynamics) 333
jax.nn library 27
jax.numpy module 62
JAX ONNX Runtime library 330
JAXopt library 328
–jax_platforms command line flag 67
JAX_PLATFORMS variable 67
Jaxpr 130–131
JAX-Privacy library 333
jax.process_index() function 67, 74

JaxPruner library 332
jax.random.normal() function 242, 244
jax.random.randint() function 248
jax.random.split() function 246
jax.scipy module 62
JaxSeq library 328
jax.stages API 144
jax_threefry_partitionable flag 259, 260
jax.tree_util package 271
jax.tree_util.register_pytree_node() function 281
jax.tree_util.tree_flatten() function 274
jax.tree_util.tree_leaves() function 268, 271
jax.tree_util.tree_map() function 268, 271
jax.tree_util.tree_reduce() function 276
jax.tree_util.tree_structure() function 274
jax.tree_util.tree_transpose() function 278
jax.tree_util.tree_unflatten() function 274, 275
jaxtyping library 329
Jax-verify library 329
jit=True flag 321
jit annotation 150
jit() function 13, 14, 38, 120–121, 123, 127, 216
JIT (just-in-time) compilation 7, 38, 121
   and pure functions 128
   compiling and running on specific
      hardware 123
   exercise 151
   internals 130
   limitations 147–151
   optimization-related arguments 127
   using jax.jit as transformation or annotation 121
   using static arguments 125
JMP library 330
jnp.broadcast_to() function 272
jnp.convolve function 81
jnp.sum() function 64, 195, 198, 210
Jraph library 331
Jumanji library 331
jvp() function 108, 110, 113
   directional derivative and jvp() 111
   forward-mode calculations 110
JVP (Jacobian-vector product) 111
j-Wave 333

K

keepdims=false parameter 224
keep_unused argument 127
Keras 3.0 library 325
KFAC-JAX library 329
kl_divergence 297

L

l2_loss 297
lax.associative_scan 81
lax.cond 81
lax.fori_loop 81
lax.map function 81
lax.scan 81, 148
lax.switch 81, 82
lax.while_loop 81
learning rate 33
Levanter library 328
Lineax library 328
linspace() function 63
LLMs (large language models) 5, 177, 314
   fine-tuning 317
   pretraining 317
LLVM 140
local_device_count() function 320
local devices 66, 208
logsumexp() function 35
loss() function 35, 205
lowering 142

M

make_jaxpr() function 131, 132
MaxText library 327
Mctx library 331
memory_analysis() function 146
merge() function 299
Mesh Transformer JAX library 326
mesh_utils.create_device_mesh() function 218
Metax library 333
Metric interface 299
metrics.Collection interface 299
MHLO (MLIR High-Level Operations) 141
MIMD (multiple instruction multiple data) 181
MISD (multiple instruction single data) 181

MLIR (Multi-Level Intermediate Representation)   141
MLP-Mixer   301
MLP (multi-layer perceptron)   4
    with tensor sharding   230–235
model.apply() function   306
model.init() function   305
model parallelism   200
models, saving and deploying   40–41
model.tabulate() method   305
modern computer vision   301
MPMD (multiple program multiple data)   181
MT19937 (Mersenne Twister)   252
multihost configurations   208–213
multinomial sampling   314
multi_transform() function   296
multivariable case   106–107
mutable argument   306

N

named arguments   164–166
namedtuple   277, 278
names axes and collectives   192
    communicating between processes   192
    nested maps   197
NAS (Neural Architecture Search)   28
ndim property   51
NetKet   334
noise
    adding to images   54
    generating random   242–245
    schedulers   319
normal() generator method   249
NumPy
    array differences with   74–80
    arrays, image processing with   48
    JAX vs.   12–15
    loading images into arrays   49
    random numbers in   248
    random numbers vs. JAX   248
numpy.ndarray   12
    objects   65
    type   47, 48, 62
numpy.random module   248
numpy.random.normal() function   242, 244
NumPyro library   331

O

Objax library   326
OpenXLA   139
optax.apply_updates() function   296
Optax library   328
OptimiSM   334
Optimistix library   328
orbax.checkpoint.CheckpointManager   309
Orbax library   329
Oryx library   331
os.urandom() function   239
OTT-JAX library   333
out_axes parameter   163, 189, 204

P

Pallas   69
parallelizing, multihost configurations   208–213
parallelizing computations   176
    controlling input and output mapping axes   187, 189, 190
    data parallel neural network training example   199–208
    pmap()   177, 180
    using names axes and collectives   192, 197
params collection   303
partial() function   127
PartitionSpec object   228
Paxml (or Pax) library   327
PCG64DXSM   252
PCG (Permuted congruential generator)   252
pdot() operation   193
PEGASUS   310
PennyLane   334
Penzai library   330
Perceiver IO   4
period of the generator   239
pickle module   65
pipeline parallelism   232
PIX library   332
pjit() function   177, 216, 232
pmap() function   13–14, 151, 167, 177, 180, 184, 185, 193, 195, 197–199, 203–204, 209–210, 213, 232, 272
pmax() function   168, 194, 197
pmean() function   168, 194
pmin() function   168, 194

PositionalSharding object   219
prepare_inputs() function   320
pretrained models   319
primals, defined   110
PRNGs (pseudorandom number generators)   238
    seeds and states in NumPy   249
process_index attribute   67, 74
prompt engineering   316
psum() function   168, 194, 195, 196, 198, 205
pure functions   41, 147
PyTorch, comparing with JAX   15–17
PyTreeDef type   274
pytrees   265, 266
    creating custom pytree nodes   280–282
    custom pytree nodes   280–282
    flattening/unflattening   274–276
    functions for working with   274–280
    representing complex data structures as
        266–271
    transposing   277–280

Q

quantumrandom module   239
qujax   334

R

RAG (retrieval-augmented generation)   317
randint() function   248
random_augmentation() function   169, 261
random.get_state() function   250
random_noise function   54
random.normal() function   249, 251
random numbers   237
    advanced JAX PRNG configuration   259
    generating random data   238–248
    in NumPy   248
    in real-life applications   260–262
    JAX PRNG   253
    NumPy vs. JAX   248
    seeds and states in NumPy   249
random.PRNGKey(seed) function   244, 253
random.split() function   255
random.SystemRandom() generator   239
ravel_pytree() function   276
Rax library   333
RBG (XLA Random Bit Generator)   259

reduce function   276
Reduce pattern   194
reduce_sum primitive   131
ReLU (rectified linear unit)   28
replicate(axis=NUMBER) method   223
ResNets (residual networks)   301
reverse mode   114
    autodiff   108
    calculations   114
    generalization   115
revision parameter   314
RLax library   331
RL (reinforcement learning)   330
RNG (random number generator)   42, 238
rot90() function   54

S

safetensors package   40
Saxml (or Sax) library   329
scan primitive   131
Scatter pattern   194
Scenic library   332
scikit-image   49, 50
SELUs (scaled exponential linear units)   28, 120
sequential equivalent guarantee   250, 258
SGD (stochastic gradient descent)   33
ShapedArray tracer   132
shape property   51
ShardedDeviceArray   63
sharding.replicate(0) parameter   235
sigmoid function   28
single_from_model_output() function   299
SISD (single instruction single data)   181
softmax_cross_entropy   297
special tensor types   80
split() function   255
SPMD (single program multiple data)   181
SPMD (single-program multiple-data)   177, 181
StableHLO   141
state, managing in Flax   302
stateful PRNGs   250
static_argnames parameter   125
static_argnums parameter   125, 127
static arguments   125
static_broadcasted_argnums parameter   194
Stax library   326

stop_gradient() function   104

Swish activation function   27

switch conditional   131

T

T5X library   328

tangents   110

temperature parameter   315

TensorFlow, comparing with JAX   15–17

tensor parallelism   232

tensors   31

tensor sharding   215–216

   basics of   217–220, 223, 226–227, 229

   MLP with   230–235

TF2JAX library   330

Threefry PRNG   252

to_bf16() method   314

to_fp16() method   314

torch.func APIs   15

torch.nn   16

total exchange   194

TPUs (tenor processing units)   5, 66

   preparing   72

   running computations on   71

tracing   128, 131

training a new large model from scratch   317

TrainState   306

transformer encoder-decoder   314

Transformer Engine library   330

transformers library   310

Trax library   326

tree_flatten() function   276

tree_map() function   271–275, 281, 282

Tree-math library   330

tree_reduce() function   276

tree_structure() function   274

tree_transpose() function   278

tree_unflatten() function   275

two-way tensor parallelism   232–235

type promotion semantics   80

U

UMT5 (T5 family)   310

uncommitted data   67

UnshapedArray tracer   133

V

VAE (variational auto-encoders)   237

value_and_grad() function   36, 270, 306

vectorizing

   controlling vmap() behavior   160–168

   real-life use cases for vmap()   168–175

vectorizing functions, speed comparisons   158–159

Veros   334

visu3d library   332

ViT (Vision Transformer)   4, 301

vjp() function   108

VJP (vector-Jacobian product)   115

vmap() function   13, 14, 105, 160, 162, 165, 167, 175, 179, 187, 219, 278

   controlling behavior of   160–168

   real-life use cases for   168–175

   transformation   32, 145, 151, 171, 185

W

weak_type property   83

while loop   131

Whisper   311

X

XLA (Accelerated Linear Algebra)   7, 12, 138

   and JAX   141

   origins and architecture   139

xla_call primitive   128, 131

–xla_force_host_platform_device_count flag   179, 219

xmap() function   177, 216

xmap operator   311

RELATED MANNING TITLES

Deep Learning with Python, Second Edition
by Francois Chollet

ISBN 9781617296864
504 pages, $59.99
October 2021

Inside Deep Learning
by Edward Raff
Foreword by Kirk Borne

ISBN 9781617298639
600 pages, $59.99
April 2022

Math and Architectures of Deep Learning
by Krishnendu Chaudhury
with Ananya H. Ashok, Sujay Narumanchi, Devashish Shankar
Foreword by Prith Banerjee

ISBN 9781617296482
552 pages, $69.99
April 2024

Deep Learning with PyTorch, Second Edition
by Luca Antiga, Eli Stevens, Howard Huang, and Thomas
Viehmann

ISBN 9781633438859
600 pages (estimated), $59.99
Spring 2025 (estimated)

For ordering information, go to www.manning.com